编委名单

主　编　顾雪梁　钱建萍　徐中意

副主编　胡祝恩　詹　蔚　魏莉芳

编　委　王　敏　王丽娜　樊　云

黄　艳　魏良庭　郭安琪

浙江省重点教材建设项目

浙江景点文化双语教程

主编　顾雪梁　钱建萍　徐中意

ZHEJIANG UNIVERSITY PRESS
浙江大学出版社

前 言

　　浙江的山水似画，它的每一座山岳都萦绕着天地灵秀，每一脉江河都流淌着古今风流；浙江的人文如诗，它的每一间古宅都镌刻着厚重历史，每一条小巷都留存着千古遗迹。浙江果然物华天宝，人文荟萃，山水竞秀，史话葱茂，无愧为文化之珠，旅游之圣。若把浙江的山水景观、人文诗篇编撰成一部中英文双语的教材，让学子们去体认，去领悟，去陶冶，去流播，那对开阔他们的文化视野，提升他们的人文素养，修炼他们的鉴赏内功，无疑是一件十分有益之事，是一个极有价值之举，也是一条值得探究之路，这正是我们编写《浙江景点文化双语教程》之初衷。

　　鉴于文化和地域归类的需要，我们把美丽浙江划分成七大"景域（Scenic Zone）"。遵循"景物辉映，人文荟萃，推陈出新，旧貌新颜"的编撰理念和原则，我们对众多景点进行筛选，从中选取了100多个自然景致和人文景观作为本书撰写蓝本，其中既吸纳了部分传统的经典景点，更撷取了大量新生的人文景观，力图博采而不失主旨，践新而不囿人文，立异而不缺内涵，选景而不乏美奂，犹如一匹匹新织就的锦缎，轻盈飘逸，风韵明媚，让人心旷神怡，耳目一新。

　　全书共有八个篇章(Chapter)，其中前七章为"景域篇"，最后一章为"特产篇"，前后相辅相成，彼此互衬互辉。本书的每一个"景域篇"都是由"旅游景点(Scenic Spots)""旅游文化(Tourism Culture)""讲解技能(Narration Tactics)"和"翻译技巧(Translation Skills)"等四个不同层面的小节(Section)构成，节节相扣，环环相连，情景交融，浑然一体。

　　"旅游景点(Scenic Spots)"一节重在凸显景点风貌。该节对每一个景点除用英汉双语讲解之外，还专门配有"生词与词组(Words & Expressions)"和"知识拓展(Knowledge Extension)"。尤其是后者，以"他山之石，为我所用"，收录了不少与该景点相关的知识和信息，深化了章节内涵、拓展了人文知识，可谓烘云托月，珠联璧合。

"旅游文化(Tourism Culture)"一节重在突出景点文化内涵。该节因不同文化而各有侧重，分别为"历史文化(Historical Culture)""宗教文化(Religious Culture)""名人文化(Celebrity Culture)""山水文化(Landscape Culture)""建筑文化(Architectural Culture)""特产文化(Local Special Product Culture)"和"民俗文化(Folk Culture)"七类。每一种文化侧重不同，视角各异，形散而神合，分叙而贯通。

"景点讲解技能(Narration Tactics of Scenic Spots)"一节重在强化解说技能。人们说，"看景不如听景"，巧用讲解艺术和讲解技能，方能妙语解颐，引人入胜；方能情以物兴，情随景移。本节引荐了景点讲解常用的方法，分别解析诸如突出重点法、名人效应法、制造悬念法、虚实结合法、诗词歌赋借用法、问答法和触景生情法等讲解技艺，以期他玉我赏，机变如神。我们还配以"课后练习(Exercises)"和"练习参考答案(Keys to the Exercises)"，以检查与巩固所学。

"翻译技巧(Translation Skills)"一节重在点化翻译悟性。该节讲授应有的翻译技能和方法，对旅游翻译技巧、旅游广告翻译技巧、景点翻译技巧、山水文化翻译技巧、建筑文化翻译技巧、土特产文化翻译技巧和民俗文化翻译技巧等不可或缺的翻译技能进行一一分述，细细解析，目的在于开拓译路，破解译疑，掌握译技，技为译用。唯此，方可从容应对，信手破译，蹊径独辟，妙语连珠。

本书既具学术性、知识性，又具趣味性、可读性；既可作为旅游专业、英语专业之教材，亦可作为导游人员、翻译工作者、旅游爱好者、英语学习者以及外国游客之品读、学习、参阅用书。

本书是浙江省高校重点建设教材，由顾雪梁教授担纲主编、策划、编撰和主审；钱建萍老师担任主编，承担了大量艰巨的后期工作，并负责第三章的撰写；徐中意副教授担任主编，分担了本书繁杂的前期组织、策划和审稿工作，并负责第二章的撰写。魏莉芳老师负责第一章的撰写，詹蔚老师负责第四章的撰写，王丽娜老师负责第五章的撰写，王敏老师负责第六章的撰写，樊云老师负责第七章的撰写，胡祝恩老师负责第八章的撰写。黄艳老师、魏良庭老师和郭安琪老师在本书的编写过程中曾作出许多努力。

　　好事多磨，本书的问世一波三折，幸在编写、出版过程中得到浙江大学出版社张琛和吴惠卿两位女士的大力扶助以及韦伟女士的倾心编辑，得获浙江越秀外国语学院英语学院的资助，得益钟绿芳女士、葛乃文先生和陈冠柏先生的竭诚相助，方使本书拨云见日，特在此深表感谢。

　　本书在撰写中参阅了有关书籍、资料和网络，特在此向原作者致以深深的感谢和敬意。

　　樊云老师在完成书稿的撰写后不幸病故，令人扼腕，谨此悼念。

　　我们编撰双语教材乃初次尝试，经验不足，相关新景点资料匮乏，故对景域分合、景点取舍、内容腴瘠、注释详略等的分寸深浅皆难把握，加之时间仓促，水平有限，因而本书挂一漏万、谬误瑕疵恐在所难免，敬请读者不吝指正，以期再版时修改。是盼。

顾雪梁

杭州玉翠斋

2015 年夏

CONTENTS 目 录

第一章　杭州景域

Chapter One　Hangzhou Scenic Zone

第一节　旅游景点

Section 1　Scenic Spots

1. 富春江 The Fuchun River

富春江全长 68 千米，富阳境内 52 千米，山奇水异，天下独绝。古老而又悠远的富春江绘就了秀丽、迷人的富春山水，孕育了一代又一代富阳名人，也给予了富阳丰厚的文化底蕴和历史积淀。

这一段风景区两岸山色青翠秀丽，江水清澈碧绿，而在山水之间还分布着许多名胜古迹。风景区东线有富春江国家森林公园等，是回归自然旅游线；南线以"地下艺术宫殿"为主，是科普考察旅游线；西线以"华东明珠"——新安江水电站等景点为旅游点，是千岛湖山水风景的旅游线；新安江城又以"风凉、水清、雾奇"三绝闻名，是江南地区著名的城镇避暑胜地。

胥江野渡，又被称为"子胥渡"，位于建德市白沙镇东北 42 千米七里泷北岸胥溪和泷江交汇的地方。传说是春秋时期伍子胥为躲避楚平王迫害沿胥溪过江的地方，故以其名命名。泷江一带的风光，大多以纯粹的自然山水风光取胜，唯有这"胥江野渡"，却是流传千古的人文景观，是游客们畅游泷江的必到之处。渡口处石壁耸立，上有摩崖石刻"子胥渡"三个大字。"胥岭""胥江"和"胥溪"等地名的由来，无一不与伍子胥这一历史上著名的忠义之士有关。当地老百姓还修建了子胥庙和子胥亭来纪念他。子胥庙中伍子胥铜像正气浩然，令人景仰；子胥亭中有一巨碑，前面镌有"胥江野渡"几个大字，后面题写着伍子胥渡江的传说。

The Fuchun River, with a total length of 68 kilometers and 52 kilometers in Fuyang, possesses peculiar mountains and water and unique landscape in the world. The Fuchun River, with its long and ancient history, depicts beautiful and charming scenery in Fuyang. It not only **breeds** many **celebrities** in Fuyang generation after generation, but also adds rich cultural heritage and historical accumulation to Fuyang.

Along the banks of this scenic spot are emerald and beautiful mountains and clear and dark green water, and between the mountains and rivers are many places of interest. The east line includes the Fuchun River National Forest Park and other scenic spots, which is a route to return to nature. The south line includes "underground artistic palace", which is a route for scientific exploration. The west line is well-known for "Pearl of East China"—Xin'anjiang Hydropower Station, and some other tourist attractions, providing a route for enjoying the landscape. Xin'anjiang City, famous for its "cool wind, clear water and unique fog", is a reputed summer resort city in Jiangnan (the south of the lower reaches of the Yangtze River).

Xujiang **Ferry**, also called Zixu Ferry, is situated where the Xuxi Stream and the Longjiang River join together. It is said to be the place where Wu Zixu, an official of Wu Kingdom in the Spring and Autumn Period (770 BC–476 BC), crossed the river in order to escape from the **persecutions** from King Ping of Chu. That is why the ferry is named after the official. The Longjiang River is mostly famous for its beautiful natural scenery, but Xujiang Ferry is enriched with cultural landscape for years. It is a must-go place for tourists during their stay by the Longjiang River. Around the ferry stand steep cliffs, on which inscribed three large Chinese characters "子胥渡" (meaning "Zixu Ferry"). The names of the Xuling Mountain, the Xujiang River, and the Xuxi Stream are all in honor of Wu Zixu, the famous loyal officer in history. Local people have also built Zixu Temple and Zixu Pavilion to **commemorate** him. In Zixu Temple the bronze statue of Wu Zixu is in noble spirit for the later generations to visit. Inside the Zixu Pavilion is a large stele inscribed with 4 Chinese characters "胥江野渡" (Xujiang Natural Ferry), with its back inscribed with the story of Wu Zixu.

★生词与词组 Words & Expressions

breed /bri:d; brid/ *v.* 养育
ferry /'feri/ *n.* 渡船，渡口
commemorate /kə'meməreit/ *v.* 纪念

celebrity /si'lebriti/ *n.* 名人
persecution /pə:si'kju:ʃn/ *n.* 迫害

◆ 知识拓展 Knowledge Extension

胥江野渡：相传春秋时楚国伍子胥受楚平王谋害，逃奔吴国，后经此渡口赴吴国都城姑苏。渡口石壁危立，上有摩崖石刻"子胥渡"三个大字。此处江面开阔，悄悄寂寂，古道萦回，故名"胥江野渡"。

2. 虎跑梦泉 Dreaming of the Tiger Spring

位于西湖西南隅大慈山脚下的虎跑泉，被茶圣陆羽称为"天下第三泉"。传说唐代高僧性空曾住在附近的寺庙里，后来因水源短缺，准备迁走。有一天，他在梦中得到神仙的指示：二虎将会移泉到此地。第二天，果见二虎从衡山跑来做穴，泉遂涌出，虎跑梦泉由此得名。

此泉水是来自地底深层的溪流，有调查显示，泉水对人体健康有益。这里的泉水，水质纯净，甘洌醇厚，用虎跑泉泡龙井茶，色香味俱佳，历来被人们所称赞。最有趣的是，在盛满水的杯子中轻轻放入硬币，硬币将会浮在水面而不下沉。即使水面高出杯口达三毫米，水也不外溢。这是虎跑泉泉水面积张力较大的科学体现。龙井茶、虎跑泉素称"西湖双绝"。

青翠的山谷，环绕的山峰，蜿蜒的小径，红花绿草，共同创造出一个独特的世外桃源，在这里听泉、观泉、品泉、试泉，甚至梦泉，都能让你其乐无穷。

沿着小路走，你会看到茂盛的绿色悬崖下有一个老虎雕像，在悬崖的左边就是泉眼，在这里观赏会是一段愉快的经历。人们常说，来到这里却没有尝过一杯龙井茶，不算到过虎跑。在赏泉的同时，来一杯西湖龙井茶，味道会更好。

The Tiger Spring is situated at the foot of the Daci Hill southwest to the West Lake, with the title of "the Third Best Spring in China" given by Lu Yu, the Sage of Tea. **Legend** has it that a monk named Xingkong lived in Daci Temple during the Tang Dynasty (618–907). He made plans to leave the temple due to lack of water; however, **coincidentally**, one night he dreamed that an **immortal** told him that two **mighty** tigers would move a fountain there. To his surprise, two mighty tigers did come on the following day from Hengshan Mountain and dug a hole in the spot where the spring immediately **gushed** forth. This is where the name of "Dreaming of the Tiger Spring" came from.

The spring came from underground streams. Surveys show that the water is **conducive** to people's health. The spring water tastes pure, sweet, and cold. People of all ages highly praise it after tasting a cup of Longjing Tea made of the water from the Tiger Spring. Most interestingly, the spring water rises three millimeters above a bowl edge without overflowing even if a coin is put into the bowl. This is a scientific phenomenon made possible by the high surface **tension** of the spring water. No surprise then that Longjing Tea and the Tiger Spring are acknowledged as "Two Wonders of the West Lake".

Verdant valleys, surrounding hills, winding path, red flowers and green trees together make a good combination to create a land of idyllic beauty. The pleasure to be gained by listening to the spring, viewing the spring, tasting the spring, feeling the spring, even dreaming the spring enables every thought about the spring to come to mind.

Along the track of the hill, you will see a tiger statue at the foot of the **luxuriant** green cliff. From the left side of the cliff is the source of the spring and it will be a pleasant experience to watch the spring here. It is said that those who came to this place without drinking Longjing Tea wouldn't have been there. Have a seat in a tea house and enjoy a cup of Longjing Tea, you will find the spring water tastes better.

★生词与词组 Words & Expressions

legend /'ledʒ(ə)nd/ *n.* 传说	coincidentally /kəʊˌinsi'dentəli/ *adv.* 巧合地
immortal /i'mɔːt(ə)l/ *n.* 神	mighty /'maiti/ *adj.* 强大的
gush /gʌʃ/ *v.* 涌出	conducive /kən'djuːsiv/ *adj.* 有益的

tension /'tenʃ(ə)n/ *n.* 张力　　　　　　　　verdant /'vɜːd(ə)nt/ *adj.* 青翠的
luxuriant /lʌɡ'ʒʊəriənt/ *adj.* 繁茂的

◆ 知识拓展 Knowledge Extension

虎跑泉：是地下水流经岩石的节理和间隙汇成的裂隙泉。它从连一般酸类都不能溶解的石英砂岩中渗透、出露，水质纯净，总矿化度低，放射性稀有元素氡的含量高，是一种适合饮用，具有相当医疗保健功用的优质天然饮用矿泉水，故与龙井茶叶并称"西湖双绝"。

3. 黄龙吐翠 Yellow Dragon Cave Dressed in Green

坐落在栖霞山脚下北部的黄龙吐翠是西湖的十大景点之一，古时这里有一片桃林为之添色。黄龙洞，又称无门洞、飞龙洞。相传南宋时期，江西黄龙山高僧慧开，字无门，对这里的环境很满意，所以决定在这里建寺修行。风雨交加的一天，人们听到一声巨响，赶到山的后面，发现一块巨石断裂，就说慧开肯定带了一条黄龙来到这里，这就是黄龙洞和无门洞的由来。

黄龙洞背靠葱郁的山丘，小溪、山洞、亭子以及庭园山石的和谐布局使这里充满着尊贵和神秘之美。黄龙洞四周绿荫浓密，曲径通幽，以竹景取胜。在山坡上有 30000 平方米的竹园。竹园内种植着各种各样的竹子，有紫竹(是制作手杖和书架的好材料)、凤尾竹(可做篱笆)、斑竹(可用于装饰、手杖和笔杆)、大叶竹(用于端午节包粽子的粽叶)等，株株吐翠。

几经历史变迁，黄龙洞由佛寺变为道观，又由道观变为仿古园。如今此地已建成以"缘"为主题的圆缘民俗园，每天吸引着大批的游客。"缘"指的是"运气"，或者应该是"好运"。在这个好运园里，我们能经历4种不同的运气：结识到志趣相投、情投意合的人；带来吉祥；得到婚姻的幸福；获得好运。黄龙洞还成为现代人寻古探幽的好去处。

As one of the ten views of the West Lake, Yellow Dragon Cave Dressed in Green which is situated at the northern foot of the Qixia Ridge was dotted with a grove of peach trees in the old days. Yellow Dragon Cave is also known as No Gate Cave or Flying Dragon Cave. It got its names from the legend that an eminent monk in the Southern Song Dynasty called Hui Kai whose courtesy name was Wu Men came here from the Yellow Dragon Mountain in Jiangxi Province. Being content with the surroundings, he decided to set up a Buddhist temple in this location. One stormy day, people heard a loud sound from the back of the hill. They rushed there, only to find a big rock cracking in the middle, and concluded that the monk must have brought a yellow dragon to the site. **Hence** it is called Yellow Dragon Cave and No Gate Cave.

With wooded hills behind, this park features serene and mysterious beauty highlighted by harmoniously arranged streams, caves, pavilions and rockeries. Moreover, with green bamboos growing in the surrounding hills, Yellow Dragon Cave seems to be dressed in green. The rare square bamboo has aroused great curiosity among visitors. There are about 30,000 square meters of bamboo forest on the hillsides. Various kinds of bamboos are available, such as black bamboo, which is good for making walking canes and bookshelves; fern leaf hedge bamboo, which is used to erect fences; **mottled** bamboo, which is ideal for **ornaments**, walking **canes** and penholders; and big-leaf bamboo, whose leaves are especially used for wrapping zongzi, a **pyramid**-shaped dumpling made of **glutinous** rice eaten during the Dragon Boat Festival. All the bamboos are dressed in green.

Through numerous vicissitudes in history, Yellow Dragon Cave has changed from a Buddhist temple into a Taoist Temple, and then into a pseudo-classic garden. At present, a special garden of **folk** custom has been developed with the theme of one Chinese character—Yuan (缘), which attracts countless tourists every day. The character "Yuan", simply speaking, refers to "luck", or "good luck". In this Good Luck Garden, we will experience four different kinds of luck: **congeniality**, auspiciousness, **marital felicity**, and good luck. Yellow Dragon Cave is also a place where modern people are longing to explore the history and find quietness.

★生词与词组 Words & Expressions

hence /hens/ *adv.* 由此	mottled /'mɑtld/ *adj.* 斑驳的
ornament /'ɔ:nəm(ə)nt/; *n.* 装饰	cane /kein/ *n.* 手杖
pyramid /'pirəmid/ *n.* 角锥状的东西	glutinous /'glu:tinəs/ *adj.* 粘质的
folk /fəuk/ *adj.* 民间的	congeniality /kəndʒi:ni'æliti/ *n.* 和谐；情投意合的人
marital /'mærit(ə)l/ *adj.* 婚姻的	felicity /fi'lisiti/ *n.* 幸福

◆ 知识拓展 Knowledge Extension

栖霞岭：又名履泰山或赤岸，在葛岭西面、岳王庙的后面。相传岭上旧时多桃花，到了春日桃花盛开，犹如满岭彩霞，故称栖霞岭。

4. 九溪烟树 & 满陇桂雨 Nine Creeks in Misty Forest & Sweet Osmanthus Rain at Manjuelong Village

九溪烟树是新西湖十景之一，位于西湖西边群山中的鸡冠垅下，一端连接烟霞三洞(即石屋洞、水乐洞、烟霞洞)，一端贯连钱塘江。沿鸡冠垅拾级而上，可直达山顶望江亭。在亭前眺望钱塘江，之字形弯曲的江流尽收眼底，远处烟波浩渺，水天一色。九溪的主景是水。九溪的水源自杨梅岭，沿途汇合了青湾、宏法、唐家、小康、佛石、百丈、云栖、诸头、方家等9个山坞的溪流，曲曲折折、忽隐忽现地流入钱塘江。这里的山和树，都因有了这纵横交错、蜿蜒曲折而又奔流不息的水而被点活，构成了狮峰、龙井、灵隐、五云山、虎跑、梅家坞一带肥沃的土地。

杭州最著名的赏桂胜地——满陇桂雨，自然风光迷人，人文景观独特，集名山、名水、名洞、名刹、名茶、名花、名人古迹于一身，尤以桂花闻名中外，享誉八方。

早在五代吴越时期，这里就建有佛寺满觉院和石屋寺，满觉陇也因此得名。明代以后，满觉陇广植桂花，绵延不息，此地赏桂已为西湖七大花事之一，观者如云。一代文豪胡适、巴金、徐志摩、郁达夫，科学泰斗胡明复、竺可桢、李四光等都在此留下过足迹。

1983 年，中国十大名花之一的桂花被评为杭州市花，满陇桂雨遂成杭州的"市花园"。此后，满陇桂雨又被评为杭州"新西湖十景"之一。

Lying under the Jiguan (meaning "**Crest**") Ridge which is to the west of the lake, Nine **Creeks** in Misty Forest is one of the "Ten New Views of the West Lake", with Three Caves in Yanxia (i.e. Shiwu Cave, Shuile Cave and Yanxia Cave) on the one side and the Qiantang River on the other. Along the Jiguan Ridge, there stands Wangjiang Pavilion, from which you can overlook the Qiantang River with all the surrounding scenery. The main scenic spot of Nine Creeks is the water which comes from the Yangmei Ridge and consists of the nine streams named Qingwan, Hongfa, Tangjia, Xiaokang, Foshi, Baizhang, Yunqi, Zhutou, Fangjia and all of the water will flow into Qiantang River, cultivating Lion Mountain, Dragon Well, Lingyin, Mount Wuyun, the Tiger Spring and Meijiawu into their fertility.

The best place for appreciating osmanthus is the Sweet Osmanthus Rain at Manjuelong Village where the scenery is quite attractive and the scenes and signs there are full of cultural interest. Besides, the Sweet Osmanthus Rain at Manjuelong Village is surrounded by famous mountain, water, temple, tea, flower and is also frequented by celebrities. What's special is **osmanthus**.

It can be dated back to the Wuyue Period of the Five Dynasties when the Buddhist temples such as Manjue Temple and Shiwu Temple were built here, and because of this, Manjuelong Village became famous. After the Ming Dynasty, Osmanthus flowers have been widely planted in Manjuelong Village and then appreciating the osmanthus in Manjuelong Village has become one of the seven great events of West Lake. Furthermore, it is said that the **literary** giants such as Hu Shi, Ba Jin, Xu Zhimo, and Yu Dafu and the scientists such as Hu Mingfu, Zhu Kezhen, and Li Siguan once visited here one after another.

One of the ten famous flowers—osmanthus flower was recognized as the city flower of Hangzhou in 1983. Consequently, Sweet Osmanthus Rain at Manjuelong Village has become the "Park of Hangzhou". Afterwards, Sweet Osmanthus Rain at Manjuelong Village has been accepted as one of the "Ten New Views of the West Lake".

★生词与词组 Words & Expressions

crest /krest/ *n.* 鸡冠	creek /kriːk/ *n.* 溪
osmanthus /ɔz'mænθəs/ *n.* 桂	literary giant 大文豪

◆ 知识拓展 Knowledge Extension

数字"九"：古时候人们常喜欢用"九"字来表示数量众多，其实，这座山区的溪流一路上穿林绕麓，不知汇合了多少细流。十八涧，原是指这条山区溪流的源头龙井一带的无数山涧泉流。所以，十八涧也是古时人们用"九"的倍数来形容山涧泉流众多的意思，并非只有十八条山涧。严格地说，"溪中溪"是"九溪"和"十八涧"两条水流的汇合点，往下形成湍急的九溪河水，流入钱塘江。

5. 雷峰夕照 Leifeng Pagoda in Evening Glow

雷峰塔始建于公元 975 年，但在 1924 年，它因年久失修而轰然倒塌。在 2002 年的时候，千年胜迹雷峰塔重建落成，现在它已成为西湖的十大景观之一。雷峰塔在夕阳的笼罩下显得分外壮丽雄伟，也正因如此，此景也被命名为"雷峰夕照"。传统美学的建筑风格与当代建筑科技的完美结合，使观光者站在雷峰塔上就能一览西湖全景。

雷峰塔坐落于净慈寺北，为吴越国王钱弘俶为庆祝黄妃得子所建，亦称"黄妃塔"。塔身七级，为清时重建，因夕阳西照，塔影横空，彩霞披照，景色十分瑰丽。康熙御题为"雷峰夕照"。与保俶塔"南北相对峙，一湖映双塔"。

雷峰塔也因其深远的佛教文化而为人所知，是中国境内三处存放有佛祖舍利的地方之一。传说《白蛇传》中许仙和白娘子在雷峰塔有一段动人的爱情故事，这也使雷峰塔显得更加神秘，成为爱情文化圣地之一。

Leifeng Pagoda was originally built in the year of 975; however, without being repaired regularly, it fell down in 1924. In 2002, Leifeng Pagoda was reconstructed; and now it is one of the Ten Views of the West Lake, as the Pagoda looks especially **majestic** when surrounded by the golden **hues** of the setting sun. It was therefore named as "Leifeng Pagoda in Evening **Glow**". With the combination of a traditional **aesthetic** style and modern architecture techniques, Leifeng Pagoda offers a view of the West Lake in its entirety.

Leifeng Pagoda is located in the north of Jingci Temple, originally seven-storied. Leifeng Pagoda was built by Qian Hongchu, ruler of the Wuyue Kingdom, to celebrate Imperial **Concubine** Huang giving birth to a son, so it is also named "Concubine Huang Pagoda". It was rebuilt in the Qing Dynasty, as the sunset glows westwards, the shadow of the pagoda looks like crossing through the sky under the rosy clouds. In a word, the scenery is really **fabulous**. Emperor Kangxi inscribed and named it "Leifeng Pagoda in Evening Glow". It is faced with Baochu Pagoda like "Facing each other between south and north, two pagodas were reflected in the lake".

Leifeng Pagoda is also known for its **profound** culture of Buddhism. It is one of the three places which **deposit Buddhist relics** in China. It is **rumored** that Leifeng Pagoda is the place where the love story of a man named Xu Xian and a snake named Bainiangzi took place. This story not only makes Leifeng Pagoda more mysterious, but also makes it a place of romance.

★生词与词组 Words & Expressions

majestic /mə'dʒestik/ *adj.* 雄伟的
glow /gləu/ *n.* 光辉
concubine /'kɔŋkjubain/ *n.* 妾，妃子
profound /prə'faund/ *adj.* 深邃的

hue /hju:/ *n.* 色彩
aesthetic /i:s'θetik; es-/ *adj.* 美学的
fabulous / 'fæbjuləs/ *adj.* 极好的，绝妙的
deposit /di'pɔzit/ *v.* 存放

rumour /'ru:mə/ *v.* 谣传　　　　　　　　　　　Buddhist relics 舍利

◆ 知识拓展 Knowledge Extension

雷峰：就是现在杭州的夕照山。明《西湖游览志》："雷峰者，南屏之支脉也。"

《白蛇传》：此传说源远流长，家喻户晓，是中国四大民间传说之一（其余三个为《梁山伯与祝英台》《孟姜女》《牛郎织女》），都被列入"第一批国家级非物质文化遗产"。据明末《警世通言》载，传说南宋绍兴年间，有一修炼千年的蛇妖化作一位名叫白素贞的美丽女子，与其侍女青青(也称小青、青鱼、青蛇)在杭州西湖和药商许宣(或名许仙)邂逅，同舟避雨，一见钟情，白蛇逐生欲念，欲与书生缠绵，乃嫁与他。遂结为夫妻。婚后，经历诸多是非，白娘子屡现怪异，许不能堪。镇江金山寺高僧法海赠许一钵盂，令罩其妻。白、青被罩后，显露原形，乃千年成道白蛇、青鱼。法海遂携钵盂，置雷寺峰前，令人于其上砌成七级宝塔，名曰雷峰，永镇白、青于塔中。

6. 临安天目山 Mount Tianmu in Lin'an

"天目三千丈，东南第一峰"，天目山是浙江西北部的主要山脉。发源于南岭山系，自西南向东北延伸，延绵 500 千米，没入东海。天目主体由东西两山组成，东边叫东天目山，西边叫西天目山。天目山古名浮玉山，"天目"之名始于汉代，有东西两峰，两峰之巅各天成一池，宛若双眸仰望苍穹，因而得名。东峰大仙顶海拔 1480 米，西峰仙人顶海拔 1506 米。天目山地质古老，地貌独特，地形复杂，茂林蔽日，素有"江南奇山"之称。

天目山历史悠久，拥有璀璨夺目的绿色文化、宗教文化，是儒、道、佛等文化融于一体的名山。东汉道教大宗张道陵出生于天目山并在此修炼多年，现有遗迹"张公舍"；梁代昭明太子萧统隐居于天目山太子庵分经读书，留有"洗眼池""太子庵"等景点；唐代李白、宋代苏轼、元代张羽、明代刘基等文人墨客曾都上天目山游览并留下优美的诗章，现存"太白吟诗石"等人文景观；清代乾隆皇帝也曾上山览胜，并赐封"大树王"，赋予了天目山丰富的文化内涵，使其更具魅力。

"The length of Mount Tianmu looks more than three thousand miles, and it is the top peak of the Southeast." Mount Tianmu, a main mountain in the northwest of Zhejiang Province, is originated from the Nanling Mountain and stretches out from the southwest to the northeast for 500 kilometers and sinks to the East Sea. It consists of two parts, one is the East Tianmu Mountain, and the other is the West Tianmu Mountain. Mount Tianmu, once called Mount Fuyu, got the name of "Tianmu" from the Han Dynasty. The peaks of the west and east mountains look like a pair of eyes looking up to the sky, so the name—Tianmu (meaning "the eyes of the heaven") came into being. The altitude of the east peak of Mount Tianmu is 1,480 meters, and that of the west peak is 1,506 meters. Mount Tianmu, with ancient geology, unique landforms, complex **terrain** and abundant plants and forests, is known as a "**miraculous** mountain of Jiangnan".

The **historic** Mount Tianmu has a bright green culture and religious culture, with Confucianism, Taoism and Buddhism perfectly integrated. The great Taoist Master Zhang Daoling was born here in the Eastern Han Dynasty and **cultivated** himself for many years, with his **remains** of "Zhang's **Shelter**" till now. Xiao Tong, namely Prince Zhao Ming of the Liang Dynasty, once **lived in seclusion** and studied in a temple, leaving the scenic spots of "Eye-washing Pond" and "Prince Temple". Numerous well-known poets and scholars, such as Li Bai in the Tang Dynasty, Su Shi in the Song Dynasty, Zhang Yu in the Yuan Dynasty and Liu Ji in the Ming Dynasty visited here, writing a lot of poems praising the beauty of the mountain. Qianlong, **Emperor** of the Qing Dynasty, once paid a visit to it and even **conferred** a giant **ginkgo** tree the name "Giant Ginkgo King". And thus, the mountain becomes full of rich culture and attractions.

★生词与词组 Words & Expressions

terrain /tə'rein/ *n.* 地形
historic /hi'stɔrik/ *adj.* 历史上有名的，有历史意义的
remains /ri'meinz/ *n.* 遗迹，遗物
emperor /'emp(ə)rə/ *n.* 帝王，皇帝
ginkgo /'giŋgəu/ *n.* 银杏树

miraculous /mi'rækjuləs/ *adj.* 奇迹般的
cultivate /'kʌltiveit/ *v.* 提升；修炼
shelter /'ʃeltə/ *n.* 住所；庇护所
confer /kən'fɜ:/ *v.* 赐给，授予
live in seclusion 隐居

◆ 知识拓展 Knowledge Extension

天目山佛教：自东晋传入，已有 1500 余年的历史，是我国佛教名山之一，有"天目灵山"之称。鼎盛时期全山有寺院庵堂 50 余座，僧侣千余人。建于 1279 年的狮子正宗禅寺和建于 1425 年的禅源寺均为江南名刹。天目山是韦陀菩萨道场。

7. 龙井问茶 Enquiring about Tea at Longjing Well

龙井泉位于浙江省杭州市西湖西面风篁岭上，是杭州三景之一，也是新西湖十景之一。龙井泉本名龙泓，又名龙湫。井旁有龙井寺，初建于五代后汉乾祐二年(949)，已有 1000 多年的历史。龙井附近曾有"八景"之说，现仅存三处。在东北的公路下面，有一凉亭，原称二老亭，相传是北宋主持龙井寺的高僧辩才出风篁岭迎接苏轼的地方。苏轼曾多次到龙井游览。

龙井村是世界上著名的西湖龙井茶的五大产地之一。而龙井泉历史悠久，由于大旱不涸，古人以为与大海相通，有神龙潜居，所以名其为龙井。

龙井泉水出自山岩中，水味甘甜，四季不干，清如明镜。龙井泉的水由地下水与地面水两部分组成。地下水比重较大，因此地下水在下，地面水在上。如果用棒搅动井内泉水，下面的泉水会翻到水面，形成一圈分水线，当地下泉水重新沉下去时，分水线渐渐缩小，最终消失，非常有趣。据说这是泉池中已有的泉水与新涌入的泉水间的比重和流速有差异之故。

龙井除泉、景外，更以盛产品质优良、驰名天下的"龙井茶"而名扬中外，游人慕名来

游龙井，不少是想品尝一下龙井茶的清香茶味的。游客观水赏景，品茗休憩，络绎不绝。

Longjing Spring lies to the west of the Fenghuang Ridge in Hangzhou. It is noted as not only one of the best-known three scenic spots in Hangzhou, but also as one of the "Ten New Views of the West Lake" scenic spots. It used to be named as Longhong as well as Longqiu. Beside the well, there is a Longjing Temple, which was built in 949 during the Five Dynasties and now it has a history of more than 1,000 years. Longjing Spring is also famous for its eight scenes, but only three of them have been preserved. There is a pavilion named Erlao and it is the place where the poet Su Shi had been welcomed by the monk, Biancai by name, who lived at Dragon Well Temple. Su Shi had visited there for many times.

Longjing Village is one of the five places in the world which produces famous Longjing Tea. Longjing Spring has a long history. It is said that it never became dry when drought visited Hangzhou in ancient times. Then this made people believe the well must lead to the sea where dragons lived. So it got the name of dragon well (Longjing).

The spring water gushes out from a rock and the water itself tastes good and is fresh and clear during all seasons. The spring water consists of surface water and underground spring water. and the latter one is the main part. So what is interesting to see is a "dividing line" on the surface of the well water when it is **stirred**, which separates the two levels of the water. It is said the line results from the difference in the flowing speed and specific gravity between the surface water and the underground spring water.

As we all know, Longjing Spring is also well known for its Longjing Tea. Most of the tourists come to visit Longjing Spring with the purpose of having a taste of the tea. And as time goes by, more and more people come here to have a look at the Longjing Spring and a drink of the tea.

★生词与词组 Words & Expressions

stir /stə:/ v. 搅拌

◆ 知识拓展 Knowledge Extension

龙井茶：因产于杭州西湖山区的龙井而得名。西湖龙井茶，位居我国十大名茶之首。龙井，既是地名，又是泉名和茶名。龙井茶以色绿、香郁、味甘、形美"四绝"闻名于世。西湖龙井，正是"三名"巧合，"四绝"俱佳。龙井茶现在的扁形特点相传源于清乾隆皇帝。据传乾隆巡游杭州时，乔装打扮来到龙井村狮峰山下的胡公庙前，老和尚献上西湖龙井茶中的珍品——狮峰龙井请乾隆品饮。乾隆饮后顿感清香阵阵，遂亲自采茶，并在匆忙中将所采之茶放入衣袋带回京城。时间一长，茶芽夹扁了，却备受太后赞赏。乾隆传旨封胡公庙前茶树为御茶，每年炒制成扁形龙井进贡，供太后享用。其实这只是一个美丽的传说，一般认为，龙井茶的扁形，是明末清初，受临近的安徽大方茶制作的影响所致。

十八棵御茶：相传在清朝年间，乾隆皇帝非常喜欢云游四海。当他第六次下江南时，他来到了杭州，游玩西湖后，他想去看看自己最爱的茶。当看到翠绿的茶树，品了龙井之后，他非常喜爱，就模仿着采茶，后来便将那十八棵茶树称为"十八棵御茶"。

8. 平湖秋月 The Autumn Moon over the Calm Lake

平湖秋月景区位于白堤西端，孤山南麓，濒临外西湖，西湖美景可尽收眼底。直到清朝康熙帝游玩杭州后才命名了西湖十景之一的"平湖秋月"。这里是一片美丽壮观的园林，亭台楼阁错落其间，点缀假山叠石，遍植四季花木。在中秋夜晚，平湖秋月是一个最佳去处。在这里，你可以静静地赏月，沉浸在微风中。凭临湖水，登楼眺望秋月，在恬静中感受西湖的浩渺，洗涤烦躁的心境，是平湖秋月的神韵所在。

清康熙三十八年(1699)立碑亭，题名为平湖秋月。从此以后这湖边景点就成为中秋时节湖上划船旅行的代名词。中秋月夜，悠闲地坐在宁静的湖面上划船成为人们体验大自然的最好经历。置身亭台楼阁的最高处，眺望西湖景色，湖光山色尽收眼底。

秋夜时分，在此纵目高眺远望，但见皓月当空，水月相融，金风送爽，湖天一碧，垂柳多姿，百花争艳，人和月亮私语，不知今夕何夕。能在此夜相逢，是人生之乐。自 1950 年以来，该景区经重新翻修，多次扩建。如今这里百花争艳，绿树成荫，假山叠石和亭台楼阁错落其间，使游客心旷神怡，更加宜赏月，宜品茗，宜休闲。

Situated at the west end of the Bai Causeway and on the southern foot of the Solitary Hill, this scenic spot, the Autumn Moon over the Calm Lake, is near the **Outer Lake**. So it affords the broadest view of the West Lake. It was not until the Qing Dynasty when Emperor Kangxi finished his sightseeing in Hangzhou and named it the Autumn Moon over the Calm Lake, which is one of the Ten Views of the West Lake. It is a **spectacular** garden with delicate pavilions, odd-shaped rockery and a rich variety of plants. On the night of Mid-Autumn Festival, there would be no better place where you can **lounge** quietly appreciating the bright moon and enjoying the cool breeze. Near the lake, standing at high stairs to enjoy the **moon** can help you feel the vastness of the West Lake and clear all your worries, and this is also the charm of the Autumn Moon over the Calm Lake.

A stone tablet was erected with the "Autumn Moon over the Calm Lake" inscription in the Qing Dynasty (1699) ruled by Emperor Kangxi. Since then the lakeside spot has been the symbol for the autumn night boat trips on the lake. A boat trip on the lake or sitting leisurely by the placid lake at a moonlit night has long been acknowledged as one of the best human experiences of nature. Autumn Moon over the Calm Lake is the best location for such a night. Leaning over the window on the top floor of the pavilion-like waterfront building, you can command a broad view of all the lake and its surrounding hills.

On an autumn night, when you are looking out here, the moon is bright over the calm lake, the water and the sky **merge** in one color; cool breeze, the lake and the moon are of one; **willows** and flowers show different charms in the moonlight; people and the moon have a private conversation. Time and space are beyond human reach, but seeing someone at such a night on the lake is a pleasure. Since 1950, the scenic spot has been renovated and enlarged for several times. Now blossoms of colourful flowers and shadows of green trees, dotted with rockeries and pavilions, make tourists heartily enjoy the moon, the tea and their relaxation much better.

★生词与词组 Words & Expressions

spectacular /spek'tækjulə/ *adj.* 壮观的，引人入胜的   lounge /laun(d)ʒ/ *v* 闲逛，闲荡

merge /mə:dʒ/ *v.* 相融，融入   willow /'wiləu/ *n.* 柳树，柳木

outer lake *n.* 外湖

◆ 知识拓展 Knowledge Extension

中秋节：每年农历八月十五日，是传统的中秋佳节。这时是一年秋季的中期，所以被称为中秋。在中国的农历里，一年分为四季，每季又分为孟、仲、季三个部分，因而中秋也称仲秋。八月十五的月亮比其他几个月的满月更圆，更明亮，所以又叫"月夕"或"八月节"。此夜，人们仰望天空如玉如盘的朗朗明月，自然会期盼与家人团聚。远在他乡的游子，也借此寄托自己对故乡和亲人的思念之情。所以，中秋又称"团圆节"。

秋暮夕月：我国人民在古代就有"秋暮夕月"的习俗。夕月，即祭拜月神。到了周代，每逢中秋夜都要举行迎寒和祭月。设大香案，摆上月饼、西瓜、苹果、红枣、李子、葡萄等祭品，其中月饼和西瓜是绝对不能少的。西瓜还要切成莲花状。在月下，将月亮神像放在月亮的那个方向，红烛高燃，全家人依次拜祭月亮，然后由当家主妇切开团圆月饼。切的人预先算好全家共有多少人，在家的、在外地的，都要算在一起，不能切多也不能切少，大小要一样。

中秋拜月：相传古代齐国丑女无盐，幼年时曾虔诚拜月，长大后，她以超群品德入宫，但未被宠幸。某年八月十五赏月，天子在月光下见到她，觉得她美丽出众，后立她为皇后，中秋拜月由此而来。月中嫦娥，以美貌著称，故少女拜月，愿"貌似嫦娥，面如皓月"。

三潭印月：又称小瀛洲，与湖心亭、阮公墩合称为湖上三岛，是西湖三岛中最大的一个岛。外湖造有三座小型的瓶状石塔，成三角形排列，形状都是葫芦形。塔尖是一个玲珑剔透的宝顶，犹如一座小小的佛牙塔，但又与佛牙塔不尽相同。每年中秋，人们总会在石塔里点起火，再在圆洞上蒙上薄薄的白纸。皓月当空之时，熊熊火光透过白纸投影在湖面上，十五个闪烁的玉盘，再加上月宫仙子的倒影，十六个月亮倒映于碧水之上，飘荡于波光之间，此情此景，真令人叹为观止。

9. 千岛湖 The Thousand Islands Lake

千岛湖位于浙江省杭州市西郊淳安县境内。它是 1959 年为建造新安江水电站而筑坝蓄水形成的人工湖，以前被称为新安江水库。湖区山水风光旖旎，1078 个岛屿星罗棋布，故得名千岛湖。千岛湖主要景点不下十处，有梅峰观岛、龙山岛、温馨岛等。此外，千岛湖外围景

点也很多，其中赋溪石林被誉为"华东第一石林"。

千岛湖，即新安江水库，在正常水位情况下，面积约 580 平方千米，比杭州西湖大 104 倍，为华东地区最大的人工湖泊。蓄水量可达 178 亿立方米，比西湖大 3000 多倍。

千岛湖分东南湖区、中心湖区、西南湖区、西北湖区和东北湖区等。东南湖区是千岛湖自然风光的精髓，是千岛湖开发最早的景区。主要景点有天池观鱼、密山岛、桂花岛、羡山岛等。在中心湖区你可以尽情地划水乘船，享受岛上野餐。西南湖区湖面广阔，岛屿众多，可领略千岛风光。西北湖区人文景观丰富，主要景点有方腊起义遗址——方腊祠、陈硕真起义遗址、流湘瀑布、长岭石柱、金坞幽谷。东北湖区则湖面狭窄，港汊深邃，历史悠久，名人辈出。

千岛湖湖水清澈，岛屿千姿百态，景区树木茂密，动物繁多，景观独特，物产丰富。千岛湖山水天下秀，优美的自然风光和良好的生态环境使千岛湖展现出广阔的发展前景。

The Thousand Islands Lake is located in Chun'an County, a west suburb of Hangzhou, Zhejiang Province. It was an artificial lake formed in the construction of Xin'anjiang **hydropower station** in 1959, and then known as Xin'anjiang **Reservoir**. The scenery around the lake is fairly beautiful with 1,078 small islands in total, so it has got the name of the Thousand Islands Lake. There are more than ten main attractions including Meifeng Island, Longshan Island, Wenxin Island and so on. In addition, there are also many scenic spots surrounding the lake, among which Fuxi Stone Forest is reputed as the "top stone forest in East China".

The Thousand Islands Lake, i.e., Xin'anjiang Reservoir, occupies an area of about 580 square kilometers, 104 times larger than the West Lake in Hangzhou and is ranked as the largest artificial lake in eastern China; its storage **capacity** is 17.8 billion cubic meters, **equivalent** to more than 3,000 times of that of the West Lake in Hangzhou.

The Thousand Islands Lake consists of the Southeast Lake, the Central Lake, the Southwest Lake, the Northwest Lake, and the Northeast Lake and so on. The Southeast Lake, the essential scenic spots of the Thousand Islands Lake, was the first scenic spot in the Thousand Islands Lake. The main sightseeing attractions are Watching Fishes in Tianchi Pool, Mishan Island, Sweet-scented Osmanthus Island, Xianshan Island, etc. In the Central Lake, you can go boating and have picnic on the island. In the Southwest Lake, you can enjoy the scenery of the thousand islands with spacious lakes and numerous islands. The Northwest Lake is abundant in human landscape, and it is known for the relics of sites of Fang La Movement—Fang La Ancestral Temple, sites of Chen Shuozhen Movement, waterfalls and valleys, etc. In the Northeast Lake, the surface of the lake is narrow, and there are many famous persons in the long history.

The Thousand Islands Lake boasts its clear and crystal water with islands of various shapes. Inside the scenic spots there are a lot of trees and various kinds of animals. It also has a unique landscape with rich resources. The scenic spot of the Thousand Islands Lake is famous all over the world, and the beautiful scenery and the perfect environment guarantee a promising development for it in the future.

★生词与词组 Words & Expressions

reservoir /'rezəvwɑː(r)/ *n.* 水库

capacity /kə'pæsiti/ *n.* 容积

equivalent /i'kwiv(ə)l(ə)nt/ *adj.* 相同的

hydropower station 水电站

◆ 知识拓展 Knowledge Extension

赋溪石林：我国四大石林景观之一，总面积 20 余平方千米，由蓝玉坪(以石城见长)、玳瑁岭(以石狮为胜)、西山坪三部分石林组成。景区以"幽、迷、奇、险"和"怪石、悬崖、灵洞、古道"等千姿百态的自然景观而著称。作为喀斯特地貌的集中分布区，它集地表石芽和地下溶洞于一体，拥有岩溶漏斗、天生桥、竖井、石笋、石幔等众多的地貌特征，是研究地表岩溶和地下岩溶形成的典型标本，被誉为"华东第一石林"，吸引了无数的海内外游人。

方腊(? —1121)：又名方十三，宋代歙州(治歙县，即徽州)人，北宋末年农民起义领袖。

陈硕真(620—653)：睦州雉山梓桐源田庄里(今浙江省杭州市淳安县梓桐镇)人，早年丧夫，有些书上又写作陈硕贞，唐代浙东农民起义军女首领。义军终因寡不敌众而败，陈硕真等被俘杀。

10. 阮墩环碧 Ruangong Islet Submerged in Greenery

阮墩环碧是位于西湖中的一座绿色小岛。它是西湖三座人造岛屿中最小的一座。它于1800 年在浙江巡抚阮元的带领下，由民工挖淤泥堆积而成。阮元是晚清著名学者和大学士。为纪念他治理西湖的功绩，人们为该岛起名为阮公墩岛。许多年来，岛上由于土壤过于松软而不宜建造房屋，一直被当作野生生物的避难所。也正因为如此，岛上一直保持着自然特色，还生长着繁盛的植物。当你划船环顾这个小岛时，不经意间会惊动躲藏在芦苇等植物中的野鸭、灰色的海鸥，还有白鹭。

20 世纪 80 年代，一个环湖而立的村庄建成了，此村庄体现了中国古代的建筑风格并以此作为一个晚间社交活动的场所。在 1985 年，此景被选为"新西湖十景"之一，命名为"阮墩环碧"。这里独特而自然，拥有复杂的园林建筑(此建筑通过小径连接起来)。这里创造出了一个令人陶醉、幽静安谧、远离喧嚣的环境。从划艇上上岸，你便会漫步于多种多样的植物中，被枫树、柳树、樟脑树等植物所包围。阵阵芳香伴随着鸟儿的歌唱不时地袅袅飘来。当你安然地坐在幽静的竹屋中，手捧着一杯茶，欣赏着周围的美景，你会隐隐约约地在烟雾中发现其他两座小岛。这两座小岛倒映在清澈的湖水中，正如那神话故事中的水晶宫。

North of the West Lake lies a green **islet** called Ruangong Islet, the smallest of the three man-made islands in the West Lake. First built from lake-bottom silt in 1800 under Zhejiang Provincial Governor Ruan Yuan, a **renowned** scholar and grand academician (in the central government) during the late Qing Dynasty, the islet was named in memory of him. It stood for many years as a wildlife **refuge** since the soil was too soft to support buildings. Covered with luxuriant **vegetation**, it remained as natural as it could be. While one **paddled** a boat around the islet, quite a few ducks, gray **gulls** and white **egrets** would be **startled** to skim over **indigo** plants and **clover ferns**.

In the 1980s, a village around-the-lake was set up as a **venue** of a **gala** night featuring an ancient Chinese style. The spot was chosen in 1985 as one of the "Ten New Top Views of the West Lake", called "Ruangong Islet **Submerged** in Greenery". It appears unique yet natural with the complex of all-bamboo buildings, linked to each other by stone paths, creating an **intoxicating** serenity and remoteness from the **bustling** world outside. Getting **ashore** from a rowing boat, one immediately finds himself wandering in the mist of the wisteria-twined maples, willows, **camphor** trees, with bamboos, roses and osmanthus trees protruding here and there from the tree grove. From time to time, a gentle breeze stirs up the fragrance of the flowers, which is coupled with the occasional melody of birds nestling among the trees. When you sit in a quiet bamboo hut, with a cup of tea, and appreciate the beautiful scenery, you may find the other two islands **shrouded** in haze. With their distinct reflections in the clear lake water, they resemble beautiful crystal palace that could only be imagined in fairy tales.

★生词与词组 Words & Expressions

islet /'ailit/ n. 小岛
refuge /'refju:dʒ/ n. 避难所
paddle /'pæd(ə)l/ v. 用桨划船
egret /'i:grit; 'e-/ n. 白鹭
indigo /'indigəu/ adj. 靛蓝色的
fern /fə:n/ n. 蕨类植物
gala /'gɑ:lə; 'geilə/ adj. 欢乐的
intoxicating /in'tɔksiˌkeitiŋ/ adj. 令人陶醉的
ashore /ə'ʃɔ:/ adv. 上岸
shroud /ʃraud/ v. 隐藏

renowned /ri'naund/ adj. 著名的
vegetation /ˌvedʒi'teiʃ(ə)n/ n. 植被
gull /gʌl/ n. 鸥
startle /'stɑ:t(ə)l/ v. 使吓一跳
clover /'kləuvə/ n. (植)红花草
venue /'venju:/ n. 聚会地点
submerge /səb'mə:dʒ/ v. 没入（水中）
bustling /'bʌsliŋ/ adj. 喧扰的
camphor /'kæmfə/ n. 樟脑

◆ 知识拓展 Knowledge Extension

阮墩：又称为"阮公墩"，是位于西湖中一座绿色小岛，漂浮于粼粼碧波之上，是西湖著名的三岛之一。由于岛上泥土松软不宜建造别墅，荒芜了百余年。20 世纪 80 年代，园林部门对该岛进行了布局，营建了青竹结构的亭、轩、堂、阁，造型朴素而典雅，现岛上建有云水居、忆芸亭、环碧小筑等竹屋茅居。因岛外碧波粼粼，岛上草木葱葱，故名环碧庄。环碧庄形成颇具特色的"绿树花丛藏竹舍"的水上园林，被称为"阮墩环碧"。现已成为西湖第一垂钓区。阮公墩的特色是每年夏秋季节举办的仿古夜游。

11. 双塔凌云 Twin Pagodas Soaring the Sky

双塔凌云是建德市梅城镇现有古迹中最为亮丽的风景名胜。梅城古称严州，风景秀丽，地理位置十分重要，是一座具有 1000 多年历史的古城和游览胜地。古严州城以南，是新安江、富春江、兰江的汇合处，这里江面辽阔，景色壮观。著名的"双塔凌云"景区就位于此地。两座砖塔一南一北隔江相望对峙，直入云天，塔边山峦起伏，更显得双塔颇有气势，"双塔凌云"因而得名，是古"严陵八景"之一。

双塔始建于隋代，被称为南北峰塔，而当地老百姓也习惯称之为"夫妻塔"。现在的南峰塔重建于明朝的嘉靖年间，这座七层八角空心砖塔高约 57 米。游人可以拾阶而上，从塔底经盘梯登上塔顶，一览山中秀美的风光，而不远处的梅城古镇也尽收眼底。塔周围还有丰富的历史人文景观，如严陵文化碑廊、先贤堂、报恩寺、潇洒亭等。严陵文化碑廊收录了历代著名诗人描写建德山水的传世名作，徜徉其间，可以感受到厚实凝重的文化积淀，体味源远流长的古严州历史气息。

相较建在山腰上的南峰塔，北峰塔地势更高一些。北峰塔下有一古迹"方腊点将台"，是北宋年间农民起义领导人方腊在此为求良将而设立的。登台眺望，可以一览三江口波澜壮阔的风光。

Twin Pagodas Soaring the Sky is the most attractive scenic spot in the old city of Meicheng town in the City of Jiande. Meicheng town, which was called Yanzhou in the ancient times, **possesses** beautiful landscapes and an important geographical location. It is an ancient city with a long history of more than one thousand years and is also a good tourist destination. To the south of the ancient Yanzhou city, where the Xin'anjiang River, the Fuchun River and the Lanjiang River join together, lies a vast expanse of river and forms magnificent view. It is here where the famous Twin Pagodas stand. The two high pagodas standing on each side of the river face each other and tower to the sky. And the mountain ranges around make them more **imposing**. That's how they got their Chinese name "Shuangta Lingyun" (meaning two pagodas tower into the sky), and it is known as one of the "Eight Scenic Spots in the Ancient Yanzhou".

The twin pagodas were first built in the Sui Dynasty (581–618), and are called the North and South Pagodas or Husband and Wife Pagodas by the local people. The South Pagoda we see today was rebuilt during the **reign** of Emperor Jiajing of the Ming Dynasty (1368–1644). It was made of hollow brick, 57 meters high from the ground. Tourists can walk to the top of the tower by winding stairs and have a bird view of the beautiful sceneries of the mountain as well as the whole Meicheng ancient town. Around the pagoda exists rich cultural landscape, such as the Gallery of Yanling Culture, Xianxian Hall, Bao'en Temple and Xiaosa Pavilion, etc. In the Gallery of Yanling Culture, tourists can take a look at the poems of the landscape of Jiande City written by poets of various dynasties, which can help them feel the deep cultural heritage and long history of ancient Yanzhou.

The North Pagoda stands higher than the South Pagoda. At the foot of the North Pagoda is a terrace, where Fang La, the leader of a peasant uprising in the Northern Song Dynasty (960–1127) called the master roll of officers and assigned them tasks. At the terrace, tourists can enjoy the gorgeous river view of Sanjiangkou.

★生词与词组 Words & Expressions

possess /pə'zes/ *v.* 有，拥有

reign /rein/ *n.* 任期，当政期

imposing /im'pəuziŋ/ *adj.* 庄严的，令人印象深刻的

◆ 知识拓展 Knowledge Extension

新安十景：即千岛浮翠、紫金锁澜、白沙奇雾、灵栖洞天、慈岩悬楼、严陵问古、双塔凌云、胥江野渡、七里扬帆、葫芦飞瀑。

12. 万松书院 Wansong Academy

万松书院位于凤凰山北的万松岭上，书院始建于唐贞元年间(785—804)，前身为报恩寺。"万松"字面上的意思是一万棵松树，但实际上，它在古代中国暗示数量极多。所以，字面理解该书院名为万松。万松书院也因其宏大的规模，悠久的历史，深远的影响而成为杭州最有名的书院。据说，清朝时，康熙和乾隆每次微服私访必经此地，而且康熙帝为书院题写"敷文"，所以万松书院又名敷文书院。此外，为大多数中国人所熟知的爱情故事——梁祝，其中的两位主人公，梁山伯和祝英台曾在此学习了三年。所以万松书院又名梁祝学院。据史料记载，万松书院为明清两朝培养了大量的人才。现今，该书院还存有相当数量的文化遗产。

万松书院包括前门、仰圣门、毓粹门、明道堂和大成殿等。仰圣门是万松书院的主要建筑之一。"仰圣"即表示人们对孔子的尊崇和景仰。"毓粹"意为培养多才多艺的人。大成殿主要是用来展示孔子的行教图。

尽管万松书院在明清时期（1368—1911）遭反复破坏和整修，但综合来看，它一直以杭州著名四大书院之首著称。现在，我们所见的就是经过整修的万松书院。文化和自然景观的完美结合使万松书院更加形象。今天的万松书院经常用作大龄男女约会相亲的地方。

Wansong Academy is located on the Wansong Ridge on the north of the Phoenix Mountain, and it used to be Bao'en Temple built between 785 and 804 in the Tang Dynasty. "Wansong" literally means ten thousand **pines**, but actually the "wan" in ancient Chinese indicates **myriad**. So the name of the school is Myriad Pines Academy in its true sense. For its most spectacular scale, the longest history and the greatest influence, Wansong Academy has been ranked the top well-known academy in Hangzhou. It is said that it was a must-go place for Emperors Kangxi and Qianlong of the Qing Dynasty when they made a **incognito** visit，and Emperor Kangxi inscribed "Fuwen" to the Academy, so Wansong Academy is also named Fuwen Academy. In addition, the two main characters in the love story of Liang Shanbo and Zhu Yingtai, a romantic story popular throughout the country, both studied here for three years. That's why this is also called Liang-Zhu Academy. It is recorded in history that the academy has **nurtured** a lot of outstanding people in the Ming and Qing dynasties, and nowadays, there are still a lot of cultural relics.

Wansong Academy includes the Front Gate, the Yangsheng Gate, the Yucui Gate, Mingdao (meaning "Explaining the Principles") Hall, and the Great Hall of **Confucius**. The Yangsheng Gate is one of the main buildings, and "Yangsheng" demonstrates people's reverence and respect for Confucius. "Yucui" means to cultivate versatile people. The Great Hall of Confucius was **dedicated** to the portrait of Confucius.

Despite its repeated destruction and reconstruction during the Ming and Qing dynasties (1368–1911), Wansong Academy had comprehensively been noted as the top of the four well-known academies in Hangzhou. What you see at present is an academy renovated. The perfect combination of culture and nature leads to a more attractive image. Nowadays Wangsong Academy is also used as a place for elder single youths' dating.

★生词与词组 Words & Expressions

pine /pain/ *n.* 松树
incognito /inkɔg'ni:təu/ *adj.* 化装的；隐匿身份的
confucius /kən'fju:ʃjəs/ *n.* 孔子

myriad /'miriəd/ *n.* 极大数量
nurture /'nə:tʃə/ *v.* 培养
dedicate /'dedikeit/ *v.* 供奉

◆ 知识拓展 Knowledge Extension

万松书院：曾名太和书院、敷文书院，是明清时杭州规模最大、历时最久、影响最广的文人汇集之地。明代王阳明、清代齐召南等大学者曾在此讲学，"随园诗人"袁枚也曾在此就读。清代康熙、乾隆两帝南巡时，分别赐额"浙水敷文""湖山萃秀"。2001年7月，杭州市启动万松书院复建工程，按明代建筑风格样式修复，规划面积5万多平方米，建筑面积1200平方米。书院主体建筑包括仰圣门、明道堂、大成殿、毓秀阁等。其中毓秀阁原为接待各地访问学者的处所，现辟有"梁祝书房"，展现梁祝当年刻苦攻读、"促膝并肩两无猜"的场景。明道堂为书院讲堂，陈设展示中国历代科举文化。大成殿为祭祀孔子处，设有"孔子行教图"壁画。

《梁祝》：系梁山伯和祝英台的美丽、凄婉、动人的爱情故事，与《白蛇传》《孟姜女》《牛郎织女》并称为中国古代四大传说。

13. 西溪国家湿地公园 Xixi National Wetland Park

西溪国家湿地公园位于杭州市区西部，距西湖不到5千米，是罕见的城中次生湿地。这里生态资源丰富、自然景观质朴、文化沉淀深厚，是目前国内第一个也是唯一的集城市湿地、农耕湿地、文化湿地于一体的国家湿地公园。

湿地内河流众多，水渚密布，温度适宜，雨量充沛，植被繁多，有大面积的芦荡，众多飞禽走兽。所到之处一派田园景象，鸟语花香，空气清新。其中，洪园、秋雪庵、深潭口、藏书楼、中国湿地博物馆等为必游景点。

　　水是西溪的灵魂，园区70%的面积为水域，整个园区六条河流纵横交汇，其间分布着众多的鱼塘，形成了西溪独特的湿地景观。生态保护是西溪湿地的重中之重，湿地内设置了三大生态保护区和生态恢复区。西溪还是鸟的天堂，园区设有多处观鸟亭，群鸟欢飞的壮丽景观给游客一种视觉上的盛宴。

　　西溪自古就是隐逸之地，众多文人雅士在这里留下了大批诗文辞章。深潭口百年老樟树下的古戏台，据说还是越剧北派艺人的首演地。西溪民风淳厚质朴。每年端午节在深潭口还会举行龙舟盛会。

　　西溪湿地是一个美丽而又宁静的水乡，也是历史上的旅游胜地。这里空气清新，是一个远离繁忙都市生活的健康休闲地。

　　The Xixi National Wetland Park is situated in the west of Hangzhou, less than five kilometers from the West Lake, and it is a precious example of secondary wetland in an urban area. With rich **ecological** resources, unaffected natural landscape and deep cultural heritage, it is the first and the only national wetland with an integration of urban wetland, **plowing** wetland and cultural wetland in China.

　　Inside the wetland there are many rivers with **dense** water. It also has suitable temperature, abundant rainfall, various kinds of plants, vast areas of reed mashes and various kinds of animals. Wherever you go, you can enjoy the idyllic scene with birds twittering and fragrant flowers and feel the fresh and clean air. And the must-go places are Hong Garden, Qiuxue Convent, Deep Pool Mouth, Library and China Wetland Museum.

　　Water is the soul of the Xixi Wetland, and 70% of the area of the park is covered by water. Six creeks weave through the park with numerous fish pools scattered among them, forming a unique scene. Ecological protection is the top priority of Xixi wetland which has set up three major ecological zones of protected areas and ecological restoration. Xixi is also a heaven for birds. There are many birds watching pavilions in the park, and the magnificent scenery of flocks of birds flying together gives the tourists a feast for the eyes.

　　Xixi is also a great place for **dodging** the city crowds. Throughout history, many artists and poets had dwelt in Xixi, leaving behind a wealth of wonderful poems and **prose**. An old stage there was said to be the debut place for the artists of Northern School of the Shaoxing Opera. The customs in Xixi are simple and homely. Every year, the dragon-boat race will be held during the Dragon Boat Festival at the mouth of the Deep Pool.

　　The Xixi Wetland is a beautiful and **tranquil** water town as well as a tourist attraction in history. With fresh air, it is a healthy **respite** away from the **hectic** city life.

★生词与词组 Words & Expressions

ecological /ˈikəˈlɔdʒikl/ adj. 生态的
dense /dens/ adj. 稠密的
prose /prəuz/ n. 散文
respite /ˈrespait; -spit/ n. 暂缓

plow /plau/ n. 耕地
dodge /dɔdʒ/ v. 躲开；躲避
tranquil /ˈtræŋkwil/ adj. 宁静的
hectic /ˈhektik/ adj. 忙乱的

◆ 知识拓展 Knowledge Extension

西溪生态：西溪之重，重在生态。为加强生态保护，在湿地内设置了费家塘、虾龙滩、朝天暮漾三大生态保护区和生态恢复区。入口处设湿地科普展示馆，园区内有三个生物修复池和一块湿地生态观赏区。西溪还是鸟的天堂，园区设有多处观鸟亭，给游客呈现出群鸟欢飞的壮丽景观。

西溪人文：西溪人文，源远流长。西溪自古就是隐逸之地，被文人视为人间净土、世外桃源。秋雪庵、泊庵、梅竹山庄、西溪草堂在历史上都曾是众多文人雅士开创的别业，他们在西溪留下了大批诗文辞章。

14. 玉皇飞云 & 宝石流霞 Clouds Scurrying over the Jade Emperor Hill & the Precious Stone Hill Floating in Rosy Clouds

"玉皇"是指玉皇山，民间传说是天上的玉龙来到杭州而化作的玉龙山。明代，山上建福星观，又名玉皇宫，是道教供奉玉皇大帝的场所，成为"晚清西湖三大道观"之一。

玉皇山有盘山公路，绕山两周半，长4千多米，可直达山顶。你也可以拾级而上，共有石阶2600余级，在给你带来乐趣的同时，也是一种挑战。山顶最高处建有"登云阁"，登此阁，即飞云脚下，令游客有飘飘欲仙之感，"玉皇飞云"即从此意境而来，被选为"新西湖十景"之一。

玉皇山主要的景观有紫来洞、八卦田和七星亭。紫来洞，系西湖"七大古洞"之一，位于玉皇山山腰，洞口以下有三个高度不同的洞石，洞前有假山花园，俯首就能看见八卦田。八卦田在玉皇山南麓，相传为南宋皇帝躬耕的籍田。在紫来洞上方有七星亭，亭旁原设有七只大铁缸，排列如"北斗七星"，称为"七星缸"，以镇火龙。

宝石流霞位于西湖北岸宝石山上。初名石姥山，曾称保叔山、保所山、巨石山、古塔山等。山上奇石荟萃，有倚云石、屯霞石、凤翔石、罗星石等，吴越王封后者为寿星石。宝石山面对西湖，是西湖北面一座天然的屏障，山体岩石裸露呈灰色，系为成岩中的凝灰岩和流纹岩，色彩丰富，每当霞光映照，熠熠闪光如宝石，故称为宝石山，已列为"新西湖十景"之一，称为"宝石流霞"。

宝石山上最引人注目的景观是一座座亭亭玉立于山顶的保俶干塔，该塔始建于五代（948—960），称为"保叔塔"（现今称"保俶塔"）。现存塔身高约45米，塔身修长玲珑，风姿绰约犹如绝代佳丽，因而成了西湖的标志景观。

The Jade Emperor Hill refers to the Jade Dragon Hill in one of the West Lake folktales, in which Jade Dragon came down from heaven and turned itself into the hill. In the Ming Dynasty, when a Taoist temple called Fuxing (Lucky Star) was built on the hill and a **shrine** of Jade Emperor was put in it. It was known as one of the three Taoist temples at the West Lake in the late Qing Dynasty.

The top of the hill can be reached by a more than 4-kilometer-long road which winds its way 2.5 times around the hill, or by a 2600-step footpath which brings a lot of fun as well as a challenge to the tourist to climb up. Currently, a pavilion called "Dengyun (**Ascending** the Cloud)" was built on the top. Climbing up the pavilion, you will see clouds **scurrying** past your feet and feel that you were in paradise. Hence the name of this new scenic spot came into being. And it is one of the "Ten New Views of the West Lake".

The major attractions on the hill include Zilai Cave, Eight **Trigrams** Field and Seven-star Pavilion. Zilai Cave, one of the "seven ancient caves of the West Lake", is located half-way up the hill and has three travertines of different sizes. In front of the cave, there is a nice garden with rockery. Looking down from the garden, you can see the Eight Trigrams Field. This field is situated at the southern foot of the Jade Emperor Hill and it is said to have been tended by an emperor himself during the Southern Song Dynasty. Above the Zilai Cave, there is Seven-star Pavilion. Originally, seven iron **vats** which were arranged in the form of the Big **Dipper** stood beside the pavilion. It was believed that this kind of arrangement can control the Fire Dragon.

The Precious Stone Hill Floating in Rosy Clouds is situated on the Precious Stone Hill on the north bank of the West Lake, originally named Shimu and used to be called Baoshu, Baosuo, Jushi, Ancient Pagoda and so on. There are many special stones, such as Yiyun stone, Tunxia stone, Fengxiang stone, Luoxing stone and so on; king of the Wuyue Kingdom called the latter one Shouxing stone. The Precious Stone Hill faces the West Lake and it is the barrier of the West Lake, and unlike the **limestone** to be found in most surrounding mountains, they are **tuff** and rhyolite rocks. Purple red or reddish brown, these weather-beaten **boulders** are usually **inlaid** with gray stuff, which shines dazzlingly bright in the sun like real **jasper**. That's why the hill was called the Precious Stone Hill. The hill was made into one of the "Ten New Views of the West Lake"—the Precious Stone Hill Floating in Rosy Cloud.

There stands Baochu Pagoda **atop** the Precious Stone Hill and it attracts much attention. It is said that Baochu Pagoda was first built in the Five Dynasties (948–960) and was **nominated** as "Baoshu", and at present people call it "Baoshu Pagoda". Now known as the landmark of Hangzhou, the 45-meter-high pagoda appears to be a pretty girl standing slim and graceful especially at the early dawn.

★生词与词组 Words & Expressions

shrine /ʃrain/ *n.* 圣坛；神殿
scurry /'skʌri/ *v.* 急赶；急转
vat /væt/ *n.* 缸
limestone /'laimstəun/ *n.* (地)石灰岩
boulder /'bəuldə/ *n.* 大块石
jasper /'dʒæspə/ *n.* 碧玉
nominate /'nɔmineit/ *v.* 命名

ascend /ə'send/ *v.* 攀登；登上
trigram /'traiˌgræm/ *n.* 卦
dipper /'dipə/ *n.* (天)北斗七星
tuff /tʌf/ *n.* (矿)凝灰岩
inlaid /in'leid/ *adj.* 镶嵌的
atop /ə'tɔp/ *prep.* 在……顶上

◆ 知识拓展 Knowledge Extension

八卦田：八卦田是南宋年间开辟的"籍田"，呈八卦状，九宫八格，总面积约 90 余亩。八卦田齐齐整整有八只角，把田分成八丘。八丘田上种着八种不同的庄稼。一年四季，八种庄稼呈现出八种不同的颜色。目前，按卦位分别种植了籼稻、糯稻、大豆、茄子、绿豆、粟、红辣椒、四季豆等农作物。八卦田四周种植了大量的乔灌木植物作软隔离，水面上种植了野茭白、芦苇、荷花等水生植物。

紫来洞：由清代福星观道长紫东在玉皇山顶用人工依势开辟而成，又名飞龙洞。特点是洞中有洞，深邃幽奇，湿润凉爽，是夏日消暑胜地。斜壁上写有"紫气东来"四个大字，巧妙地嵌入"紫来"二字。

七星缸：在玉皇山侧按北斗星座形状放置的七口铁缸。最为人们津津乐道的是"七星缸"的来历和缸体上所镌刻的八卦图所蕴含的深刻文化内涵。相传，旧时杭城火患频频，前人信形家之言，谓玉皇山山势如龙所致，乃铸缸七口，置于玉皇山紫来洞东北角，以镇"离龙"，消除火灾。

15. 云栖竹径 & 吴山天风 Bamboo-lined Path at Yunqi & Heavenly Wind over the Wu Hill

云栖竹径是"新西湖十景"之九，它位于西湖之西南，钱塘江北岸，五云山云栖坞里。由于地理环境的特殊性，五云山上的五彩祥云常飞集坞中栖留，并经久不散，称"云栖"。此地距杭州市区约 20 千米，远离市井，山深林神秘，竹林满坡，素以竹景的"绿、清、凉、静"四胜而著称于世。

云栖竹径，四季皆含画意。春天，破土竹笋、枝梢新芽，一片盎然生机；夏日，丝丝凉意，幽雅之感；秋天，黄叶绕地，古木含情；冬日，林寂鸣静，飞鸟啄雪。蝉鸣声声的炎夏暑期，是云栖竹径一年中的最佳时节。行走在幽幽山道上，犹如潜泳在竹海碧波之中；这里有树龄千年以上的枫香树，树干三人合抱，高近 40 米，是西湖著名古树。霜降后满树红叶如映日彩霞。

吴山在西湖东南面，山体由十个或更多的山峰组成，延伸数米直入市区，又被称为"城隍山"。这里一年四季耐人游赏、风景各异、绿树成荫、百花争艳。这里多有奇特的岩石和摩崖石刻。又因这些岩石酷似十二生肖中的动物，也称十二生肖石，象征着人们出生于不同的年份——鼠、牛、虎、兔、龙、蛇、马、羊、猴、鸡、狗、猪年，又可称为吴山十二峰。山上樟树丛生，其中最大的一株是宋朝的樟树，位于山顶的茶楼前，有 800 多年的历史。

吴山位于西湖和钱塘江之间，山巅有一个观亭，可远眺钱塘江及西湖。走出观亭，一块很大的岩石上篆刻着南宋著名教育学家顾禧"吴山第一峰"的诗句。那里可以观看观亭的全景。吴山向多古树，有四季常青的樟树、银杏、枫树，还有宋朝的古樟树，新老交融，面貌一新，恰好点明了吴山天风的佳景。

The Bamboo-lined Path at Yunqi is the ninth of the "Ten New Views of the West Lake". It is located to the southwest of the West Lake, the north of the Qiantang River, a **basin**-like place in Mount Wuyun, Yunqi. Due to the special geographical environment, the colorful clouds around the top of Mount Wuyun stay here constantly and never **disperse** with prolonged time, so it is called

"Yunqi". It is about 20 kilometers from Hangzhou, far from the urban district, and the high mountains are full of mystery, bamboos can be caught sight of around the slope, it is famous with the "green, clear, cool, quiet" bamboo forest in the world.

Bamboo-lined path at Yunqi is as pretty as a picture no matter which season it is. In the spring, bamboo shoots break through the soil, and buds are on the branches, everything is in an abundant life. In the summer, everyone can enjoy the sense of coolness. In the autumn, fallen leaves lie on the ground and age-old trees appear to be full of tenderness. In the winter, the forest is silent with birds **pecking** in the snow. The hot summer is the best time for visiting here. Walking alone the peaceful path is just like diving in the green waves of bamboos. Here stands a liquidambar tree of over a thousand years old, and its trunk could be encircled by three persons, in height of 40 meters. This tree is famous as an ancient tree at the West Lake. After Frost's Descent, the red leaves are as beautiful as the rosy clouds.

The Wu Hill is situated at the south-east of the lake, which is made up of 10 or more peaks. It stretches for several miles and extends into the downtown. Besides, it is locally called the Chenghuang Hill. It is also a place where you can enjoy different scenes in different seasons for it is covered with a rich variety of trees and flowers. There are a lot of **odd-shaped** rocks and inscriptions on the hill. A strange cluster of rocks which is known as the "Twelve Animal Stones" appears like the twelve animals in the Chinese lunar calendar symbolizing the different years in which people are born: rat, ox, tiger, hare, dragon, snake, horse, sheep, monkey, rooster, dog and pig, and it is also called the "Twelve Peaks of the Wu Hill". On the hill, there are many **camphor** trees. One of them, the oldest one, "Song Camphor", stands in front of a teahouse on the top of the hill, is more than 800 years old.

On the top of the Wu Hill, there is a **pavilion** where you can have a view of both the Qiantang River and the West Lake as the mountain is located between the Qiantang River and the West Lake. Walking out of the pavilion, you can see an **inscription** lauding a huge rock as "No.1 Peak of the Wu Hill" by Gu Xi, a famous educationist of the Southern Song Dynasty. From there you could also have a **panoramic** view of the pavilion. Furthermore, ginkgo, **Chinese sweet gum**, pine tree and evergreen camphor were planted all over the hill to accompany the "Song Camphor". All these create a more attractive appearance of the Wu Hill because the new scenery blends perfectly with the old.

★生词与词组 Words & Expressions

basin /beis(ə)n/ *n.* 盆地
peck /pek/ *v.* 啄
camphor /'kæmfə/ *n.* 樟树
inscription /in'skripʃ(ə)n/ *n.* 碑文
Chinese sweet gum 枫香树

disperse /dispə:s/ *v.* (云雾等)消散
odd-shaped /'ɔdʃeipt/ *adj.* 奇怪的，奇特的
pavilion /pə'viljən/ *n.* 亭，阁
panoramic /ˌpænə'ræmik/ *adj.* 全景的

◆ 知识拓展 Knowledge Extension

云栖：吴越时，这里曾建云栖古寺，竹林深处可闻钟磬声，初名"云栖梵径"。寺地尚存，旁有回雁峰、宝刀陇、壁观峰，均属于云栖六景。尽管云栖地处偏远，但贵如康熙、乾隆二帝，每到西湖，必游云栖。如今竹径主干道的路面，便是仿康熙年间原状重修的。路中间一色青石板，两旁镶以卵石块。青石板与卵石块之间，以黑砖嵌出两条黑线。据说，黑线为当年御道款式，只有皇上才配行走，一般人众须在其外抬脚落步，谁若敢越黑线一步，轻则鞭杖，重则论死。

吴山城隍庙：宫殿式建筑的城隍庙是吴山上最大的神庙，旧时庙内庭园古木参天气象萧森，威严自生，令人们心生敬畏，连山名也因此而改叫城隍山了。今日更在城隍庙的遗址高台上修建起斗拱飞檐，城隍阁似仙山琼阁般耸立于吴山之巅，又新添了令人眼前一亮的标志性景观。城隍阁高 41.6 米，面积 3789 平方米，七层仿古楼阁，整体造型具有南宋和元代建筑风格，飞檐翘角，凌空飞升，如凤凰展翅，给人以"龙飞凤舞到钱塘"的联想。其气势足以与黄鹤楼、岳阳楼、滕王阁相媲美，俨然江南第四名楼。

第二节　旅游文化——历史文化

Section 2　Tourism Culture—Historical Culture

杭州是中国著名的风景旅游和历史文化名城，也是中国七大古都之一。中国有句谚语："上有天堂，下有苏杭。"来过杭州的意大利旅行家马可·波罗称杭州为"世界上最为美丽、华贵的天城"。这也促使其成为整个国家最著名的旅游胜地之一。

Hangzhou has long been a famous tourist attraction with rich historical heritage and colorful cultures. It is also one of the seven ancient capitals in China. As shown in the widely expressed Chinese proverb, "in heaven there is paradise and on earth there are Hangzhou and Suzhou." The famous Italian traveler Marco Polo commented Hangzhou as "the finest and most splendid city in the world", which has helped to make Hangzhou one of the most famous tourist attractions in the entire country.

1. 古都文化 Ancient Capital Culture

杭州作为我国七大古都之一，有它的历史文化足迹。它曾经是吴越国和南宋王朝两代的建都地。杭州古称钱塘。隋朝开皇九年(589)废钱塘郡，置杭州，杭州之名首次在历史上出现。杭州作为南宋的都城开始繁荣昌盛。公元 1107—1187 年，宋朝在懦弱的皇帝高宗的统治下，被迫南移，从开封迁都至杭州。

Hangzhou, one of the seven ancient capitals in China, has its own historic footmark. It used to be the capital for Wuyue Kingdom and the Southern Song Dynasty. Originally known as Qiantang,

Hangzhou was established as a city in the Sui Dynasty (589), thus the name "Hangzhou" first appeared in the history. Hangzhou rose to its prominence as the capital of the Southern Song Dynasty (1127–1279). Forced to flee before the invasion took place, the imperial court under the rule of the pusillanimous Emperor Gaozong (1107–1187) moved its capital southwards from Kaifeng to Hangzhou.

2. 吴越文化　Wuyue Culture

　　吴越文化是江南文化的主体，是中华文化体系中的重要组成部分。吴越文化由吴文化和越文化构成。吴文化，主要指以江苏无锡梅里为核心的环太湖区域的吴地文化；越文化，主要指以浙江绍兴为核心区域的越地文化。

　　吴文化和越文化同属江南文化，它们同宗同源，具有很大的相容性。这种相容性既体现在两地相通的吴语体系，又体现在相似的生活方式和相近的社会习俗以及宗教信仰等方面。在五代十国期间，这里正式成立了以钱镠为国王的吴越国，从而实现了吴越政治、经济、文化的高度一体化。

Wuyue Culture is the cultural subject of Jiangnan and also an important part of the system of the Chinese culture. The so-called Wuyue Culture is formed by Wu Culture and Yue Culture. Wu Culture mainly refers to the culture of Wu Kingdom, the core of which used to be located in Wuxi Meili of Jiangsu Province and along the Taihu Lake. Yue Culture mainly refers to the culture of Yue Kingdom, the core of which used to be in Shaoxing of Zhejiang Province.

Both Wu Culture and Yue Culture belong to the culture of the south of Jiangnan. They have the same origin and are compatible with each other, especially in the system of Wu language and similar lifestyle, customs, religions, etc. Kingdom of Wuyue was founded formally when Qian Liu was named the King of Wuyue during the Five Dynasties and Ten Kingdoms, then the integration of Wu and Yue's policy, economy and culture was actually realized.

3. 运河文化　Canal Culture

　　中国的大运河与万里长城一样，被列为世界最宏伟的四大古代工程之一，且已录入世界文化遗产。它创始于春秋时期，吴王夫差开凿的从江都到末口的南北水道沟，距今已有2400多年的历史。此后经过不断的开凿整修，直至公元 1293 年，才完成了一条由杭州直达北京纵贯南北的人工大运河。大运河全长 1782 千米，跨越北京、天津、河北、山东、江苏、浙江四省二市，沟通了钱塘江、长江、淮河、黄河、海河五大水系，比巴拿马运河长 21 倍，比苏伊士运河长 10 倍，比这两条运河开凿的时间早 2000 多年。

　　独具特色的运河文化不仅是中华民族多元一体文化的重要组成部分，而且对中华民族多元一体文化的形成和发展起着重要的推动作用。运河文化以其博大的包容性和统一性，强大的凝聚力和向心力，增进了中国传统思想文化发源地齐鲁地区与中原地区、江南地区的文化交融，更把汉唐的长安、洛阳，两宋的开封、杭州和元、明、清的北京连为一体，从而使各个区域文化融合为中华民族的多元一体和大一统文化；同时，也使运河区域成为人才荟萃之地，文风昌盛之区。

Just like the Great Wall, the Grand Canal is widely recognized as one of the four greatest ancient construction projects in the world and has been recorded in the World Cultural Heritage List. Tracing back over 2,400 years to the Spring and Autumn Period, Fuchai, King of Wu Kingdom, ordered the canalization from Jiangdu to Mokou. The subsequent digging work had been kept on until the artificial Grand Canal running from Hangzhou to Beijing came into being in 1293. With a total length of 1,782 kilometers, the canal, linking the Qiantang River, the Yangtze River, the Huaihe River, the Yellow River and the Haihe River, flows through Beijing, Tianjin, Hebei Province, Shandong Province, Jiangsu Province and Zhejiang Province. It is 21 times longer than the Panama Canal, 10 times longer than the Suez Canal, and 2,000 years earlier than the above-said two canals.

The unique canal culture is an essential part of China's multi-national culture integration; it also pushes forward the formation and development of this integration. The tolerance, unification, proliferation, openness, cohesiveness and centripetal force of canal culture has not only strengthened the ties of Chinese traditional ideology among Shandong, Middle region and the south of Jiangnan, but also integrated the cultural centers led by Chang 'an and Luoyang in the Sui and Tang dynasties, Kaifeng in the Northern Song Dynasty, Hangzhou in the Southern Song dynasty, Beijing in the Yuan, Ming and Qing dynasties. In the mean time, the canal region has also become a place to cultivate talented people with academic successes.

4. 良渚文化 Liangzhu Culture

良渚文化是我国长江下游太湖流域一支重要的古文化。

经半个多世纪的考古调查和发掘，初步查明在余杭的良渚、安溪、瓶窑三镇的地域内，分布着以莫角山遗址为核心的 50 余处良渚文化遗址，有村落、墓地、祭坛等各种遗存。20 世纪 80 年代以来，反山、瑶山、汇观山等高台土冢与祭坛遗址相复合，以大量殉葬精美玉礼器为特征的显贵者专用墓地的发现，莫角山大型建筑基址的发现，显示出良渚遗址已成为实证中华五千多年文明史的最具规模和水平的遗址之一。

良渚文化社会形态发生变革的一个重要方面是以用玉制度为核心的礼制的产生。以用玉制度为主要特征，表明了良渚文化礼制的产生，这无疑是社会发生质变的表现，说明良渚社会已从荒蛮的史前期踏入文明的社会。

Liangzhu Culture is an important sect of ancient Chinese culture in the area of the Taihu Lake, residing at the lower reaches of the Yangtze River.

More than half a century's archaeological investigation and excavation has preliminarily identified three towns—Liangzhu, Anxi and Pingyao, with more than 50 relic sites of Liangzhu Culture, which contain villages, tombs and altars. Since the 1980's, some altars and tombs on the Fanshan Mountain, the Yaoshan Mountain and the Huiguan Mountain have been found to be closely related to those relic sites. The discovery of nobles' tombs with exquisite jade burials and the large-scale Mojiao Mountain Structure relic proves the fact that Liangzhu cultural site is one of the most outstanding regions to display the 5000-year Chinese history.

The ritual system centred on jade usage system was the key to the social reforms in Liangzhu society. The use of jades marked the beginning of Liangzhu cultural ritual system, reflected the substantial change in the society. Liangzhu society was a step from the barbarian prehistoric phase towards civilization.

第三节　景点讲解技能——诗词歌赋借用法

Section 3　Narration Tactics of Scenic Spots—Borrowing Poems

诗词歌赋借用法就是在向游客介绍景点的时候，借助历史文人的诗词歌赋，以丰富游客的历史知识，使他们运用形象思维更好地了解眼前的景观。诗词歌赋的应用可将景点的自然美加以理想化，赋予景点一种诗意的意境美。诗词歌赋还包含了丰富的社会文化信息，它不仅对城市意象的塑造产生重要影响，同时又成为城市意象的一种传媒因素。

我国古代诗词歌赋所表现出来的物我一体、返璞归真、宁静和谐以及追求精神自由等休闲思想实际上是古人的一种生存智慧，是一种尽情享受生活乐趣的快乐哲学。

杭州作为一个风景旅游城市，西湖不仅是城市中优美的自然景观，更是几千年里人类按照自身愿望，与自然环境相互作用的结果，符合人们的理想和传统。在景点介绍过程中，大量描写西湖的诗词歌赋增加了西湖的文化内涵。

苏轼在《饮湖上初晴后雨》中对西湖的描述为："欲把西湖比西子，浓妆淡抹总相宜。"在这两句诗中，诗人用一个奇妙而又贴切的比喻，写出了西湖的神韵。西施无论浓施粉黛还是淡描娥眉，总是风姿绰约的；西湖不管晴姿雨态还是花朝月夕，都美妙无比，令人神往。这个比喻得到后世的公认，从此，"西子湖"就成了西湖的别称。

白居易还在《忆江南》(之二)中写道：

江南忆，最忆是杭州。

山寺月中寻桂子，郡亭枕上看潮头。

何日更重游？

该诗的上句写诗人跑去寺里寻找那美丽的传说，下句写自己悠然躺在床上看澎湃的钱塘潮，一动一静。从中我们可以一窥作者内心蕴涵的种种心理活动，也许可以感受到杭州的难忘。

杨万里在《晓出净慈寺送林子方》中描写的正是曲院风荷的景色：

毕竟西湖六月中，

风光不与四时同。

接天莲叶无穷碧，

映日荷花别样红。

诗人写六月的西湖，不写山，不写水，却抓住了夏日西湖的荷花来写，既合时令特色，又合地理特点。全诗色彩鲜明，清新秀丽，诗中有画，于写景中流露出诗人陶醉于大自然美景的情趣。

描写灵泉洞内唐诗有云，"石上生灵笋，泉中落异花"，而这两句诗所描绘的正是洞中钟乳石琳琅满目，倒映在水中状如异花的奇特溶洞景观。而清风洞则"盛夏之日，风从口出，寒不可御"。霭云洞，云气袅袅，蔚为壮观，洞内精巧灵奇、百态千姿，为三洞之冠。"山青、水清、洞奇、石美、雾幻"，仙境般的灵栖洞让游客流连忘返。

总而言之，杭州景点与诗歌紧密相融。徜徉在美妙的诗歌中，游客们回味古老的历史韵味，更深刻地体会景点的妙处和神韵。

◆ **综合练习**

请运用所学的"诗词歌赋借用法"景点讲解技巧，选一个杭州地区的景点分小组进行中英文讲解练习。

第四节 旅游翻译技巧——词类的转换与增减

Section 4　Translation Skills of Tourism

—Conversion of Parts of Speech & Word Addition and Omission

1. 汉语写作的特点 Features of Chinese Writing

1.1　行文用词华美

汉语旅游材料讲究四言八句，言辞华美。显得"文采浓郁"，辞藻的渲染加上汉语言常采用的对偶平行结构和连珠四字句，使得文字达到音形意皆美、诗意盎然的境效，给人以美感。

1.2　文化上强调"意与境"相混

汉民族的写作美学一贯追求那种客观景物与主观情感高度和谐、融为一体的浑然之美，因而人们常常将景物的内在意蕴依附于其外在的表象之上，使具体的景象获得抽象的人格与情感，做到情与景相融、虚与实相生、意与境相谐，在描绘外界自然美的同时无时无刻不在传递一种内在和朦胧之美。其语言表达常常人文色彩浓郁，物我一体，一景一物，皆有灵性，主观色彩极浓。

汉语语言表达常常伴有大量的对偶平行结构和连珠四字句，以求行文工整，声律对仗，文意对比，达到意境美、色彩美、音韵美和情感美，以及诗情画意、情意盎然的效果。

2. 汉语旅游材料的翻译策略　Translation Strategies of Chinese Tourism Materials

汉语旅游材料文本的多样性决定了翻译策略的多重性，常用的翻译技巧主要有以下几种：

2.1　适当的增添

由于地域、历史、文化背景不同，两个民族对同一事物的理解也存在着很大差异。有些内容在原语国家可能众所周知，但外国人却一无所知。在这种情况下，对原文中一些带有原语文化色彩和历史背景的重要信息，就可以添加解释性翻译，将这部分知识补充出来，避免译语读者的误解甚至不解，做到内外有别。例如：

例 1　传说白娘子曾经在这里修炼。

It was said to be the very place where Lady White, the legendary heroine of *The Story of the White Snake*, cultivated herself according to Buddhist doctrine.

这句话如果完全按照原文翻译，可译作：There once was a cave which was said to be the very place where Lady White cultivated herself. 这样的译文外国人也能看懂，但很可能产生不解：白娘子是谁？为什么会在一个不足一平方米的洞里修炼？添加了 legendary heroine of *the Story of the White Snake*，游客不但容易理解，还会对传说故事有所了解，从而提高了旅游兴趣，加深景点印象。在实践中甚至还能不时见到译员将整个故事进行介绍的情形。

在旅游翻译中，传统节日也经常需要类似的解释性翻译。特别是当游客对传统节日、风土民俗很有兴趣时，节日的来历和习俗就成了十分重要的补充内容。比如"端午节"也可以译作：Dragon Boat Festival—a festival to memorize Qu Yuan—a famous poet and statesman of Chu Kingdom in the Warring States Period, who finally killed himself by plunging into the Miluo River on the fifth day of the fifth lunar month in the year of 295 BC. 粽子可译作 zongzi, a pyramid-shaped dumpling made of glutinous rice eaten during the Dragon Boat Festival。在译文中，采用适当阐释或加注释的形式来明确原义，能够避免译语读者的误解或不解。

从理论上说，增添的内容可以很广泛，只要是与原文相关或理解原文内容所需要的背景知识都可以加入，比如历史年代、人物身份、生卒时间及其历史贡献、地理位置、音译名称在原文语言中的含义等。但是在实际工作中，翻译的侧重点、游客兴趣、必要性以及时间等因素却往往限制了增添的内容和详略程度。

2.2　适当的删减

中国人在描述完一个景色之后，常会引用一段名人的话或者中国古诗作验证，这样会让读者或听者加深印象，并从中得到艺术享受。可是这类补充性信息对外国人和译员来说，却往往是不小的负担。甚至有时候这些描述不但对原文理解没有帮助，还会让游客更觉糊涂。在旅游翻译时，如果没有特别目的和要求，这样的文字常可删去。

另一种情况是，汉语在介绍美景时倾向于使用华丽的辞藻和各种各样的修辞格，甚至几个连用的词表示的都是类似的意思。在英语口语中，这种华丽并不实用，意义相似甚至雷同给人的感觉也不一定美，所以翻译的时候可做适当删减，只要把美好的感觉传达给客人就可以了。

比如在虎跑梦泉有这样一段话：

例 2　这里的泉水，水质纯净，甘洌醇厚。

The spring water tastes pure, sweet and cold.

原文中作了详细介绍，辞藻华丽、句式整齐，读起来让人身临其境、沁人心脾。但是翻译成英文时却可以适当地删减。

例3　在冬天，那些树也是绿意盎然，挺拔苍翠。

The trees are still green and vigorous in winter.

2.3　词类转换

词类转换是常用的英汉翻译技巧。我们在翻译时不可太拘泥于句法形式和词类的对应。即是说，在按照原语的方式来进行理解和按照接受语的方式进行表达时，我们往往需要进行必要的词类转换，采用不同的句法结构，以实现动态对等，这样才能准确表达原义 (the intended meaning)。

在汉译英时，常用到的词类转换形式有：汉语动词转换为英语名词、英语介词短语、英语形容词，汉语名词转换为英语动词等。

2.3.1　汉语名词转译为英语动词

例4　他在**梦**中得到神的指示：二虎将会移泉到此地。

He **dreamed** one night that an immortal told him that two mighty tigers would move a fountain there.

例5　……而桥的阴面却还是**白雪皑皑**.

... while the snow on the shady side still **lingers**.

2.3.2　汉语动词转译为英语名词

例6　在山顶，看海上飘云的日出，可以**享受**其宁静之美。

It is a serene **enjoyment** to watch at the hilltop the sunrise in drifting clouds over the sea.

例7　西湖之美给我留下了深刻的**印象**。

The beauty of the West Lake **impresses** me deeply.

2.3.3　汉语动词转译为英语介词或介词短语

例8　我们都**赞成**这个旅游计划。

We are all **in favor of** this trip plan.

例9　沿着山路**走**，你会看到茂盛的绿色悬崖脚下有一个老虎雕像。

Along the track of the hill, you will see a tiger statue at the foot of the luxuriant green cliff.

2.3.4.　汉语形容词转换为副词

例10　这里的美丽自然风景是**少见的**。

The natural scenery here is **exceptionally** beautiful.

2.3.5　汉语形容词转换为动词

例11　山深林**神秘**，竹林满坡，素以竹景的"绿、清、凉、静"四胜而著称于世。

The high mountains are full of **mystery**, bamboos can be caught sight of around the slope, it is famous with the "green, clear, cool, quiet" bamboo forest in the world.

例12　宝石山上**最令人注目的**景观是山顶的保俶塔。

There stands Baochu Pagoda atop the Precious Stone Hill and it **attracts much attention**.

词类转换的翻译方法在英汉互译中使用非常普遍，而且，转换具有可逆性，即，有英译汉时的英语动词转换为汉语名词，就有对应的汉译英时的汉语名词转换为英语动词。因此，研习了英译汉的各词类转换，也就不难在汉译英时逆向思考并使用相对的转换方式。另外，两种语言体系互译时，词类转换的运用不是随意发生的。运用与否既与原词语所在句子需要表达的语义有关，与其所在的语境有关，也与译者本身的语言素养、语言习惯和译者目标语言的文化背景有关。

◆ 课后练习 Exercises

把下面的句子翻译成英语(Put the following Chinese sentences into English)

1. 在这里我们可以欣赏到内湖和孤山的景色。

2. 这里是一片美丽壮观的园林，亭台阁楼错落其间，点缀假山叠石，遍植四季花木。

3. 相传《白蛇传》中的白娘子曾被镇压在此塔下。

4. 密林掩藏起伸向远处的曲径小道，呈现出一幅欣欣向荣的优雅景致。

5. 夏日，丝丝凉意，幽雅之感。

6. 马家浜文化作为长江下游地区史前文化在中国史前文化中有着重要地位，为研究长江下游地区在中国文明起源中的作用提供了宝贵的实物资料。

第二章　宁波、舟山景域

Chapter Two　Ningbo & Zhoushan Scenic Zone

第一节　旅游景点

Section 1　Scenic Spots

1. 阿育王寺 Asoka Temple

阿育王寺又名广利寺，是中国现存唯一以印度阿育王命名的千年古寺。阿育王寺位于宁波鄞县太白山麓的育王山，始建于西晋武帝太康三年(282)，至今已有1700多年历史。

阿育王寺占地80000多平方米，集古建筑、雕刻、园林、文物、景点、绘画等文化与艺术之大成，寺内建筑雄伟，金碧辉煌，主要建筑有舍利殿、大雄宝殿、云水堂、藏经楼等600余间，建筑面积14000平方米，规模宏大。

璀璨辉煌的舍利殿，顶上铺着黄色琉璃瓦，金碧辉煌。寺内的舍利塔，佛光闪熠，塔内供奉镇寺之宝舍利，是一颗释迦牟尼佛真身舍利(在我国仅三颗)，藏于一座精致玲珑的铜塔内。该塔据传是古印度阿育王在各地所建的84000个宝塔之一。舍利塔在中外佛教界中享有盛誉，是寺内最宝贵的遗迹。寺后侧壁的石雕"四大金刚"及法堂两侧壁上的"十六王子"砖雕，神态逼真，气韵多姿。寺院附近还有佛迹亭、极目亭、仙人岩和七佛潭等胜迹。

阿育王寺保存的珍贵文物众多，其中有元代上、下塔、有唐代范的所书大唐阿育王寺"常住田碑"，宋代苏轼撰书"宸奎阁碑"，宋代张九成撰写"妙喜泉铭"以及钦赐龙藏经卷7247卷。此外，悬挂在寺内的匾额中的还有一些是清高宗、宋孝宗和宋高宗等御笔题词的珍品，见证了寺庙的辉煌历史。阿育王寺在我国佛教史上有着重要地位，现为佛教全国重点寺院。

Asoka Temple is also called Guangli Temple is the only temple extant in China named after Asoka (a king of ancient India). Situated on Asoka Hill of Mount Taibai in Yin County of Ningbo, it was first built in the Western Jin Dynasty (282), over 1,700 years from now.

Covering an area of over 80,000 square meters, Asoka Temple is a culture and art complex of ancient architecture, sculptures, gardens, cultural relics, scenic spots and paintings, etc. The temple is of grand and splendid architecture style, with more than 600 rooms, including the Hall of Stupa, the Hall of Sakyamuni, the Hall of Yunshui and the Scripture-storing Tower, etc., covering a total floor area of 14,000 square meters.

The Hall of Stupa is **resplendent** and glorious, with its roof paved by yellow glass tiles. The Stupa is glittering with Buddha's light，inside of which the Buddhist relic was enshrined and worshiped. The Buddhist relic here is the real relic of Sakyamuni (one of the three in China), stored in an exquisite bronze pagoda. As the most valuable relics of the temple, the stupa here is said to be one of the 84,000 stupas all over the world initiated by Asoka, which enjoys a high reputation in the Buddhist circles in both China and abroad. Stone statues of "Four Warriors" on the sidewall behind the temple and brick sculptures of "Sixteen Princes" on the sidewalls of Hall of Dharma are both carved with a style of realism and a variety of artistic conceptions. Besides, there are other famous historical sights near the temple, such as the Pavilion of Buddha's Footprint, the Pavilion of Unlimited View, the Rock of **Immortals** and the Pond of Seven Buddhas, etc.

A great number of rare cultural relics are preserved in the temple, including the Upper Pagoda and Lower Pagoda of the Yuan Dynasty, the tablet of Asoka Temple written by Tangfan in the Tang Dynasty, the tablet written by Su Shi in the Song Dynasty, the tablet inscription written by Zhang Jiucheng in the Song Dynasty and 7,247 *Tibetan Dragon Sutras* bestowed by emperors. Besides, there are some precious horizontal inscribed board hung in the temple, inscribed by the Emperor Gaozong of the Qing Dynasty, the Emperor Xiaozong and the Emperor Gaozong of the Song Dynasty, being a witness of the glorious history of the temple. Asoka Temple has a significant position in the history of Buddhism, which is on the list of national key Buddhism temples.

★生词与词组 Words & Expressions

resplendent /ri'splend(ə)nt/ *adj.* 华丽的   immortal /i'mɔːtəl/ *n.* 神仙

◆ 知识拓展 Knowledge Extension

阿育王(约公元前 304 年—前 232 年)：AsoKa，音译阿输迦，意译无忧，故又称无忧王，是印度孔雀王朝的第三代君主，频婆娑罗王之子，是印度历史上最伟大的一位君王。据说，阿育王由于在征服羯陵伽国时目睹了大量屠杀的场面，深感悔恨，于是停止武力扩张。后半生是"白阿育王"时代，他在全国努力推广佛教，终于促成了这一世界性宗教的繁荣。阿育王在全国修了 8.4 万座佛舍利塔，多次帮助僧团，布施供养三宝。由于阿育王后来幡然悔悟，并且积极地爱护人民，保护生命，护持佛教，所以他被人们尊为"护法名王"。

"舍利子"：原称为"舍利"，后来才称为舍利子。舍利原是印度语，译为"设立罗"等各种不一之名称，其意义为遗留物或灵骨，说明修行者已得成果的见证，可以坚定弟子修行。因此佛徒看到舍利即像看到佛菩萨，顶礼参拜，诚心供养。舍利塔，是中国几千年文明史的载体之一，被佛教界人士尊为佛塔。礼拜舍利宝塔是人们表达对诸佛皈依和感恩的方式。

2. 慈城古建筑群 Cicheng Ancient Building Complex

慈城镇位于宁波市江北区，是中国历史文化名镇。慈城是江南极少数保存较为完好的县城，保存了完整的传统生活结构，保留下来的传统建筑中有大量的民居建筑等历史建筑。慈城古建筑群是其中最优秀、最具有代表性的，2009 年获联合国 "文化遗产保护荣誉奖"，是全国重点文物保护单位。

慈城古建筑群主要包括孔庙、甲第世家、福字门头、冯岳彩绘台门、姚镇故居、冯宅、桂花厅、刘家祠堂、莫骖马宅、程氏余庆堂、方家砖雕台门、恩荣坊、东官坊、世恩坊、贞节坊等古建筑。

其中孔庙始建于北宋(1048)，布局完整，规模宏大，为浙东地区现存最为完整的文庙，反映了儒学在传统生活中的重要性及其深远的影响。现占地 17565 平方米，保存的建筑大多建于清中晚期。

甲第世家始建于明嘉靖年间，为嘉靖进士钱照住宅。该宅坐北朝南，平面布局为长方形。该宅从平面布局到建筑特点都具有明代民宅建筑的特有形式，是保存较完整的一组建筑群，是研究明代晚期住宅建筑之典型。

冯岳彩绘台门为明嘉靖南京刑部尚书冯岳故居，为万历帝所赐建，台门所有梁、柱、枋、额、斗拱上都有粉彩的孔雀牡丹、鹤、荷花叶图案，部分斗拱上还有龙、凤、麒麟、灵芝、如意等透雕木刻。该台门从建筑风格与构造特征看是典型的明代原物，是明代南方建筑彩画的最佳实例之一。

慈城古建筑群周围保留了完整的传统街区，至今仍保留着 "一街一河双棋盘" 的中国传统县城的完整形态，从很大程度上体现了慈城明清时期的建筑风格和生活气息。

Situated in Jiangbei District of Ningbo, the town of Cicheng is a nationally famous town of historical culture, and one of the few well-preserved towns in Jiangnan, retaining the **intact** traditional life structure. It not only contains a lot of civilian houses, but also a large number of historical constructions. Being the best and most representative constructions of the town, Cicheng Ancient Building Complex won the honorary award of cultural relics preservation given by the United Nations in 2009 and it was also one of the national key cultural relic protection units.

Cicheng Ancient Building Complex consists of many ancient constructions, including the **Confucius** Temple, Aristocratic Family of Jiadi (Jiadi here means a family of which many members succeeded in the highest imperial examinations), the House Gate with the Character of Fu, the Coloured Drawing House Gate of Feng Yue, the Former Residence of Yao Mo, Feng's Former Residence, the Hall of **Osmanthus Fragrans**, the Ancestral Hall of Liu's Family, The Residence of Family Mo of Emperor's Son-in-law, the Yuqing Hall of Cheng's Family，the Brick Sculpture House Gate of Fang's Family, Enrong Lane, Dongguan Lane, Shi'en Lane and the Memorial Archway of **Chastity**, etc.

First built in the Northern Song Dynasty (1048) with a complete layout and grand size, the Confucius Temple in the complex is the best-preserved temple of its kind in East Zhejiang, reflecting the profound impact that the Confucianism has on the traditional Chinese lifestyles. It now occupies an area of 17,565 square meters, and most of its constructions were built during the middle and late Qing Dynasty.

Aristocratic Family of Jiadi is the residence of Qian Zhao, a Jinshi (a successful candidate in the highest imperial examination) in the Ming Dynasty (1545). The house sits north to south, with a plane layout of rectangle. It is of unique architecture style of the Ming Dynasty both in its layout and construction features, being a set of well-preserved houses as well as a typical example of studying the residence of the late Ming Dynasty.

The Coloured Drawing House Gate of Feng Yue is the former residence of Feng Yue, a Ministry of Penalty in Nanjing of the Ming Dynasty, which was granted by the Emperor Wanli. The beams, pillars, horizontal inscribed board and brackets of the house gate are all decorated with **pastel** peacock and peony, crane and lotus; some of the brackets have **hollowed-out** wood carvings with patterns like dragon, phoenix, **kylin**, **lucid ganoderma** or Ruyi. The house gate should be an original one of the Ming Dynasty judged from its construction style and features, which is one of the best examples representing the colored drawing art of architecture in South China in the Ming Dynasty.

The whole traditional streets are well preserved around the complex, remaining a complete form of traditional Chinese town, that is "one street, one river and double chessboards", mirroring Cicheng's architecture feature and life style during the times of the Ming and Qing dynasties to a great extent.

★生词与词组 Words & Expressions

intact /in'tækt/ *adj.* 未受损的
aristocratic /ærɪstə'krætik/ *adj.* 贵族的
hollowed-out /'hɔləud'aut/ *adj.* 中空的
osmanthus fragrans 桂花

chastity /'tʃæstiti/ *n.* 贞节；节操
pastel /pæs't(ə)l/ *adj.* 粉彩的
kylin /'ki'lin/ *n.* 麒麟
lucid ganoderma 灵芝

◆ 知识拓展 Knowledge Extension

宋式彩画：是中国宋代建筑木构件上所绘的一种彩画。宋式彩画的纹样有花纹、琐纹、云纹、飞仙、飞禽、走兽和人物。宋式彩画除了用于檐下外，也在柱子上广泛地使用。《营造法式》上对此有记载，现实例已不多。

3. 河姆渡遗址 Ruins of Hemudu Culture

河姆渡遗址位于浙江省余姚市河姆渡镇，是距今 7000 年前新石器时代的古文化遗存。遗址以其悠久、独特而又丰富的文化内涵，被学术界命名为"河姆渡文化"。河姆渡遗址面积 4 万多平方米，共出土 7000 余件文物，为全国重点文物保护单位，国家级爱国主义教育基地。

河姆渡遗址景区由博物馆、遗址挖掘现场和原始聚落展示区以及原始生态区组成。博物馆内共展出文物 400 余件，设有 3 个基本陈列厅和 1 个临时展厅。其中河姆渡生态环境的模型，十分逼真地再现了 7000 年前河姆渡人的生活。

河姆渡遗址由四个文化层组成，从 5000 年前的第一文化层开始，到 7000 年前的第四文化层，前后延续 2000 年左右。在遗址第三、四文化层中，发现了大片木构建筑遗迹，是目前发现最早的"干栏式"建筑，是中国南方传统木结构建筑的祖源。这里还存在着稻谷、谷壳、稻秆和稻叶、米粒等的堆积，保存较为完好。

河姆渡遗址出土石、骨、木、陶质的各种生产工具几千件，以骨器为主。河姆渡遗址还出土了大量精美艺术品，不少都饰有鸟和太阳结合的图案，有些是用骨、角、兽牙和玉石材料制成的。其中出土的 8 支木桨是目前所知世界上最早的水上交通工具。出土的近 20 种象牙雕刻，也各具特色。这集中地反映了先民们丰富的精神生活和文明程度。

Located at Hemudu Town in Yuyao, Zhejiang Province, Ruins of Hemudu Culture is a site of ancient culture of the Neolithic Age (New Stone Age) 7,000 years ago. The site is named as "Hemudu Culture" by academia for its long-standing, unique and rich cultural connotation. It covers an area of over 40, 000 square meters, with more than 6,700 unearthed cultural relics. It is one of the national-level historic preservation units and a national base for patriotic education.

The site of Ruins of Hemudu Culture consists of four sections: the museum, the excavating sites, the exhibition area of **primitive** tribes and the primitive ecological area. The museum has three primary exhibition halls and one temporary exhibition hall, displaying more than 400 cultural relics. In particular, the model of Hemudu ecological environment is a vivid reproduction of the life of Hemudu residents 7, 000 years ago.

Four culture levels are included in Ruins of Hemudu Culture, from the first culture level of 5,000 years ago to the fourth culture level of 7,000 years ago, lasting around 2,000 years. Many architectural remains of wood structure are discovered in the third and the fourth culture levels, regarded as the earliest architecture of "stilt style" and the origins of the traditional architecture in the south of China. Besides, the piles of rice, **chaff**, rice straws, rice leaves and rice grains are also in good preservation here.

Thousands of manufacturing tools made of stone, bone, wood and pottery are excavated in Ruins of Hemudu Culture, most of which are bone objects. A lot of exquisite works of art are also unearthed, many of which are decorated with the patterns integrating birds and the sun, some of which are made of bone, horn, animal teeth and jade. Among them, the unearthed 8 wooden paddles are believed to be the earliest **aquatic** vehicles in the world. Moreover, nearly 20 ivory sculptures are unearthed, each with its distinctive characteristics. All of these reflect the rich spiritual life and the civilization of the ancestors.

★生词与词组 Words & Expressions

primitive /'primitiv/ *adj.* 原始的   chaff /tʃæf/ *n.* 糠

aquatic /ə'kwætik/ *adj.* 水上的

◆ **知识拓展 Knowledge Extension**

河姆渡文化：河姆渡文化是中国长江下游地区年代较早的新石器时代文化遗存，其文化特征在考古学上有一定的代表性，遂于 1976 年命名之。河姆渡文化的发现与确立，扩大了中国新石器时代考古研究的领域，说明在长江流域同样存在灿烂古老的新石器时代文化。

河姆渡的骨器：河姆渡文化的骨器制作比较先进，有耜、鱼镖、镞、哨、匕、锥、锯形器等器物，经精心磨制而成，一些有柄骨匕、骨笄上雕刻花纹或双头连体鸟纹图案，可谓是精美绝伦的实用工艺品。

4. 黄坛古民居 Huangtan Ancient Housing

黄坛镇位于宁海城西 5000 米处，已有 1000 多年的历史，明清古建筑民居遍布全镇，蔚然成景。原有大型院落 20 多座，目前仍存近 10 座。各院落之间卵石盘根错节，清冽渠水围绕，遗世独立，悠然一派古朴幽静的古村落景象。

黄坛的大型院落多建于清代中后期，座座四合院均有精致的木、石、砖三雕装饰，手法多样、雕刻技艺精湛、表现内容题材丰富，尤以黄坛四堂为代表。

黄坛四堂的砖雕以厚诒堂的门楼为代表，台门上昂首戏球的五只狮子，翘首飞翔的两只凤凰，无不形态生动，栩栩如生。台门门头上的八仙人物故事，采用深浮雕手法，精雕细琢，构思严谨，布局巧妙，情景交融。木雕多分布于门窗、屏风、梁架、雀替、牛腿和额枋上，不仅雕刻得极为精致，而且内容丰富，形式多样，集浪漫与写实于一体。石雕主要用于台门、漏窗、柱础和门柱上，设计精巧，人物和动物生动形象、千姿百态。精美的三雕艺术，营造了厚诒堂浓郁的书卷气息和强烈的艺术氛围。

益善堂最具特色的是遍布各面墙上的十六片各式红石石花窗。后墙上有雕刻着"状元及第""寿考维祺"文字以及平安、狮子抢球、魁星等图案的石花窗；山墙上有雕刻着寿、福、双金钱、喜报等图案的石花窗。这些石花窗仿照木隔扇做法，图案复杂，雕琢精致细腻，巧妙地将文字与人物、图案融为一体，工艺难度极高，堪称一绝。

克绍堂吸收了苏州园林建筑风格，将精致细巧的园林特色与粗犷豪放的台州式建筑风貌巧妙结合起来，使民居兼具实用与审美的功能，别具一番超凡脱俗的韵味。居易堂主要特色是台门两边的五花卷草山墙，造型高大，气势雄伟，烘托出深宅大院的威严显赫。

Situated 5 kilometers away from the west of Ninghai City, the town of Huangtan has a history of more than one thousand years, with ancient houses of the Ming and Qing dynasties scattering all over the town, making it a historical resort. Nearly 10 large courtyards out of the over 20 originally built are well preserved, connected with stone pathways and surrounded by clear ditch water.

Setting itself apart from other towns, Huangtan gives a carefree and leisurely impression through its primitive simplicity and original ancient features.

The large courtyard dwellings of Huangtan were mainly built in the middle or late Qing Dynasty, and each was decorated with fine wood, stone and brick carvings, with diverse techniques, exquisite carvings, and rich contents, in particular with the Four Huangtan Halls.

The gate tower of the Houyi Hall is the representative of brick carving of the Four Huangtan Halls, taking the examples of "five lions playing a ball" and "two flying phoenixes" on the house gate, invariably natural and vivid. Another example is "the tale of the Eight Immortals" on the top of its gate, adopting a style of relief carving, with delicate craftsmanship, **rigorous** design, clever layout and scene blending with feelings. The wood carvings are mostly distributed on the windows, screens, **trusses**, **sparrow braces**, brackets and architraves, not only with exquisite craft, but also rich in content and form, combining the styles of romanticism and realism. Stone carvings are mainly used on gates, open frames, leaking windows, column bases and doorposts, exquisite in design, vivid in carved characters and animals which differ in various ways. The fine art of three carvings creates a rich cultural and artistic atmosphere for the Houyi Hall.

The most distinctive feature of the Yishan Hall is its 16 stone flower windows on each wall of the house, which are made of red stones and vary in forms. The stone flower windows on the back wall are carved with characters like "Zhuang-Yuan-Ji-Di", meaning "being No.1 in the highest imperial exam", "Shou-Kao-Wei-Qi", meaning **"longevity**-happiness-good fortune-good health", and patterns like "Safety", "Lions challenge for the ball" and "Kuixing", the god of literature. And the stone flower windows on the gables are carved with patterns like "Shou", meaning "longevity", "Fu", meaning "good fortune", "double coins" and "good news". Drawing on the craft of wooden **partition** windows, these stone flower windows are of complicated patterns and delicate carvings. Skillfully integrating characters, figures and patterns into a whole, it is extremely difficult in craftsmanship, making it the only one of its kind.

Borrowing from the architectural style of Suzhou Gardens, the Keshao Hall combines the exquisiteness of gardens with the roughness of Taizhou architecture, providing the dwellings with practical and aesthetic functions at the same time, as well as the extraordinary charm. The uniqueness of the Juyi Hall lies in the flower-grass figure gables on both sides of its house gate, lofty in design and grand in manner, adding a dignified and **illustrious** atmosphere to this grand courtyard.

★生词与词组 Words & Expressions

rigorous /'rigərəs/ *adj.* 严密的
longevity /lɔn'dʒeviti/ *n.* 长寿
illustrious /i'lʌstriəs/ *adj.* 显赫的

truss /trʌs/ *n.* 梁架，桁架
partition /pɑː'tiʃ(ə)n/ *n.* 隔板
sparrow brace 雀替

◆ 知识拓展 Knowledge Extension

黄坛四堂：指黄坛严民家族"金""石""绿""竹"四房的宅院，分别称厚诒堂、益善堂、克绍堂、居易堂四堂。四堂的艺术价值主要体现在石、砖、木、三周仙中，"三周仙"艺术在浙江省内少见，堪称一绝。

5. 普陀山——海天佛国 Mount Putuo—Buddhist Country amidst Sea and Sky

普陀山山上林木苍郁，怪石陆离，金沙铺岸，礁石嶙峋，天然风景绚丽多姿，与佛教所寻的清静、庄严、神圣的境界不谋而合，从唐代始便成为观音道场，与山西省的五台山、四川省的峨眉山以及安徽省的九华山并称为中国"四大佛教名山"。由此，"海天佛国"的普陀山天下闻名。

普济寺、法雨寺、慧济寺并称为普陀山的三大禅寺，各有各的优雅妙处。

普济寺，其前身是有名的"不肯去观音院"，始建于北宋，现为全国重点寺院。普济寺规模宏大，建筑雄伟，占地 26000 多平方米，有大小殿宇 231 间，殿宇间古木参天，宝鼎蒙烟。其中大圆通殿是寺之正殿，殿正中塑有观音像，高约九米，金碧辉煌。两边塑有观音三十二应身像，仪态不一，展现观音在十方世界以不同身份出现的各种形象，其中就有化为凡人的形象。

法雨禅寺创建于明万历八年，现存殿宇 294 间。康熙(清朝皇帝)所赐的"天华法雨"和"法雨禅寺"匾额高高悬挂于庙宇大门，使之成为当时名动江南的一代名刹。天王殿、玉佛殿、九龙殿等建筑从远处看金碧辉煌，气象超凡，使整座寺庙显得宏大高远。其中天王殿中供奉着四大天王，分别象征风、调、雨、顺，庇护当地百姓。

慧济寺俗称佛顶山寺，坐落于普陀山佛顶山上，初建于明代，占地约 13300 平方米。寺中汇集唐、宋、元、明、清等历朝名画家所绘的观音宝像，形态各异，精妙绝伦，是普陀山佛教艺术精华之一。整座寺院依山而建，以幽静称绝。大雄宝殿盖彩色琉璃瓦，阳光之下光芒四射，形成"佛光普照"奇景，煞是壮观。

普陀山南海观音立像台座三层，总高 33 米，其中佛像高 18 米，台基面积为 5500 平方米。佛像顶现弥陀，左手托法轮，右手施无畏印，雍容、慈祥，不愧为海天佛国的象征。据报道，南海观音大佛开光那天，原本天空乌云密布，风雨欲来。红布落下的一瞬，却从天空云层中裂开一道光缝，金光直射佛像，光彩夺目，似观音显灵，在场所有人都对这奇异的景象感到震惊。

Mount Putuo, with its verdant trees, odd rocks, golden beaches and **craggy** reefs, has gorgeous natural scenery which fits perfectly with the serene, **solemn** and holy atmosphere that Buddhism pursues. Hence it has become a special place to enshrine Avalokitesvara ("Guanyin" in Chinese) since the Tang Dynasty and one of the four Famous Buddhist Mountains in China, the rest being Mount Wutai in Shanxi Province, Mount Emei in Sichuan Province and Mount Jiuhua in Anhui Province. Gradually, the fame of Putuo as "Buddhist Country amidst Sea and Sky" spreads throughout the country and even the world.

Puji Temple, Fayu Temple and Huiji Temple are known as the three major temples at Mount Putuo, each endowed with its own beauty and splendor.

First built during the Northern Song Dynasty, Puji Temple originates from the "Not-willing-leave" Temple in the Tang Dynasty, and is one of the key temples in the country. Enormous in size with magnificent architecture, occupying an area of over 26,000 square meters, the temple has 231 halls of various sizes with ancient trees and huge incense burners standing in between. In the center of its main hall—Grand Yuantong Hall is a glittering 9-meter-tall statue of Guanyin, and on both sides there are 32 statues representing Guanyin's different images with some as ordinary persons.

Fayu Temple was first built in the Ming Dynasty (1580) with 294 halls. The horizontal inscribed boards with "Tian Hua Fa Yu" and "Fa Yu Chan Si" hung on the front gate, which were **bestowed** by Kangxi (an emperor of the Qing Dynasty), brought the Temple great fame at that time. Seen from the distance, the Hall of Heavenly King, Emerald Buddha Hall and the Nine-Dragon Hall are splendid and magnificent with an extraordinary scene, which makes the whole temple remarkable and spectacular. There are four Heavenly Kings enshrined in the Hall of Heavenly King, symbolizing wind, harmony, rain, and timeliness respectively.

Located on the Foding Peak, Huiji Temple was first built in the Ming Dynasty, covering an area of about 13,300 square kilometers. It has a large collection of precious sculptures of Guanyi Buddha with various patterns painted by famous artists in the Tang, Song, Yuan, Ming and Qing dynasties, delicate and peerless, contributing partly to the essence of Buddhist art of Putou. The whole temple sits along the mountain, famous for its **tranquility**. The roof of the Grand Hall is paved with colorful glazed tiles, bright and shining under the sun, forming an extraordinary and grand sight of "Buddha's Grace Illuminates All Creatures".

The standing statue of Guanyin of the South Sea at Mount Putuo has a pedestal of three layers, with a total height of 33 meters. The statue itself is 18 meters high, with a **stylobate** of 5,500 square meters. Guanyin Buddha carries Amitabha on her head, the left hand holding Dhama-Chakra and the right hand giving "abhaya mudra" (fearlessness) in a graceful and merciful manner. No wonder it's the symbol of this "Buddhist Country amidst Sea and Sky". As reported, on the day of its ceremony of consecration, the sky was filled with dark clouds and a heavy rain was coming in a minute. However, at the moment when the red curtain came down, a bunch of light **split** through the clouds. The golden light shot directly at the figure of Buddha, shining with dazzling brilliance, as if the Guanyin Buddha had revealed its power. People on the spot were all shocked by this amazing scene.

★生词与词组 Words & Expressions

craggy /ˈkrægi/ *adj.* 峻峭的
bestow /biˈstəu/ *v.* 授予；赠予
stylobate /ˈstailə(u)beit/ *n.* 柱座；台基

solemn /ˈsɔləm/ *adj.* 庄严的
tranquility /træŋˈkwiləti/ *n.* 宁静
split /split/ *v.* 裂开

◆ 知识拓展 Knowledge Extension

不肯去观音院：日本僧人慧锷活跃于九世纪中叶，曾经几次入唐，周游五台山和天台山等灵地。相传，唐咸通四年，慧锷从五台山请得观音像一尊，携带回国，经普陀莲花洋，舟触礁不能行，他求菩萨显灵，祷告说："若我国众生无缘见佛，当从所向建立精舍。"结果，船漂泊到潮音洞下，当地一个姓张的渔民看到后，将自己的茅屋献出供奉佛像，这就是最早的"不肯去观音院"。

中国佛教四大名山：山西五台山、浙江普陀山、四川峨眉山、安徽九华山。有"金五台、银普陀、铜峨眉、铁九华"之称。分别供奉文殊菩萨、观音菩萨、普贤菩萨、地藏菩萨。

6. 前童古镇 Qiantong Ancient Town

前童镇，地处浙江省宁海县西南，面积 68 平方千米，人口 2.6 万，是一个历史悠久、文化积淀深厚、地理环境独特的江南古镇，被命名为"浙江省历史文化名镇"。

前童以民居布局奇特、明清古建筑群保存完善以及人才辈出而闻名遐迩。该镇始建于宋末，盛于明清，至 2005 年仍保存有 1300 多间各式古民居。前童历代人才辈出，在科举时代，前童有功名者 200 余人，其中有 25 岁任浙江临时都督的童保暄。

这里，"家家有雕梁，户户有活水"。白溪水缘渠入村，汩汩溪水挨户环流，家家连流水小桥，户户通卵石坦途，为江南集镇独特之奇观。这里的供水系统按八卦的原理设计，国内外绝无仅有。

前童是个五匠之乡，尤其以木雕和雕刻为代表。北京故宫博物院收藏的一顶花轿和一张木雕嵌镶床皆出自前童工匠之手。前童家家户户几乎都保存着清代和民国时期的雕花床、八仙桌、红橱、篾丝箱等精致家具。古老的民居里，拱斗、雀替、柱饰造型千姿百态。山墙上堪称一绝的石花窗，林林总总 200 余扇，其图案没有一幅雷同。

前童还是欣赏浙东传统民俗文化的好去处。每到元宵节，小镇都要举行元宵文化旅游节。村民们抬着传统的鼓亭、抬阁，让孩子扮成各种戏曲人物站在抬阁上，在锣鼓、鞭炮、火铳的轰鸣声中，在火树银花的光焰中游遍村镇，以欢庆丰收，纪念先人兴修水利的功德。

前童古镇，是一座不凡的江南明清时期的民居原版，是一幅古韵浓重的乡村画，一段美轮美奂的江南丝竹调。

The town of Qiantong is located at southwest of Ninghai County of Zhejiang Province, with an area of 68 square kilometers and a population of 26,000. It is an ancient town in Jiangnan, with a long history, rich cultural relics and unique geographic environment, which has been entitled as a "Historical and Cultural Town of Zhejiang Province".

Qiantong is well-known for its unique layout of civilian houses, well-preserved architectural complex of the Ming and Qing dynasties and the people of talent coming forth in large numbers. It was first built in the Southern Song Dynasty and prospered in the Ming and Qing dynasties. Up to 2005, there still remain more than 1,300 ancient folk houses of great variety. For all ages, Qiantong **gave birth to** lots of outstanding people. In the times when there were imperial examinations, over two hundred people succeeded in winning scholarly honors or official positions, including Tong Baoxuan who was appointed as a temporary governor of Zhejiang at the age of 25.

In this town, every house has carved beams and running water. The water from the White Stream flows into the town through a ditch, gurgling from house to house, while every house is connected with bridges and pebbled roads, which is a spectacular sight for a town in Jiangnan. The water system here was designed according to the principles of the Eight Diagrams, regarded as the only one at home and abroad.

Qiantong is a town of "Five Craftsmen", in particular with wood carvings and sculptures. A bridal sedan chair and a bed with wood carving and **paneling** preserved in the Beijing Palace Museum are both produced by the craftsmen of Qiantong. Nearly every house here preserves exquisite furniture of the Qing Dynasty and the Republic of China, such as carved beds, square tables for eight people, red cabinets and chests made of bamboo slices, etc. In those ancient folk houses, you can find brackets, sparrow braces and pillar decorations with a diversity of shapes and designs. More than 200 unique stone flower windows on the gables are of great variety, and not a single similar pattern can be found here.

Besides, Qiantong is a good place to enjoy the traditional folk culture and customs in East Zhejiang. The town holds a special cultural festival at every Lantern Festival. The villagers uplift traditional drum pavilions and lift pavilions, on which children stand and act as various characters in traditional operas. They travel around the town with the **roaring** drums, firecrackers and fire spears as well as the flaming fireworks to celebrate the harvest they have got in the past year and to commemorate the ancestors for their merits in the construction of water control projects.

Qiantong Ancient Town is an original remarkable version for the folk houses of the Ming and Qing dynasties in Jiangnan, a painting of village with great ancient charm as well as a fabulous melody of traditional **stringed and woodwind music**.

★生词与词组 Words & Expressions

paneling /'pænəliŋ/ *n.* 镶板
give birth to 产生；生（孩子）

roaring /'rɔːriŋ/ *adj.* 喧嚣的
stringed and woodwind music 丝竹音乐

◆ 知识拓展 Knowledge Extension

梁皇山：原名桐柏山。南朝岳阳王携王妃、太尉、将军多人，到桐柏山避难隐居，在"稍场"的佛寺中，随同和尚念经拜佛，同时习文练武。大难不死，必有后福，他回到京城，做了梁宣帝。民间有句顺口溜："梁岩亮，金钟响，岩门开，王子出山做宣帝。"此后，驿站改为梁皇街，稍场佛寺命名为梁皇寺，桐柏山更名为梁皇山。

7. 庆安会馆 Qing'an Guild Hall

庆安会馆，即天后宫，位于宁波市区三江口东岸，是浙东清代建筑艺术的精品，又是江南现存唯一融天后宫与会馆于一体的古建筑群，是中国八大天后宫和七大会馆之最。天后即天宫的皇后，也叫妈祖，被认为是海神。庆安会馆是宁波港口城市的标志性建筑，是昔日宁波港与海外各国通商贸易的历史见证，也是妈祖文化的物证，现为全国首家海事民俗博物馆。

这个建筑群始建于清道光三十年(1850)，咸丰三年(1853)落成，是与海外做贸易的船商捐资建造的。这些船商将这里作为他们办公、交流、聚会的场所。

天后宫坐东朝西，规模宏大，占地面积约 5000 平方米，按照传统的建筑风格，宫门、仪门、前戏台、大殿、后戏台、后殿、前后厢房等建筑均沿中轴线分布。庆安会馆的建筑采用宁波传统的砖雕、石雕和朱金木雕工艺进行装饰，堪称宁波近代地方工艺之杰作，有着重要的历史文化价值。现保存有 1000 余件朱金木雕，以及 200 多件砖雕、石雕工艺品，体现了清代浙东地区"三雕"工艺技术的最高水平，不仅有很高的观赏价值，而且为研究我国雕刻艺术提供了实物例证。

每年农历三月廿三妈祖诞辰和九月九升天日，会馆都要举办隆重的仪式祭祀天后，其热闹的庙会蔚为甬上大观。

Qing'an Guild Hall, also known as "Tianhou Palace", lies at the east coast of Sanjiangkou in the city center of Ningbo. It is the essence of architecture art of the Qing Dynasty in East Zhejiang, the only ancient architectural complex existent integrating Tianhou Palace and Guild Hall, ranked the first among the eight Tianhou Palaces and the seven Guild Halls in China. Tianhou means the Queen in the heaven, and she has a name—Mazu, who is also regarded as the Goddess of Sea. Qing'an Guild Hall is a landmark of Ningbo as a seaport, the witness of ancient sea trade in Ningbo, the physical evidence of Mazu culture, and also the first national **maritime** and folklore museum.

The hall was built by the merchants dealing with sea trades during the year of 1850 to 1853 in the Qing Dynasty. It was once the site for their work, communication and get-together.

Sitting east to the west, the hall is grand in size and covers an area of about 5,000 square meters. The house adopts the traditional Chinese construction style, with all the gates, pavilions, stages, halls and wing-rooms laid out symmetrically. Its buildings are all decorated with stone carvings, brick carvings, and colorful wood carvings of traditional Ningbo style, regarded as a masterpiece of Ningbo local handcraft of modern times, which is of significant historical and cultural value. Over 1,000 colorful wood carvings, and 200 brick carvings and stone carvings are well preserved here, reflecting the highest level of the technical skills of "the three carvings" of the Qing Dynasty in East Zhejiang. It can provide us with not only high **ornamental value**, but also physical examples for studying Chinese carving art.

Every year on March 23rd and September 9th of traditional Chinese lunar calendar, grand ceremonies are held in the hall to celebrate Mazu's birth and going up to the heaven. Along with its busy temple fair, it has become a spectacular site which attracts people all over the city.

★生词与词组 Words & Expressions

maritime /'mæritaim/ *adj.* 海事的	ornamental value 观赏价值

◆ **知识拓展 Knowledge Extension**

妈祖：被尊为海上女神，又称天妃、天后、天上圣母、娘妈，是历代海洋贸易者、船工、海员、旅客、商人和渔民共同信奉的神祇，许多沿海地区均建有妈祖庙。妈祖的真名为林默，小名默娘，故又称林默娘，诞生于莆田县湄洲(今莆田市湄州岛)，诞辰日为宋建隆元年(960 年)农历三月二十三日。宋太宗雍熙四年(987 年)九月初九逝世。

三江口：姚江、奉化江汇合成甬江流入东海的交叉口，是历代商贾云集之地，也是宁波城市的象征景观。位于宁波市区中心繁华地段，素有"宁波外滩"之称。

8. 七塔禅寺 The Seven-pagoda Temple

七塔禅寺位于浙江省宁波市江东区，是宁波市区规模最大、保存最完好的寺院，1983 年被国务院批准为全国首批重点开放寺院。七塔禅寺历史上为浙东佛教四大丛林(即天童寺、阿育王寺、七塔寺、观宗寺)之一。

七塔禅寺初建于唐大中十二年(858)，寺初名"东津禅院"，距今已有 1140 余年历史。当时有江西分宁宰官任景求舍宅为寺，敦请天童寺退居方丈心镜藏奂禅师居之，是为寺院的开山始祖。此后寺院几经兴废，其间历史多已不详。明代时因迎奉普陀山观音菩萨圣像，成为"小普陀"观音道场。此后香火鼎盛，游人络绎不绝。清康熙年间，寺前立七座佛塔，代表禅宗起源，因而得名七塔禅寺。光绪十六年(1890)，另一位天童寺退居方丈慈运长老任七塔寺住持，其住寺期间大弘佛法，使得七塔禅风广传海内外。

七塔寺内除主要殿堂为古典建筑外，还保存有一批珍贵文物。寺的正中是圆通宝殿，里面供千手观音坐像，圆通宝殿的内壁嵌有佛教文化中的稀世至宝《五百罗汉石刻图》，工艺精妙，形神兼备。殿前有四棵古银杏，最大直径 1.9 米。

天王殿，正中供弥勒化身坐像，左右各供四大天王像；三圣殿，中间供有三圣立像；三圣殿之后是藏经楼，内有清雍正十三年(1735)刻印、光绪颁赐之《龙藏》一部。楼后为祖堂，堂正中供有唐开山祖师心镜藏奂禅师真身舍利塔。此外还有宋代大铜钟两口，各重达七八千斤，分别铸于南宋绍兴四年(1134)和嘉定十一年(1218)。

Situated in the Jiangdong District of Ningbo, Zhejiang, the Seven-pagoda Temple is the largest and most well-preserved temple in the urban area of Ningbo, and one of China's first temples open to the public. In history, it is one of the four Buddhism centers in East Zhejiang, the left being Tiantong Temple, Asoka Temple, and Guanzong Temple.

The Seven-pagoda Temple was first built in the Tang Dynasty (858), entitled Dongjin Temple at that time, with a history of more than 1140 years up to now. It was Ren Jingqiu (an official of Jiangxi at that time) who donated his residence and transformed it into this temple. He also earnestly invited the honored Buddhist monk Xinjingzanghuan, a retired abbot of Tiantong Temple to reside here, who then became the **initiator** of the temple. After its rise and decline of several times, some parts of the history became unclear. The temple has been honored as "Little Putuo" in the Ming Dynasty, since an icon of Guanyin Buddha from Mount Putuo was enshrined here. In the reign of Emperor Kangxi of the Qing Dynasty(1661–1722), seven pagodas representing the origin of Zen were built in front of the temple, hence it was renamed as Seven-pagoda Temple. In the year of 1890, the honored Buddhist monk Ciyun, another retired abbot of the Tiantong Temple, was invited to take the abbot of Seven-pagoda Temple. He **propagated** Buddha dharma with great efforts during his term of service, spreading the school of Seven-pagoda Temple at home and abroad.

Apart from the main buildings of the temple as historical architecture, dozens of precious cultural relics are well-preserved here. At the center of the temple is the Hall of Yuantong (Yuantong is another name of Guanyin), a seated statue of "Thousand-arm Guanyin" is enshrined inside. *The Stone Inscription of Five-hundred Arhats*, an **invaluable** treasure of Buddhnism Culture, was embedded in its inner wall, with exquisite workmanship and a unity of form and spirit. There are four old gingko trees in front of the hall, among which the largest one has a diameter of 1.9 meters.

A seated statue of the **avatar** of Buddha Maitreya is worshiped in the middle of the Hall of Heavenly King, with the statues of Four Heavenly Kings on both sides. In the middle of the Three-saint Hall are the standing statues of Three Saints of Buddhism. Behind the Hall of Three-saint is the Tower of Scripture-storing, with a precious scripture named *Longcang*(*Tibet Dragon Sutras*) preserved here, engraved in the Qing Dynasty (1735) and granted by Emperor Guangxu. Behind it is the Ancestor Hall, the Stupa of Xinjingzanghuan is enshrined here. Besides, there are two big bronze bells of the Song Dynasty, each with a weight of around four thousand kilos, made in the year of 1134 and 1218 respectively.

★生词与词组 Words & Expressions

initiator /i'niʃieitə/ *n.* 创始人

invaluable /in'væljuəbl/ *adj.* 无价的

propagate /'prɔpəgeit/ *v.* 传播；宣传

avatar /'ævə'tɑ:/ *n.* (神的)化身

◆ 知识拓展 Knowledge Extension

"千手观音"：又称千手千眼观世音、千眼千臂观世音等。千手观音是阿弥陀佛的左胁侍者，与阿弥陀佛、大势至菩萨(阿弥陀佛的右胁侍者)合称为"西方三圣"。据佛教典籍记载，千手观音菩萨的千手表示遍护众生，千眼则表示遍观世间。千手观音的形象，常以四十二手象征千手，每一手中各有一眼。

罗汉：即小乘中的极果，称"无学道位"，是断见思惑，出三界分段生死的圣者。五百罗汉，佛经中常有提及。据说，浙江天台山有五百罗汉隐迹其间，惜非凡夫俗子肉眼所能见到。

9. 上林湖越窑青瓷遗址 Ruins of Yue Kilns at the Shanglin Lake

慈溪的上林湖位于慈溪浒山镇东南 10 千米处，是我国越窑青瓷(或秘色瓷之泛称)的发祥地和唐宋越窑青瓷的生产中心，是全国重点文物保护单位。越窑是我国古代最著名的青瓷窑系，东汉时，中国最早的越窑瓷器烧制成功，这是人类文明史上的一个里程碑。

上林湖越窑始于东汉，盛于晚唐、五代至北宋早期，衰于北宋晚期，至南宋初停烧，烧造历史长达千年之久。从唐代晚期到宋代初期，这里的制瓷工艺达到其最高水平，釉层均匀，色泽淡雅，达到了如冰似玉的效果。瓷器制作精细，品种丰富，胎骨细薄，式样优美，并运用各种装饰方法来美化瓷器。

上林湖越窑青瓷不仅上贡朝廷，下供庶民，而且还远销海外，深受世界各国的钟爱。唐宋以来，以明州(宁波古称)港为主要构成港的"海上丝绸之路"和"海上陶瓷之路"将上林湖越窑青瓷远销 20 多个国家和地区。在印度、伊朗、埃及和日本等国，都有越窑上林湖生产的青瓷遗物出土，这些青瓷是古代宁波对外贸易、文化交流的桥梁和信使。

风光秀丽的上林湖畔及周围地区，散落着近 200 处古窑址和碎瓷堆，被称为"露天青瓷博物馆"和"文明的碎片"。

Located 10 kilometers away from southeast Hushan Town of Cixi City, the Shanglin Lake is the birthplace of Chinese **celadon porcelains** of Yue kilns (or generally called as "mysterious porcelain") and its production center in the Tang and Song dynasties, a historical and cultural site listed under national preservation. Yue kilns (Porcelain Kilns of the Kingdom Yue) are the most famous celadon porcelain **kilns** in ancient China. In the Eastern Han Dynasty, the success of firing the earliest celadon of Yue ware is a milestone in the history of human civilization.

Yue kilns here started from the Eastern Han Dynasty, **prospered** in the late Tang Dynasty, the Five Dynasties and the early Northern Song Dynasty, but declined in the late Northern Song Dynasty, and ceased in the early Southern Song Dynasty, with a history as long as a thousand years. The craftsmanship of porcelain making here reached its highest level during the late Tang Dynasty and the early Song Dynasty, with even-distributed **glaze**, elegant colour, achieving the effect that the porcelains look as if they are made of ice or jade. The celadon porcelains produced here are of delicate workmanship, rich variety, thin bodies and elegant styles, beautified by various forms of decoration.

The Shanglin Lake celadon wares not only were used to **pay tribute to** imperial court and to supply the ordinary people, but also commanded a ready sale overseas. Because the celadon wares here were well received overseas, they have been transported to more than 20 countries or regions through the Silk Road and the Porcelain Road since the Tang and Song dynasties, with Mingzhou (Ningbo in ancient time) harbor as the main harbor. The celadon wares of the Shanglin Lake were unearthed in many countries, including India, Iran, Egypt and Japan, which proves them as a bridge as well as a messenger between ancient Ningbo and foreign countries in trade and cultural communication.

Nearly 200 ancient kiln sites and broken porcelain piles scatter at and around the beautiful

Shanglin Lake, and accordingly, it is called "the Open Museum of Celadon Porcelain", and "the Fragments of Civilization".

★生词与词组 Words & Expressions

kiln /kiln; kil/ *n.* 窑	prosper /'prɔspə/ *v.* 繁荣；昌盛
glaze /gleiz/ *n.* 釉面	celadon porcelain 青花瓷
pay tribute to 向……进贡；歌颂	

◆ 知识拓展 Knowledge Extension

越窑：是中国古代南方青瓷窑。窑所在地主要在今浙江省上虞、余姚、慈溪、宁波等地。因这一带古属越州，故名。生产年代自东汉至宋。唐朝是越窑工艺最精湛时期，居全国之冠。隋、初唐继承南朝风格，生产碗、盘、盘口四系壶、四耳罐、鸡头壶等产品。盛唐以后产品精美，赢得声誉。越窑产品都做得很规整，一丝不苟，常将口沿做成花口、荷叶口、葵口，底部加宽，做成玉璧形、玉环形或多曲结构，十分美观。胎体为灰胎，细腻坚致；釉为青釉，晶莹滋润，如玉似冰。唐朝文学家陆羽在所著《茶经》中评价全国各地生产的茶碗，将越窑产品排在首位。

10. 天童寺 Tiantong Temple

天童寺位于宁波市东 30 千米的鄞州区太白山麓，我国禅宗"五山十刹"之一，素有"东南佛国"之誉。始建于西晋永康元年(300)，距今已有 1700 余年的历史。

关于天童寺的由来有个神奇的传说。相传，西晋僧人义兴和尚云游到此，有意在此山建寺苦修。玉皇大帝被他的虔诚感动，派太白金星化身为小孩每天给他送斋送水。最后寺院建成，小孩向义兴和尚告辞，并告之实情，说完腾云而去。后人便以太白名山，以天童名寺。

天童寺占地面积 7.64 万平方米，有殿堂楼阁 30 多幢计 999 间，殿宇建筑精美、金碧辉煌、规模宏大。内有天王殿、大雄宝殿、佛殿、法堂、藏经楼、罗汉堂等。

天王殿是由近代著名僧人圆瑛法师任天童寺住持时重建的。大殿进深六间，阔七间，高 18 米。殿中供奉弥勒佛，两边分列四大天王。

大雄宝殿，是一座重檐歇山式建筑，它是由明代密云禅师自崇祯八年(1635)开始重建，殿内供奉横三世佛，中央为释迦牟尼佛，左面是药师佛，右面是阿弥陀佛，佛像高达 13.5 米。大殿两侧是姿态各异的十八罗汉像。大殿后墙嵌有王日升所书《心经》。

天童寺四周群山峻岭环抱，重嶂叠翠，古松参天，景色秀丽，有"深径回松""凤岗修竹""双池印景""平台铺月"和"太白生云"等十大胜景。宋代任鄞州地方官的王安石曾在他的著名诗篇中赞美了天童寺的美景。

天童禅风远播海外，在日本和东南亚国家有相当影响。"曹洞宗"是日本佛教重要派别之一，其开山祖师道元禅师曾在该寺参禅得法，日本一代绘画巨匠雪舟和尚，还曾任过天童寺首座。这些在中日佛教文化交流史上有重要地位。

Situated at the foot of Mount Taibai in Yinzhou District, 30 kilometers away from the city of Ningbo, Tiantong Temple is one of the "Five Greatest Mountains and Ten Famous Buddist Temples" in China, enjoying a reputation of Southeast Buddhist Country. It was first built in the Western Jin Dynasty (300), with a history of over 1,700 years.

There was a legend about the origin of the temple. It is said that a monk named Yixing once visited here and decided to build a temple for penance. The Jade Emperor was deeply moved by his great deed, and sent God Taibai to look after him in the **incarnation** of a boy to provide him water and food everyday. After the temple has been built, the child told him the truth and disappeared among the clouds in the sky. From then on, the mountain was named "Mount Taibai", and the temple "Tiantong Temple", which means "Child from Heaven".

Occupying an area of 76,400 square meters, Tiantong Temple has 30 tall buildings and 999 rooms in total, making it elaborate, splendid and magnificent. It mainly consists of the Hall of Heavenly King, the Great Buddha's Hall, the Shrine of Buddha, the Hall of Dharma, Depositary of Buddhist Sutra and the Hall Arhat, etc.

Zen Master Yuanying, a famous monk of modern times, rebuilt the Hall of Heavenly King when he was the **abbot** of the temple. The hall has a depth of six rooms, a width of seven rooms and a height of 18 metres, with Maitreya and Four Heavenly Kings worshiped inside.

The Great Buddha's Hall with Xieshan style of **multiple-eave roof** was rebuilt by Master Miyun since the Ming Dynasty (1635). "The **Trinity** of Buddhas" are enshrined here, Sakyamun in the middle, bhaisajyaguru on the left and Amitabha on the right. The figure of Buddha reaches up to 13.5 metres. Eighteen Arhats of different shapes and sizes are on both sides. The *Heart Sutra* written by Wang Risheng was **embedded** in the back wall of the hall.

Encircled amidst mountains, peaks and old pine trees, with its beautiful natural scenery, Tiantong Temple boasts its top ten best attractions, such as "Pine Trees along the Deep Path", "Slim Bamboos at Phoenix Hillock", "Scenery Mirrored in Two Pools", "Moonlight on the Terrace" and "Growing Clouds of Mount Taibai". Wang Anshi, a magistrate of Yinzhou in the Song Dynasty, once spoke highly of the beautiful scenery of Tiantong Temple in his famous poem.

Tiantong Temple has a great influence on the history of Buddhism among Japan and the countries in Southeast Asia. It is also the origin of Soto Sect of Japanese Buddhism, whose founder Zen Master Dogen once practiced **meditation** here. Monk Sesshu, a famous Japanese painting artist was once in the seat of honor in this temple. All of these play a significant role in the history of Buddhism for the mutual communication between Japan and China.

★生词与词组 Words & Expressions

incarnation /ˌinkɑːˈneiʃ(ə)n/ *n.* 化身
trinity /ˈtriniti/ *n.* 三位一体
meditation /ˌmediˈteiʃ(ə)n/ *n.* 冥想

abbot /ˈæbət/ *n.* 住持
embed /imˈbed/ *v.* 嵌入
multiple-eave roof 重檐屋顶

◆ 知识拓展 Knowledge Extension

圆瑛(1878—1953)：俗名吴亨春，法名宏悟，别号韬光。光绪四年(1878)生于古田县平湖乡端上村农家。当代爱国名僧，佛教领袖。新中国成立后为中国佛教协会首任会长。

三世佛：是大乘佛教的主要崇拜对象，有按空间分的横三世佛和按时间分的竖三世佛。横三世佛指西方极乐世界阿弥陀佛，主管西方极乐世界。他有两位胁侍，"大勇"大势至菩萨和"大悲"观世音菩萨。中央娑婆世界的释迦牟尼，主管中央娑婆世界，他有两位胁侍，"大智"文殊菩萨和"大行"普贤菩萨。东方琉璃世界的药师王佛，主管东方琉璃光世界，他有两位胁侍，日光普照菩萨和月光普照菩萨。竖三世佛指过去佛燃灯古佛，现在佛释迦牟尼佛，未来佛弥勒佛。

曹洞宗：为禅宗南宗五家之一，由于良价禅师在江西宜丰洞山创宗，其弟子本寂在吉水的曹山传禅，故后世称为曹洞宗。

11. 天下玉苑 China Jade Garden

天下玉苑位于余姚市大隐镇，占地约 2.3 平方千米，是中国最大的以玉文化为特色的大型文化主题公园，有"新千年江南第一景"之称，融山水灵气、玉雕精品和人文胜迹为一体。

这里是玉的世界，景区收藏展出玉雕精品 10000 多件，做工精细，造型别致。其中 100 多件大型玉雕艺术品为传世佳作。重达一吨以上的玉雕精品就达 30 余件，其中传世精品 3 件，国宝级艺术珍品 8 件，列入吉尼斯世界纪录的 4 件，国家级精品达 40 余件之多，其造型之精巧，工艺之精细，气势之宏大，形象之生动，实属罕见。

天下玉苑以周边秀山丽水为背景，以丰厚的历史文化积淀为底蕴，建有秀湖、玉苑门楼、南天坛、凤凰台、西隐禅寺五大景区，大小景点 20 多个。西隐禅寺、南天坛有着千年的佛教文化底蕴。其中，西隐禅寺是玉苑最主要的建筑群，所有的建筑依山而建，是世界上第一座全部用玉石雕成佛像的寺院，堪称江南第一玉佛寺，其玉佛的数量、品质和重量均为国内外所独有。殿内供奉着释迦牟尼和东方、西方三圣玉佛。殿前立柱和走廊栏杆均用汉白玉制成，实属罕见。

天下玉苑的建筑风格迥异，集南北之精华，主景依托山水，亭、台、楼、阁等布局错落有致，建造出山外有山、园外有园、举步即景、步移景换的艺术效果。

天下玉苑获两大世界吉尼斯之最：世界最大的玉雕文化主题公园，以及世界最大的明清官式寺庙。

Located in Dayin Town of Yuyao City, China Jade Garden, the largest theme garden of Jade Culture in China, covers an area of about 2.3 square kilometers. It is regarded as the top one scenic spot in Jiangnan for the new **millennium**, a complex of natural scenery, fine jades and historical cultural sites.

This is a world of jade, displaying more than ten thousand exhibits of jade-carving works, which are of fine workmanship and unique shapes. Over one hundred big jade-carving works are masterpieces, handed down from ancient times. There are 30 pieces of elaborate jade works weighed up to one ton, including three ancient ones. Moreover, there are eight pieces of precious national art treasure among them, four of which are on the list of **Guinness Records**, and over 40 are national fine arts. Their exquisite shapes, delicate workmanship, magnificent manner and vivid images are rarely seen in other places.

Taking the surrounding beautiful natural scenery and rich historical cultural relics as its background, China Jade Garden has established five scenic areas: the Xiuhu Lake, the Yunyuan Gate Tower, the South Temple of Heaven, the Phoenix Terrace and the Xiyin Temple, including over twenty scenic spots of varying sizes. Among them, the Xiyin Temple and the South Temple of Heaven are characterized by rich Buddhism culture of thousands of years. As the main architectural complex of the garden, the Xiyin Temple is regarded as top one jade Buddhism Temple in Jiangnan. It is the first temple in the world, in which all the Buddhas are made of jade. And its jade Buddhas are **matchless** from the aspects of quantity, quality and weight at home and abroad. Three jade statues of Skamania, the East and the West are enshrined in the temple. It's also rare to see all the stand columns in front of the temples and corridor rails are made of white marble.

China Jade Garden, with its distinctive style, **incorporates** many merits of architecture styles both of the south and the north in it. And its main feature is properly arranged with landscapes, pavilions and stages, creating an artistic effect of mountain beyond mountain, garden beyond garden and scenery beyond scenery.

China Jade Garden has been honored for two Guinness Records: one is the largest theme garden of jade culture in the world, and the other is the biggest temple with the official style of the Ming and Qing dynasties in the world.

★生词与词组 Words & Expressions

millennium /mɪ'lɛnɪrm/ *n.* 千禧年

incorporate /ɪn'kɔ:pəreɪt/ *v.* 融入

matchless /'mætʃlɪs/ *adj.* 无双的；无比的

Guinness Records 吉尼斯世界纪录

◆ 知识拓展 Knowledge Extension

西隐禅寺：地处宁波余姚大隐山。禅寺坐西北朝东南，背倚龙凤山，面朝九龙山，左盘青龙，右踞白虎，是凤舞蛟腾之处，龙盘虎踞之地，是一块不可多得的风水宝地。西隐禅寺有近千年的佛文化渊源，相传南宋时，康王赵构被金兵追杀至大隐九龙山下，逃进一座尼姑庵，一位尼姑把康王藏于柴房，受佛祖庇佑，逃过一劫。康王复位后，为了感谢尼姑救命之恩，将小庵扩建，从此香火不断。清康熙年间，西隐庵改称西隐寺。

12. 溪口镇 Xikou Town

溪口，位于奉化市西北方向，距宁波市区西南方向 22 千米。这里山水如画，风景秀美，骚人墨客，寻幽探胜，古代即已形成"溪口十景"。由于名胜古迹众多，早在19世纪20年代蒋介石成为国民党领袖时，溪口即蒋的故乡就成了旅游胜地，各地游客慕名而来。

溪口的主要景点有雪窦山景区、丰镐房、文昌阁、摩诃殿等，特别是西北的雪窦山，名胜古迹众多，为浙东著名旅游胜地。汉代有人以"海上蓬莱，陆上天台"来赞美她。

丰镐房是蒋介石的故居，占地4800平方米，建筑面积1850平方米。建筑布局为传统的前厅后堂，两厢四堂格局。楼轩相接，廊庑回环，墨柱赭壁，富丽堂皇，厅堂廊庑内布满雕刻彩画。前厅及左右还有三个花园。文昌阁曾为蒋介石的私人别墅和藏书楼。摩诃殿则是蒋家女眷拜佛诵经的佛殿。

雪窦山是四明山支脉的最高峰，海拔800米，气候温暖湿润，四季分明。雪窦山山峰灵秀，岩壑雄奇，瀑布绚丽，湖谷幽深，尤以雪窦寺、妙高台和千丈岩瀑布等景点闻名遐迩。

雪窦寺始建于晋，寺内现藏有"钦赐龙藏"经书、钦赐玉印、龙袍、龙钵以及玉佛、名人画卷、书题等珍贵文物。寺西面是当年蒋介石幽禁著名爱国将领张学良将军的旧址，现为张将军事迹陈列馆。雪窦山顶上有坪如台，故名妙高台。妙高台又称妙高峰、天柱峰，海拔700余米，周围松樟翠竹蔽日，夏季气候凉爽，是理想的避暑胜地。蒋介石1928年在此建别墅，自题匾额"妙高台"。

千丈岩瀑布位于雪窦寺南边，高达186米，以雄奇、壮观而名闻浙东。

Xikou Town is situated northwest to Fenghua City and 22 kilometers away from the southwest of Ningbo City. Xikou is proud of its picturesque scenery and landscape, attracting a large number of writers and poets to explore its beauty, which has been noted for its "Ten Scenic Sights" since the ancient time. When Chiang Kai-Shek came to power as head of the Nationalist Party in China from the 1920s, Xikou, as his hometown, became an attraction to a large number of tourists around China.

The main scenic spots of Xikou Town are the Scenic Area of Mount Xuedou, Fenghao House, Wenchang Pavilion and Mohe Temple, etc. Situated in the northwest of Xikou Town, Mount Xuedou is a well-known tourist resort in East Zhejiang, with abundant scenic spots and historical sites. Dating back to the Han Dynasty, it was **extolled** as "Beautiful as the Penglai Fairy Island in the Sea and Magnificent as the Tiantai Mountain on the Land".

Fenghao House is the former residence of Chiang Kai-Shek, with an area of 4,800 square meters and 1,850 square meters of the floor area. It is of a traditional architectural layout, a pattern which consists of the front hall, the back hall, wing rooms on both sides and four halls in the middle. The halls and pavilions are connected with winding corridors, black columns and reddish brown walls demonstrating its magnificence, which are fully decorated with carvings and color paintings. There are three gardens around the front Hall and its both sides. Wenchang Pavilion was once Chiang Kai-Shek's private villa and library. Mohe Temple was built for the female members of Jiang's family to worship Buddha and **chant sutras**.

Mount Xuedou is the highest branch range of Mount Siming, with an elevation of 800 meters. The weather here is warm and humid, with a clear distinction of four seasons. With elegant peaks, spectacular rocks, magnificent waterfalls, and deep lakes, Mount Xuedou is particularly well-known for its scenic spots like Xuedou Temple, Miaogao Terrace and the Waterfall of Qianzhang Rock (Qianzhang means 1000-meters high).

Xuedou Temple was originally built in the Jin Dynasty, with a precious collection of cultural relics preserved here, including the "Longcang" scripture and the jade seal granted by the emperor, the imperial robe, the imperial **alms bowl**, the jade Buddha, scroll paintings and inscriptions written by celebrities. The house situated in the west of the temple was the site where Zhang Xueliang, a famous patriotic military officer, was confined. Now it is open to the visitors as "the Exhibition Hall of General Zhang's Deeds". There is a level ground on the summit of Mount Xuedou which is like a terrace, so it is named Miaogao Terrace, also called Miaogao Peak or Tianzhu Peak. With an elevation of more than 700 meters, surrounded by trees and bamboos, it is pleasantly cool in summer, making itself an ideal place for summer resort. In 1928, Chiang Kai-Shek built a villa here and inscribed its tablet as "Miaogao Terrace" by himself.

Located at the south of Xuedou Temple, the Waterfall of Qianzhang Rock has a drop height of 186 meters, famous for its grand scene in East Zhejiang.

★生词与词组 Words & Expressions

extol /ik'stəul/ v. 赞美　　　　　　　　　　　　chant sutras 诵经
alms bowl 钵盂

◆ 知识拓展 Knowledge Extension

雪窦山：宋时被称为"天下禅宗十刹之一"，是佛教界公认的"未来佛"弥勒佛的道场。雪窦山位于浙江省奉化市溪口镇西北，为四明山支脉的最高峰，海拔 800 米，有"四明第一山"之誉。山上有乳峰，乳峰有窦，水从窦出，色白如乳，故泉名乳泉，窦称雪窦，因此得名。

13. 月湖 The Moon Lake

月湖位于宁波市西南部，占地面积 967000 平方米，其中水域面积 90000 平方米，是宁波城内最重要的历史文化保护区，又是浙东学术文化的中心。

月湖开凿于唐贞观年间(636)，至宋已初具规模，并筑成十洲，即"月湖十景"，分别为湖东的竹屿、月岛和菊花洲，湖中的花屿、竹洲、柳汀和芳草洲，湖西的烟屿、雪汀和芙蓉洲。此外，还建有七桥和许多风格迥异的亭、榭、楼、阁。其中七桥最引人入胜，包括大厅桥、月湖桥、尚书桥、幢东桥、虹桥、袭绣桥和四明桥。

宋元以来，月湖是浙东学术中心，是文人墨客憩息荟萃之地。自南宋建都临安(即现在的杭州)，明州(即现在的宁波)成为东南重镇。月湖十洲成为四明故家大族的择居佳处，文人墨客会聚于此，退隐里居，读书讲学，成一时之风尚。著名的西湖楼氏家族，宋丞相史浩家族，以及杨简、袁燮、舒璘、沈焕等"四明学派"的著名学者，都曾在此定居或流寓讲学。十洲之上因而世家宅第林立，书楼讲舍遍布，庙堂寺院众多，园林泉石独幽，小桥流水、竹影荷香，极富江南水乡和地域文化特色。明、清以来，传统相继：范氏天一阁、徐氏烟屿楼、童氏白华堂，名人辈出，书香幽幽。唐代大诗人贺知章、北宋名臣王安石、南宋宰相史浩、宋代著名学者杨简，这些风流人物，或隐居，或讲学，或著书，都在月湖留下了不可磨灭的印痕。清代著名的学者全祖望曾写下优美篇章《湖语》，形象地记载了月湖的美景和千年文明，令人叹为观止。

The Moon Lake, located in the southwest of Ningbo city, covers an area of 967,000 square meters, including 90,000 square meters of water area, remains as the most important conservation district of historic sites in the urban area and as the academic cultural center of East Zhejiang.

During the Tang Dynasty (636), the Moon Lake began to **take shape** and gradually reached its **flourishing** period in the Song Dynasty. Ten isles were built in the lake at that time, namely "Ten Views of the Moon Lake", with the Bamboo Isle, the Moon Isle and the **Chrysanthemum** Isle in the east, the Flower Isle, the Bamboo Isle, the Willow Isle and Green Grass Isle in the middle, the Misty Isle, the Snow Isle and the Lotus Isle in the west respectively. Moreover, there are seven bridges and pavilions, each with its own distinguishing styles. Seven Bridges are the most admirable, including the "Dating Bridge", "Moon Lake Bridge", "Shangshu Bridge", "Zhuangdong Bridge", "Hong Bridge", "Gunxiu Bridge" and "Siming Bridge".

Since the Song and Yuan dynasties, the Moon Lake, with **a galaxy of talent**, has become the academic cultural center of East Zhejiang. After Lin'an (Hangzhou in ancient time) having been made the capital of the Southern Song Dynasty, Mingzhou (Ningbo in ancient time) turned into a **stronghold** of southeast China. Ten isles of the Moon Lake began to enjoy the popularity of being an ideal place for the scholars and officers from celebrated families to reside, gather, study or teach. Many celebrated families, like Lou's Family from the West Lake, Prime Minister in the Song Dynasty—Shi Hao's Family and the well-known scholars of Siming School such as Yang Jian, Yuan Xie, Shu Lin and Shen Huan all have lived or taught here. Following this, numerous mansions, libraries, schools and temples were built on the isles, decorated with nice gardens, springs, stones, bridges, streams, bamboos and lotus flowers, reflecting the typical features of watery regions and local culture. This tradition was passed on during the Ming and Qing dynasties: Fan's Family of Tianyi Pavilion, Xu's Family of Yanyu Building, Tong's Family of Baihua Hall all nurtured many talents, within the strong academic atmosphere here. A great number of great poets and scholars once lived here, gave lectures, or wrote books, leaving an **indelible** mark on the Moon Lake, including He Zhizhang, a great poet in the Tang Dynasty; Wang Anshi, a famous prime minister of the Northern Song Dynasty; Shi Hao, a famous prime minister of the Southern Song Dynasty; Yang Jian, a famous scholar in the Song Dynasty, etc. Quan Zuwang, a famous scholar in the Qing Dynasty, once wrote a wonderful article *Language of the Lake*, in which he made a descriptive record of the spectacular scenery and age-old history of the Moon Lake.

★生词与词组 Words & Expressions

flourishing /ˈflɜːrɪʃɪŋ/ *adj.* 繁荣的
stronghold /ˈstrɒŋhəʊld/ *n.* 要塞；据点
take shape 形成

chrysanthemum /krɪˈsænθɪməm/ *n.* 菊花
indelible /ɪnˈdelɪb(ə)l/ *adj.* 擦不掉的；持久的
a galaxy of talent 人文荟萃

◆ 知识拓展 Knowledge Extension

全祖望(1705—1755)：清代学者、文学家。字绍衣，号谢山，鄞州(今浙江宁波)人，学界尊称其为谢山先生。曾主讲于浙江蕺山书院、广东端溪书院。他上承清初黄宗羲经世致用之学，勤奋攻读，博通经史，为清代浙东史学名家。全祖望学贵自得、融会百家的思想有着丰富的内涵，堪称其一生的学术总结。

14. 朱家尖岛——东方夏威夷 Zhujiajian Island—Oriental Hawaii

朱家尖位于浙江省舟山市东部海域，岛屿面积 72 平方千米，与相距 1.35 海里的普陀山并称普陀山国家级重点风景名胜区，是舟山群岛核心旅游区"普陀金三角"的重要组成部分，与中国最大的渔港沈家门一脉相连。

朱家尖以沙滩闻名于世，沙滩平坦宽阔，沙质细腻柔纯，是制作沙雕作品的理想之地，被国际沙雕组织 WSSA 确认为世界上沙质和风景最好的沙滩之一，朱家尖在沙滩的沙质和景致方面都远远超过了全世界最好的避暑胜地之一的夏威夷群岛，因而拥有"东方夏威夷"的美称。朱家尖的"十里金沙"是华东地区最大的沙滩，由岛东南沿岸依次排列的东沙、南沙、千沙、里沙和青沙五大沙滩组成，绵延近 5 千米，如一条金色的项链镶嵌在青山碧海之间。各沙滩尽头，均有岬角相拥，独立成景，滩岸绿林环抱，滩前碧波万顷，滩面金黄开阔，景色蔚为壮观，在全国沿海都是罕见的。

南沙景点是朱家尖景区的精华所在，也是"十里金沙"奇观的中心。从 1999 年起，在朱家尖南沙已经成功举办了十多届中国舟山国际沙雕节，开创了我国沙雕艺术和沙雕旅游活动的先河，使朱家尖成为国内沙雕艺术的发源地。

通过海洋文化和沙雕艺术的完美结合，每年的舟山国际沙雕节已成为中国滨海旅游节庆的成功典范。

With a total area of 72 square kilometers, Zhujiajian Island is located in the eastern sea area of Zhoushan City. Zhujiajian Island is seen as the main section of Mount Putuo National Scenic Site, along with Mount Putuo, which is 1.35 sea miles away from it. It is a significant part of Putuo **Golden Tourist Triangle** in Zhoushan Archipelago Tourism Area, connecting Shenjiamen, the largest fishing harbor of China.

Zhujiajian is well-known for its sand beaches. With its flat and broad beaches, fine and smooth, soft and pure sands, Zhujiajian has become an ideal place for making sand sculptures. It has been confirmed as one of the beaches with the world's best sand quality and natural scenery by the

World Sand Sculpture Association (WSSA), which far **surpasses** Hawaii Islands, one of the best summer resorts in the world, hence winning the fame of "Oriental Hawaii". As the largest sand beaches in East China, the "Ten-mile Golden Sand Beach" is formed by five interlinked big sand beaches along the southeast coast of the island—Dongsha, Nansha, Qiansha, Lisha, and Qingsha, extending nearly five kilometers, like a golden necklace inlaid among the green mountains and the blue sea. Embraced by capes at both ends, each sand beach has its independent scenery. With green forests encircling the bank, the vast blue sea in front and its golden broad **beach faces** form a spectacular view, very rare among the coastal areas of China.

Nansha Sand Beach is the essence of Zhujiajian scenic area, also the center of the grand view of the "Ten-mile Golden Sand Beach". Since 1999, Zhoushan International **Sand Sculpture** Festival has been held here successfully for dozens of times, which initiated the artistic and tourism activities of sand sculpture and made Zhujiajian the place of origin of national sand sculpture art.

With a perfect combination of sea culture and sand sculpture art, the annual Zhoushan International Sand Sculpture Festival has become a successful model of China coastal tourism festivals.

★生词与词组 Words & Expressions

surpass /sə'pɑːs; -'pæs/ v. 胜过，优于
beach face 滩面

Golden Tourist Triangle 旅游金三角
sand sculpture 沙雕

◆ 知识拓展 Knowledge Extension

沙雕：就是把沙堆积并凝固起来，然后雕琢成各种各样的造型。它通常通过堆、挖、雕、掏等手段塑成各种造型体现自然景观、自然美与艺术美和谐统一，其体积之巨大是传统雕塑难以比拟的，具有强烈的视觉冲击力。沙雕只能用沙和水为材料，雕塑过程中不允许使用任何化学黏合剂。作品完成以后经过表面喷洒特制的胶水加固，在正常情况下一般可以保持几个月。由于沙雕会在短时间内自然消解，所以又被称为"速朽艺术"，因为无法长期保存，所以每个作品都是独一无二、永不重复的，这也正是沙雕的魅力所在。

15. 走马塘村——中国进士第一村 Zoumatang Village—China's First Village of Jinshi

千年古村走马塘位于宁波鄞州区姜山镇，被誉为"中国进士第一村"。村中明清古建筑众多，文物古迹众多，人称其为"四明古郡，文献之邦，有江山之胜，水陆之饶"。

该村建于北宋端拱年间(988—989)，距今已有 1000 多年历史。当时长洲进士陈矜任明州知府，死后葬于茅山，其子为父守陵，带家眷定居走马塘，遂成为今走马塘人的祖先，至今已传 38 代。今天存放在宁波天一阁的陈氏家谱，清楚详细地记载了这个家族的千年变迁。古村现有人口 1500 余人，几乎全为陈姓。

整个村庄群水环绕，水路四通八达，是典型的江南古村。这里有江南乡村的小桥流水和

中国传统的宗祠古宅。村中的建筑大多数是明清建筑，保存有多处石雕、木雕、砖雕，工艺精美，设计巧妙，堪称江南一绝。

此外，古村的水系也具特色。村子的四周开掘了护村河，形成了长方形的格局。村中还有大大小小的池塘十余个，这些水池能蓄能泄，防洪灌溉，还可以防火。旁有一棵千年老树，这是走马塘千年沧桑的历史见证。

村中心有保存完好的"贻谷堂"，曾是清末老中医陈松涛坐堂号脉之处，是宁波地区保存最完整的百年私人诊所。

在宋祠里，保留着陈氏历代先祖的牌位，两壁还悬挂着 10 幅明清以来祖宗的画像。村里建有新、旧祠堂，里面供奉着求学有成的先贤的牌位。据不完全统计，该村在近千年中，共走出了 161 名官吏，其中尚书 4 名，进士 76 名。

Located in Jiangshan Town in Yinzhou District of Ningbo, Zoumatang Village is honored as "The First Village of Jinshi" (Jinshi means a successful candidate in the highest **imperial examinations**). The village has dozens of ancient buildings of the Ming and Qing dynasties, with a large amount of cultural relics, enjoying the fame of "an ancient county of Siming, a state of literature, having the beautiful scenery of mountain and water".

The village was built in the Northern Song Dynasty (988–989), with a history of more than one thousand years. At that time, Jinshi Chen Jin of Changzhou died when he was the magistrate of Mingzhou, buried at the Maoshan Mountain. To guard his father's tomb, his son then settled down at Zoumatang Village with his family, who are the ancestors of this village. Up to now, there have been 38 generations of this family. Nowadays, Chen's genealogy is preserved in the Ningbo Tianyi Pavilion, having a detailed record of the long history of this family. There are more than one thousand and five hundred people living in this ancient village now, almost everyone sharing the same family name "Chen".

The village is surrounded by waters extending in all directions. It is a typical ancient village of Jiangnan, with bridges, rivers, and Chinese traditional ancestral halls. The buildings here were mainly built in the Ming and Qing dynasties. Many stone carvings, wood carvings and brick sculptures are well preserved with exquisite workmanship, known as "a wonder in Jiangnan".

Besides, the water system in this village is of characteristics with a moat around the village of the **rectangular** shape. About 10 ponds with various sizes can be found in this village, serving the functions of water supply, **irrigation**, flood prevention, and fire protection. Next to it is a thousand-year-old tree, the best witness of the long history of Zoumatang Village.

A well-preserved private clinic called "Yigu Hall" lies in the center of the village, where the famous doctor of Chinese traditional medicine in the late Qing Dynasty—Chen Songtao once practiced medicine. It is now the most well-kept private clinic with a history of hundreds years in Ningbo.

Memorial tablets of ancestors are protected well in Chen's ancestral halls. Ten portraits of ancestors since the Ming and Qing dynasties are hanging on the walls. Memorial tablets of those successful scholars are also worshipped in old or new ancestral halls. According to incomplete statistics, a history of about one thousand years of this village witnessed 161 officials, among whom there were 4 ministers and 76 Jinshi.

★生词与词组 Words & Expressions

rectangular /'rek'tæŋgjulə/ *adj.* 长方形的   irrigation /ˌiri'geiʃən/ *n.* 灌溉
imperial examinations 科举   memorial tablets 牌位

◆ 知识拓展 Knowledge Extension

"进士科"：隋朝于 605 年首次开的进士科，被视为科举的开始。隋唐时，"进士科"只是科举各科中的其一，考的是诗赋。因为进士科是常科，考取又最难，故此最为尊贵，地位亦成为各科之首。宋代以前，进士只需要通过在尚书省举行的"省试"。自宋以后，进士一律要经过由皇帝主持的"殿试"一关复核和决定名次。在明朝和清朝，殿试分录取考生为三等，称三甲。一甲三人依次为状元、榜眼、探花，称"进士及弟"。二甲若干(清朝时一般为七人)，称"进士出身"。三甲称"同进士出身"。世人统称录取者为"进士"。进士是功名的尽头，就算是对名次不满意亦不可以重考。

第二节　旅游文化——中国宗教文化

Section 2　Tourism Culture—Chinese Religious Culture

宗教文化是人类文化的一个重要组成部分，它指的是由民族的宗教信仰、意识等所形成的文化。中国的宗教文化具有自身的特点，对中国历代民众的精神生活有深远的影响。中国的宗教文化自隋朝以来逐渐发展成为融合儒、释、道三教的民俗文化。准确地说，在这里佛教、道教、儒教三教并存，因而了解佛教、道教和儒教这三种文化即掌握了一把更好地理解中国传统文化的钥匙。

As an indispensable part of human cultures, religious culture refers to the culture formed by a nation's religious beliefs and ideologies, etc. Chinese religious culture, with its unique characteristics, has a long and profound impact on the spiritual life of Chinese people in all ages. Chinese religious culture has developed into a folk culture that blends Confucianism, Buddhism and Taoism since the Sui Dynasty. To be more precise, Buddhism, Taoism and Confucianism coexist here. Therefore, to know the cultures of Buddhism, Taoism and Confucianism is to possess a key to a better understanding of traditional Chinese culture.

1. 佛教 Buddhism

佛教自公元一世纪传入中国以来一直是中国最大的宗教。中国佛教泛指从佛教传入中国以来繁荣起来的各个流派。中国佛教在繁荣时期曾有八大主要流派：1)律宗；2)禅宗；3)三论宗；4)法相宗；5)密宗；6)华严宗；7)天台宗；8)净土宗。尤其在中国佛教的全盛时期——唐朝，曾涌现出数不清的佛学大师。这些佛教流派很多融合了儒教、道教和其他中国本土的哲学思想，使这个原本外来的宗教以其独一无二的特色成为中国文化不可或缺的组成部分。佛教在审美观、政治、文学、哲学和医学等各方面都极大地影响了中国民众的心理。

Buddhism remains the largest religion in China since its introduction in the 1st century. In a broad sense, Chinese Buddhism refers to the various sects of Buddhism that have flourished in China since ancient time. The eight principal sects of Buddhism flourished in China were: 1)The Vinaya；2)The Dhyana；3)The Three Treatises；4)The Idealist；5)The Mantra or Tantric；6)The Avatamsaka or Flower Adornment；7)The Tiantai or White Lotus；8)The Pure Land. In particular, at the peak of the Tang Dynasty's vitality, Chinese Buddhism produced a large number of spiritual masters. Many of these sects integrated the ideas of Confucianism, Taoism and other indigenous philosophical systems so that what was initially a foreign religion (the buddhadharma) came to be a natural part of Chinese civilization, albeit with a unique character. Buddhism has played an enormous role in shaping the psychology of the Chinese people in the aspects of aesthetics, politics, literature, philosophy and medicine.

2. 道教　Taoism

道教是中国本土形成的传统宗教。人们普遍认为道教由张道陵天师在 1900 多年以前，即东汉顺帝年间(126—144)正式创立。事实上，道教教义的源头可追溯到先秦时期(公元前 221 以前)。因而，道教的"三祖"通常指的是黄帝、老子和张天师。

道教的核心理念是"道"，认为"道"无形无象、玄之又玄、无法言说。"道"被认为是宇宙的起源，为天地万物之始，是控制万物发展变化的法则，是道教的至高信仰。道教修行者把"道"与"德"当作他们最基本的信念与行为规范。他们不仅要修"道"，还需积"德"。因而，"道"与"德"是道教教义的根本。在"道"与"德"的基础上还衍生出了一整套的法则，包括"自然无为""清静寡欲""柔弱不争"和"返璞归真"。

Taoism is an indigenous traditional religion of China. It is generally believed that Taoism was formally established 1,900 years ago by Celestial Master Zhang Daoling during the reign of Emperor Shundi of the Eastern Han Dynasty (126–144). However, the original sources of Taoist doctrines can be traced back to the Pre-Qin period (before 221 BC). Thus the "Three Ancestors" usually refers to Huangdi, Laozi and Celestial Master Zhang.

The core of Taoism is, of course, "Tao" (the Way), which is beyond description. It is said that Tao is the origin of the universe, the basis of all existing things, the law governing their development and change, and the ultimate god of Taoism. Taoists regard Tao and Virtue as the general principles of their beliefs and behavior. They should not only cultivate Tao but also accumulate Virtue. Therefore, both Tao and Virtue serve as the basis of Taoist doctrines. A whole set of principles are derived from the foundation of Tao and Virtue, including non-action, non-passion and non-desire, non-struggle, and the pursuit of simplicity and truth.

3. 儒教 Confucianism

儒家思想(或称为孔子学说或儒教)是由中国哲学家孔子(孔夫子)的学说发展而来的一套伦理和哲学体系。

儒家思想的核心是"仁"。孔子把"仁"作为最高的道德原则、道德标准和道德境界。在实践中，构成儒家伦理思想的其他规范随之形成。其中比较经典的有五常，由五方面构成：仁(仁慈)、义(正义)、礼(礼仪)、智(学问)、信(正直)；以及四字，由四方面构成：忠(忠诚)、孝(孝道)、节(节制)、义(正义)。此外，还有很多其他的规范，如诚(诚实)、恕(善良与宽恕)、廉(正直和清白)、耻(羞耻、判断和是非之心)、勇(勇敢)、温(和蔼、温和)、良(好心)、恭(有礼貌、恭敬)、俭(节俭)、让(谨慎、谦虚)。在儒家思想的所有原则中，"仁"和"义"是最基本的。因而，有时道德可等同为仁义。

儒家维护"礼治"，提倡"德治"，重视"人治"。这对中国封建社会的影响很大，被封建统治者长期奉为正统思想。

Confucianism is a Chinese ethical and philosophical system developed from the theories of the Chinese philosopher Confucius (Kongfuzi).

Humanity is the core in Confucianism. Confucius regarded Humanity as the highest moral principle, moral standard and moral realm. In practice, other elements of Confucianism came into being over time. One of the classical norms of Confucianism is "Wuchang", consisting of five elements: Ren (Humanity), Yi (Righteousness), Li (Ritual), Zhi (Knowledge), Xin (Integrity), and another one is "Sizi" with four elements: Zhong (Loyalty), Xiao (Filial Piety), Jie (Continency), Yi (Righteousness). There are still many other elements, such as Cheng (honesty), Shu (kindness and forgiveness), Lian (honesty and cleanness), Chi (shame, judgment and sense of right and wrong), Yong (bravery), Wen (kindness and gentleness), Liang (being good, kindhearted), Gong (being respectful, reverent), Jian(being frugal), Rang (being modest, self-effacing). Among all the elements in Confucianism, Ren (Humanity) and Yi (Righteousness) are fundamental. Sometimes morality is interpreted as Ren and Yi.

It is necessary to maintain "rule of rites", to advocate "rule of virtue" and to value "rule of man" in Confucianism, which has exerted a great impact on Chinese feudal society, and regarded as orthodox by feudal rulers for ages.

第三节 景点讲解技能——突出重点法

Section 3 Narration Tactics of Scenic Spots

—Highlighting Priority

俗话说："看景不如听景。"导游讲解在导游工作中占有极为重要的地位。导游员只有根据景点和游客的不同情况，灵活地使用导游资料，运用导游艺术和讲解技巧，才能使导游内容生动而又富有生命力。本章主要讲导游讲解技巧中的"突出重点法"。

所谓"突出重点法"，就是导游在讲解时避免面面俱到，而是突出某一方面的讲解方法，主要分为以下四种讲解技巧。

1. 突出代表性 Highlighting on Representativeness

游览大的景点前，导游员必须做好周密的计划，确定重点景观。这些景观既要有自己的特征，又能概括全貌。到现场游览时，导游员主要讲解这些具有代表性的景观。

例如介绍普陀山的景观时，可以突出讲解普陀山作为观音菩萨道场的历史典故和普陀三宝(多宝塔、普陀鹅耳枥、明代杨枝观音石刻碑)。普陀山上有大小寺庙 20 多座，讲解时要突出普陀山最具代表性的三大寺庙：普济寺、法雨寺和慧济寺，三大寺庙中又以普济寺为代表，其前身为"不肯去观音院"，有深厚的宗教历史文化。

带游客到杭州西湖游览时，由于景点众多，很难面面俱到，要选定最具代表性的苏堤、白堤和断桥等景观进行重点讲解，其他景点根据需要可以一语带过。

2. 突出与众不同之处 Highlighting on Distinctiveness

不同的佛教寺院，其历史、宗派、规模、结构、建筑艺术、供奉的佛像各不相同，导游员在讲解时应突出介绍其与众不同之处，以有效地吸引游客的注意力，避免产生雷同的感觉。例如介绍宁波的"阿育王寺"时，可以突出该寺的珍宝和历史渊源：寺内珍藏着一座含有舍利珠的佛祖舍利宝塔，是中国现存唯一以印度阿育王命名的千年古寺；介绍杭州的灵隐寺时，可突出该寺的宗派：为我国佛教史上著名禅宗丛林，在宋代被列为禅宗五山之一。

3. 突出"……之最" Highlighting on Superlatives

人们对"……之最"感兴趣，也喜欢追求"……之最"。适应这一心理，把游览项目中最显著的特点充分表达出来，抓住游客注意力，引起游客兴趣。面对某一景点，导游员可根据实际情况介绍这是世界(中国、某省、某市、某地)最大(最长、最古老、最高、最小)的……

例如介绍宁波市的"天一阁"时，可突出"天一阁"是中国现存年代最早的私家藏书楼，也是世界上现存最古老的三大家族图书馆之一，是宁波作为历史名城的主要标志之一，使游客马上认识到"天一阁"在中国所有藏书楼中的重要地位和其藏书的历史价值，并对后面的讲解产生极大的兴趣。

4. 突出旅游者感兴趣的内容　Highlighting on Tourists' Interest

旅游者因客源地、年龄、性别、职业、爱好、宗教信仰等方面的差异，对景观有各自不同的兴趣。导游如能在讲解前适当地了解游客群体的特点和兴趣爱好，然后根据具体情况调整讲解内容，进行针对性的讲解，可更好地吸引游客的兴趣，达到事半功倍的导游效果。

就客源地来说，小桥流水、古典园林、石库门建筑等景致最能吸引东亚及东南亚游客的兴趣，其中日韩的游客对中国的书法、佛教文化和古典历史文化最感兴趣；而欧美的游客则对黄山、九寨沟、西湖等自然景观和故宫、长城等宏伟的建筑艺术更感兴趣。

国内的游客也因居住环境不同而在旅游中喜欢体验别样的风情，如北方的游客喜欢游览江南水乡的古镇风情、南方的游客则对北方的大漠苍穹和雪域高原情有独钟。

就同一景区而言，讲解时也要根据游客的兴趣突出重点，如在介绍绍兴沈园的时候，学者和教师旅游团对陆游的生平和他的诗词如"钗头凤"等有较大的兴趣，而女性游客则可能对陆游和唐琬的爱情故事更感兴趣。

总之，导游在运用"突出重点法"讲解景点时应灵活机动，根据不同游客的兴趣抓住重点、突出景区的与众不同之处，才能吸引游客的注意力，从而达到事半功倍的效果。

◆ 综合练习

请运用所学的"突出重点法"景点讲解技巧，选一个宁波或舟山地区的景点分小组进行中英文讲解练习。

第四节　旅游广告的翻译技巧

Section 4　Translation Skills of Travel Advertisements

广告语言拥有自己独有的语言表达规律和形式，因而能产生一种特殊而难忘的，有时是持久的效果。广告的原则可用速写的 AIDMA 来表示，即注意(attention)、兴趣(interest)、愿望(desire)、记忆(memory)、行动(action)，因此广告的创作与翻译就要力求自然(natural)、准确(exact)、醒目(striking)、易懂(plain)。

用词准确、造句洗练、修辞手法独到的旅游广告语不但能够准确体现旅游经营机构的经营理念、形象定位、产品卖点等，还能够有效地吸引潜在旅游者实施旅游行为。

1. 旅游广告的分类　Classification

旅游广告的种类很多，按广告的内容主要可分为旅游产品广告和旅游服务广告。

旅游产品广告又可分为观光旅游产品(自然风光、名胜古迹、城市风光等)、度假旅游产品(海滨、山地、温泉、乡村、野营等)、专项旅游产品(文化、商务、体育健身、业务等)和生态旅游产品等。

旅游服务广告则是指旅行社、旅馆、饭店、航线、游轮等有关旅游企业提供的旅游服务方面的广告。

2. 旅游广告的语言特点　Language Features

根据功能翻译理论，功能靠形式体现，而形式是由词汇、句法(即句型结构)和修辞技巧来体现的。因而在讨论翻译技巧之前我们必须先了解旅游广告的语言特点，即词汇、句法及修辞特点。

2.1　旅游广告的词汇特点

中英文旅游广告中均大量使用带有褒义形容词的描述性语言来吸引读者的注意力，但中文的旅游广告侧重于对具体物象的描写，常使用华丽的书面化的形容词来表达意境，如汉语的四字词语美轮美奂、闻名遐迩、苍翠欲滴等，而英文的旅游广告则习惯使用口语化的简单词汇表达亲切的口吻，简洁亲切，如best、fresh、gorgeous、friendly、fantastic、bright等。

2.2　旅游广告的句法特点

旅游广告为了达到通俗易懂、简单明了的目的，所用的句子多为省略句、简单句和祈使句。

祈使句能拉近与读者的距离，如：Please join us throughout the holiday.(请与我们共度佳节。)有时也使用反问句以引起读者的注意和兴趣，例如：Why don't you come and enjoy yourself leisurely?(何不来此享受一下休闲时光呢？)

省略句语言凝练、意味深长，给读者留下足够的想象的空间，如：You'll enjoy relaxed sunny days. Warm crystal clear lagoons. Cool green foliage. Waterfalls. Flowers. Exotic scents.(您会享受这阳光明媚的轻松时光。温暖、清澈的环礁湖，清凉、碧绿的树叶，瀑布，花丛，异样的芬芳。)这段文字采用了许多省略句，给旅游者留下无限遐思和向往。

旅游广告标语大多使用省略句或祈使句的形式来代替完整的句子，使语言更加精练，令人过目不忘，例如：

(1)香港：购物者的天堂！Hong Kong: Shopper's Paradise!

(2)巴厘：人间天堂！Bali: A Paradise on the Earth!

(3)阿拉斯加：阿拉斯加，一见倾心！Alaska: Alaska—Love at First Sight!

2.3　旅游广告的修辞特点

旅游广告中常用双关、比喻、拟人、排比和押韵等修辞手法，使语言生动形象，更富美感，起到良好的吸引和说服读者的作用。

2.3.1　比喻

比喻是中文旅游广告中比较常用的一种修辞手法，它将抽象枯燥的事物与生动具体的事物进行类比，形成鲜明生动的意象，唤起消费者情感上的共鸣。但在英译时要考虑外国读者的可接收性，而比喻部分也可省略不译，如：

黄山巨松……或耸立挺拔，似擎天巨人；或凌空倒挂，似雄鹰展翅；或虬根盘结，如蛟龙出海。

Pines on the mountain are clinging to the rock surface instead of taking roots in soil. The ancient pines in fantastic shapes rise high into the sky or hung upside down.

2.3.2　排比

景点广告中经常同时使用排比和比喻的修辞手法来描绘优美的意境，引发读者美好的想象。如：

这里3000座奇峰拔地而起，形态各异，有的似玉柱神鞭，立地顶天；有的像铜墙铁壁，巍然屹立；有的如晃板垒卵，摇摇欲坠；有的若盆景古董，玲珑剔透……神奇而又真实. 迷离而又实在。不是艺术创作胜似艺术创作，令人叹为观止! (黄成洲，2008：147)

3,000 crags rise in various shapes. They look like whips or pillars propping up the sky; or huge walls, solid and sound; or immense eggs piled on an unsteady board; or lovely miniature rocky or curios…Fantastic but actual, dreamy but real! They are not artistic works, but more exquisite than artistic works. One cannot help marveling at the acme of perfection of Nature's creation.(贾文波，2004: 120)

本例句通过四个排比句将各座山峰的形态刻画得惟妙惟肖，令人神往。

2.3.3　对偶

对偶在中文旅游广告标语中使用频率很高，恰当的使用可以使广告朗朗上口，节奏感强，令人过目不忘，例如：

(1)上有天堂，下有苏杭。

While there is paradise in heaven, there are Suzhou and Hangzhou on the earth.

(2)中国：远古的珍藏，现代的奇迹!

China: Ancient Treasures, Modern Wonders!

3. 旅游广告的翻译原则与技巧　Principle and Skills

旅游广告翻译所遵循的主要原则应该是"译文的读者效应"，是原、译语间功能的传递，而不仅仅是语言形式上的对应，即译文更应顺从译语文化环境的规范和标准。

根据以上翻译原则，下面分析几种常见的旅游景点翻译技巧：

3.1 四字词语的翻译

根据上文提到的中英文形容词使用的特点，中文景点广告中使用的四字词语，在英译时根据不同的语境可转换成单个的形容词、转译成名词、对词义进行简化或删减，如：

(1) 转换成单个形容词："美轮美奂"可译为"fantastic"；"五彩缤纷"可译为"colorful"。

(2)转译成名词："朦朦胧胧"可转译成名词"half-lights"；"神奇美妙"可转译成名词"magic"。

(3)简译或减译："玲珑剔透"可简译为"exquisite"；"苍翠欲滴"可减译为"green"。

3.2 传统文化词汇的翻译

在翻译中国传统文化词汇时，要在尽可能保留我国传统文化特色的基础上，采用音译、直译和意译相结合的方法处理，如，武术：wushu / Chinese Martial Arts (音译/意译)；麻将：mahjong (音译)；对联：Spring Couplets (意译)；《易经》：*Yi Ching*/ *The Classic of Changes* (音译/意译)等。

此外，必要时还需加注，增译其社会意义或附带意义等以促进读者的理解，如宗教术语的翻译。佛教中很常用的术语"涅槃"翻译成梵文"nirvana"后，可添加其特殊的宗教意义以促进读者的理解，即"the extinction of desire and suffering"；道教中的术语"阴—阳"若简单音译成"Yin-yang"，则难以体现其深层的宗教意义和哲学意义，故可添加"the basic principle of the universe in Taoism"来说明它是道教学说中关于宇宙的基本原则；而儒家思想中的术语"仁"如仅仅翻译成"Ren；Humanity"，会让外国的读者一头雾水，根据需要可增译"the highest moral principle in Confucianism"以说明它是一种道德标准及其在儒家学说中的地位。

3.3 句法和修辞手段的翻译

旅游景点广告翻译的难点和要点首先是要区分开中文旅游广告中哪些语言是客观存在的景观，哪些语言是作者的主观感受或想象，然后将客观存在的景观按照英文的逻辑思路和表达方式进行组织和表达，而将表达作者的主观感受方面的语言进行选择性的翻译。同时，要注意到中文使用了很多的比喻和排比等修辞手法，翻译成英语时要根据英文的习惯选择适当的表达方式，不一定保留原有的修辞手法。例如，上文中提到的关于使用排比和比喻修辞手法描写黄山松树的例子：

黄山巨松……或耸立挺拔，似擎天巨人；或凌空倒挂，似雄鹰展翅；或虬根盘结，如蛟龙出海。

Pines on the mountain are clinging to the rock surface instead of taking roots in soil. The ancient pines in fantastic shapes rise high into the sky or hung upside down. (黄成洲，2008：147)

从这个例子中，我们很显然能够区分出"耸立挺拔""凌空倒挂"和"虬根盘结"等语言描写的是客观存在的景观，而"似擎天巨人""似雄鹰展翅"和"如蛟龙出海"等比喻句描写的是作者的主观感受和想象。因而，译者在翻译中就省略了这些比喻句，只翻译了客观描写部分。从功能语言学的角度来说，这样的翻译是可行的，已经达到了功能对等的目的。但从意义对等的角度来讲，本句的翻译忽略了原文中要表达的意境和美感。

总之，翻译时要朝着兼顾形式对等和功能对等的方向努力。

◆ 课后练习 Exercises

一、将下列句子翻译成英文(Put the following Chinese sentences into English)

1. 千姿百态的各式彩龙在江面游弋,舒展着优美的身姿,有的摇头摆尾,风采奕奕;有的喷火吐水,威风八面。

2. 在节假日期间旅店显得鲜艳夺目:美不胜收的圣诞装饰、热烈亲切的气氛、令人惊叹的热带植物园。

3. 阳光、沙子、大海、浪花……在蓝天和棕榈树之间,我们流连忘返。

4. 这儿的峡谷又是另一番景象:谷中急水奔流,穿峡而过,两岸树木葱茏,鲜花繁茂,碧草萋萋,活脱脱一幅生机盎然的天然风景画。

5. 她(黄河)奔腾不息,勇往直前,忽而惊涛裂岸,势不可挡,使群山动容;忽而静如处子,风平浪静,波光潋滟,气象万千。

二、将下列中文旅游广告短文翻译成英文(Put the following Chinese Travel Advertisements into English)

金沙湾海滨度假村

金沙湾海滨度假村位于象山一小岛之上,以海上狩猎而盛名,故被称为海上狩猎岛。岛内遗留着七千万年前火山喷发形成的火山熔岩,处处闪动着大自然的神秘灵光。岛内的生态环境良好,岩崖形态奇特,岛内种植了果树、蔬菜、花草,鸟语花香,景色优美。在这里,果园观光、果品采摘是女人的天堂。岛上的狩猎中心也放养了许多野猪、野鸡、野鸭、野兔、野鹦鹉等野生动物,在这里海岛狩猎、出海捕捞是男人的"战场"。在这里踏金沙、戏海水、品海鲜、拾海贝便是孩子们的乐园。这里的茶苑品茗,海景观光等也是老人们的向往。无论是跟亲人还是朋友一起出游,这一综合性海岛生态风情度假村都可让人尽情享受。

第三章　绍兴景域

Chapter Three　Shaoxing Scenic Zone

第一节　旅游景点

Section 1　Scenic Spots

1. 曹娥庙 Cao–E Temple

曹娥庙位于上虞市百官镇曹娥江西岸。曹娥庙，早年叫灵孝庙、孝女庙，始建于公元151年，是为了宣扬东汉时上虞孝女曹娥的精神而建的一处纪念性建筑。相传，东汉时，上虞人曹盱失足坠江而亡。他十四岁的女儿曹娥遂沿江寻找父亲的尸体，但是，多日也没有结果，最后她投江而溺亡。数天过后，令人称奇的是，曹娥的尸体竟然驮着其父浮上了水面。正是因为这种舍身寻父的孝行，曹娥被世人尊为孝女。

曹娥庙现有庙宇布局严谨，错落有致，气势恢宏。它背依凤凰山，面向曹娥江，占地6000平方米，建筑面积达3840平方米。其主要建筑分布在三条轴线上。北轴线依次有：石牌坊、饮酒亭、碑廊、双桧亭、曹娥墓；中轴线分布有：罩墙、御碑亭、山门、戏台、正殿、曹府君祠；南轴线上则分布着：山门、戏台、土谷祠、沈公祠、戏台、东岳殿、阎王殿。

曹娥庙的主要景点包括正殿、暖阁、后殿、双桧亭、曹娥墓等。

正殿是人们瞻仰、纪念孝女曹娥的主要场所。暖阁位于正殿中央，富丽堂皇。后殿历史上是供奉孝女曹娥父母雕像之所。双桧亭是旧时达官贵人在曹娥墓前举行祭祀仪式的厅堂，因落成后亭前植有两棵桧树而得名。

曹娥庙文化积淀厚重，艺术品位颇高。庙内现存的"曹娥碑"载有"中国最早的字谜"。该庙还以雕刻、壁画、楹联和书法"四绝"饮誉海内外，它也因之被誉为"江南第一庙"。

Located in the west bank of Cao-E River in Baiguan Town, Shangyu City, the Cao-E Temple, also called the **Filial Piety** Temple or the Filial Daughter Temple in the early years, was first built in 151 as a memorial building to commend the filial daughter Cao-E of the Eastern Han Dynasty. It is said that in the Eastern Han Dynasty, a Shangyu man Cao Xu slipped into a river and died, his 14-year-old daughter Cao-E sought her father's **corpse** everywhere but failed. Several days later, she jumped into the river to look for her father's corpse. As a result, she was drowned. However, to the world's **astonishment**, several days later, Cao-E's corpse came up with his father on her back. Because of this, the contemporaries considered Cao-E the filial daughter.

The present temple is laid out strictly with proper distribution and very extensive scale. The Cao-E Temple lies against Mount Phoenix and faces the Cao-E River, with an area covering 6,000 square meters and a built-up area of 3,840 square meters. The main buildings scatter on three axes. Along the north axis are the dolmen, wine-drinking pavilion, tablet corridor, double Chinese **juniper** pavilion, and Cao-E Grave. The middle axis has the cover wall, pavilion of stone tablets, main hall, stage, and the Caos' Ancestral Temple in proper order. Along the south axis are the gate, stage, Tugu Temple, Shen Temple, Eastern Mountain Hall and the Death King Palace.

The major scenic spots in the Cao-E Temple are the main hall, the warm room, the back hall, and the double Chinese juniper pavilion.

The main hall is the place where people worship and commemorate Cao-E. The warm room is located in the center of the main hall with splendid furnishing. The back hall is the place where the statues of Cao-E's parents are placed and admired. The double Chinese juniper pavilion which was named after two Chinese junipers planted in front of the hall is the the place where the rich men in ancient times held sacrificing ceremonies.

The Cao-E Temple is of great cultural value and various works of art are exhibited here. The "earliest riddle about a character" is preserved here on the "Cao-E Tablet". The temple has won a good reputation at home and abroad especially for its sculpture, **fresco**, calligraphy and **couplets** written on scrolls and hung on the pillars of a hall. Because of all these, the Cao-E Temple is recognized as "the top temple in Jiangnan".

★生词与词组 Words & Expressions

corpse /kɔːps/ *n.* 尸体

juniper /'dʒuːnipə/ *n.* 杜松；桧树

couplet /'kʌplit/ *n.* 对联；对句

astonishment /ə'stɔniʃmənt/ *n.* 惊讶；令人惊讶的事物

fresco /'freskəu/ *n.* 壁画

filial piety 孝顺；孝心

◆ 知识拓展 Knowledge Extension

曹娥碑：东汉年间人们为颂扬曹娥的美德，纪念她的孝行而立的石碑。开始由蔡文姬的父亲蔡邕书写此碑，历经千百年风雨沧桑，又由宋朝王安石的女婿蔡卞重新临摹，一直保存至今。今天的曹娥碑其实是宋朝的石碑，高 2.1 米，宽 1 米，上面的字体为行楷体。围绕这块石碑，有一个非常有趣的传说。话说三国时，曹操和杨修一起来曹娥庙祭拜。看到碑上"黄绢幼妇，外孙齑(jī)臼"八个字感到很奇怪，不解其意，最后还是杨修破译了这个谜语，说答案便是"绝妙好辞"。他给曹操解释说：黄绢是有颜色的丝绸，那便是"绝"字；"幼妇"是少女，即"妙"字；外孙是女之子，那是"好"字；"齑"是捣碎的姜蒜，而"齑臼"就是捣烂姜蒜的容器，用当时的话说就是"受辛之器"，"受"旁加"辛"就是"辞"的异体字。

所以"黄绢幼妇,外孙齑臼",谜底便是"绝妙好辞"。因为有了这个故事,便成就了"曹娥碑"作为"中国最早的字谜"的美誉。也正因为曹娥碑隐含着中国第一个字谜,是中国文字隐语的图腾,字迹的鼻祖,历代的文人墨客都喜欢到这里参读研究这块石碑。罗贯中、曹雪芹都把曹娥碑的故事写入了自己的作品中。

2. 穿岩十九峰风景区 The Chuanyan Nineteen Peaks Scenic Area

从新昌县城出发,向西南 20 多千米就到了穿岩十九峰景区。整个景区由十九峰、千丈幽谷、重阳宫、台头山、倒脱靴五个分景区组成。景区内人文与自然景观交相辉映,以雅、幽、奇、险为特色,融峰、谷、洞、溪、瀑为一体,是地质学上典型的丹霞地貌和国内罕见的最大的丹霞群之一,也是硅化木国家宝库、国家级地质公园。景区内处处是风景,各个皆不同:群山绵亘、台地高峻、深谷险壑、叠瀑飞泉、清溪碧潭,兼具"桂林之秀、漓江之美、雁荡之奇",素有"小桂林""浙东张家界"之美誉。

"十九峰头云作巾,峰峰都是玉嶙峋",十九座山峰鱼贯列队,形态各异。清江如带,绕山而行,倒影生姿,如同人间仙境,世外桃源。十九峰中以望海峰为最高,海拔约 400 米,仅有一石铺小径,有台阶 99 级,人称"一步即登天"。马鞍峰半腰有岩洞,高约 5 米,深广约为 240 平方米,东西贯通,有诗云:"半天高插万余丈,一洞可容千数人",穿岩之名由此而得。缆船峰相传为大禹治水系缆船处;新妇峰犹如新妇出嫁,亭亭玉立;而其他诸峰也都以其独特的风光而得名。十九峰从南到北分别为:香炉、缆船、马鞍、新妇、棋盘、卓剑、覆钟、望海、笔架、泗洲等,十九峰之名都寄托着人们对幸福生活的向往。

千丈幽谷位于十九峰之东,千岩竞秀,万壑争流,是一处大自然的造化之地。谷内红崖断壁,奇岩怪石,流溪浅滩,沿途有二龙锁江、一指峰、珠落玉盘、铜墙铁壁、三象入浴、金猴献桃等诸多景点,山情野趣,浑然天成。

It is almost 20 kilometers away from the southwest of Xinchang County towards Chuanyan Nineteen Peaks Scenic Area, which consists of five parts: Nineteen Peaks, Qianzhang **Glen**, Chongyang Palace, Mount Taitou and Downright Boot Rock. The scenery, of which the cultural and natural landscapes add **radiance** to each other, is characterized with elegance, **seclusion**, peculiarity and steepness with the integration of peaks, valleys, caves, streams and waterfalls. The Chuanyan Nineteen Peaks Scenery is famous for "the scene of mountains and rivers". It is a typical Danxia landform as one of the biggest Danxia **physiognomy** sights, and also the national **solidified** woods treasury and geological park. In this area you can see different scenic spots everywhere: stretching mountains, tall platforms, deep canyons, cliffside waterfalls, clear streams, all of which form the perfect combination of "the elegance of Guilin, the beauty of the Lijiang River and the peculiarity of the Yandang Mountain". Thus, it has won a good reputation of "Zhangjiajie in the east of Zhejiang" and "Small-scaled Guilin".

As a saying goes, all the nineteen peaks in clouds can be the craggy jades, the towering cliffs stand in a line as an army with various images. And the scene that the clear river, like a ribbon, flows around the mountain and forms its vivid reflection is similar to human's fairyland. Among all the peaks, the Wanghai Peak ranks the highest with a height of 400 meters. It has only one way up with 99 stone-steps. People claim that one is only one step away from the heaven. In the middle of the Ma'an Peak, there is a cave, 5 meters high and 240 square meters wide, which links the east to the west. It is proved that the scenic area got its name "Chuanyan" from a poem which says the peak stands at the height of ten thousand meters and the cave can accommodate thousands of people. Speaking of the Lanchuan Peak, it is said that this peak is the spot where Dayu tied the ship when managing the floods. Xinfu Peak resembles a bride, slim and graceful, and other peaks are named after their unique features as well. The nineteen peaks are arranged in order from the south to the north: the Xianglu Peak, the Lanchuan Peak, the Ma'an Peak, the Xinfu Peak, the Qipan Peak, the Zhuojian Peak, the Fuzhong Peak, the Wanghai Peak, the Bijia Peak, the Sizhou Peak, etc. And all names of the nineteen peaks are entrusted with people's yearning for a happy life.

The Qianzhang Glen lies in the east of Chuanyan Nineteen Peaks. It is a piece of land favored by nature, where thousands of rocks vie with each other, and myriad streams struggle to flow. Inside the glen, there are red cliffs and **dilapidated** walls, odd rocks and shallow creeks, along with many scenic spots such as the Two Dragons Setting River, One Finger Peak, Pearls Falling into a Jade Plate, Bastion of Iron, Three Bathing Elephants, Golden Monkey Offering Peaches, which provide an **inclination** of the **unadulterated** peculiarity of nature.

★生词与词组 Words & Expressions

glen /glen/ *n.* 峡谷

seclusion /si'klu:ʒ(ə)n/ *n.* 隐居

solidified /sə'lidifaid/ *n.* 木化的

inclination /inkli'neiʃ(ə)n/ *n.* 倾向

radiance /'reidiəns/ *n.* 光辉

physiognomy /ˌfizi'ɔ(g)nəmi/ *n.* 地貌

dilapidated /di'læpideitid/ *adj.* 荒废的

unadulterated /ʌnə'dʌltəreitid/ *adj.* 纯粹的

◆ 知识拓展 Knowledge Extension

丹霞地貌：20 世纪 30 年代被命名的一类地貌类型，形成丹霞地貌的岩层是一种在内陆盆地沉积的红色屑岩，后来地壳抬升，岩石被流水切割侵蚀，山坡以崩塌过程为主而后退，保留下来的岩层就构成了红色山块。中国境内已发现的丹霞地貌约有 780 多处，分布广泛。共有 9 个省的十几家风景名胜区提出加入丹霞地貌捆绑申遗行列，最终入选的 6 个提名地是中国亚热带湿润区丹霞地貌的最佳代表。

3. 峰山道场 Fengshan Bodhimanda

峰山道场位于上虞市百官镇梁巷村境内东北方，东临曹娥江，古为百官渡西岸泊船处。峰山海拔高 40.3 米，东西近 230 米长，南北近 180 米宽，山上绿树成林，且有竹园相衬。

峰山并不高大，但有它自己的地域特色。峰山在会稽东岳之西，是古代明州至越州的水陆中转码头，交通十分便捷。由于其得天独厚的地理优势，很有利于佛教文化的交流，因而峰山一度成了江南佛教文化弘扬与交流的重要之地。

峰山道场因唐朝时峰山密宗第三代传人顺晓大师在峰山研修佛理弘法而得名。

峰山道场还是日本国天台宗初祖最澄大师在华学习密宗受法的圣地。唐贞元廿年(804)日本国僧最澄法师随第 12 次遣唐使入唐求法，求经未得之归途于峰山遇峰山密宗第三代传人顺晓大师，遂与其共研佛理。最澄得到顺晓大师的授法灌顶，授曼陀罗和印信经书102部(115 卷)，最澄终于求法成功。最澄返回日本后，创立日本佛界最早的门派天台宗。后来，他回到峰山为其先师顺晓雕像，归国时，还从越州上虞带得《茶经》及茶籽引种至日本，使日本成为最早得到中国茶种的国家。

峰山道场作为中日文化交流的重要见证，已成为日本宗教朝拜的圣地。

Fengshan Bodhimanda is located in the northeast of Liangxiang Village, Baiguan Town, Shangyu City. On its east is the Cao-E River, where the ancient officials **berthed** their boats on the west bank. Fengshan is 40.3 meters high, 230 meters long and 180 meters wide, covered with thick forests and some bamboo gardens.

Fengshan is not high at all, but the mountain has its own geographic advantages. Located in the west of the East Kuaiji Mountain, it was the water dock between ancient Mingzhou County and Yuezhou County, enjoying convenient transportation. Thanks to its unique geographic location which was beneficial to the exchange of Buddhist culture, it became a very important place for the communication and exchange of Buddhism in Jiangnan.

It is famous for a great Buddhist **master** named Shun Xiao, Fengshan's third descendant, who studied **esoteric doctrine** here in the Tang Dynasty.

Fengshan is also a holy land, where Saicho, the creator of Japanese Tendai sect, studied the esoteric doctrine. In 804, Saicho came to China with the twelfth group of **envoys** to study Buddhism. But he failed. On the way back home, he **came across** Shun Xiao, Fengshan's third descendant. Then they began to study Buddhism together and at last Saicho got Esoteric Buddhism from Shun Xiao. Saicho went home after that and established the earliest Buddhism **paction** of Tendai sect in Japan. He also brought tea seeds with him back home to Japan, as a result of which, Japan became the first country to learn from China to grow tea.

That's why Fengshan is the witness of Sino-Japanese friendship and a holy place for Japanese people to visit.

★生词与词组 Words & Expressions

berth /bə:θ/ *v.* 使停泊　　　　　　　　master /'mɑ:stə/ *n.* 大师

esoteric /ˌesə'terik/ *adj.* 秘传的　　　doctrine /'dɔktrin/ *n.* 教义

envoy /'envɔi/ *n.* 使者　　　　　　　　paction /'pækʃən/ *n.* 协议书

come across 偶遇

◆ 知识拓展 Knowledge Extension

日本最澄大师(767—822)：日本佛教的先祖，是天台宗最忠实的信徒之一。他是日本近江国(今滋贺县)滋贺郡人。781 年在京都比睿山靖草庵修行，研习鉴真东渡时带去的天台教典，大受教益。为了进一步研习教义，他决心入唐求法。唐贞元二十年(804)，最澄带着弟子义真乘坐日本第十二次遣唐使藤原葛野磨吕的使船入唐求法。当年九月二十六日到达天台山，从道邃、行满大师受学，并"卖金货纸"，抄写天台教典，延请了几十名经生帮助抄经，共抄得 128 部 345 卷。后至绍兴龙兴寺(属密宗)求经未得，归途遇峰山密宗第三代传人顺晓大师，与其共研佛理并向最澄授金刚界和胎藏两界灌顶，授曼陀罗和印信经书 102 部(115 卷)，遂求法成功，最澄返回日本后，"台、密、禅、戒"兼修，创立日本佛界最早的门派天台宗。最澄创日本天台宗后再回峰山为其先师顺晓雕像。

4. 府山 Fushan Hill

府山是绍兴古城内的主要名山，因形状若卧龙，又名卧龙山；越国大夫文种死后葬于龙山之上，故又称文种山。因历来为府治所在，又名府山；今辟为府山公园。山上古迹众多，据记载，在全盛时的宋代，山上共有 72 处楼台亭阁。现存越王台、越王殿、南宋古柏、清白泉、飞翼楼、风雨亭、文种墓、樱花园、摩崖石刻等文物景点十余处。

府山是范蠡所筑山阴小城的核心，越王勾践以此为王宫 19 年。五代吴越国王钱镠在山上始建王宫，北宋仍为越州州署，作王宫时间长达 74 年，范围遍及全山。山上山下文物古迹众多。东南麓的越王台是为纪念越王勾践卧薪尝胆的故事而建。越王台古称点将台，相传越王勾践曾在古越王台点将出兵伐吴。与越王台相对的是宏伟庄严、富丽堂皇的越王殿，殿内有巨大的越王勾践卧薪尝胆图，文种、范蠡、西施等人的画像，集中了卧薪尝胆、十年生聚、十年教训、投醪欢送等令人扼腕的故事。殿与台之间，今存南宋古柏一株和范仲淹的清白泉，并有"龙湫泉"一口。

府山东北隅有文种墓，文种墓曾经被毁，目前的墓冢于 1981 年重修，墓呈圆形，东北向。文种，字少禽，楚国人，曾为越国大夫，为勾践兴越灭吴的主要谋士。勾践是一个可以共患难，不可同安乐的人。文种自灭吴后，仍留在勾践身旁为官，终遭勾践猜忌，赐剑命文种自杀，葬于龙山。

府山里的一草一木、一岩一石、一亭一台背后都有历史，被列为浙江省文物保护单位。

Fushan Hill, one of the most famous mountains in Old Shaoxing, has another two names. One is the **Coiling** Dragon Mountain for its shape is just like a coiling dragon; the other is the Wenzhong Hill for the senior official of Yue named Wenzhong was buried here after his death. Its present name is Fushan Hill because it has always been the capital (Fu in Chinese). There are various **historical** relics on the Fushan Hill. As documented, during the **flourishing** Song Dynasty, the number of Towers and Pavilions was over 72. There still remain dozens of them, such as King Yue's Terrace, King Yue's Palace, Ancient Cypress of the Southern Song Dynasty, Qingbai Spring,

Feiyi Tower, Fengyu Pavilion, Wenzhong Tomb, Cherry Blossom Garden, the **Inscription** on **precipice** and other spots of cultural relics.

Fushan is the core of the small town built by Fanli, which had been a palace of the King of Yue, Goujian for 19 years. King Qianji of Wuyue Kingdom in the Five Dynasties set up his palace in the Fushan Hill originally and it was still the office building of Yuezhou in the Northern Song Dynasty, the whole mountain being a palace for 74 years. A large number of historical and cultural relics are scattered all over the hill. The Terrace of King Yue is a famous memorial structure in honor of the story of the King of Yue who took revenge on the King of Wu by working for him as a servant, sleeping on brushwood and tasting gall. It lies at the southeast foot of Fushan Mountain and named Call-officers-roll Platform in ancient time. As legend goes, the King of Yue **dispatched** troops to fight with Wu State here. Facing it stands the magnificent and grand King Yue's Palace, inside of which has a huge picture depicting King Yue's hard time and portraits of Wenzhong, Fanli, Xishi etc., describing the stories of "the King of Yue spent a whole decade on drawing the lesson from the failure of a war against Wu, undergoing self-imposed hardships so as to strengthen his resolution to wipe out the national **humiliation**" and so on. Between the two buildings are the ancient Cypress, Qingbai Spring and Longqiu Spring.

Wenzhong Tomb, round-shaped, lying at the northeast of the hill, was once ruined, and repaired in 1981. Wenzhong, styled as Shaoqin, Chu-state's people, used to be the senior official in Yue and played an important role as a **counselor** in the process of booming Yue and **annihilating** Wu. Goujian, a person for one to share hardships with but not fortune **was suspicious of** Wenzhong finally and ordered him to commit suicide with a sword. After death, Wenzhong was buried in the Coiling Dragon Mountain.

Fushan Hill, with historical stories behind each building and each plant, is a cultural relic of Zhejiang Province.

★生词与词组 Words & Expressions

coiling /ˈkɔiliŋ/ *adj.* 卷绕的
flourishing /ˈflʌriʃiŋ/ *adj.* 繁荣的
precipice /ˈpresipis/ *n.* 悬崖；绝壁
humiliation /hjuˌmiliˈeiʃn/ *n.* 丢脸；耻辱
annihilate /əˈnaiileit/ *v.* 歼灭；战胜

historical /hiˈstɔrik(ə)l/ *adj.* 历史的
inscription /inˈskripʃ(ə)n/ *n.* 题词；刻印
dispatch /diˈspætʃ/ *v.* 派遣；分派
counselor /ˈkauns(ə)lə/ *n.* 顾问；参事
be suspicious of 怀疑

◆ 知识拓展 Knowledge Extension

文种(？—前472)：也作文仲、字会、少禽，一作子禽，春秋末期楚之郢(今湖北江陵附近)人，后定居越国。春秋末期著名的谋略家，越王勾践的谋臣，和范蠡一起为勾践最终打败吴王夫差立下赫赫功劳。

范蠡(前536—前448)：字少伯，春秋战国末期的政治家、军事家和经济学家。公元前496

年前后入越，辅助勾践廿余年，终于使勾践于公元前 473 年灭吴，范蠡以为大名之下，难以久居，于是急流勇退，毅然弃官，乘舟泛海而去。

西施：本名施夷光，是中国古代"沉鱼落雁，闭月羞花"四大美人中的"沉鱼"，春秋末期的浙江诸暨一带人氏，又称西子，是家喻户晓的美人。

5. 镜湖国家城市湿地公园 Jinghu National Urban Wetland Park

镜湖国家城市湿地公园是浙江省首个淡水湖泊型国家级城市湿地公园，位于绍兴大城市越城、柯桥、袍江三大城市组团的中心，是绍兴大城市"绿心"的核心部分。

公园东起解放北路西侧河流及梅山公园，西至张家潭等河流，南临鸭沙滩、荸荠泾，北依狭猕湖路，总占地面积15.6平方千米。公园具有独特的荷叶地地形，充分展示了平原河网地区丰富的湿地景观，分布有植物65科、132属、151种及相关浮游生物。

东侧的梅山，早在越国时期，越工勾践就在山上建有斋戒之台；至唐代，在山的西侧建有永觉寺，历代有巫山之穴、梅子真泉、适南亭、尚书墓、茶坞等名胜古迹。经过前期的复绿，目前山上动植物众多，成群的白鹭在此集聚栖息，其中黄嘴白鹭是国家二级保护动物。

西侧的东浦古镇，是典型的江南水乡古镇，形态保存基本完好，"小桥、流水、人家"，216座形态各异的桥梁、36条水色澄清的河流、徐锡麟故居、东浦老街等等，可谓古镇风貌，酒乡风情，名人故居。

北侧的狭猕湖是绍兴最大的天然淡水湖，以狭猕鱼为名，独具地方特色，现存面积2.23平方千米，湖上有省级文保单位避塘，湖底有近1米的泥炭层，是绍兴此类矿产最丰富之地，湿地作为碳库，可以降低大气中的二氧化碳，缓解温室效应。

Jinghu National Urban Wetland Park is the first wetland park of fresh water lake in Zhejiang Province, located in the center of the three major cities of Greater Shaoxing, that is, Yuecheng District, Keqiao and Paojiang, the core of the "Green Heart" as well.

The total land area of the park is 15.6 square kilometers with a **unique topography** of the lotus leaf fully displaying the rich wetland landscape of the plains of the river network. Around the park are distributed more than 65 branches, 132 genres, 151 kinds of plants and relevant **planktons**.

East of the park is the Meishan Mountain, on which a fasting platform was built by King Goujian of Yue. In the Tang Dynasty, Yongjue Temple was built in the west of the mountain along with other such as the Tomb of the Wushan Mountain, the True Spring of Meizi, Shinan Pavilion, Shangshu Tomb and the Tea House and other places of interest. After the green recovery project, many plants and animals begin to appear on the mountain, and flocks of egrets are the most eye-catching sight in this **habitat**. Besides, Chinese egret is a second class national protected animal.

On the west side of the park is Dongpu Town, an ancient town with typical water scenery famous for 216 bridges with different shapes, 36 clean and clear rivers, old buildings and streets, rice wine as well as many former **residence** of celebrities such as Xu Xilin's Former Residence, Dongpu Street and so on.

On the north side of the park is the Angsang Lake which is the largest natural freshwater lake in Shaoxing. Covering an area of 2.23 square kilometers, the lake has a one-meter thick peat layer on the lakebed, which can be used as a carbon reservoir, reducing CO_2 in the atmosphere, **alleviating** the greenhouse effect.

★生词与词组 Words & Expressions

unique /juːˈniːk/ *adj.* 独特的

plankton /ˈplæŋ(k)t(ə)n/ *n.* 浮游生物

residence /ˈrezidəns/ *n.* 住宅，住处

topography /təˈpɒgrəfi/ *n.* 地形学

habitat /ˈhæbɪˌtæt/ *n.* 栖息地，产地

alleviate /əˈliːvieit/ *v.* 减轻，缓和

◆ 知识拓展 Knowledge Extension

浮游生物(plankton)：在海洋、湖泊及河川等水域的生物中，自身完全没有移动能力，或者有也非常弱，因而不能逆水流而动，而是浮在水面生活，这类生物总称为浮游生物。

6. 柯岩风景区 Keyan Scenic Area

柯岩风景区位于绍兴市城西，AAAA级旅游景区，占地3平方千米。柯岩以石文化见长，景区融自然和人文景观于一体，以奇岩、清潭、幽洞、秀山的巧妙组合而取胜。景区是在绍兴古采石场上建立起来的观光型景点，紧邻中国轻纺城，是一处以古越文化为内涵，融绍兴水乡风情、古采石遗景、山林生态于一体的名胜景区。它始建于汉代，距今已有1800多年历史，至清代，形成著名的"柯岩八景"，素为越中名胜。自1995年经别具匠心的营造，形成石佛景区、镜水湾景区和越中名士苑三大景点，游览面积达1.2平方千米。

三国时期，这里曾是一处采石场，经历代能工巧匠的不断开凿，鬼斧神工般地造就了姿态各异的石岩、石洞、石潭和石壁。千百年来，随着宗教的介入，文人名流的渲染及后人的开发，现已形成天工大佛、炉柱晴烟、七星岩、八卦台、文昌阁、蚕花洞、莲花听音、越女春晓、镜水飞瀑、三聚同源等胜景奇观，特别是两"柱"孤岩，一左一右，一胖一瘦，浑然兀立。左者谓江南最大的圆雕石佛——天工大佛。佛像高20.8米，为弥勒佛盘坐造像，法相敦厚慈祥，仪表文静端庄，两耳相通，背面悬壁，雕刻工艺，造诣颇高；右者号称天下第一石——云骨，奇石高30余米，底围不足4米，可由三人合抱，底部扁形直立，最薄处不足1米，上丰下削，凹凸险峻，远远望去，宛如一柱烟霭，袅袅长腾。奇石上有两个隶书大字：云骨，系清光绪年间所刻。岩顶长着一棵古柏，已逾千年，令人惊叹不已。

镜水湾是一处人工建筑，从古纤道路的高桥上看下去，其状如一位着长裙、靠右侧卧的少女。在桥上还能看到人工瀑布、水乡戏台等。

Located at west of Shaoxing, Keyan Scenic Area is one of the first national "AAAA level tourist spots". This scenic spot, harmoniously integrated with the other two great scenic spots of Keyan and Jianhu, extends the sightseeing area up to 3 square kilometers, and has become a high level tourist destination. It boasts its largest size, most comprehensive functions, combining food, accommodation, transportation, sightseeing, entertainment and shopping into a whole. It is a place famous for its ancient Yue state culture at its core, integrating the features of the Shaoxing watery regions, the relics of the ancient **quarry** as well as mountains forestry ecology into a whole. It was first built in the Han Dynasty with a history of over 1,800 years. In the Qing Dynasty, the well-known "eight scenic spots of Keyan" came into being, and has been places of great interest since then in Shaoxing. Keyan is the key area of the Keyan Scenic Spot. Since the development and scenery recovery in 1995, the three key scenic spots, including Stone Buddha, Jingshui Bay and Garden of Celebrities in Yue (Shaoxing) have been completed covering a sightseeing area of up to 1.2 square kilometers.

In the Three Kingdoms Period, it was once a quarry. The continuous cutting and superlative craftsmanship of skillful craftsmen in all the **successive** dynasties have created the stone rocks, caves, ponds and walls of various gestures and shapes. For thousands of years, with the **interposition** of religions, propaganda of bookmen and celebrities and the development of the **descendants**, now the whole scenic spot includes many scenery and landscape of great wonders, such as the excellent-carving Grand Buddha, Smoke Rising Upward from Rocks, Seven-star Rock, the Eight Diagrams Platform, Wenchang Pavilion, Silk-worm-flower Cave, Sound Heard on the Lotus Flower, Spring Dawn of Yue State, Jingshui Flying Waterfall and Same Source of Three Religions Get-together. What is worth our particular attention is the two "poles" of solitary rocks, one on the left and the other on the right, one fat while the other thin, standing upright and solemn. The one on the left is the largest round stone Buddha figure in Jiangnan—an excellent carved Grand Buddha. It is leg-crossed sitting Maitreya, a 20.8 meters high statue, looking honest and sincere, quiet and elegant, with two interlinked ears and a wall as his back. Its carving technique is of pretty high level. The one on the right is the "cloud bone", which claims to be the No. 1 rock under the sun. This **marvelous** rock is over 30 meters high while the bottom diameter is less than 4 meters. Three people can hold it around with their arms at full length. The bottom is erect and flat with the thinnest part less than 1 meter. It is huge in the upper part while sharp in the lower part, unsmooth and **precipitous**, looking like a **surge** of smoke curling upward into the sky from a distance. Two big characters "Cloud Bone" have been carved on this rare stone, which was done in Guangxu reign of the Qing Dynasty. On the top of it is an old cypress tree of over 1,000 years, which astonishes people a lot.

Jingshui Bay is an **artificial** lake. Overlooked from the high bridges of ancient towpath it is like a girl wearing a long dress and lying aside to the right. Artificial waterfalls and opera stages built in the water can be seen from the bridges as well.

★生词与词组 Words & Expressions

quarry /ˈkwɔri/ *n.* 采石场

interposition /intəpəˈziʃ(ə)n/ *n.* 涉入，介入

marvelous /ˈmɑːrvələs/ *adj.* 了不起的；非凡的

successive /səkˈsesiv/ *adj.* 连续的

descendant /diˈsend(ə)nt/ *n.* 后裔；子孙

precipitous /priˈsipitəs/ *adj.* 险峻的；急躁的

surge /sə:dʒ/ *n.* 大浪　　　　　　　　　　artificial /ˌɑ:ti'fiʃəl/ *adj.* 人造的

◆ **知识拓展 Knowledge Extension**

　　中国轻纺城：总占地面积 77.8 万平方米，总建筑面积达 326 万平方米，商行 1.6 万余家，营业用房 1.9 万间。是目前全国规模最大、设施最齐、经营品种最多的纺织品集散中心，也是亚洲最大的轻纺专业市场。

7. 兰亭 The Orchid Pavilion

　　兰亭位于绍兴城西南的兰渚山麓，据传春秋时越王勾践种兰于此，东汉时建有驿亭，因而得名。"此地有崇山峻岭，茂林修竹，又有清流急湍，映带左右。"公元 353 年，东晋著名书法家王羲之在此书写了著名的《兰亭序》，更使兰亭闻名遐迩。

　　兰亭的魅力，不仅来自山水风光的瑰丽，更来自历史文化的厚重。先是鹅池旁的"鹅池"碑，相传其"鹅"字系王羲之一笔而就，"池"字由王献之从容续成，父子合璧，千古称奇；接着是"兰亭"碑，系清康熙所题，曾一度遭受破坏，劫后重生，难能可贵；随后是有"东南第一大碑"之誉的"御碑"，碑阳为康熙1693年手书《兰亭序》，碑阴为乾隆1751年游兰亭时所书《兰亭即事诗》手迹，祖孙二帝手迹同碑，世所罕见，令人叹为观止。

　　兰亭融秀美的山水风光、雅致的园林景观、独享的书坛盛名、丰厚的历史文化积淀于一体，以"景幽、事雅、文妙、书绝"四大特色而享誉海内外，成为中国一处重要的名胜古迹。

Located at the foot of the Orchid Hill, the Orchid Pavilion is in the southwest of Shaoxing. During the Spring and Autumn Period, King Goujian of Yue planted orchids here and later a pavilion was **constructed** here during the Eastern Han Dynasty. In 353, the noted calligrapher Wang Xizhi wrote some of his celebrated works here, among which the *Orchid Pavilion Prologue* is the most famous. Since then, the Orchid Pavilion has been known as a home to calligraphy.

The attraction of the Orchid Pavilion not only comes from its **magnificent** landscape and graceful southern China gardening sights, but also derives from its profound historical culture and its unique and vast reputation in the calligraphic field. First, the famous Goose Pond stone **stele**. Two Chinese **characters** "鹅池(Goose Pond)" are carved on the stele. It is said that the two characters were written respectively by Wang Xizhi and his son, Wang Xianzhi—a famous calligrapher as well. It is **extraordinary** that the two characters on the stone stele have different styles written by the father and the son, both well-known calligraphers. Second, the Orchid Pavilion Stele on which there are two characters written by Emperor Kangxi of the Qing Dynasty. The stele was once broken into four pieces and was not mended until 1980. Though both the carved characters on the stele are damaged, it can still be seen that they were well written. Third, the Imperial Stele with a **magnificently** carved top. On the face of the stele carved the whole *Orchid Pavilion Prolog* copied by Emperor Kangxi in 1693. The handwriting was natural and graceful in style. On the back of the stele was the **script** of the *Orchid Pavilion Poem* by Emperor Qianlong when he visited the Orchid Pavilion in 1751. Emperor Qianlong was good at calligraphy, and this poem showed the much-toured Emperor's admiration for the Orchid Pavilion. It is very rare that the scripts of the grandfather and the grandson are carved on the same stele. It is really a national treasure.

The Orchid Pavilion not only has beautiful scenery and elegant landscape, but enjoys a unique reputation of calligraphy, rich history and cultural background. Being characterized by these features, the Orchid Pavilion has become a key place of interest known both at home and abroad for its quiet surroundings, elegant sceneries, wonderful articles and spectacular calligraphy.

★生词与词组 Words & Expressions

construct /kən'strʌkt/ *v.* 建造

stele /sti:l; sti:li/ *n.* 石碑

extraordinary /ik'strɔ:dnri/ *adj.* 特别的，非凡的

magnificent /mæg'nifis(ə)nt/ *adj.* 壮丽的，华丽的

character /'kærəktə/ *n.* 字符

script /skript/ *n.* 手迹

◆ 知识拓展 Knowledge Extension

王羲之(303—361)：字逸少，号澹斋，原籍琅琊临沂(今属山东)，后迁居山阴(今浙江绍兴)，中国东晋书法家，有书圣之称。为南迁琅琊王氏贵胄，后官拜右军将军，人称王右军。

王献之(344—386)：字子敬，书法家、诗人。祖籍山东临沂，生于会稽(今浙江绍兴)，王羲之第七子。官至中书令，为与后世书法家王珉区分，人称王大令。与其父并称为"二王"。传世墨迹有《中秋帖》《十二月帖》《鸭头丸帖》《廿九日帖》《玉版十三行》，等等。

8. 南山风景区 Nanshan Scenic Area

南山风景区位于嵊州西南，以奇峰、林海、秀湖为特色，是江南最大的火山大峡谷，也是迄今为止国内发现的海拔最低的古冰川遗迹。景区分为南山湖、火山口、冰川谷、天兴潭、金银湾、鹿门书院等六大景区，包含火山弹、冰臼群、冰漂砾、古松林、斤丝潭飞帘等多个独具特色的景点，是一处集碧湖、奇岩、飞瀑于一体的山水风光旅游胜地。

南山湖烟波渺渺，湖中岛屿如海市蜃楼，穿梭云中。沿湖四周，古木参天，多红枫青松。象鼻山南麓之盆地，三面临山，一面临湖，有桃林一片。每当阳春三月，花香四溢，人面桃花相映成趣，恍若置身桃源仙境。

天兴潭，古称三悬潭，因其周围悬岩如削，瀑布飞泻，组成三汪清潭而得名。远望此地，只听得瀑声轰鸣，只闻其声，不见其形。待寻声而至，入眼即是重峦叠翠，涧流碧澄，藏风聚气。再深入其间，只见里潭瀑布凌空飞泻，声若雷鸣，如白龙入海。里潭与中潭并列，水流过石棱而注入中潭，又汇于外潭。外潭有巨石一方，明太守白玉曾祈雨于此，故名拜龙石。周围尚有猴面壁、九龙滩、观瀑亭等景点。

鹿门书院是南宋理学家吕规叔创立。理学大师朱熹曾授学于鹿门书院，宣传其理学思想。

南门上书"古鹿门",北门上题"贵门",均系朱熹手笔。南北两洞的背面的"隔尘""归云"是书法家赵睿荣所提。书院四周茂林修竹,怪石清泉,随处可见,其中山光水影,令人游目骋怀。

Nanshan Scenic Area, located in the southwest of Shengzhou, is characterized by its odd rocks, immense forests and blue lakes. It is not only the largest volcanic grand canyon in Jiangnan, but also the ancient **remnants** of **glaciations** at the lowest **elevation** in China so far. This resort is divided into six areas, namely, the Nanshan Lake, Crater, Glaciated Valley, Tianxing Pond, Golden-silver Bay and Lumen **Academy**. It also includes Volcanic Bombs, Moulin Group, Ice Group, Ancient Pines, Flying Waterfall Curtain on Jinsi Pond and some other unique tourist sites, forming a tourist resort with an integration of lakes, rocks and waterfalls.

When the Nanshan Lake is dimly seen in mist, the islands in the middle are like a **mirage**, shuttling back and forth between clouds. Around the lake, there are many ancient trees towering to the sky, most of which are maples and pines. The basin at the southern foot of the Elephant Trunk Hill faces mountains from three sides and another side is adjacent to the lake as if one is in a fairyland.

Tianxing Pond, called Sanxuan Pond as well, gets the name for the cliffs around it, plunging waterfalls and three clear ponds. Looking out here, you can only hear waterfalls roaring, but can not see its appearance. Then getting close to it tracing its sound, you will see many steep mountains with clear streams flowing, all natural elements gathering here. Going deeper, you can find the **vaporous** and roaring waterfalls drop from the perilous peaks with a thunder, which presents the most spectacular view, like a white dragon diving into the sea. The inner pond parallels with the middle pond, and clear water fills into the inner pond and then flows to the outer one. The outer pond has a huge rock called Dragon Worship Stone. It is said that Bai Yu, a prefecture officer in the Ming Dynasty had prayed for rain here. So came the name. What's more, there is Monkey Face Wall, Nine Dragon Shoal, Waterfall-watching Pavilion and other attractions around it.

The famous Lumen Academy was set up by Lü Guishu, a **neo-Confucianist** in the Southern Song Dynasty. Zhu Xi, an excellent scholar in this field, once **propagandized** his thoughts about neo-Confucianism here. The words "Gu Lu Men" were carved on the south gate, while "Gui Men" **inscribed** on the north gate, which were both written by Zhu Xi. On the back of south and north caves were calligrapher Zhao Ruirong's handwriting "Ge Chen" and "Gui Yun". Around the academy, there exist thick forests and slender bamboos, odd rocks and clear waters, especially the mountains' **reflections** on the river make one's eyes travel over the great scenes in fancy.

★生词与词组 Words & Expressions

remnants /remnants/ *n.* 残留部分
elevation /ˌeli'veiʃ(ə)n/ *n.* 海拔
mirage /'mirɑːʒ; mi'rɑːʒ/ *n.* 海市蜃楼;幻想
neo-Confucianist /ˌniːəukən'fjuːʃənist/ *n.* 理学家
inscribe /in'skraib/ *v.* 题写;雕

glaciation /ˌgleisi'eiʃən/ *n.* 冰川
academy /ə'kædəmi/ *n.* 学院;研究院
vaporous /'veipərəs/ *adj.* 空想的;多蒸气的
propagandized /ˌprɔpə'gændaiz/ *v.* 宣传
reflection /ri'flekʃ(ə)n/ *n.* 倒影

◆ *知识拓展* Knowledge Extension

贵门更楼：位于贵门乡贵门村北，是一座坐北朝南的四合式二层建筑，下层是石砌的台基，中有天井，南北两面各有拱券洞门，为旧时人婺往来之通道；上层楼房四面相向，回廊相连，登楼北望，南山湖风光尽收眼底。更楼是概称，东为"更楼"，西则为"鹿门书院"。更楼旁有两棵大枫树称姐妹枫，高逾十丈，径围八尺，分列于贵门更楼北门口两旁。贵门更楼洞左100米，有古松五六棵，皆需两人伸臂方可围合。

朱熹(1113—1200)：南宋著名哲学家、教育家，婺源县城人，字元晦，又字促晦，号晦庵，别号紫阳，小名沈郎，小字季延。朱熹曾于绍兴二十年春和淳熙三年二月，两次回婺源故里省亲扫墓。今"文公山"上的古杉群即朱熹手植。

9. 斯氏古民居建筑群 Ancient Si Family House Complex

清代民宅，主要由斯盛居、发祥居和华国公别墅组成，系斯姓房族聚居之所，其中千柱屋、发祥居、华国公别墅3处已被列入了国家重点文物保护单位。

斯盛居建于清嘉庆戊午年(1798)，其名源自"于斯为盛"的门额，又因屋内墙柱有999根，俗称"千柱屋"。斯盛居为当地巨富斯元儒(1753—1832)的住宅。斯盛居建筑群规模恢宏，纵横交织，门户重重，屋宇宽敞，砖、石、木雕精湛细腻，其中《百马图》砖雕，堪称艺术精品。

千柱屋正厅门楼制作讲究，其门额以青石制作，上镌"于斯为盛"四字。斯盛居内廊柱林立，玲珑剔透，令人目不暇接，有入五里雾中之感。斯盛居背倚松啸湾，拾级而上有"林泉之胜，甲于一邑"的笔峰书屋，书屋依山势而建，系斯氏家塾。书屋门前有盘槐两株，枝干老态龙钟，曲虬横卧，一若青狮，一若白象，颇具观赏价值。屋前古木参天，均数百年也，依然苍翠欲滴，生机盎然。

发祥居因门厅有"长发其祥"门额而名，俗称"下新屋"。建于清嘉庆壬戌年(1802)，为斯元儒胞兄元仁的住宅。平面对称布局，中轴建筑三进，为门厅、大厅、座楼。左右两侧设东、西厢楼，边门出入。其建筑木雕工艺精细，间缀砖雕与石雕。

华国公别墅因门额镌刻"华国公别墅"而名，建于清道光庚子年(1840)，系后人为追念斯华国而建的兼家庙与学塾为一体的建筑群。依山势而建，中轴建筑共三进，依次为门厅、中厅和后厅，两侧配置厢房和附房，其中厅为学塾之讲堂，后厅即家庙。

斯氏古民居建筑群建造讲究、保存完整，且建筑时代风格明显，梁、柱、窗、墙均有雕饰，颇具特色，堪称民居艺术瑰宝。

The Ancient Si Family House Complex was built in the Qing Dynasty. It is made up of Sisheng Housing, Faxiang Housing and Huaguogong Villa, where the Sis' generations once lived. Three places of this **complex** have been preserved as scenic spots at the national level, among them are One-thousand-pillar House, Faxiang Housing and so on.

The Sisheng Housing, namely, the Thousand-Pillar House for there are 999 **pillars** supporting the whole housing, was built in 1798. It was the residence of Si Yuanru (1753–1832), a rich man. This complex is of great **scale** and the houses are extremely wide. The bricks, stones and wooden sculptures are all fine and exquisite, of which a brick sculpture the *Picture of a Hundred Horses* is a classic artwork.

The main hall of Thousand-Pillar House is exquisitely constructed with "Start to Boom" written in square characters above its **lintel**, which is bluestone-made. Visitors may feel like lost in the dense fog when going inside. The porch columns stand at intervals, the **adjoining** rooms and the whole beautifully wrought layout may have a dazzling effect on one's eye. The Sisheng building is against the Songxiao Bay at the back. Ascending the stairs, one can reach Bifeng Study inscribed with "the Ideal Place for Woods and Springs" by an ancient poet, which was built as Si Family's private school at the foot of mountain. The two locust trees in the front door, whose limbs are old and inflexible, are well worth appreciating as their branches crunch low, looking like a blue lion and a white elephant. In front of the old building, the ancient trees, verdant and **exuberant**, are towering to the sky, which are hardly to imagine that they are all centuries of years old.

The Faxiang Housing, also called Xiaxinwu, was Si Yuanren's house, which was built in the Renxu Year of Jiaqing reign of the Qing Dynasty in 1802. The house is **symmetrically** built and made up of the lobby, hall, and main building. It is **exquisitely** made and dotted with fine brick and stone sculptures.

Huaguogong Villa, named after the inscription "Hua Guo Gong Bie Shu", was built in the Gengzi Year of Daoguang reign of the Qing Dynasty in 1840, which was a building complex as a study and family temple in honor of Si Huaguo. The housing lies on the hill, **comprised** of the lobby, mid-hall and back-hall, with the mid-hall used as a private study and the back-hall the family temple.

The Ancient Si Family House Complex is built **daintily** and of the special times' style with all the beams, windows, and pillars decorated with sculptures. It is the gem of the folk housings.

★生词与词组 Words & Expressions

complex /'kɔmpleks/ *n.* 综合设施
scale /skeil/ *n.* 规模
adjoining /ə'dʒɔiniŋ/ *adj.* 邻接的；毗连的
symmetrically /si'metrik(ə)li/ *adv.* 对称地
comprise /kəm'praiz/ *v.* 包含；由组成

pillar /'pilə/ *n.* 柱子
lintel /'lint(ə)l/ /'lintl/ *n.* [建]过梁
exuberant /ig'z(j)u:b(ə)r(ə)nt/ *adj.* 繁茂的
exquisitely /'ekskwizitli/ *adv.* 精致地
daintily /'deintili/ *adv.* 讲究地；优美地

◆ 知识拓展 Knowledge Extension

《百马图》：唐代韦偃的《百马图》共描绘各种马 95 匹、牧马的奚官与圉人 41 人在一条河中及岸边洗马、戏马、驯马、饲马的场面。这幅图中所描绘的近百匹黑、白、红、花等各色马，有动有静，姿态各异，生动活泼。画家对马的描绘，极善抓住动态和神情，运动中的马被表现得活泼顽皮，静立时的马又被表现得庄重威武，画中笔法清秀温雅，敷色清淡，可以看出唐法向宋元法变化的痕迹。

10. 宋六陵 Six Mausoleums of the Song Dynasty

宋六陵"在会稽县东南三十里，旧名宝山，一名上皋山，今谓之攒宫山，宋永以下诸陵皆在"。宋六陵即高宗永思陵、孝宗永阜陵、光宗永崇陵、宁宗永茂陵、理宗永穆陵、度宗永绍陵。其实它还包括了北宋哲宗皇后孟氏、北宋最后一个皇帝徽宗及南宋皇后与皇室大臣的坟墓，共占地 2.25 平方千米，是江南一带规模最大的皇陵区。南宋绍兴元年(1131)，宋高宗驻跸越州，以州署为行宫。六月，元祐太后孟氏在行宫逝世，遗诏丧葬从简，"权宜就近择地攒殡，俟军事宁息归葬陵园"，于是就选择会稽县宝山南麓殡之地。

每座陵寝均设上下宫，功能齐备，结构完善。以高宗永思陵为例，据宋周必大所著《思陵录》记载，永思陵分为上下宫。下宫有外篱门、棂星门、围墙、殿门、大窑子、献殿等。元至正二十二年(1362)，江南释教总统杨琏真珈，两次率人盗掘宋六陵，破椁裂棺，窃取随葬珍宝，不计其数。六陵被盗，引起南宋遗民们的强烈不满，所以当元朝政权被推翻后，朱元璋下诏将流失在北方的理宗颅骨和其余诸陵归葬旧陵，立碑植树，绕以墙垣，以纪念义士唐珏等人。

现在宋六陵已列为浙江省重点文物保护单位。

Six **Mausoleums** of the Song Dynasty lie 15 kilometers Southeast of Kuaiji County. In the past, it was named Mount Baoshan, and Mount Shanggaoshan while its present name is Mount Cuangong, in which the mausoleums of six emperors of the Southern Song Dynasty lie here. The Six emperors are named Gao, Xiao, Guang, Ning, Li, Du. In fact, the mausoleums of the empress surnamed Meng and the last emperor named Hui of the Northern Song Dynasty and the **empresses** and ministers of the Southern Song Dynasty are also here. The mausoleums have an area of 2.25 square kilometers and are called the largest imperial tombs area in Jiangnan. In Primary Year of Shaoxing reign the Southern Song Dynasty (1131), Emperor Gao stopped over Yue state (today's Shaoxing), and made his Imperial Palace here. In June, Yuanyou Queen's mother surnamed Meng died in the palace and left her **testamentary edict** saying: Her funeral should be conformed to the principle of simplicity. After discussion she was buried nearby temporarily. But once the lost territory was reoccupied, the **reliquary** would be returned to the imperial cemetery. So the tomb was located in the south of Kuaiji County.

Each mausoleum has been found with upper and lower palaces of perfect structures and complete functions. Taking Gao's mausoleum for an example, it is documented that the lower palace **consists of** Waili Door, Lingxing Door, Bounding Wall, Palace's Door, Dayaozi, Xian Palace and etc. Up to 1362, the president of Buddhism in Jiangnan named Rin-chen-skyabs, led a group of people to illegally excavate and rob the mausoleums twice, breaking the coffins and taking away numerous **funerary** treasures, which caused the strong dissatisfied motion of the adherents of the Southern Song Dynasty. Therefore, when the Yuan Dynasty's **regime** was overthrown, Zhu Yuanzhang gave formal order to bury the lost Emperor Li's skull and other mausoleums to the former ones and set up the steles and bounding walls and planted trees to commemorate Tang Jue, a chivalrous scholar in the Song Dynasty and the others.

Six mausoleums of the Song Dynasty are the key protected cultural relics of Zhejiang Province.

★生词与词组 Words & Expressions

mausoleum /ˌmɔːsəˈliːəm/ *n.* 陵墓

testamentary /ˌtestəˈment(ə)ri/ *adj.* 遗嘱的

reliquary /ˈrelikwəri/ *n.* 遗骨匣

regime /reˈʒim/ *n.* 政权，政体

empress /ˈempris/ *n.* 皇后；女皇

edict /ˈiːdikt/ *n.* 法令；公告

funerary /ˈfjuːn(ə)(rə)ri/ *adj.* 埋葬的；葬礼的

consist of 由构成

◆ 知识拓展 Knowledge Extension

周必大(1126—1204)：南宋大臣，文学家。官至左丞相，封益国公。著有《益国周文忠公全集》200 卷，有清咸丰刻本。

11. 沈园 The Shen's Garden

沈园是唯一保存至今的宋式园林，园内风景秀丽，景致宜人，是江南著名的私家园林。因为主人家姓沈，所以称为"沈氏园"。

相传南宋年间，一个踌躇满志的诗人在此邂逅了他的前妻——一个美丽聪颖，对诗词有相当修养，与他情趣相投的女子，一个他一生中最为珍爱的人。他们就是当时伟大的爱国诗人陆游与其表妹唐琬。两人曾在沈园经历过一番伤心的遭遇。陆游 20 岁时同表妹唐琬结婚，夫妻感情深厚。但陆母不喜欢唐琬，逼儿休妻。母命难违，陆唐两人只得饮泣吞声，依依分别，各自嫁娶。五年后的一个春天，两人在此邂逅重逢，唐琬对陆游非常殷勤，派家人给陆游送去了酒菜，回忆往事，陆游无限悲戚。临别之时，陆游再也控制不住自己，将满腔悲愤诉诸笔端，在园壁上题下了千古绝唱《钗头凤》，极言痛苦之情。唐琬见词，衷肠寸断，伤感难抑，相传回家之后和词一阕，诉尽对陆游的无限思念。作为赵氏之妻，她一直以来只能将思念深埋在心底，但经过此番刺激，身心再也无法承受，不久便忧郁而死，当时大约是 30 岁左右。此事在陆游的心底埋下了深深的创伤，使他终生难以释怀，沈园从此成了梦魂萦绕的伤心之地。之后，陆游多次重游故地，追思往事，写下多首怀念唐琬的诗词。沈园因此成为爱情的象征，常有许多年轻男女到此表达对对方的爱意。

沈园经历 800 年的兴衰，至绍兴解放之时，仅存一隅。现在沈园是在原址修复、重建和扩建后的仿宋园林，占地 38000 平方米，分为古迹区、东苑和南苑三大部分。沈园内色调庄重典雅，景点互为映衬，很有宋代风味。因陆游一生爱梅，园内古迹区栽植有大量的腊梅树。

The Shen's Garden, the only Song-Dynasty-style garden preserved till now, with elegant and pleasant scenery, is a famous private garden in Jiangnan. Shen is the family name of the garden's former owner, hence the name, "The Shen's Garden".

According to the legend, during the Song Dynasty, an **agloat** poet **encountered** his first wife in this garden, who was pretty and smart, well cultured in poem and verse, also **temperamentally compatible** with him. They were the great patriotic poet, Lu You and his female younger cousin,

Tang Wan, who had a sad experience here. Lu You, at the age of 20, married Tang Wan. They loved each other deeply, but his mother disliked Tang and forced her son to divorce. For it was not allowed to disobey mother at that time, they had no way but to separate with sadness. They later both married others. Five years after separation, on a spring day, they encountered each other here. Lu was **hospitably** treated with wine and dishes by Tang, and he couldn't help looking back the past with endless sadness. When departing time came, with full grief and **indignation**, he composed the well-known poem entitled "**Phoenix Hairpin**" on the garden's wall, expressing his great pains completely. Seeing the poem, Tang fell into great sorrow and became heartbroken deeply. She wrote a poem in reply and expressed her great feeling of missing Lu. Since she became Zhao's wife, she could only bury her sentiment of missing Lu in heart in her daily time. This meeting stimulated her a lot. Both her body and mind couldn't bear the torture any more. Before long she died in melancholy at the age of about 30 and her death left a deep wound in Lu You's heart throughout his life, never cured. The Shen's Garden **henceforth** became the place for his dream-soul to **linger over**. Later on, Lu revisited the garden to recall the past for many times and wrote many poems and verses to **yearn** for his beloved, Tang Wan. The Shen's Garden thus becomes the symbol of love, and young couples often come here to display their love to each other.

The Shen's Garden, experienced 800 years of prosperity and decline, only left a corner after Shaoxing's **liberation**. The present Shen's Garden is an imitation of the Song Dynasty garden after rebuilding, reconstruction and **extension** of the original one, occupying an area of 38,000 square meters. It is divided into the Historical Site Area, the East Garden and the South Garden. The scenic area, with a tone of elegant and **solemn**, scenic spots complementing mutually, has a great flavor of the Song Dynasty. Out of Lu You's special love for plum, massive Chimonanthus Praecox trees are planted in the historical site area.

★生词与词组 Words & Expressions

agloat /ægləut/ *adj.* 踌躇满志的

temperamentally /ˌtemprə'mentəli/ *adv.* 气质地

hospitably /ˌhɔspi'tæbli/ *n.* 好客；殷勤

phoenix /'fi:niks/ *n.* 凤凰

henceforth /hensfɔ:θ/ *adv.* 今后；自此以后

liberation /libə'reiʃ(ə)n/ *n.* 解放

solemn /'sɔləm/ *adj.* 庄严的

encounter /in'kauntə/ *v.* 遭遇；遇到

compatible /kəm'pætib(ə)l/ *adj.* 兼容的

indignation /indig'neiʃ(ə)n/ *n.* 愤慨；愤怒

hairpin /'hɛəpin/ *n.* 钗

yearn /jə:n/ *v.* 渴望；思念

extension /ik'stenʃən/ *n.* 延长；伸展

linger over 细细思考

◆ 知识拓展 Knowledge Extension

陆游(1125—1210)：南宋诗人、词人、文学家、史学家。字务观，号放翁，越州山阴(今浙江绍兴)人。与王安石、苏轼、黄庭坚并称"宋代四大诗人"，又与杨万里、范成大、尤袤合称"中兴四大诗人"。今尚存诗九千三百余首，是我国现有存诗最多的诗人。

唐琬(生卒年月不详)：字蕙仙。陆游的表妹，陆游母舅唐诚的女儿，自幼文静灵秀，才华横溢。她是陆游的第一任妻子，与陆游两情相悦，后因陆母偏见而被拆散，也因此写下著名的《钗头凤·世情薄》。写下此词不久后，便抑郁而终。

12. 汤江岩景区　Tangjiang Rock Scenic Area

汤江岩是国家级风景名胜区，地处诸暨市西南，与斗岩景区相距不足 10 千米。因景区世居汤姓，浦阳江流经段称汤江，江边山林中屹立的摩天巨岩，也就称汤江岩。

汤江岩景区面积 14 平方千米。三面青山一面湖，由汤江岩、虎洞山、灵屏寺、五指山、安华湖等主要景点构成。汤江岩为整个景区的主要景点，岩高 300 多米，在汤江边拔地而起，孤耸雄峙，悬崖壁立，气势磅礴，岩壁上的条条纵纹裂隙，将巨岩切割成无数奇特的崖石群，千姿万状，引人遐思。

崖壁之下建有一庙，旧称胡公庙，相传是纪念元末新州守将胡德济而建。大岩向右，盘桓一道，由平缓逐渐转陡，曲屈陡峭。沿途只见岩下坠石如屋，堆叠成景，奇形怪状。有像狮、猴的，有似苍鹰归栖的，有状如天门迎客的，真是数不胜数。道旁形成了众多叠石岩洞，洞中洞，洞连洞，洞洞相穿，曲折深邃，较有名的如"神仙洞""星月洞"等。

Tangjiang Rock, a national scenic area, lies in the southwest of Zhuji City, less than 10 kilometers from the Douyan Rock Scenic Spot. Since ancient times the Tang Family has been living in this place, a part of the Puyang River which flows through this area is called the Tang River. The giant rock stands by the side of the Tangjiang River, so it is called Tangjiang Rock.

Covering an area of 14 square kilometers and **surrounded** by mountains and a lake, the spot is comprised of Tangjiang Rock, Tiger Cave, Lingbing Temple, Mount Wuzhi and Lake Anhua, of which Tangjiang Rock is the major one. It is more than 300 meters high, standing by the river **abrupt** and **majestic**. On the rock are lines of **crannies** which divide the rock into clusters of rocks which are of different shapes beyond imagination.

There is a temple called Hugong Temple at the foot of the rock to honour a guarding general Hu Deji in Xinzhou of the late Yuan Dynasty. On the right of the steep rock is a path on both sides of which you can see many stones of different shapes, some resembling lions, monkeys, eagles flying in the sky and some resembling pine trees that welcome the tourists. Along the path there are chains of caves which are zigzagging, deep and quiet. These caves are connected together with small holes in big holes. Among these caves the famous ones are "Gods Cave" and "Stars and the Moon Cave".

★生词与词组 Words & Expressions

surround /sə'raund/ v. 围绕；包围
majestic /mə'dʒestik/ adj. 庄严的；宏伟的

abrupt /ə'brʌpt/ adj. 陡峭的
cranny /'kræni/ n. 裂隙，裂缝

◆ 知识拓展 Knowledge Extension

胡德济(生卒年月不详)：字世美，明朝初期军事将领。胡大海养子。跟随养父胡大海追随朱元璋，并在攻占婺州时候担任诱兵，活捉元将季弥章。

13. 五泄 Five Waterfalls

五泄即五瀑布，是浙江省级风景名胜区，位于诸暨市西北 23 千米处，由 72 峰、36 坪、25 崖、10 石、5 瀑、3 谷、2 溪和 1 湖构成，素有"小雁荡"之称。

五泄景区为国家级森林公园，主要由五泄湖、桃源、东源和西源峡谷等四个景区组成。

五泄(瀑布)风景区最壮观的景色当推五泄瀑布，它以神态奇特、变幻莫测的姿态闻名于世。在地壳剧烈变动时期，五泄涵漱峰与碧云峰之间撕裂了一道口子，岩底逐段曲折下沉，造成长 334 米，落差 80 余米，宽窄不一的峡谷。五瀑布从高 1000 余米的天堂岗下流，经十几千米的长途跋涉，将涓涓细流，汇集成浩浩荡荡的溪水，经紫阆、张家，穿陡岩，劈溪流，跌入峡谷，曲折奔放，成为五级瀑布，呈现出雄壮、幽静、俏美和飘逸等特色。

五泄瀑布久负盛名，早在 1400 年前的北魏就闻名于世，郦道元的《水经注》里，就有着详细的记载。唐代五台山高僧灵默禅师慕名到此创建了五泄禅寺，佛教曹洞宗创始人良价在此出家。历代文人墨客，都曾来此游览，留下了画稿、诗文。始建于唐朝的五泄禅寺、摩崖石刻等古迹也成为经典风景胜地。

Wuxie, namely Five **Waterfalls**, is a **provincial** scenic spot located in Zhuji City, 23 kilometers northwest of the city center. It is made up of 72 mounts, 36 level grounds, 25 cliffs, 10 stones, 5 waterfalls, 3 valleys, 2 streams and 1 lake with the name of "Small Yandang Mountain".

Wuxie Scenic Spot, which is a national forest park, is mainly made up of four areas, including the Wuxie Lake, Taoyuan, and Dongyuan and Xiyuan two valleys.

The most spectacular scenery in Wuxie Scenic Spot is surely the five waterfalls, which are famous worldwide for their strange postures and unpredictable shapes. During the period of drastic changes of the crust of the earth, there appeared a wide stripe between Hanqiu Peak and Biyun Peak of Wuxie. The bottom of the rocks sank part by part, resulting in a valley with varied width, which is 334 meters long and more than 80 meters deep. The five waterfalls flow down the Tiantanggang at the **altitude** of 1,000 meters, winding its way more than 10 kilometers, running along Zilang, Zhangjia, collecting drips of streams and at last forming five falls characterized with **grandness**, peacefulness, beautifulness or **elegance**.

It has been a long time since the Five Waterfalls got famous. As early as 1,400 years ago in the Beiwei Period, it was recorded in Li Daoyuan's *Shui Jing Zhu*. Attracted by its fame, the famous monk of Mount Wutai Master Lingmo built Wuxie Temple in the Tang Dynasty. Liangjia, the founder of Cao Dong School chose to become a monk in Wuxie as well. Lots of famous scholars once came here to visit and left drawings and poems behind about this scenic spot, the Wuxie

Temple which was set up in the Tang Dynasty and the cliff sculptures also become classic scenic spots.

★生词与词组 Words & Expressions

waterfall /'wɔ:təˌfɔ:l/ *n.* 瀑布	provincial /prə'vinʃ(ə)l/ *adj.* 省级的
altitude /'æltitju:d/ *n.* 高度	elegance /'elig(ə)ns/ *n.* 典雅；高雅

◆ 知识拓展 Knowledge Extension

郦道元(470—527)：北朝北魏地理学家。字善长，范阳人。有《水经注》四十卷。《水经注》看似为《水经》之注实则以《水经》为纲，详细记载了一千多条大小河流及有关的历史遗迹、人物掌故、神话传说等，是中国古代最全面、最系统的综合性地理著作。

14. 新昌大佛寺景区　The Great Buddhist Temple

大佛寺景区坐落于新昌县的石城大峡谷中，主景区内石壁金相、楼台水榭与奇岩怪石、幽谷清泉相映成趣。"僧过不知山隐寺，客来方见洞开天"，整个景区怪石争奇、古树参天，苍松翠柏星罗棋布，使得它置身闹市，却清幽之极，进入山门不见大殿，曲洞四环，真佛面容才得以现。

整个景区以大雄宝殿为正殿，宝殿内供释迦牟尼坐像。此佛像由南朝始(486—516)，历经三代，终成旷代之鸿作，被誉为"江南第一大佛"。这尊大佛是我国早期石窟造像在南方仅存的伟绩。该佛像通高 16 米，两膝相距 10.6 米，结跏趺坐，作禅定印，秀骨清相，婉雅俊逸，表情沉静慈祥，超脱睿智。南朝著名文学家，《文心雕龙》作者刘勰曾作碑记，称之为"不世之宝，无等之业"。龛外殿阁，为清代晚期重建，殿依山作势，靠窟构阁，佛龛大殿浑然一体。

寺内另一处建有千佛院。千佛院又称千佛岩，因千佛琢于峭壁之上而得名，初建于东晋(345—350)，后经扩建，另筑小佛千余尊，又有"江南敦煌"之称。佛像造型纤巧优雅，线条流畅，多着通肩服饰，个别则是褒衣博带，腰束络带，重现古人古朴形象。在众多的雕像中，有一尊观音像最引人注意。观音头戴化佛宝冠，身披天水，腰系长裙，冠带绕双肩下垂两边，手持折柳宝瓶立于莲花宝座上，全身笼罩在一轮透明的圆形月光之中，双目凝视前方，显出悠然自若的神情。

景区内另有晋代高僧支遁墓、晋昙光尊者舍利塔、隋智者大师纪念塔、放生池、大悲阁，以及出自历代名家手笔的众多石刻、碑匾、楹联与唐宋众多名流学者题咏的诗文等。

The Great Buddhist Temple is located in Shicheng Gorges of Xinchang County. The main scenery spot of **metallographic** rockeries, pavilions, terraces, waterside houses, odd rocks and clear springs gives one unique impression. An old saying goes "Monks had not known that the temple was hidden in the mountain, while the guests to the temple saw the cave open to the sky." With peculiar rocks and **towering** old trees, the whole attraction is scattered all over by dark-green cypresses and pines, exposed to the noisy downtown but manifesting the quietness of great scenic beauty. When entering the gate, one cannot see the main hall directly, the real Buddha only comes to one's eyes until they reach the end of the **zigzag** routes.

The Grand Hall, the central part of the whole attraction, **enshrines** Sakyamuni's seated statue, who is the founder of Buddhism. The statue was firstly built in the Southern Dynasties (486–516), as a masterpiece, came into being through three generations, and later was renowned as "The First Buddhist Statue in Jiangnan". It is a piece of great achievement in making statues remaining in the southern China at early times. The statue has a height of 16 meters, and the distance between the two knees is 10.6 meters. The statue has been sitting there for **meditation**, delicate and elegant, showing the expression of seclusion, kindness, **detachment** and wisdom. Liu Xie, the great writer in the the Southern Dynasties and author of *Dragon-Carving and the Literary Mind*, spoke highly of it as a priceless art treasure. The palaces and halls outside the shrine were rebuilt in the late Qing Dynasty and stood **perilously** on the **topographical** features of mountains. The statues and the hall fit perfectly as an integrated whole.

Thousand-Buddha Temple was constructed in another place of the Great Buddhist Temple. Also known as the Thousand-Buddha Cliff, the temple got its name for the thousands of Buddha sculptures carved into the cliff. Initially built in the Eastern Jin Dynasty (345–350), it had an expansion of over one thousand small Buddhist statues later. Thus, it has always enjoyed its laudatory title "The Mogao Caves in Jiangnan". The sculptures are properly shaped with delicate and graceful images in smooth lines, most with dresses covering over shoulders, very few with a band around the waist, which represent the plain figures in ancient times. Among all these sculptures, a figure of Mercy **Bodhisattva** is the most attractive. She carries the holy water and wears a long skirt with a crown of Buddha on her head and a string of hat around her shoulders flowing down on two sides, holding the Willow **Aquarius** in her hand and standing on the Lotus Throne. Against the transparent circular moonlight, she is gazing at something in front of her with a natural and carefree expression.

Other scenic spots include the Tomb of Zhidun, an eminent monk of the Jin Dynasty, Mahakasyapa, Tanguang Stupa, Monument of Master Suizhi, Life-Free Pond, the Great Mercy Pavilion and **multitudinous** stone inscriptions, horizontal boards, and couplets by famous men of letters, and poems and essays autographed by numerous and famous educators in the Tang and Song dynasties.

★生词与词组 Words & Expressions

metallographic /ˌmitæləˈgræfik/ *adj.* 金像的
zigzag /ˈzigzæg/ *adj.* 蜿蜒的
detachment /diˈtætʃm(ə)nt/ *n.* 超脱
perilously /ˈperiləsli/ *adv.* 危险地
Bodhisattva /ˌbɔdiˈsɑːtvə/ *n.* 菩萨
multitudinous /ˌmʌltiˈtjuːdinəs/ *adj.* 大量的

towering /ˈtauəriŋ/ *adj.* 高耸的
enshrine /inˈʃrain/ *v.* 供奉
meditation /mediˈteiʃ(ə)n/ *n.* 沉思
topographical /ˌtɔpəˈgræfikl/ *adj.* 地貌
Aquarius /əˈkweəriəs/ *n.* 宝瓶(星)座, 宝瓶宫

◆ **知识拓展 Knowledge Extension**

刘勰(约 465—520)：字彦和，生活于南北朝时期，中国历史上著名的文学理论家。晚年在山东莒县浮来山创办(北)定林寺。刘勰虽任多官职，但其名不以官显，却以文彰，一部《文心雕龙》奠定了他在中国文学史上和文学批评史上不可或缺的地位。

我国的大佛：除新昌大佛之外，我国还有其他 13 座大佛，他们是四川乐山大佛、烟台南山大佛、海南观音、九华山地藏菩萨大铜像、雪窦山露天弥勒大佛、连云港伊山大佛、无锡灵山大佛、香港天坛大佛、山西云岗大佛、洛阳龙门大佛、太原蒙山大佛、河南平顶山鲁山大佛、峨眉山四面十方普贤金像。

15. 越王陵 The Mausoleum of Yue's King

印山越王陵是 1998 年中国十大考古发现之一，是越王允常的陵墓，现为全国重点文物保护单位。其规模之大，结构之殊，保存之完整，不仅被誉为"江南第一大墓"，还获得了"北有秦陵，南有印山"的高度评价。

越王陵平面略呈方型，立面高耸似印，所以被当地百姓称之为印山。越王陵地处印山南半部，是一座从岩层中挖凿而成的长方形竖穴岩坑木椁墓，由隍壕、墓道、墓坑，墓室等组成，占地 10 万平方米，规模宏大。隍壕设置在陵墓外围四周，代表着王权的尊严与产物。它们虽历经 2000 多年的历史沧桑，至今保存相当完好，对王陵起到防御保护作用的同时，也明确界定了墓域的四至，构成了明确的陵园范围。墓坑口大底小，墓道上大下小，两者形成了狭长的"凸"字形平面布局，总长度达 100 米。墓坑与墓道相连，构成"中"字形平面布局。墓室建于墓坑内，横断面呈三角形。内部用栋梁和木板分隔成前、中、后室，在中室安放着木椁独木棺木，长 6 米，宽 1 米多，呈东西向摆置，墓室与独木棺构成了越国王陵的鲜明特色，有"中国第一大木质金字塔"之美誉。

越王陵墓室的结构、设计、用材还有出土文物为国内罕见，可以与西安的秦始皇陵相提并论。

The Mausoleum of Yue's King is regarded as one of the ten major **archaeological** discoveries in 1998 in China and said to be the mausoleum of Yue's King named Yunchang, which is one of the national key cultural relic protection unit. With its large scale, unique structure, intact preservation, it is praised as the "the largest tomb in Jiangnan" and its value is also highly praised as "in the north there is the Qin's Mausoleum, in the south there is Mount Yin".

The mausoleum, for its surface is slightly square-shaped and its facade is **skyscraping** like a stamp (Yin), is called Mount Yin. Located at the southern part of Mount Yin, it is a **vertical petrous shaft** of a rectangular plan wooden funeral chamber tomb, which consists of the trench, the tomb passage, the tomb pit, and the tomb chamber and so on, occupying an area of 100,000 square meters. The trenches are located around the tomb, standing for the dignity and the outcome of the monarch's power and, well preserved though they have experienced over 2,000 years' historical changes, which both has protective functions and defines the mausoleum's area clearly. With big opening and small bottom, large superior surface and narrow undersurface, the tomb pit and a tomb passage presents a long and narrow surface layout like the Chinese character "凸" with a total length of 100 meters. The tomb pit is linked with tomb passage and forms the plane layout like the Chinese character "中". The tomb chamber is in the tomb pit and its **transverse section** is triangle-shaped. The inside is separated into a front chamber, a middle chamber and a rear chamber by pillars and boards. In the middle chamber, there is a wooden **coffin chamber** which is 6-meter long and over 1-meter wide, facing east-west. The tomb chamber and the coffin chamber form **distinct** characteristic of the mausoleum, which is called "The Greatest Wooden Pyramid in China".

The structure, the design, the material and the unearthed relics of the mausoleum are rare in China, which **is comparable to** the Qin's Mausoleum in Xi'an.

★生词与词组 Words & Expressions

archaeological /ˌɑrkiə'lɔdʒikl/ adj. 考古学的
vertical /'vɜːtik(ə)l/ adj. 垂直的
shaft /ʃɑːft/ n. 轴
distinct /di'stiŋ(k)t/ adj. 明显的，显著的
transverse section 横切面

skyscrape /'skaiskreip/ n. 摩天大楼
petrous /'petrəs/ adj. 岩石的
transverse /trænz'vɜːs/ adj. 横断的；横向的
be comparable to 比得上……的
coffin chamber 墓室

◆ 知识拓展 Knowledge Extension

越王允常：越国历史上第一位颇有作为的君主，是越国霸业活动的开创者、奠基者。

第二节　旅游文化——名人文化
Section Two　Tourism Culture—Celebrity Culture

绍兴是首批国家级历史文化名城，历史悠久，人文荟萃，文化积淀深厚，遗存丰富，名胜古迹众多，是江南著名的水乡、桥乡、酒乡，也是著名的戏曲之乡、书法之乡。在历史文献中记载的历代各个领域的代表人物中，绍兴人数不胜数。从舜、禹传说开始，历朝历代名人辈出，政治名人如勾践、范蠡、文种、谢安、王思任、葛云飞、徐锡麟、秋瑾、陶成章、周恩来等；人文艺术名人如王羲之、王献之、王冕、贺知章、陆游、张岱、徐渭、赵之谦、鲁迅等；学者如王充、王守仁、刘宗周、蔡元培、马寅初、马一浮、范文澜、胡愈之、杜亚泉、竺可桢、陈建功、钱三强等；而美女西施、孝女曹娥、情女祝英台、才女唐琬、侠女秋瑾也各以其独有的女性美流芳百世。

在绍兴出生或者成名的人物数量之大、影响之广在中国是很少见的。而绍兴之奇特，也

许还不仅仅在于名人之多，而在于每个时期都有名人毫不间断地出现。绍兴文化之精粹，即历代名人名士为民族之复兴，为国家之强盛，敢于上下求索，成为政治、经济、文化的思想先驱。他们一生追求的是真理和光明，追求的是民族、社会的文明进步，他们留下的思想和文化遗产，引导和激励后人去实现新的理想追求。

Shaoxing is one of the first state-level historical and cultural cities. With a long history, profound cultural background and rich historic artifacts, Shaoxing is famous for its rivers, bridges, wine, operas as well as Chinese calligraphy. From the historical documents, Shaoxing has representative figures in almost every field ranging from literature to politics. From the period of Great Emperors Shun and Yu, Shaoxing has celebrities in nearly all Chinese dynasties. The political celebrities include Goujian, Fanli, Wenzhong, Xie An, Wang Siren, Ge Yunfei, Xu Xilin, Qiu Jin, Tao Chengzhang, Zhou Enlai, etc.; the arts and humanities celebrities include Wang Xizhi, Wang Xianzhi, Wang Mian, He Zhizhang, Lu You, Zhang Dai, Xu Wei, Zhao Zhiqian, Lu Xun, etc.; the well-known scholars include Wang Chong, Wang Shouren, Liu Zongzhou, Cai Yuanpei, Ma Yinchu, Ma Yifu, Fan Wenlan, Hu Yuzhi, Du Yaquan, Zhu Kezhen, Chen Jiangong, Qian Sanqiang, etc. Apart from the above celebrities, there are also many female celebrities in Shaoxing such as Beauty Xishi, Filial Daughter Cao-E, Royal Lover Zhu Yingtai, Talented Woman Tang Wan, the Great Revolutionist Qiu Jin and so on.

Shaoxing is unique for its great number of famous figures born in each era of China with their wide influence spread all over the country. The essence of Shaoxing's celebrity culture is that for centuries these people have been striving hard for the nation's renaissance, for the country's strength, thus becoming the political, economic, cultural and ideological pioneers. They live in pursuit of truth and light for the civilization and progress of the society. Their moral wealth and cultural heritage will guide and inspire the future generations to realize their vision.

第三节　景点讲解技能——名人效应法

Section 3　Narration Tactics of Scenic Spots

—Celebrity Effect

国外的许多心理学家通过大量的实践证明：著名领袖以及名人的效应要比一般无名气的人更具影响力和说服力。导游员借助著名领袖人物以及名人的业绩对旅游名胜进行精彩的讲解，以达到游客对景点的兴趣和满足，这种表达方式称之为"名人效应法"。

1. 要感动别人，首先要感动自己 To Be Convictive

在运用名人效应法时，既要通过名人的言行，也要通过名人的感人事迹，使游客真正感受到名人的伟大之处。一段名言、一个故事，都要重点突出其闪光点，如果能加上亲身的感受，就会收到更佳的讲解效果。如在为游客讲解三味书屋时，就可以将鲁迅小时候在书桌上刻"早"字的故事穿插其中。

三味书屋是清末绍兴城里的一所著名的私塾，鲁迅十二岁时到三味书屋跟随寿镜吾老师学习，在那里攻读诗书近五年。鲁迅十三岁时，他的祖父因科场案被逮捕入狱，父亲长期患病，家里越来越穷，他经常到当铺卖掉家里值钱的东西，然后再去药店给父亲买药。有一次，父亲病重，鲁迅一大早就去当铺和药店，回来时老师已经开始上课了。老师看到他迟到了，就生气地说："十几岁的学生，还睡懒觉，上课迟到，下次再迟到就别来了。"鲁迅听了，点点头，没有为自己作任何辩解，低着头默默回到自己的座位上。第二天，他早早来到学校，在书桌右上角用刀刻了一个"早"字，心里暗暗地许下诺言：以后一定要早起，不能再迟到了。以后的日子里，父亲的病更重了，鲁迅更频繁地到当铺去卖东西，然后到药店去买药，家里很多活都落在了鲁迅的肩上。他每天天不亮就早早起床，料理好家里的事情，然后再到当铺和药店，之后又急急忙忙地跑到私塾去上课。虽然家里的负担很重，可是他再也没有迟到过。

2. 着重突出名人的闪光点 Highlighting the Key Points

在介绍或讲解名人事迹时要做到实事求是，不要为了艺术效果而有意编造故事。为此，导游员要结合景点挖掘名人那些不被人们注意的小事情、小故事，做到出奇制胜。其次，要运用好名人效应法，导游在自己的语言表达上要有讲究，言语要精练生动，讲解层次要分明有序，其"闪光点"要吸引人、感动人。如在介绍"八字桥"的时候，可以顺便把绍兴其他名桥及故事介绍一下，如绍兴的"题扇桥"：

题扇桥位于浙江省绍兴城区蕺山街。相传与晋代右将军、会稽内史王羲之有关。王羲之每次从宅第出来途经蕺山街走上小桥，总看见有位老婆婆在桥头摆小摊卖六角扇，但买的人却很少。有一天，王羲之又过小桥，见婆婆守着扇摊，一脸愁容，顿生恻隐之心，所以提笔在她的扇子上各题了五个字。老婆婆看到了，脸上立刻露出了愤怒的神色。王羲之笑着对她说，你只要对人说这是王右军题的字，每把扇子必能卖出百钱的好价格。老婆婆将信将疑，按照王羲之的嘱咐卖扇。不一会儿，由王羲之题过字的扇子便被行人抢购一空了，有的甚至还多给了一些钱，老婆婆高兴得嘴巴也合不拢了。从此以后，这座桥就被称为题扇桥了。

3. 严防"出轨" Keeping to the Point

在运用名人效应法的同时，要特别注意和防止负面效应的影响。讲解好名人的业绩，千万不要冲淡这个主题，更不要偏离主题。如在讲解"沈园"景区时，就可以给游客讲一下陆游和唐琬分手的真正原因。

南宋的大词人陆游在娶了他的表妹唐琬的第二年，唐琬就被逐出家门，原因是"不当母夫人意"，"二亲恐其惰于学，数遣妇，放翁不敢逆尊者意，与妇诀"。就是说唐琬在夫家，与婆婆不合；或说因为夫妻两人太恩爱，公婆认为会妨碍陆游的上进之心，所以常常责骂唐琬，而造成二人的分手。但真相是因为唐琬不孕，而遭公婆逐出。陆游与唐琬是相爱的，他们分手以后，陆游又被迫娶妻，而唐琬也改嫁了皇族赵士程。而两人的哀情传世的一段，就是两人相别十年后，在绍兴城外的沈氏园中重逢。那是一个春日，陆游来此赏春，唐琬和丈夫赵士程也来此游春，因而在此意外地重逢。两人重逢，又无法当面相诉离情。随后，唐琬派人送来一些酒菜，默默示以关怀。当她与丈夫离去，陆游伤心之余，在园子的墙壁上题下了一首哀怨的《钗头凤》。两人重逢后没有多久，唐琬就因心情忧伤而死。陆游在死前一年(84岁，1208 年)，又来到沈园，写下了"沈家园里花如锦，半是当年识放翁；也信美人终作土，不堪幽梦太匆匆"的诗句以表达对唐琬最深的怀念。第二年，陆游终于也追随着唐琬去另一个世界了。

◆ 综合练习

请运用所学的"名人效应法"讲解技巧，围绕绍兴地区某一景点或特产设计提问并分小组进行中英文讲解练习。

第四节　翻译技巧——正说、反说、叠词

Section 4　Translation Skills—Positive Expression, Negative Expression & Reduplicated Words

导游在向游客介绍绍兴的景点时除了应当忠实地表达原文习语的意义外，还应尽可能运用多种翻译技巧，使游客对介绍的景点印象深刻，增进了解，因此翻译时可采用正说、反说、叠词等多种方法。

1. 正说和反说 Positive Expression & Negative Expression

由于英汉两种语言都有各自独特的表达方式，因此无论是语意、词汇、语法、惯用习语，还是修辞方法，彼此都有大量的不同之处。有时英语语言本身存在许多形义相悖的现象，即用肯定的形式表达否定的意义或用否定的形式表达肯定的意义，而汉语也同样存在着这种现象，因此英汉互译时有些句子就不能拘泥于原文表层结构上的肯定或否定形式。

英语和汉语都有从正面和反面的方式来表达一种概念的现象。在英汉互译过程中，只有这样处理，译文才能确切表达原意并符合译入语的规范。这种把正说处理为反说，把反说处理为正说的译法，叫正反、反正表达法。这种正说和反说的相互转换是翻译中常见的一个重要方法。

1.1 正、反翻译法

正、反翻译法就是原文从正面表达，译文从反面表达的一种翻译法。

在英文句子中假如没有出现如 no、not、none、nothing、nobody、neither、nowhere 或 barely、hardly、seldom、rarely、little、few 等这些带有否定意义的单词，也没有出现带有否定意义前后词缀的单词，如 de-、dis-、im-、in-、ir-、non-、un-或-less，但是句子表达的内容却是否定意思，我们在把它们译成中文时，通常采用"不""没""没有""非""无""未""否"等否定词。

汉译英的正反翻译法

汉语中有些词语是肯定(正说)的，但译成英语却是否定(反说)的。例如：

1) 吼山的棋盘石很**特别**。

The Chessboard Stone of the Houshan Mountain is very **unusual**.

2) 这些志士们相信革命**肯定**会成功。

The revolutionists believed that it was **all to nothing** that they would succeed.

1.2 反、正翻译法

反正翻译法就是原文从反面表达，译文则从正面来表达的一种翻译法。

汉译英的反正翻译法

汉语中有些词语是否定(反说)的，但译成英语却是肯定(正说)的。例如：

1)湖区西南部还有多处优质泉眼，清泉四溢，终年**不枯**。

Many sweet springs are dotted in the beauty spot. All of them overflow and **keep running** all the year round.

2)他 14 岁的女儿曹娥遂沿江寻找父亲的尸体，但是，多日也**没有结果**。17 天以后，她投江而溺亡。

His 14-year-old daughter Cao-E sought her father's corpse everywhere but **failed**. Seventeen days later, she jumped into the river to look for her father's corpse. As a result, she was drowned.

英汉互译中的正反、反正翻译法如能够运用得当，就能确切地表达原文意义，传达出语言的情态，使句子流畅、传神。

2. 叠词的使用 Reduplicated Words

语言的基本构成是词语，词语是声音和意义的结合。语言讲究声音美，词语的声音和谐有助于意义的表达。重叠是英语和汉语都有的一种语言现象，是加强语言表现能力的一种有效手段。叠词的重复翻译可以使译文形式整齐、结构均衡，可以加强译文的节奏感和韵律感。

1.1 汉语叠词的翻译可选用对应的英语叠词、谐音叠词或同义词的重叠

汉语叠词英译时，有的可选用对应的英语叠词，有的可译成英语的谐音叠词，但更多的可译成英语的同义词的重叠。例如:

马马虎虎—so so，反反复复—again and again，地地道道—through and through，磨磨蹭蹭—dilly-dally，昏昏沉沉—dizzy and sleepy，哼哼唧唧—groan and moan，孤孤单单—lonely and single，和和气气—polite and amiable，等等。

1.2 汉语叠词的翻译可舍形求义

汉语中的大多数叠词很难选用对应的英语叠词进行翻译，所以只能舍弃其形式而翻译其意义，用比较贴切、自然的译文表达出原文的语意和体现重叠后词的词义变化。例如：平平静静—in quiet；试试(试试看，试一试)—have a try，等等。又如：

1)**一群一群**的人蜂拥进入该风景旅游区。

Crowds of people swarmed into the tourist area.

2)About this, he **thought and thought**, **brooded and brooded**.

他对此事，**想了又想，盘算再盘算**。

◆ **课后练习 Exercises**

将下列句子用正说、反说和叠词等方法翻译成英文。

1. 在安昌，你还可以看到浓浓的江南民俗风情，绍兴几千年的民俗风情在这里展现得淋漓尽致：热闹的水乡社戏、喜庆的船上迎亲、传统的手工酿酒、穿梭的乌篷小船……乃至祝福、裹粽子、串腊肠、扯白糖等江南风俗一应俱全。

2. 古纤道既是古人行舟背纤的通道，又是来往船只躲避风浪的屏障。

3. 舜王庙以殿宇宏伟、结构独异、雕刻精湛闻名于世，受到国内外建筑学家和艺术家的珍视。

4. 王羲之故居是省级文保单位，坐落于幽幽山谷之中，是一个以书法朝圣为主题，融寻幽访古、休闲观光、修学交流为一体的文化旅游区。

5. 香林花雨气候冬暖夏凉，四季花果不断，植被覆盖郁郁葱葱，山谷涧溪蜿蜒曲折，常年水流不绝。

6. 仓桥直街的商贸也是"无心插柳柳成荫"，至今，整条街上已经有350多家商铺。

7. 大禹治水"八年于外，三过家门而不入"。

8. 徐渭一生不得志，连应八次乡试，都因不拘礼法而失败，曾九次自杀、七次下狱，最后贫困潦倒而死。

9. 登上香炉峰顶南望复岫回峦，逶迤起伏；向北俯视，河湖港汊，阡陌良田以及千年古城，一览无遗。

10. 南山湖烟波纱纱，湖中岛屿如海市蜃楼，穿梭云中。

第四章 温州景域

Chapter Four   Wenzhou Scenic Zone

第一节 旅游景点

Section 1   Scenic Spots

1. 百丈漈——飞云湖景区 Baizhang Waterfall—Feiyun Lake Scenic Area

百丈漈——飞云湖景区面积 170 平方千米，由百丈飞瀑、刘基故里、铜铃山峡、朱阳九峰、天顶湖、峡谷景廊、龙麒源、岩门大峡谷、飞云湖、双龙等十大景区构成，为国家重点风景名胜区。

百丈飞瀑位于海拔 300 米以上，为"V"形深壑巨涧，涧长 1200 米，落差达 353 米，形成三折瀑布，俗称头漈、二漈、三漈，因三级瀑布高度合计 272 米，折合鲁班尺 100 丈盈 2 米，故名"百丈"。自古就有"头漈百丈高，二漈百丈深，三漈百丈宽"的说法。

一漈百丈高。高 207 米，宽 30 余米，素有"天下第一瀑"之称。瀑布从千仞绝壁上直泻而下，如银河垂地，水珠飞溅，咆哮如雷，如烟似雾。

二漈百丈深。瀑高 65 米，瀑分上下二折，当中折处有一个高 27 米，深 8 米，长 50 米的岩廊，可容 300 多游人观光。廊中观瀑，瀑流如帘，飘飘洒洒，犹如花果山水帘洞。

三漈百丈宽。高为 12 米，漈口宽达 80 余米，在蝙蝠山西，瀑流大，旁边多巨石。传说女娲造雁荡山，吕洞宾造三漈与女娲相比，造就一漈、二漈；女娲得知后下凡，此时吕洞宾正赶着大群巨石造三漈，仙法被女娲所破，巨石便散布滩上不动了。

飞云湖景区位于飞云江中游，属珊溪水利工程拦江截流而成，拥有 35.4 平方千米的水域面积。飞云湖是浙南地区最大的湖泊。景区内分别由葫芦岛、七星岛、梅坑底、洞背洞等自然景观构成。飞云湖碧波浩渺、青山屏立、白鹭栖息、云虹飘渺。

Baizhang Waterfall—Feiyun Lake Scenic Area covers an area of 170 square kilometers. As a national park, it consists of 10 sub-scenic areas, namely the Baizhang Waterfall, Liu Ji Hometown, Tongling Valley, Zhuyang Nine Peaks, the Summit Lake, Scenery Corridor Canyon, the Source of Longqi, the Yanmen Gorge, the Feiyun Lake, and the Double Dragon.

The waterfall lies 300 meters above the sea level in a "V" shaped **ravine** of 1,200 meters deep, forming a three-step waterfall because of a drop of 353 meters. The three steps of the waterfall are commonly known as the first, the second and the third section. They are 272 meters long in total, which is equivalent to Luban's (Master Carpenter in ancient China)measurement of 100 Zhang (a length measure in China) and 2 meters. Thus, Baizhang Waterfall got its name. There has always been a statement that "the first section is 100 Zhang high, the second is 100 Zhang deep and the third is 100 Zhang wide".

The first section, 207 meters high and 30 meters wide, is known as the "Number One Waterfall in China". The water runs vertically down from the cliff high above, splashing with the sound of thunder.

The second section, 65 meters high, is divided into two folds by a rock corridor in the middle. The corridor, which is about 27 meters high, 8 meters deep and 50 meters long, can hold over 300 visitors. Viewing from the corridor, one can see the waterfall running down like a curtain. Hence it is also known as the "Curtain Water Cave in the Mountain of Flowers and Fruits".

The third section is 12 meters high with its mouth of more than 80 meters wide. It is in the west of the Bat Mountain with big rocks piling around. The legend has it that Lü Dongbin, one of the Eight Immortals, created a waterfall in order to compete against the goddess Nüwa's Yandang Mountain. He fortunately finished the first and second sections of the waterfall. But just as he started to make the third one with the rolling big rocks, the Goddess came and broke his **magic spell**. The rocks were then frozen on the beach.

Formed by the **closure** of Shanxi Water Conservancy Project, Feiyun Lake Scenic Area lies in the middle reaches of the Feiyun River. Covering a water area of 35.4 square kilometers, it is considered the largest lake in the south of Zhejiang. The area consists of the **Gourd** Island, the Seven-star Island, the Meikeng Gully and the Bottom-and-Back Cave, and other natural landscapes, where people can see blue waves, green mountains, egrets as well as beautiful clouds and even rainbows.

★生词与词组 Words & Expressions

ravine /rə'viːn/ *n.* 既深且狭、坡度很大的山谷　　closure /'kləʊʒə/ *n.* 关闭

gourd /gʊəd/　*n.* 葫芦　　magic spell 咒语

◆ 知识拓展 Knowledge Extension

鲁班尺：亦作"鲁般尺"，为建造房宅时所用的测量工具，类似现在工匠所用的曲尺。它从左至右共分四排，分别是传统的寸、鲁班尺、丁兰尺、厘米四种标尺。鲁班尺长约46.08厘米，相传为春秋鲁国公输盘所作，后经风水界加入八个字，以丈量房宅吉凶，并呼之为"门公尺"。这八个字分别是："财""病""离""义""官""劫""害""本"，在每一个字底下，又区分为四小字，来区分吉凶意义。

2. 洞头风景名胜区　Dongtou Scenic Area

洞头风景名胜区是温州唯一一个以县名冠名的省级风景名胜区，与雁荡山和楠溪江互为辉映，构成浙南"一山一江一海"旅游金三角。全区总面积 200 多平方千米，其中陆域面积 21.94 平方千米，分半屏山、仙叠岩、大瞿岛、竹屿、大门岛、海中湖、东沙等 7 大景区，共 400 多处景点。

"神州海上第一屏"位于半屏山景区。半屏岛西部为渔村，东部海岸则有一片长 1200 米、高 100 至 200 米的断崖峭壁，犹如刀削斧劈，直立千仞。这里集中了半屏岛的主要景观，如渔翁扬帆、擎天柱、海螺石、龙宫门等，是目前为止在全国发现的最大的海上天然岩礁画屏。洞头半屏山与台湾半屏山遥遥相望，传说是被龙劈成两半的，民谣曰："半屏山，半屏山，一半在洞头，一半在台湾。"

位于东沙景区的东沙妈祖宫是浙江沿海建筑最完善、保存最好的妈祖宫，为省级文物保护单位。妈祖宫初建于清朝乾隆年间，民国初年增修。妈祖宫建筑面积约 400 平方米，木结构，有戏台、两厢、天井与大殿，结构古朴，有闽南风格。因洞头岛居民的祖籍大多在福建沿海，便把发源于福建莆田的海神——妈祖请到了洞头来。这里常年香火不断，每逢渔汛期来临，南来北往的各地渔民都要到此朝拜。

此外，在洞头还有位于仙叠岩景区被誉为"东海庐山"的南炮台山；位于大瞿岛景区的郑成功校场遗址；位于东沙景区的海霞军事主题公园；位于湖中海景区的洞头最古老的寺院——宁海禅寺；位于竹屿景区被誉为"东海美人"的大竹屿及位于大门岛景区的洞头海岛第一沙滩马岙潭海滨浴场等等。

百岛洞头气候宜人，年平均气温 17.3℃，海岛风光旖旎，石奇、滩佳、礁美、洞幽、鱼丰、鸟多，是一个集自然风光、海上运动、渔乡风情、避暑度假为一体的海岛风景旅游度假胜地。

Dongtou Scenic Area is the only provincial key scenic area named after its county. The area, together with the Yandangshan Mountain and the Nanxi River, forms a tourism golden triangle of "one mountain–one river–one sea". It covers an area of more than 200 square kilometers, of which the land area is 21.94 square kilometers. There are no less than 400 scenic spots in 7 scenic areas, including the Banping (half screen) Mountain, Xiandie Rock, Daqu Island, Bamboo Islet, Dameng (big door) Island, Haizhonghu (lake in the sea) and Dongsha.

"The No.1 Sea Screen of China" lies in the Banping Mountain Scenic Area. In the west of Banping Island, there is a fishing village. On the east coast, there is a **bluff** of 1,200 meters long and 100–200 meters high. The bluff, which seems to be a half-cut from the mountain, contains the main sceneries of Banping Island, including the Fisherman Setting His Sail, Sky Pillar, **Conch** Rock, Gate of Dragon King's Palace and so on. It is considered the biggest natural **ledge** painted screen on the sea in China. The Banping Mountain in Dongtou, facing another Banping Mountain far away in Taiwan, is said to be cut by a dragon. There is a **ballad** going like this, "Mount Banping, Mount Banping, half in Dongtou, half in Taiwan".

Located in Dongsha Scenic Area, Dongsha Mazu Temple is the best constructed and preserved

Mazu temple along the coast of Zhejiang Province. As a provincial cultural relic protection unit, it was built during Qianlong reign of the Qing Dynasty and restored in early Republican era. It is a wood construction with an overall **floorage** of about 400 square meters, including the stage, two wing rooms, the courtyard and the hall. The whole structure is simple and unsophisticated, which is of a style of southern Fujian. The ancestral homes of the residents in Dongtou are mainly from the coastal area of Fujian, that's why the Sea Goddess Mazu originating from Putian, Fujian was brought here. There is an endless stream of pilgrims at the temple throughout the year. Before the fishing seasons, fishermen from different places, usually come here to worship.

In addition, there are also many other scenic spots in Dongtou, including the South Battery Mountain, known as "the Lushan Mountain in East China Sea", in Xiandie Rock Scenic Area; the Relic Site of Zheng Chenggong's Drill Ground in Daqu Island Scenic Area; the Haixia Military Theme Park in Dongsha Scenic Area; Ninghai Temple, the oldest temple of Dongtou, in Huzhonghai Scenic Area; the Big Bamboo Islet, praised as "the Beauty of East China Sea", in Bamboo Islet Scenic Area and Ma'aotan Bathing Beach, the No.1 beach of Dongtou, in Damen Scenic Area.

Dongtou has agreeable climate with an annual average temperature of 17.3℃. The islands with charming sceneries are full of exotic rocks, superb beaches, pretty reefs, quiet caves, a large number of fishes and birds. It is a tourist island that integrates natural scenery, marine sports, **piscatorial** customs, as well as vacation.

★生词与词组 Words & Expressions

bluff /blʌf/ *n.* 断崖
ledge /ledʒ/ *n.* 壁架
floorage /'flɔːridʒ/ *n.* 占地面积

conch /kɔŋk; kɔn(t)ʃ/ *n.* 海螺壳
ballad /'bæləd/ *n.* 民谣
piscatorial /ˌpiskə'tɔːriəl/ *adj.* 渔业的

◆ 知识拓展 Knowledge Extension

楠溪江：位于浙江省温州市北部的永嘉县境内，干流全长 145 千米，呈典型河谷地貌景观。

宁海禅寺：别称"和尚寺"，又叫泗洲宁海禅寺，位于洞头县霓屿乡长坑龙村田岙自然村,建于清末民初，黄墙青瓦，呈古朴典雅气象。

3. 江心屿 Jiangxin Island

江心屿位于温州市区北面瓯江之中，与厦门鼓浪屿、漳州东门屿、台湾兰屿并称"中国四大名屿"。

该屿东西长，南北狭，全岛面积约 190000 平方千米。屿内风景秀丽，历史古迹、人文景观丰富，是瓯江上的一颗璀璨明珠，被誉为"瓯江蓬莱"。千百年来，无数文人墨客，历代名贤留有咏叹江心屿的著名诗篇，故还有"名人之岛""诗之岛"之美誉。

瓯江江心有东西双塔，东塔建于唐代，西塔建于北宋，历来是温州的标志。它们一东一西立在江心屿的两端，既是佛塔，同时也是瓯江上重要的航标灯塔。它们已经被列入了"世界历史文物灯塔"的名单。

国家 4A 级旅游区——温州江心屿公园位于瓯江中游，总面积约 7 万平方米。屿中名胜古迹众多，如宋文信国公祠、浩然楼、谢公亭、澄鲜阁等。其中江心寺为屿上最大的建筑群。江心屿原本为东西两岛，东有普寂禅院，西有净信讲寺，往来不便。宋绍兴七年(1137)，两岛间的江流被填塞并于其上建寺，称江心寺。现在的江心寺系清乾隆年间所重建，占地面积 5100 平方米，主要由前、中、后三殿及方丈室组成。寺内留有宋、清皇帝御书。1983 年经国务院批准，江心寺被列为全国 142 个重点开放寺院之一。

此外，数百年来流传至今的江心屿十景：春城烟雨、瓯江月色、孟楼潮韵、远浦归帆、沙汀渔火、塔院筼风、海眼泉香、翠微残照、海淀朝霞、罗浮雪影等更是让游客流连忘返。

Jiangxin Island lies in the Oujiang River, north of the **city proper** of Wenzhou. Jiangxin Island in Wenzhou, Gulang Island in Xiamen, Dongmen Island in Zhangzhou and Lanyu Island in Taiwan are regarded as China's four famous islands.

The Island is shaped long from east to west, narrow from south to north and covers about 190,000 square kilometers in total. The Island, praised as "a shining pearl on the Oujiang River" for its **picturesque** scenery, historical sites and abundant cultural sights, has been known as "Penglai Fairyland of the Oujiang River". Famous poets have left their remarks on the island in successive times. Therefore, the Island has also long been known as "the Island of Celebrities" and "the Island of Poems".

East Pagoda and West Pagoda, the symbols of Wenzhou, were built in the Tang Dynasty and the Northern Song Dynasty **respectively**. Standing on the eastern and western **tips** of the Island respectively, two pagodas also serve as important lighthouses. The twin **pagodas** have already been listed among the World Historical and Cultural Relic Lighthouses.

The Park of Jiangxin Island, the National 4A Grade Scenic Spot, lies in the middle of the Oujiang River on the Island and covers an area of 70,000 square kilometers. What's more, there are many historical and cultural sites in the Park, such as the Memorial Temple of Wen Tianxiang, the Memorial Pavilion of Xie Lingyun, the Memorial Tower of Meng Haoran, Chengxian Hall Pavilion, etc. Jiangxin Temple, built in the year of 1137 (the 7th year of Shaoxing reign of the Song Dynasty), is the largest building group on the Island. Jiangxin Island was originally two separated islands in ancient times. At that time, there was a Puji Temple on the east island and a Jingxin Temple on the west island. **For the sake of** convenience, people filled the gap between the two islands and built Jiangxin Temple. The current temple was rebuilt during Qianlong reign of the Qing Dynasty. Covering an area of 5,100 square kilometers, the temple mainly consists of the anterior hall, the middle hall, the posterior hall and the Buddhist abbot's room, in which emperors of the Song and Qing dynasties have left their inscriptions. In 1983, Jiangxin Temple was listed as one of the 142 national key temples open to public by the State Council.

For hundreds of years, Top Ten Views of Jiangxin Island have attracted hundreds and thousands of tourists. The ten views are City in Spring Misty Rain, Moonlight over the Oujiang River, Rhythm of Tide around Haoran Tower, Returning Fishing Boats of Yuanpu in Sunset, Fishing Boat Lights on the Oujiang River, Breezing Wind through Bamboo Forest, Sweet Spring from Haiyan Well, Cuiwei Mountain in Evening Glow, Rosy Dawn in Haidian and Mount Luofu dressed in Snow.

★ 生词与词组 Words & Expressions

picturesque /ˌpɪktʃəˈresk/ *adj.* 美如画的
tip /tɪp/ *n.* 尖端
city proper 市区

respectively /rɪˈspektɪvli/ *adv.* 分别地
pagoda /pəˈgəʊdə/ *n.* 塔
for the sake of 由于，为了

◆ 知识拓展 Knowledge Extension

蓬莱：又称为蓬莱山、蓬莱仙岛等。传说渤海中有三座神山：蓬莱、瀛洲、方丈，为神仙居住的地方，自古便是秦始皇、汉武帝求仙访药之处，"八仙过海"的神话传说也发生在这里。相传八仙在蓬莱阁醉酒后，展示各自的宝器，凌波踏浪、渡海而去。"八仙过海，各显神通"的传说便由此流传。

4. 南麂列岛 Nanji Islands

南麂列岛位于平阳以东海域，属国家级海洋自然保护区，在 1998 年就被列入了联合国教科文组织世界生物圈保护网络，是中国十大美丽岛屿之一。因其贝藻类丰富，拥有海洋贝类 400 余种，海洋藻类 170 余种，又被誉为"贝藻王国"。南麂列岛由 23 个海岛、14 个暗礁、55 个明礁组成，总面积约 201 平方千米，海域面积约 190 平方千米。

南麂岛为南麂列岛的主岛，面积达 7.64 平方千米，海岸线曲折绵延 24.8 千米，年平均气温 16.5℃。有大沙岙、三盘尾、竹柴百屿等景区，人称"碧海仙山"。

大沙岙在南麂岛南部，海滩宽 800 米，长 600 米，由千百年来贝壳的碎屑堆积而成，是全国罕见的贝壳沙质海滨大浴场。沙滩沙质纯净，色金黄，行之如毯，海水湛蓝透明，能见度 2 米，浴场两旁的山脉绵延入海达数百米，可同时容纳千人海浴。在大沙岙还可观海上日出，"海市蜃楼"也时而可见。

在大沙岙东北面山坳里，有昔日宋美龄在南麂岛的寓所——美龄居。美龄居建于 1954 年，采用大石块、钢筋、水泥结构，共有三间平房，约 80 平方米。中堂作会客室、活动室，两边是卧室，屋后两厢一为卫生间，一为厨房间，像一座坚实的碉堡。

三盘尾是南麂列岛自然景观中观望海景最佳之处。三盘尾景区有三绝，即天然壁画、天然草坪和风动岩。"天然壁画"位于三盘尾南部东侧峭崖处，整个岩面宛然是一幅天然山水画。画壁宽约 40 米，高 30 余米，气势恢宏，层次分明，被专家誉为"国宝"和东海奇观。三盘尾的天然草坪因海风带来的养分和水分而一年四季常绿，不因季节改变而变化。风动岩

高7米，宽4米，重50多吨，形如铜钟，却裂成两瓣，一瓣是"静若处子"，另一瓣遇上大风，便随风摇动，发出号角声。

南麂列岛具有独特的海岛风情。优良的自然条件使其形成了特殊的生态环境，具有重要的科研和生态价值。

Nanji Islands, one of China's **marine** nature reserves, is located in the eastern part of Pingyang County. It is a part of UNESCO's World Network of **Biosphere** Reserves and known as one of the Ten most Beautiful Islands in China. Rich in shellfish and **algae**, it is also billed as the Kingdom of Shellfish and Algae with over 400 species of shellfish and more than 170 types of algae living in the adjacent surrounding area. Nanji Islands is composed of 23 islands, 14 **submerged reefs** and 55 reefs, with a total area of about 201 square kilometers and a sea area of about 190 square kilometers.

The biggest island of the reserve, covering an area of 7.64 square kilometers, is the Nanji Island with an annual average temperature of 16.5℃. Along the 24.8 kilometers-long coastline, there are Dasha'ao, Sanpanwei and Zhuchai Baiyu Scenic Areas. It is renowned as Fairy Mountains in the Blue Sea.

Formed by the **fragments** of shells through centuries, Dasha'ao Beach has a stretch of fine and soft shell sand 800 meters long and 600 meters wide. It is a shell sand bathing beach, which is rare nationwide. Walking on the pure golden sand, you can feel as if you were walking on a soft carpet. The seawater is so transparent that you can see as far as two meters below water while the mountains along the beach stretch hundreds of miles into the sea. It is such a big beach that it can hold more than one thousand people at the same time. On the beach, you can also enjoy the beautiful sunrise and even the **mirage**.

Located in the valley of northeastern Dasha'ao, Meiling Residence is once the residence of Song Meiling. In 1954, Meiling Residence was built. It is an 80-square-meter bungalow of big stones and **reinforced** concrete structure. The central room is served as a parlour and activity room with two wing rooms as bathroom and kitchen. There are bedrooms on both sides. The whole bungalow is just like a fort.

The **vantage** point to see the seascape around Nanji Islands is Sanpanwei. There are three wonders in Sanpanwei, namely the Natural **Murals**, the Natural Lawn and the Fengdong Rock. The Natural Murals is at the cliff of southeastern Sanpanwei. The whole surface of the cliff is like a vivid landscape painted with distinct layers. This spectacular natural mural, which is about 30 meters high and 40 meters wide, is therefore considered by experts a national treasure and the wonder of the East China Sea. The Natural Lawn in Sanpanwei is green all year round because of the water and **nutrient** brought by the sea breeze. The Fengdong Rock, weighing more than 5 tons, is about 7 meters high, 4 meters wide. It is shaped like a bronze bell which is split into two parts, with one part standing still and another swinging and horning by strong wind.

Nanji Islands' excellent natural conditions here have made these islands form a special ecological environment valuable for scientific research and studies.

★生词与词组 Words & Expressions

marine /məˈriːn/ *adj.* 海的

algae /ˈælɡədʒiː/ *n.* (alga 的复数) 海藻

mirage /ˈmirɑːʒ/ *n.* 海市蜃楼

vantage /ˈvɑːntidʒ/ *n.* 优势;有利地位

nutrient /ˈnjuːtriənt/ *n.* 滋养的(物质)

biosphere /ˈbaiə(u)sfiə/ *n.* 生物圈

fragment /ˈfræɡm(ə)nt/ *n.* 碎片

reinforced /riːinˈfɔːst/ *adj.* 加固的;加筋的

mural /ˈmjuər(ə)l/ *n.* (大型)壁画

submerged reefs 暗礁

◆ 知识拓展 Knowledge Extension

宋美龄(1897—2003):出生于中国上海,广东文昌县人(今海南省),与宋蔼龄、宋庆龄并称为宋氏三姐妹,父亲为富商宋嘉澍。宋美龄是蒋介石的第三任妻子,中华民国时期的第一夫人。凭借孔宋家族的强力支援与美国留学背景,活跃于政治、外交等领域,对近代中国历史与中美关系产生了深远的影响。宋美龄晚年长期定居美国,于北京时间 2003 年 10 月 24 日在美国逝世,享年 106 岁。

5. 楠溪江古村落 The Ancient Villages along the Nanxi River

在永嘉县楠溪江中下游的绿色森林中隐藏着大大小小 200 多座古村落,大部分的村落保存着完整的历史特点和许多传统文化遗迹。其规划布局、建筑风貌体现了传统的儒家思想,同时渗透着阴阳五行学说与风水学。在这里,游客不仅可以欣赏到自然的田园风光,还可以感受到浓厚的耕读文化气息。

在所有古村落中,芙蓉村历史最为悠久,超过 1200 年,系全国重点文物保护单位。芙蓉村始建于唐代末年,现存村庄系元至正年间重建,为陈姓聚居的大型村寨。因村西有三个高崖,其色白里透红,状如三朵含苞待放的芙蓉,故此得名。整个村子犹如一座小城堡,略呈正方形,四周有用卵石砌成的寨墙,长 2000 余米,高 2 米。村内道路交汇点有高 0.2 米、面积 2~3 平方米的方形平台,称为"星";村内水渠交汇点有众多方形水池,水池称作"斗",故有"七星八斗"之说,意为天上星星与地上人才相对应。另外,村内还有 30 余处明清古民居,5 处明代大宅遗址,18 座大小宗祠。

芙蓉古村建筑精华之一——陈氏大宗祠坐落在如意街的北侧,属礼制建筑,因而格局严谨,形制完备。陈氏大宗祠建筑坐西朝东,前面有一个大院子,院子的南北各有一门,南门叫"光宗门",北门叫"耀祖门"。院的前方开有一方小池名叫"相承池",池的东岸有一照壁,上雕"八仙乘槎图"。陈氏宗祠的主体建筑为七开间,两进建筑,正厅左右为宽敞的廊间。与享堂正对着的是宗祠中最为精美的大戏台,它向院内凸出,三面开敞临空,便于观众于三个方向看戏。戏台的屋顶为歇山顶,檐口高,翼角飞扬,木结构上有雕成神仙人物的斜撑、精美的花篮柱、覆莲式的梢子,雕工非常精美,像这样的建筑,在全国也属罕见。

除了芙蓉村,楠溪江畔还有以"文房四宝"结构布局的苍坡村,以明代水利系统闻名的岩头村,以古祠古树为特色的岩龙村等等。这些古村落民居在我国民居中独树一帜,被专家誉为民居中的"活化石"。这些古建筑群与远山、近水、滩林达到高度统一，构成一幅精美的中国山水画，给风景区增添了浓厚的人文气息，赋予楠溪江丰富的文化内涵。

Along the middle and lower reaches of the Nanxi River in Yongjia County, there are about more than 200 ancient villages that are hidden among the green forest. Most of the villages have preserved complete historical features and many traditional cultural relics. The layout and the style of those villages embody the traditional culture of Confucianism, the theory of Yin-Yang and five elements as well as geomantic omen. Here, the visitors can enjoy the natural **pastoral** scenery while experiencing ancient farming-reading culture.

Of all the villages along the Nanxi River, Furong Village is the oldest. With a history of over 1,200 years, it is a state-level major cultural relic preservation site. The village was initially built in the late Tang Dynasty and then rebuilt during Zhizheng reign of the Yuan Dynasty with the Chen Clan living in it. In the west of the village, there stand three cliffs, with the color of reddish white. Because the three cliffs look so much like three budding **hibiscus**, the village was then named Furong (hibiscus). Surrounded by a pebble wall of about 2 meters high and 2,000 meters long, the square-shaped village is like a small fortress. At the **junctions** of the roads, there are platforms of 0.2 meters high and 2–3 square meters large, which resemble "xing"(stars). At the junctions of the water channels, there are square ponds, which resemble "dou". The layout of "qi xing ba dou", meaning the stars and constellations in the sky, implicates that the talented people in the village are as many as the stars in the sky. What's more, there are about more than 30 ancient residences of the Ming and Qing dynasties, 5 relic sites of big mansions and 18 **clan temples** of different sizes.

The Chen Clan Temple, one of the best constructions in the village, lies to the north of Ruyi Street. As an **etiquette** building, it has precise layout and perfect structure. The temple faces east with a big yard in front of it. In the yard, there is the Guangzong Gate in the south and the Yaozu Gate in the north. Xiangcheng Pond, with a mirror wall of "the Eight Immortals on a Raft" to its east side, is in the front of the yard. The main building of the temple has two rows which consist of 7 rooms in total. There are spacious rooms on both sides of the main hall. Opposite to the **funerary** hall, there is a grand stage which is the most exquisite part of the temple. It is projecting inward with three sides open wide. So the audience can enjoy the operas from different directions. There are nine roof ridges with wing butts of the eave flying upwards, **diagonals** braces with woodcarving of the immortal, pillars with basket-shaped top and pin bolts with lotus patterns. The fine carving of this kind is rare throughout the whole country.

Apart from Furong Village, there are Cangpo Village featured with a construction layout of "four treasures of the study", Yantou Village featured with water-**conservancy** system of the Ming Dynasty and Yanlong Village featured with ancient clans and ancient trees. The residences in these ancient villages are so unique that they are praised as the living fossils of the traditional residences. The ancient building complex, together with the mountains, water and the forests makes the scenery a beautiful **scroll** of Chinese landscape. The Nanxi River is therefore enriched so much by the rich culture.

★生词与词组 Words & Expressions

pastoral /ˈpɑːst(ə)r(ə)l/ *adj.* 田园的
junction /ˈdʒʌŋ(k)ʃ(ə)n/ *n.* 汇合
funerary /ˈfjuːn(ə)(rə)ri/ *adj.* 丧葬的
conservancy /kənˈsɜːv(ə)nsi/ *n.* 保存
clan temple 祠堂

hibiscus /hiˈbiskəs/ *n.* 芙蓉花
etiquette /ˈetiket/ *n.* 礼仪
diagonal /daiˈæg(ə)n(ə)l/ *n.* 对角线
scroll /skrəʊl/ *n.* 画卷

◆ 知识拓展 Knowledge Extension

阴阳五行：阴阳五行学说是中国古代朴素的唯物论和自发的辩证法思想，它认为世界是物质的，物质世界在阴阳二气作用的推动下滋生、发展和变化；并认为木、火、土、金、水五种最基本的物质是构成世界不可缺少的元素。这五种物质相互滋生、相互制约，处于不断的运动变化之中。这种学说对后来古代唯物主义哲学有着深远的影响，在长期医疗实践的基础上，将阴阳五行学说广泛地运用于医学领域，用以说明人类生命起源、生理现象、病理变化，指导着临床的诊断和防治，成为中医理论的重要组成部分，对中医学理论体系的形成和发展起着极为深刻的作用。

耕读文化：耕读生活早期作为文人的一种理想，起源于隐逸，是儒家"穷则独善其身"和道家"复归返自然"的人格结构，在中国传统的文化中有着很高的道德价值，意味着高尚、超脱，是古代士人这个知识阶层陶情冶性的寄托。特别是以老子、庄子为代表的道家思想，在崇尚自然、追求虚静、逃避现实和向往一种原始自然状态的生活方面，似带有更浓厚的浪漫色彩。

6. 蒲壮所城 Puzhuangsuo Fortress

蒲壮所城位于苍南县蒲城乡浙闽交界处附近的山麓，为唐宋以来戍守要地。蒲壮所城为明代东南沿海的抗倭名城，保存基本完整，为国家级重点文物保护单位。

明初，倭寇屡犯闽浙沿海，明太祖朱元璋命信国公汤和筑城防御，设金乡卫，下辖蒲门、壮士、沙园等千户所。蒲门所城于明洪武十七年(1384)兴筑，历时三年筑成。为"濒海筑城五十有九"之一，其后壮士所并入蒲门，遂改称"蒲壮所"。

所城依山临海，形势险要。城墙周长2千米，高4.5～7米，底宽8～12米，顶宽4～8米，城门三座，设有护城(瓮城)，城堞611口，敌台6座，窝铺22座。城外设有南堡烽火墩，由北向南分列于顶魁山、大尖山、对面山，直至霞关烟墩多处，海上敌情，通过多处烽火墩可以迅速传到所城。现存所城，平面为正规则长方形，北面城墙依山而筑，其余东、南、西三门依次为威远门、正阳门、挹仙门，有护城河环绕。城门均作拱券形，由石板错缝砌成。城楼均为三开间硬山顶式木构建筑。城内建筑布局，号称"一亭二阁三牌坊，三门四巷七庵堂，东南西北十字街，廿四古井八戏台"。现在的街巷尚保存当时格局，城西南角的社仓巷、铁械局、马房巷等，为当时后勤装备区域。城内通绕东、南、西之间城墙的跑马道，则保存如旧。

所城内现保存陈后英庙、墓及建成时开掘的古井、嵌在城墙的数通碑记。此外东城门边节孝石牌坊为清代建筑，柱头圆雕蹲狮，面额浮雕朱雀、草花，神态各异，栩栩如生。建成时嵌于街心的奠基石，图刻纵横，引人遐思；东南角的文昌阁巷有清末张蔚(孙锵鸣女婿)所创蒲门学校原址，校门保存完整，古风犹存；城外东侧的东庵，重建于清同治，依山而筑，高台楼阁，曲栏地沼，错落有致；城北龙山上西竺寺，重建于清代，寺旁茂林修竹，寺后泉水一泓，风景幽雅。

Puzhangsuo Fortress is located in Pucheng Town of Cangnan County. It is at the foot of the mountains around the boundaries of Zhejiang and Fujian provinces, which has been of strategic importance since the Tang and Song dynasties. Puzhuangsuo Fortress, built to defend against Japanese invaders, is a famous fortress in the southeast coastal area of China in the Ming Dynasty. The fortress has been well-preserved and is now a state-level key unit of cultural relic protection.

In early Ming Dynasty, the Japanese pirates constantly invaded the coastal areas of Fujian and Zhejiang. Zhu Yuanzhang, the founder and the first emperor of the Ming Dynasty, ordered Duke Tang He to build the fortifications. Jinxiang Wei was therefore set up, with Qianhu Suo Pumen, Zhuangshi and Shayuan under its command. Pumensuo began to be built in the 17th year of Hongwu reign (1384), which was one of the 59 fortresses built along the coast during the Ming Dynasty. Later, Pumensuo changed its name into Puzhuangsuo when Zhuangshisuo was merged into it.

The fortress is built strategically between mountains and the sea. The wall, 2 kilometers in circumference, is 4.5~7 meters high. The base of the fortress is 8~12 meters wide, while the top is only 4~8 meters wide. There are 3 gates with barbican entrances, 611 battlements, 6 defending towers and 22 sheds. Outside the fortress, there are **beacon towers** in South Fortress stretching on the Dingkui Mountain, the Dajian Mountain, and the Duimian Mountain from north to south till the beacon tower of Xiaguan, through which the enemy's situation was quickly transmitted. The fortress was structured in a plane of regular rectangle. The present fortress with its north wall built against the mountain, has the Weiyuan Gate, the Zhengyang Gate and the Yixian Gate in the east, south and west respectively. The arch gates are of **herringbone slate work** with gate towers of 3 rooms of a flush-gable-roof style. The construction layout of the fortress is known as one pavilion, two hall pavilions and three memorial archways; three gates, four alleyways and seven nunneries; east, south, west and north four crossways, twenty-four wells and eight stages. The alleys yet have kept their original styles, for example, Shecang Alley, Weapon Bureau and Mafang Alley in the south corner of the fortress were the areas for **logistical** equipment at that time. And the race course around east, south, and west gates has also been well-preserved.

Besides, there are other historical sites worth visiting in the fortress. For instance, there is the temple and tomb of Chen Houying, a hero fighting against the Japanese invaders during the Ming Dynasty. The ancient wells and tablet inscriptions on the wall have witnessed the history. What's more, the stone memorial archway of **fealty** around the east gate is of the Qing Dynasty. It has circular engraving of lions on the column cap, and reliefs of vivid birds and plants on the surface. The foundation stone inlaid in the center of the street crisscrossed by the engravings arouse tourists' reverie. The Wenchang Pavilion Alley in the southeast corner is the original location of the relic site of Pumen School founded in late Qing Dynasty by Zhang Wei, son-in-law of the great scholar Sun Qiangming. The school gate has been well-preserved with its old style. To the east of the fortress, there is the East Temple, which was reconstructed during the Tongzhi reign of the Qing Dynasty. The temple built against the mountain with terraces and pavilions, is well-spaced. Titled as the "Best Scenery of Pumen", Xizhu Temple is located on the Dragon Mountain which is to the north of the fortress. The temple was reconstructed during the Qing Dynasty. It is now embraced by woods and bamboos with a spring at the back of the temple, which is of its special charm.

★生词与词组 Words & Expressions

herringbone /'heriŋbəun/ *adj.* 箭尾形的

fealty /'fi:əlti/ *n.* 忠诚

beacon tower 烽火台

logistical /lə'dʒistikl/ *adj.* 后勤方面的

slate work 石板瓦工程

◆ 知识拓展 Knowledge Extension

倭寇：一般指 13 世纪至 16 世纪期间，以日本为基地，活跃于朝鲜半岛及中国大陆沿岸的海上入侵者。由于这批海盗最初都来自日本(当时称为倭国)，所以被统称为"倭寇"。

陈后英(生卒年不详)：蒲城民间抗倭英雄。生于明嘉靖年间，是一名樵夫。因平时为人正直厚道，处事公正无私，人称"陈公道"。当时蒲城屡遭倭寇侵犯，陈后英只身抗倭，为全城人做好抵抗工作赢得了宝贵时间，但终因寡不敌众，壮烈牺牲。1565 年，当地人民为纪念陈后英抗倭英勇牺牲特建陈后英庙。该庙位于苍南县蒲城乡后英巷中段，墓、庙均依山而建，墓、庙相连，前为后英庙，后为后英墓。

汤和(1326—1395)：安徽钟离城(今凤阳东乡东湖村)人，字鼎臣，幼习弓马，武艺高强，勇冠一乡。1352 年 2 月率族众投郭子兴领导的濠州义军反元，推荐幼年好友朱元璋参加起义军。为明朝开国名将、抗倭英雄。

孙锵鸣(1817—1901)：字韶甫，号蕖田，晚号止庵，为孙衣言仲弟。道光二十一年(1841)进士，入翰林，是李鸿章的房师。著有《海日楼诗文集》《东瓯大事记》。

7. 顺溪景区 Shunxi Scenic Area

顺溪镇因溪水顺流而下而得名。

顺溪木构古屋建筑群，也称顺溪老屋，位于平阳县顺溪镇的顺溪村和溪北村，地处国家级重点风景名胜区南雁荡山腹地，属全国重点文物保护单位。顺溪老屋共有 10 座，多建于清乾隆至嘉庆年间，系陈氏聚居之处。各屋样式、布局相似，面积大小不同，总建筑面积达 2.52 万平方米，是温州地区少有的整体格局至今保存完好的古建筑群落。它最初的修建者是生活在 200 多年以前的陈嘉询、陈永千父子。雍正二年(1724)，陈氏父子营建了顺溪第一座大屋——陈氏祖屋，之后后人各立门户，择地重建大屋。村中 90%的居民为陈姓，是浙南罕见的聚族而居的大家族。现各大屋保存基本完整，祖屋还保留了较多的传统木作遗制，堪称古代木作的"活化石"，有很高的艺术价值。顺溪老屋被建筑专家称之为"独具风格的明清江南古宅"及"浙南清中晚期民居博物馆"。

青街初建于元至正十八年(1358)，长210米，宽约3米，全部由青石板铺就。街呈弧线，部分面溪见山，呈半边街形，建筑物多为清末民初遗风。富有畲乡风格的古廊桥和桥旁直径达1.5米的樟抱梅古树，更为小街添景生色。畲族自治乡村落最具特色的是竹林，一片连着一片，宛如绿色海洋，享有"毛竹之乡"的美誉。种植毛竹迄今已有300多年的历史。

此外，在顺溪还有堪称"顺溪一绝"的眉峰山、龙湫洞、万壑笙钟摩崖石刻、云祥寺、冰廊、三叠瀑潭、白云瀑等景点，构成了一个集古老民俗、深厚人文与原始自然生态为一体的风景名胜区。

Shunxi Town gets its name because of the water running down the stream.

The ancient wood construction complex of Shunxi, also known as Shunxi Old Houses, is located in Shunxi Town, Pingyang county. It lies in the Shunxi Village and Xibei Village of Shunxi Town, which is the central region of the South Yandang Mountain, a national park. As a state-level key cultural relic protection unit, the old houses were mainly built from Qianlong reign to Jiaqing reign of the Qing Dynasty. The old houses are the places of inhabitation for the Chen Clan. Covering a total construction area of 25,200 square meters, the 10 old houses are of similar style and layout with different land coverage. It is a rare construction complex in Wenzhou, whose overall structure is so well-preserved. Their initial constructors were Chen Jiaxun and his son Chen Yongqian. In the 2nd year of Yongzheng reign (1724), they built the first big house in Shunxi, which was named the ancestral house of Chen Clan. From then on, their **descendants** started to build their own houses. 90% of the residents in the village are of the Chen Clan, a large clan **inhabiting** in the south of Zhejiang. Now, the original look of the old houses are basically kept. Besides, there are lots of woodwork with high artistic value still kept well in the old houses, which is considered as the living fossil of the ancient woodwork. The old houses in Shunxi are praised by experts as "ancient houses with unique style of the Ming and Qing dynasties in Jiangnan" as well as "the museum of folk residences of middle and late Qing Dynasty in the south of Zhejiang".

Qingjie Street was built during 18th year of Zhizheng reign of the Yuan Dynasty (1358). The main street is about 210 meters long and 3 meters wide. It is an **arc** street made of cyan **slabs** with some parts facing the stream and the mountain. The constructions there are mostly of the style of late Qing Dynasty and early era of the **Republic of China**. The ancient covered bridge of She (an Ethnic Minority Group) style and the 1.5 meters high old camphor tree with **prune** trees growing side by side of the bridge lend more charm to the village. The bamboo forest rolling up one another like green sea is the most typical feature of the Autonomous Village of She Ethnic Minority Group. The history of planting moso bamboo can be traced back to 300 years ago.

In addition, there are other scenic spots worth visiting, including the Wonder of Shunxi—Meifeng Mountain, Longqiu Cave, Cliff Carving of "Wan He Sheng Zhong (Flute-shaped Peak and Bell-shaped Peak among the Mountains)", Yunxiang Temple, Ice Corridor, Three-step Waterfall and Pool, Baiyun Waterfall and so on. All these have made Shunxi an area integrating ancient customs, rich culture and primitive natural **ecology**.

★生词与词组 Words & Expressions

descendant /di'send(ə)nt/ *n.* 子孙	inhabit /in'hæbit/ *v.* 居住于
arc /ɑːk/ *n.* 弧形	slab /slæb/ *n.* 平板
prune /pruːn/ *n.* 梅脯；梅干李干	ecology /i'kɔlədʒi/ *n.* 生态
Republic of China 民国	

◆ 知识拓展 Knowledge Extension

陈嘉询祖屋：平面建筑，形似"东"字，以中心纵轴为主体，横轴为副，依次建有门台、前厅、中厅和后厅，两边横厢均有走马楼，横厢后边又有廊厢别院。每厅9开间，厅间为宽敞天井。建筑群以回环廊道分隔为六个庭院，彼此形似独立，却又毗连沟通。门户相对，回廊串接，四通八达，错落有致。祖屋共有大小天井6个，套房99间，四周围以高墙，总面积为4200平方米。门台为长条粗石砌成，悬山顶，铺圆筒瓦，门台前两旁竖立旗杆石。大厅悬有古匾，房子为穿斗抬梁式混合结构，屋脊悬山顶，饰吻兽，门窗雕镂精致，形象生动，柱子粗壮，础为方形青石，排列有序。山乡小镇萃聚多座庞大古建筑，世所罕见，故平阳民间长期流传"青街毛竹、顺溪大屋"的民谚。其设计之独特，工艺之精湛，令人赞叹不已。1997年，陈嘉询祖屋被列为浙江省第四批文物保护单位。

8. 泰顺廊桥 Covered Bridges in Taishun

被誉为"廊桥之乡"和"中国桥梁博物馆"的泰顺县在中国桥梁建筑史上的地位非常重要。境内现存各式古桥梁500多座，其中保存完好的木质结构古廊桥33座，以泗溪的北涧桥和溪东桥最具代表性。它们被建筑学家誉为"世界上最美的廊桥"，并被载入《中国桥梁史话》。因两座桥的结构与造型基本相同，且相距不远，当地人称之为"姐妹桥"。现两桥均为国家级重点文物保护单位。

北涧桥，又称下桥，因横跨北溪而得名。始建于清康熙十三年(1674)，后经6次重修，至今容颜不改。北涧桥长51.7米，宽5.37米，高11.22米，净跨29米。桥屋20间，为宫殿式重檐，结构精巧，造型古朴。

溪东桥，又称上桥，因横跨东溪而得名。始建于明隆庆四年(1570)，于清乾隆十年(1745)、道光七年(1827)重修。为叠梁式木拱桥，桥长41.7米，宽4.86米，高10.35米，净跨25.7米。桥拱上建有长廊式桥屋15间，中央三间为宫殿式楼阁，两头翼角飞挑，盘龙卧虎，斗角绕云，青龙绕虚，颇有吞云吐雾之势。溪东桥近处有狮子峰、将军峰，处在"将军逗狮"的风水宝地之中。

廊桥其实并不仅仅是过河的工具，它还兼有休息亭、驿站、拜神祈福、社交、交通运转、物资贸易等大量民俗、文化、经济、社会方面的功能。廊桥代表着一种文化，是明清时期浙南山区政治、经济、文化、民俗等诸多内容的重要载体。

Taishun County, honored with titles of "Home of Covered Bridges" and "Bridge Museum of China", plays a very important role in the history of bridge construction in China. Currently, there are more than 500 ancient bridges of various styles, including 33 well-preserved wooden covered bridges in Taishun. Beijian Bridge and Xidong Bridge are the most representative ones. Praised as the "most beautiful covered bridges in the world" by architects, the two bridges have already been recorded in the book of *A History of Chinese Bridges*. Because of their similar structures and close locations, local people named them "Sister Bridges". The two bridges are both state-level key units of cultural relic protection.

Beijian Bridge, also known as the Lower Bridge, spans the North Stream hence getting its current name. Built initially during the 13th year of Kangxi reign (1674), the Qing Dynasty, Beijian Bridge has undertaken 6 times of reconstruction, therefore it has kept its original style. With a span of 29 meters, it is 51.7 meters long, 5.37 meters wide and 11.22 meters above the **stream bed**. The bridge, with ingenious structure and **primitive** and simple style, has 20 rooms with double eaves of **palatial** style.

Xidong Bridge, also known as the Upper Bridge, is spanning the East Stream hence getting its current name. The bridge was built initially during the 4th year of Longqing reign (1570), the Ming Dynasty and rebuilt during the 10th year of Qianlong reign (1745) and the 7th year of Daoguang reign (1827), the Qing Dynasty, As a **laminated** wooden beam arch bridge, it is 41.7 meters long, 4.86 meters wide and 10.35 meters above the stream bed with a span of 25.7 meters. There are 15 rooms of palatial style built on the bridge, which are combined to form a long alley. Three pavilions are built in the middle of the bridge, with the **wing butts** of vivid tigers and dragons **towering** into the sky. Near the bridge, there is the Lion Peak and the General Peak which form a good landscape geomancy of "the general playing with the lion" according to the traditional Chinese geomancy.

In fact, a covered bridge is not just a tool for getting across the river. It is also served as a rest stop, a postal relay station and a place for worshiping, social contact, transportation, trading, etc. The covered bridge represents a kind of culture and is an important carrier of politics, economy, culture and folklore in the mountainous areas of southern Zhejiang during the Ming and Qing dynasties.

★生词与词组 Words & Expressions

span /spæn/ *v.* 跨越　　　　　primitive /ˈprimitiv/ *adj.* 简单的
palatial /pəˈleiʃ(ə)l/ *adj.* 宫殿的　laminated /ˈlæmineitid/ *adj.* 层压的
tower /ˈtauə/ *v.* 高耸　　　　stream bed 河床

◆ 知识拓展 Knowledge Extension

廊桥：亦称虹桥、蜈蚣桥等，为有顶的桥，可保护桥梁，同时亦有遮阳避雨、供人休憩、交流、聚会等作用。廊桥在中国已有 2000 多年的历史，汉朝已有关于"廊桥"的记载；中国木拱廊桥现存 200 余座。廊桥主要有木拱廊桥(可分为编木拱桥和编木拱梁桥)、石拱廊桥、木平廊桥、风雨桥、亭桥等。木拱廊桥亦被学者称为"木拱桥",在泰顺境内当地人则称之为"蜈蚣桥"。世界各地,譬如欧洲(以中欧为多)、北美、亚洲等地也都有廊桥,各具特色。2009 年 9 月 30 日,由福建省屏南县、寿宁县、周宁县和浙江省泰顺县、庆元县联合申报的"中国木拱桥传统营造技艺"被列入联合国教科文组织《急需保护的非物质文化遗产名录》。

9. 乌岩岭国家级自然保护区 Wuyan Ridge National Nature Reserve

乌岩岭国家级自然保护区是我国距离东海最近的森林生态与野生动物类型的自然保护区,总面积 188.615 平方千米。1975 年经浙江省人民政府批准建立省级自然保护区,1994 年经国务院批准晋升为国家级自然保护区,被确定我国唯一的黄腹角雉自然保护区。

乌岩岭国家级自然保护区内动植物资源丰富,拥有"天然生物基因库"和"绿色生态博物馆"的美称,其中属国家一级保护野生植物的有中华水韭、南方红豆杉、伯乐树、莼菜等4 种,属国家二级保护野生植物的有金毛狗、福建柏、华东黄杉、浙江楠等 20 种;动物 1300多种,其中属国家一级保护野生动物的有黄腹角雉、云豹、白颈长尾雉等 8 种,属国家二级保护野生动物的有短尾猴、大灵猫等 42 种。

乌岩岭拥有白云尖、南麂岗、米筛潭、龙井潭等数十处景点。位于保护区内西部边陲的白云尖,为境内千米以上 17 座山峰的主峰,海拔 1611.3 米,被称作浙南第一高峰,也是浙江省八大水系飞云江的发源地。尖顶经常处于云雾之中,云海茫茫,犹似天上仙宫。

乌岩岭国家自然保护区内气候温润宜人,年平均气温 15.2℃,区外围还有举世闻名的古廊桥和古民居、浙南大温泉等景区、景点。

Wuyan Ridge National Nature **Reserve**, the closest reserve of forest ecology and wildlife to the East China Sea, has a total area of 188.615 square kilometers. In 1975, the People's Government of Zhejiang Province approved of setting up a provincial level nature reserve in the Wuyan Ridge. In 1994, the reserve was **upgraded** to national level and became the only nature reserve of the **tragopan caboti** in China.

The reserve with rich animal and plant resources is titled the "Natural Biological **Gene** Bank" and the "Green Ecological Museum". In the reserve, there are wild plants under first class protection, such as the **isoetes sinensis**, the **taxus chinensis var mairei**, the **bretschneidera sinensis** and the **water shield**. The 20 species of wild plants under second class protection are the **cibotium barometz**, the **fokienia hodginsii**, the **pseudotsuga gaussenii flous**, the **phoebe chekiangensis** and so on. Besides, there are more than 1,300 animal species, among which 8 wildlife species are under the first class protection, namely the tragopan caboti, the **neofelis nebulosa**, the **syrmaticus ellioti** and so on. The **stump-tailed macaque** and the **viverra zibetha** belong to the 42 species of the wildlife under second class protection.

In the reserve, there are more than 10 scenic spots, such as the Baiyun Peak, the Nanji Ridge, the Mishai Pool and the Longjing Pool. The Baiyun Peak, 1,611.3 meters above the sea level in the west of the nature reserve, is the major peak among 17 peaks with an altitude of more than 1,000 meters. It is considered the highest peak in the south of Zhejiang and is the source of the Feiyun

River, one of the eight major river systems of Zhejiang Province. The peak is wreathed in clouds and mist all year round, making it a wonderland on the earth.

The reserve, with **agreeable** climate, has an annual average temperature of 15.2°C. Near the reserve, there are other scenic areas and spots such as the famous Covered Bridges, the Ancient Folk Residences, the Hot Spring of Southern Zhejiang and so on.

★生词与词组 Words & Expressions

reserve /ri'zə:v/ *n.* 保护区

gene /dʒi:n/ *n.* 基因

tragopan caboti 黄腹角雉

taxus chinensis var mairei 南方红豆杉

water shield 莼菜

fokienia hodginsii 福建柏

phoebe chekiangensis 浙江楠

syrmaticus ellioti 白颈长尾雉

viverra zibetha 大灵猫

upgrade /ʌp'greid/ *v.* 提升

agreeable /ə'gri:əb(ə)l/ *adj.* 宜人的

isoetes sinensis 中华水韭

bretschneidera sinensis 伯乐树

cibotium barometz 金毛狗

pseudotsuga gaussenii flous 华东黄杉

neofelis nebulosa 云豹

stump-tailed macaque 短尾猴

◆ 知识拓展 Knowledge Extension

黄腹角雉：学名 Tragopan caboti，别名角鸡、吐绶鸟，是我国特产的一种鸟，主要分布于浙江。全长约 50(雌)～65(雄)厘米。雄鸟上体栗褐色，满布具黑缘的淡黄色圆斑。头顶黑色，具黑色与栗红色羽冠。飞羽黑褐色带棕黄斑。下体几乎为纯棕黄，因腹部羽毛呈皮黄色，故名"黄腹角雉"。有翠蓝色及朱红色组成的艳丽肉裙及翠蓝色肉角，于发情时向雌鸟展示。雌鸟大都通体棕褐色，密布黑、棕黄及白色细纹，上体散有黑斑，下体多有白斑。食物以蕨类植物的果实为主。

10. 仙岩 Xianyan Scenic Area

据史料记载，仙岩早在南宋时期就已是著名的旅游胜地，有五潭二井之秀、九狮一象之奇。道家称仙岩为"天下第二十六福地"。

仙岩有三大景区，各自具有代表性的特色景观资源，即以人文景观为特色的仙岩景区，以洞景怪石为特色的化成洞景区和以水景为特色的天河景区，总面积 30.45 平方千米。三个景区内目前共分 12 大景区，总计 108 个景点。景区内众多景点中又以梅雨潭与圣寿禅寺最为出名。

仙岩明珠梅雨潭位于翠微岭上，雷响潭下。拾级而上，只见梅雨瀑水光摇曳，似撒落的珍珠，似初夏的梅雨，从峭壁悬崖上洒落，故称梅雨瀑。飞瀑下是梅雨潭，著名散文家朱自清先生在 20 世纪 20 年代曾到此一游，写下了不朽名篇《温州的踪迹·绿》，文中称赞梅雨潭有"醉人的绿""奇异的绿"。

仙岩最著名的古刹是浙南最大的寺院圣寿禅寺(俗名仙岩寺)，坐落在积翠峰之麓。圣寿禅寺始建于唐贞观年间，历经沧桑，屡毁屡建。北宋大中祥符二年(1009)真宗敕赐"圣寿禅寺"匾额。明永乐十三年(1415)，鉴空禅师奉旨进京，钦赐紫袍还山，此后梵刹大兴。现存的建筑系清代以来陆续重建，共5进，有天王殿、大雄宝殿、法堂等，包括楼、阁、轩、居和禅房等百余间，占地面积3万多平方米。整个寺院飞檐斗角，气势宏伟。寺前有放生池，寺后有流米岩。相传流米岩有一洞能天天流米出来，不多也不少，刚好供寺院里的僧人食用，后来有一僧贪心，想让岩洞多流米出来，擅自拿口袋去接米，并给自己留了下来，哪知从此以后，此洞就再也没有一粒米流出了。

此外，弘一大师游览过的伏虎寺，为纪念南宋永嘉学派奠基人之一陈傅良而建的"陈文公节祠"，唐代名士刘冲隐居地罗隐洞及随处可见的唐宋以来的摩崖石刻等，都为仙岩增添了无限魅力。

According to historical records, since the Southern Song Dynasty, Xianyan has become a well-known tourist **resort**. It is renowned for its five lakes and two wells, nine lion-shaped mountains and an elephant-shaped mountain. It therefore has been given the title of the "26th Fairyland on Earth" by the **Taoists**.

There are three scenic areas with their respective typical features in Xianyan, namely Xianyan Scenic Area **featuring** cultural attractions, Huacheng Cave Scenic Area featuring caves and strange-shaped rocks and Tianhe Scenic Area featuring waterscape. The three scenic areas with their total area of 30.45 square kilometers include 108 scenic spots in 12 sub-scenic areas. Among the numerous scenic spots, the Meiyu Pool and the Shengshou Temple are the most popular ones.

The Meiyu Pool, known as the pearl of Xianyan, is located beneath the Thunder Pool, in the Cuiwei Ridge. Going up the stairs of the ridge, you will see the sparkling water of the Meiyu Waterfall sprinkling from the cliff, which is like scattered pearls and the raindrops of the rainy season. That's how the Meiyu Waterfall got its name. Beneath the waterfall, there is a pool named the Meiyu Pool. In the 1920s, the famous **essayist** Zhu Ziqing visited the pool and wrote an essay about it—*The Trace of Wenzhou: Green*. In his essay, he praised the beautiful color of the pool, describing it as "intoxicating green" and "fantastic green".

Shengshou Temple, known as Xianyan Temple, is the biggest temple in the south of Zhejiang. The temple, located at the foot of the Jicui Peak, was built during Zhenguan reign of the Tang Dynasty. However, it has undergone several times of destruction and reconstruction. In the 2nd year of Dazhong Xiangfu of the Northern Song Dynasty (1009), Emperor Zhenzong bestowed a board with the inscription of "the Shengshou Temple". In the 13th year of Yongle reign, the Ming Dynasty (1415), the monk Jiankong went to the capital under the **imperial's** order and came back with the **robe** bestowed by the emperor. After that, Jiankong started construction and expansion of the temple. The existing constructions in the temple are the ones that have been rebuilt in succession since the Qing Dynasty. There are 5 rows of the building, including the Heavenly King Palace, the Great Buddha's Hall, the Dogma Hall as well as over a hundred storeyed buildings, pavilions and **meditation abodes**. The magnificent temple covers a total area of more than 30,000 square meters. Besides, there is a releasing pond in front of the temple and a "Rice Flowing Rock" at the back of the temple. It is said that there was once a hole in the Rice Flowing Rock from which the rice flowed every day. Amazingly, the amount of the rice was just enough for the monks in the temple. However, a greedy monk who wanted more picked up the rice and kept it for himself. Since then, there has been no more rice coming out of the hole.

Besides, there are also other scenic spots worth visiting. Fuhu Temple is the temple that the **eminent** monk—Great Master Hongyi has ever visited. The Temple of Chen Fuliang was built to commemorate one of the founders of Yongjia School of the Southern Song Dynasty. The Luoyin Cave is the place where Liu Chong, a learned celebrity of the Tang dynasty, has ever lived. In addition, there are also **cliffside carvings** from the Tang and Song dynasties which can be found everywhere in the scenic area. All these have lent more charm to Xianyan.

★生词与词组 Words & Expressions

resort /ri'zɔ:t/ *n.* 度假胜地
feature /'fi:tʃə/ *v.* 以……为特色
imperial /im'piəriəl/ *adj.* 皇帝的
eminent /'eminənt/ *adj.* 卓越的；著名的
cliffside carving 摩崖石刻

Taoist /'tɑ:əuist/ *n.* 道家思想者；道士
essayist /'eseiist/ *n.* 散文家
robe /rəub/ *n.* 礼服；官服
meditation abode 禅房

◆ 知识拓展 Knowledge Extension

天下第二十六福地：指神仙居住之处。道教有七十二福地之说。亦指幸福安乐的地方，旧时常以此称道观寺院。

鉴空禅师(生卒年不详)：别号慧心，乐清人，俗姓方。受业于白鹤毓禅师，精通五经四书、儒家学说，深研戒、定、慧三学，书法超众，为当时一代高僧。永乐十三年，钦赐紫衣云履回山，重建仙岩大殿。明永乐十六年(1418)九月初一日，鉴空禅师上殿礼佛后，沐浴更衣，端坐圆寂，火葬后得五色舍利。永乐皇帝追封称阐教禅师。

紫袍：紫色朝服，高官所服。唐代白居易《初授秘监并赐金紫闲吟小酌偶写所怀》诗曰："紫袍新秘监，白首旧书生。"清代孙枝蔚《白纻词》云："东家年少着紫袍，君若遇之暂逡巡。"

弘一大师(1880—1942)：即李叔同，谱名文涛，幼名成蹊，学名广侯，字息霜，别号漱筒；出家后法名演音，号弘一，晚号晚晴老人。精通绘画、音乐、戏剧、书法、篆刻和诗词，为现代中国著名艺术家、艺术教育家，中兴佛教南山律宗，为著名的佛教僧侣。

陈傅良(1137—1203)：南宋著名学者。字君举，人称止斋先生，浙江温州瑞安湗村(今署塘下镇罗凤街道)人。永嘉学派的主要代表之一，与同时期的学者陈亮近似，世称"二陈"。

11. 雁荡山(北雁)Mount Yandang (The North Yandang Mountain)

雁荡山是全国十大名山之一，素有"寰中绝胜""海上名山"之美誉，号称"东南第一山"。因其"岗顶有湖，芦苇丛生，结草为荡，秋雁宿之"而得名。2005 年，雁荡山被联合国教科文组织列为世界地质公园。

雁荡山闻名始于初唐，盛于北宋。含北雁荡、中雁荡与南雁荡，通常人们说的指北雁荡。雁荡山总面积450平方千米，最高海拔1150米。共有8大景区，550个景点，其中，北雁的灵峰、灵岩和大龙湫被誉为"雁荡三绝"。

灵峰因其远望像一对紧紧拥抱的夫妻，故也称夫妻峰。灵峰是雁荡山的东大门，当东来的游客进入东大门时，一抬头就能看到一块叫"接客僧"的巨石。因其外形酷似一个光头合掌的和尚，形象逼真生动，被誉为雁荡山一大胜景。雁荡之绝美在于夜景——灵峰的夜景移步换形，变化多姿，有雄鹰敛翅、夫妻峰、犀牛望月、相思女等。

灵岩景色之美，为全山之冠。画楼似的灵岩底层有灵岩寺、小龙湫；中层有龙鼻洞、天窗洞；上层的卧龙谷、双珠谷，各有声色，皆有独到之处。"灵岩飞渡"的杂技表演令人惊心动魄。

大龙湫，又名大瀑布，位于雁荡最高峰海拔1056米的百港尖，水从峭壁上凌空飞泻而下，单级落差197米，是我国单级落差最高的瀑布，为中国四大名瀑之一。盛夏季节，雷雨之后，大龙湫在空中、潭底幻成两条龙，腾飞翻卷，仪态万千，变化无穷，故而得名。

除此以外，雁荡山还有5个值得一游的景区，即拥有美丽神话的仙桥、雁荡山的摇篮雁湖、雁荡山最险峻的显胜门、蕴含中国本土道教文化的羊角洞和发现死火山的三折瀑。

Mount Yandang, one of the major ten mountains in China, gets its name from the lake of beautiful view on the top of the mountain where the wild geese come and live in the **reed** in autumn. It is referred to as "Unsurpassed Wonder in the World", "Famous Mountain Above the Sea" and "No.1 Mountain of Southeast China". In 2005, Mount Yandang was announced as a World Geopark by the UNESCO.

The mountain became known in the early Tang Dynasty and enjoyed greater fame during the Northern Song Dynasty. It consists of North Yandang, Middle Yandang and South Yandang. Normally, what people talk about is North Yandang. Covering an area of 450 square kilometers, Mount Yandang is about 1,150 meters above the sea level. It is divided into 8 scenic areas, consisting of 550 scenic sites. The most famous areas are the Three Wonders, namely the Spiritual Peaks, the Spiritual Rocks and the Big Dragon Waterfall.

The Spiritual Peak (Lingfeng Peaks) is also called Husband and Wife Peak because it looks like a couple in each other's arms. It is at the eastern gate of Mount Yandang. Entering the eastern gate, you can easily find the Old Monk Rock. Facing the southeast, the "old monk" **salutes** with hands folded. It's so vivid that the rock has been considered as one of the most significant scenic spots at Mount Yandang. The sight of the peak at night is breath-taking and even more attractive than that in the daytime. When night falls, with a little imagination, you can see many beautiful scenes from different positions under the moonlight, such as "an eagle retracting its wings", "wife and husband", "**rhino** looking at the moon", "love-sick maiden" and so on.

Among the Three Wonders of Mount Yandang, the Spiritual Rock is the most magnificent and fascinating. At its bottom, there are Lingyan Temple and the Small Dragon Waterfall; in the middle, the Cave of Dragon Nose (Longbi Cave) and the Cave of Clerestory (Tianchuang Cave); and at its top, the Valley of Crouching Dragon (Wolong Valley) and the Valley of Double Pearls (Shuangzhu Valley). Apart from the beautiful and grand scenery, the marvelous "flying person" performance of ferry in the air which is put on show every day is also very amazing.

The Big Dragon Waterfall (Dalong Qiu), also known as the Great Waterfall, is one of the four most famous waterfalls in China. Its water comes from the highest peak of Mount Yandang–Bai Gang Peak whose altitude is 1,056 meters. The Big Dragon Waterfall is about 197 meters, which is the longest of all waterfalls in China. After a heavy rain in summer, the Big Dragon Waterfall **conjures** an image of a dragon flying swiftly upward and the other one **seething** in the pond water below. Thus, the name "dragon" is given to it.

There are five other scenic areas also worth visiting. The Immortal Bridge (Xianqiao Bridge) is well-known as a setting in fairy tales. The Wild Goose Lake (Yanhu Lake) gives Mount Yandang its name. The Wonder-displaying Gate (Xiansheng Gate) is considered to be the steepest rock in Mount Yandang. The Goat-horn Cave (Yangjiao Cave) embodies the Chinese traditional religion of Taoism. The Three-step Waterfall (Sanzhe Waterfall) is the most peculiar among all the waterfalls in Mount Yandang because of the dead **volcano** found there.

★生词与词组 Words & Expressions

reed /ri:d/ *n.* 芦苇丛	salute /sə'l(j)u:t/ *v.* 致意，打招呼
rhino /'rainəu/ *n.* 犀牛	conjure /'kʌndʒə/ *v.* 令人想起
seethe /si:ð/ *v.* 冒泡 (使沸腾)	volcano /vɔl'keinəu/ *n.* 火山

◆ 知识拓展 Knowledge Extension

江湜(1818—1866)：咸丰时县学诸生，曾游雁荡山写下骚体《大龙湫题壁》："嶂连云兮山四围，仰飞瀑兮从天来，倾万斛之珠玑，为我心兮写哀。噫! 风尘溷洞兮故里为灰，非龙湫之宴坐将余生兮焉归？"一生坎坷多舛，郁郁不得志，倾其全力作诗，病卒杭州，得年49岁。

12. 永昌堡 Yongchang Fortress

永昌堡位于龙湾区永昌镇，建于明嘉靖年间，是浙江省仅存的一座民建古城堡。明代，中国东南沿海倭寇猖獗，温州经常成为海盗的袭击目标。公元 1553 年至 1563 年的短短 11 年间，温州遭倭患 28 次之多。抗倭首领王沛、王德叔侄组织起一支纪律严明、士气高昂、战斗力强的抗倭队伍，使得倭寇 4 年内不敢进犯温州一带。王沛和王德牺牲之后，王德的侄子王叔果、王叔杲两兄弟继承了抗倭事业，并建造城堡作为抗倭根据地。

城堡呈长方形，城墙高 8 米，南北长 738 米，东西阔 445 米，周长 2366 米。城外环护城河，城内凿有二渠，居民分住渠之两岸。南北两座城门旁还有一道水门，一大一小两条河自南向北从永昌堡的中心横穿而过，巧妙地构成了水上交通网络。

永昌堡内的古宅目前还有 40 余处，住着 3000 余名居民，大多是王氏后裔。其王氏祠堂建于明嘉靖二十一年(1542)，占地 13 余亩，是堡内规模最大、保存最完整的古建筑，其布局严谨、结构宏伟，素有"江南故宫"之称。另外，堡内的布政司堂、状元第、都堂第、王绍志故居等十余幢明清年代古民居内涵丰富、古风浓郁。

2001 年 6 月永昌堡被国务院列入全国重点文物保护单位。

Yongchang Fortress, which lies at Yongchang Town of Longwan District, was built in Jiajing reign, the Ming Dynasty. It is the only existing nongovernmental-built ancient fortress in Zhejiang Province. During the Ming Dynasty, Japanese **pirates** invaded China's southeast coastal area and Wenzhou was constantly targeted. In the short period from 1553 to 1563, Wenzhou had been attacked by the pirates 28 times. Wang Pei, together with his nephew Wang De, organized a well-disciplined force with great **morale** and combat power which prevented the pirates' invasion for 4 years **running**. After Wang Pei and Wang De died, Wang Shuguo and Wang Shugao, the nephews of Wang De, continued their career and built a fortress as their base.

The Fortress, being rectangular, stands at 8 meters high and extends 783 meters long from south to north and 445 meters long from east to west, with a **circumference** of 2, 336 meters. The Fortress **is fortified with** a **moat** outside and two canals inside, with people living on both sides of the canals. The water gates were built near both the south and north gates of the fortress with a small river and a big river going through the center of the fortress from the south to the north. Thus, a water transport network has been **dexterously** set up.

At present, there are more than 40 ancient houses in the fortress where more than 3,000 residents live there. Most of the residents are descendants of Wang Family. The Ancestral Hall of Wang Family which covers more than 13 *mu* (about 0.87 hectare) was built in the 21st year, Jiajing reign, the Ming Dynasty (1542). It is the largest and best-preserved ancient building in the fortress. The hall enjoys a fame of "the Imperial Palace in Jiangnan" for its precise layout and magnificent structure. Besides, the folk houses of Ming and Qing dynasties such as the Colonial Hall, the Number One Scholar's Mansion, the Imperial Censor's Mansion of the Ming Dynasty and the Former Residence of Wang Shaozhi all involve rich culture.

Yongchang Fortress was listed by the State Council as the national key unit of cultural relic protection in June, 2001.

★生词与词组 Words & Expressions

pirate /'pairət/ *n.* 海盗
running /'rʌniŋ/ *adv.* 连续地
moat /məut/ *n.* 护城河
be fortified with 设防

morale /mə'rɑːl/ *n.* 士气
circumference /sə'kʌmf(ə)r(ə)ns/ *n.* 周长
dexterously /'dekstrəsli/ *adv.* 巧妙地

◆ 知识拓展 Knowledge Extension

王沛(1485—1558)：字子大，号仁山，永强二都英桥里(今温州市永中街道新城村)人。倭寇扰我沿海，王沛为了保卫乡闾田园，号召乡人奋起抵抗。嘉靖三十一年(1552)初，当倭贼向永强进犯时，他组织了一支千余人的抗倭队伍，从而阻止了敌人的这次入侵。不久，其从侄王德由粤谢官归里，再协助增募勇士千人，使队伍扩充到二千五百余人。

王德(1517—1558)：字汝修，号东华。嘉靖二十九年(1550)适逢倭寇骚扰，帮助其叔父王沛募兵抗倭。明朝廷为褒奖王氏叔侄的爱国行动，后来追赠王沛为太仆寺丞，王德为太仆寺少卿。温州人民在温州郡城内兴文街、康乐坊分别建立褒忠祠和愍忠祠以纪念。

王叔果(1516—1588)：字育德，号西华。嘉靖二十九年(1550)中进士，翌年，倭寇猖獗，其叔王德和三叔父王沛都抗战而死。他上疏请筑永昌堡，得到准许，于是筹集资金，由其弟叔杲尽力督造。第二年落成，一乡得到保障。

王叔杲(1517—1600)：字阳德，号旸谷，比兄叔果少一岁。嘉靖廿二年举人。嘉靖三十七年(1558)，叔果率乡人兴筑永昌堡，坚持地方集资。全部费用七千余金，大半由他拿出来。王叔果王叔杲兄弟二人为官清正廉洁，为国为民贡献卓著，才华旷世，故被后人称之为"东瓯双璧"。

13. 玉海楼 Yuhailou Library

位于瑞安的玉海楼是浙江四大著名藏书楼之一，其建筑最大的特点是集藏书楼功能、浙南优秀民居特点和私家园林风范于一体。其规模之宏大，保存之完整，在清代名人纪念建筑中实不多见。

玉海楼坐北朝南，总占地面积约8000平方米。在东西3条轴线上分别布列玉海书楼、百晋陶斋、居室、后花园。三面环河，前后两进，左右回廊，庭院清幽，花木扶疏。

玉海楼的主人是清代经学家、文字训诂学家孙诒让，与黄以周、俞曲园合称"清末三先生"，著有中国第一部甲骨文考释专著《契文举例》、墨子研究《墨子间诂》和儒家经典研究的《周礼正义》等重要著作，整理了大批珍贵的地方文献。玉海楼就是1888年其父孙衣言供孙诒让潜心著述而建的藏书楼。因孙氏父子敬慕南宋学者王应麟著作宏富，故以其巨著《玉海》作为楼名，以为自家藏书亦如玉之珍贵，若海之浩瀚。台门石额"玉海楼书藏"及长篇跋文为清代礼部侍郎李文田所书。初建时，藏书八九万卷，大部分是同治七年后的十余年间所购，多为苏、浙、皖故家世族散出的元、明、清珍善本。藏书多以名家批校本、多瓯郡乡帮文献和孙氏父子手批校本的特点闻名于世。以经史子集四部插架，管理严格，订有《藏书规约》16条揭之堂壁，定下流通方法和保护措施。

1963年，玉海楼被列为浙江省文物保护单位，1996年被列为全国重点文物保护单位，先后四次修缮，使其焕发出昔日风采，吸引了众多中外著名人士和华侨、港、澳、台胞莅临参观。

Yuhailou Library, located in Rui'an, is one of the four famous libraries in Zhejiang Province. It features as a combination of library, outstanding residence and private garden of South Zhejiang. This commemorating building of the Qing Dynasty is of a grand scale and luckily well-preserved, which is rather rare among its kind.

Covering an area of about 8,000 square meters, Yuhailou Library faces to the south. On its three east-west axes, there are Yuhai Library, Baijintao Studio, the Bedroom and the Back Garden. The whole construction is surrounded by the river on its three sides. There are two main buildings connected with corridors on both sides. The whole courtyard with luxuriant trees and flowers is fascinatingly tranquil and beautiful.

The owner of Yuhailou Library is Sun Yirang, a Confucian **classicist** and textual researcher of the Qing Dynasty. Sun Yirang, Huang Yizhou and Yu Quyuan are known as the three great scholars in the late Qing Dynasty. Sun's important works are *Qiwen Juli*, the first work of **decipherment** of the **Oracle**, *Mozi Jiangu*, a corrected, definitive edition of Mozi, and *Zhouli Zhengyi*, an important **commentary** on *The Rites of Zhou*. Besides, he also devoted himself to the classification of local documents. The library was built by his father Sun Yiyan in 1888. It was named after the masterpiece of *Yu Hai* by the Southern Song Dynasty scholar Wang Yinglin, whom the Family of Sun admired. That's why the family took its name for their collection of rarity, meaning as precious as jade and **voluminousness,** meaning as vast as sea. Near the gate, there is a stone carved with the letters of "Yuhailou Library" and a long **epilog** written by Li Wentian, the vice minister of the Board of Ritual of the Qing Dynasty. At the very beginning, there were about 80,000 to 90,000 volumes of books, most of which were bought in 10 years after the 7th year of Tongzhi reign of the Qing Dynasty. The books were mostly from the **aristocracy** of the Yuan, Ming, Qing dynasties in Jiangsu, Zhejiang and Anhui Provinces. The library is known for its collection of local documents and books **collated** by the celebrities and by Sun Yirang and his father. The books in the library were categorized into the Confucian classics, history, philosophy and belles-letters on different shelves. The management is strict for there are 16 rules proclaimed, including the circulation methods and measures of protection.

In 1963, Yuhailou Library was listed as a key unit of cultural relic protection of Zhejiang Province and in 1996 as a state-level key unit of cultural relic protection. The library then undertook four times of renovation, restoring to its ancient style. Since then, it has attracted many celebrities both at home and abroad, overseas Chinese, and compatriots from Hong Kong, Macao and Taiwan of China.

★生词与词组 Words & Expressions

axis /'æksis/ *n.* 轴
decipherment /di'saifəmənt/ *n.* 解读
commentary /'kɔmənteri/ *n.* 注释
epilog /'epəˌlɔg/ *n.* 跋
collate /kə'leit/ *v.* 校对

classicist /'klæsisist/ *n.* 古典主义者
Oracle /'ɔrək(ə)l/ *n.* 甲骨文
voluminousness /və'lumənəsnəs/ *n.* 广博
aristocracy /ˌæri'stɔkrəsi/ *n.* 特权阶级

◆ 知识拓展 Knowledge Extension

孙衣言(1814—1894)：字绍闻，号琴西，晚号逊披，斋名逊学，浙江瑞安人。清代官吏、学者、藏书家。道光三十年进士，授编修；光绪间，官至太仆寺卿，寻以及乞归。生平努力搜集乡邦文献，刻《永嘉丛书》，筑玉海楼以藏书。有《逊学斋诗文钞》。

王应麟(1223—1296)：字伯厚，号深宁居士，祖籍河南开封，后迁居庆元府鄞县(今浙江鄞县)，是南宋著名的学者、教育家、政治家。博学多才，对经史子集、天文地理都有研究，是南宋末年的政治人物和经史学者。

李文田(1834—1895)：字畲光、仲约，号若农、芍农，谥文诚，广东顺德均安上村人。学问渊博，生平嗜学不倦，工书善画，经史、兵法、天文、地理，无一不晓。清代著名的蒙古史研究专家和碑学名家。

14. 泽雅 Zeya Scenic Area

素有温州"西雁荡"之美誉的泽雅景区总面积 128.6 平方千米。区内景观以群瀑、碧潭、幽峡、奇岩为特色，融淳朴的山村风情为一体，有七瀑涧、金坑峡、珠岩、西山、龙溪、崎云、高山角、五凤八大景区，230 多处名胜景点。

泽雅，顾名思义，"泽"为水，"雅"为美，当是多秀水之处。比如以瀑布为特色的七瀑涧景区一涧七瀑，一折高一折，一瀑胜一瀑，形态各异，气势磅礴。另外，以山为特色的金坑峡天门峰，壁立千仞，鬼斧神工。以岩洞为特色的高山角景区有清静幽邃的鸳鸯洞，冬暖夏凉的清风洞。而在莽莽大山中生长的 82 属 245 种植物，名贵的如银杏、百年银桂、红豆杉、活跃在山间的长毛猴、野鹿等三十多种野生动物也倍增泽雅山水的魅力。

然而，令泽雅备受瞩目的却是宋代延续至今素有"中国造纸术的活化石"之称的纸山文化。温州造纸历史悠久，始于唐代，明宣德年间大量生产屏纸，以致泽雅山区俗称纸山。据水碓坑村的潘氏族谱记载：元末，泽雅先民为避战乱，从福建南屏一带逃迁而来，同时也带来了造纸术。经明、清，泽雅纸农已近 10 万人，约占当地人口的 80%。泽雅屏纸在工艺上同古法造纸术一脉相承，其流程几乎与《天工开物》中记载的完全相同。在古老的泽雅，有西岸村、横阳村、石桥村等十几个明清时的古村落，那里到处可见依山而建的水碓房、捞纸房和淹纸槽，它们与古民居，元代的寂照寺，明代的漫水桥、永宁桥融为了一体。而坐落在石桥村南斗山之阴，龙溪东岸的"四连碓"成为纸山屏纸生产的典型作坊，于 2001 年被列为全国文物保护单位。

泽雅丰厚的人文景观与原始、野韵的自然风光相依相融，共同构筑了这一方宁静、古朴的清幽之地。

Zeya, known as "the West Yandang", has a 128.6 square kilometers land coverage. Zeya is renowned for its waterfalls, lakes, gorges and rocks as well as its **unsophisticated** folk customs. There are more than 230 scenic spots in eight scenic areas, namely the Seven-step Waterfall Ravine, the Jinkeng Gorge, the Pearl Rock, the West Mountain, the Dragon Stream, the Qiyun Mountian, the Gaoshanjiao and Wufeng.

In Chinese, "ze" means water, while "ya" means beautiful. "Zeya" is just what the name implies—the place where the beautiful water flows. For example, the Seven-step Waterfall Ravine features its magnificent waterfalls which are falling down one upon another. Besides, there is the Jinkeng Gorge which features its splendid mountains, especially the Tianmen Peak. What's more, the Gaoshanjiao features its caves of various kinds. The Yuanyang Cave is quiet and deep while the Qingfeng Cave is cool in summer and warm in winter. In the lush mountains, there are about 245 different **species** of plants which belong to 82 genera. There are, for example, ginkgo, hundred-year latifolius and taxus. In addition, animals such as shaggy monkeys and wild deer in the mountains have added more charm to the landscape of Zeya.

However, it is the Culture of Paper Mountain that has made Zeya more **prominent**. It is known as the living **fossil** of Chinese papermaking technique which has been developed since the Song Dynasty. Papermaking in Wenzhou has got a long history which can be traced back to the Tang Dynasty. And during Xuande reign of the Ming Dynasty, the Nanping Paper was made in large quantities. That's why the mountainous area of Zeya was called the Paper Mountain. According to the **genealogy** of Pan Clan in Shuiduikeng Village, in the late Yuan Dynasty, the **ancestors** of Zeya from Nanping of Fujiain Province sought **refuge** during the war. They came to Zeya, bringing their technique of papermaking. After the Qing and Ming dynasties, the number of people who made paper in Zeya was about 100,000, accounting for approximately 80% of the local population. Surprisingly, the papermaking technique of Zeya is exactly the same as the ancient one recorded in *Exploitation of the Works of Nature*, the greatest technique **encyclopedia** of the Ming Dynasty. In Zeya, there are more than 10 ancient villages, such as Xi'an Village, Hengyang Village, and Shiqiao Village. In the villages, there are water **ram** workshops, paper collecting workshops and **dunking** bathes which seem to be a natural part of the scenery of the folk houses of the Ming and Qing dynasties, the Jizhao Temple of the Yuan Dynasty, and Manshui Bridge and Yongning Bridge of the Ming Dynasty. The Connected Four Water Rams, located at the eastern bank of the Dragon Stream of the North Nandou Mountain in Shiqiao Village, is considered as a typical workshop of making Nanping Paper. It is listed as a state-level unit of cultural relic protection in 2001.

The abundant human landscape and the natural scenery have made Zeya a place of quietness and simplicity.

★生词与词组 Words & Expressions

unsophisticated /ˌʌnsə'fistikeitid/ *adj.* 简单而自然的	species /'spiːʃiz/ *n.* 物种
prominent /'prɔminənt/ *adj.* 显著的	fossil /'fɔs(ə)l/ *n.* 化石
genealogy /dʒiːni'ælədʒi/ *n.* 宗谱	ancestor /'ænsestə(r)/ *n.* 祖先
refuge /'refjuːdʒ/ *n.* 避难(处)	encyclopedia /inˌsaiklə(u)'piːdiə/ *n.* 百科全书
ram /ræm/ *v.* 将某物夯入某物	dunk /dʌŋk/ *v.* 泡；浸

◆ **知识拓展 Knowledge Extension**

屏纸：又称为"南屏纸"。其制作流程有 20 多道工序，其中一些生产环节比古籍《天工开物》记载更原始、更详尽，被专家称为中国造纸术的活化石。现留存的水碓、纸坊于 2001 年列入第五批全国文物保护单位，并于 2007 年列入第二批浙江省非物质文化遗产名录。

造纸术：中国四大发明之一，人类文明史上的一项杰出的发明创造。我国古人以上等蚕茧抽丝织绸，剩下的恶茧、病茧等则用漂絮法制取丝绵。漂絮完毕，篾席上会遗留一些残絮。当漂絮的次数多了，篾席上的残絮便积成一层纤维薄片，经晾干之后剥离下来，可用于书写。这种漂絮的副产物数量不多，在古书上称它为赫蹏或方絮。

纸山文化：古法造纸自宋末元初传入泽雅以来，被完好地保留至今。是中国目前保留的最原始、最完整的古法造纸术，素有中国造纸术活化石之誉。以竹为主要原料，依靠水力资源沿溪构筑水碓，沿袭古法造纸，制造泽雅屏纸，尤其以"四连碓造纸作坊群"为泽雅古法造纸的典型代表与精髓。它是国内仅存最好的古法造纸作坊群，不仅体现传统工艺的完整性，同时体现人与自然和谐相处的纸山和纸文化的独特性。泽雅纸山已形成其内涵丰富、博大精深的纸文化。

《天工开物》：初刊于明崇祯十年(1637)，作者是明朝科学家宋应星，是世界上第一部关于农业和手工业生产的综合性著作，作者在书中强调人类要和自然相协调、人力要与自然力相配合。它是中国古代一部综合性的科学技术著作，有人也称它是一部百科全书式的著作，外国学者则称它为"中国 17 世纪的工艺百科全书"。

15. 中国木活字印刷文化村 China Wood Movable Type Printing Culture Village

被誉为中国至今发现的唯一尚存木活字印刷的村落——中国木活字印刷文化村是一个著名历史古迹。

自北宋庆历年间(1041—1048)著名发明家毕昇发明泥活字印刷以来，活字印刷已有近千年的历史。据东源村保存的《太原郡王氏宗谱》记载，东源村王氏祖宗原住河南，唐末时有一房进入福建。从元代开始，其祖先王法懋用木活字印刷术技艺印刷家谱，后从福建省移居平阳，再移瑞安东源村，并将祖传的"梓辑"(修编族谱并用木活字进行印刷的全套工艺的总称)手艺带到了东源。此后，村民世代传承，并不断精益求精，成为远近闻名的家谱印刷村。

坐落在村内的"中国木活字印刷文化展示馆"是由古宅改造而成。古宅建于明末清初，占地 1670 平方米，不仅陈列了详尽的文字图片资料及印刷模具，还专门聘请专业谱师现场演示印刷流程。在东源村印刷制作家谱的字模采用老宋体，是明朝以来的官方字体，用它印在宣纸上显得美观大气。做谱采用雕刀、雕盘、印版、上手刷(棕刷)、下手刷、白蜡等工具，整个工艺流程有 15 道工序，除开丁(登记)、誊清(理稿)等文稿环节外，印刷环节有字模、捡字、排版、校对、印刷、切谱(裁边)、装订等。字模是采用不易开裂、质地细腻、附着墨汁性能好的上好棠梨木，经雨淋日晒自然干燥后，制成一个个的木活字，以备排版用。其整个操作流程，与元代农学家王祯《农书》上记载的印刷流程如出一辙。

东源村木活字印刷术是我国已知唯一保留下来且仍在使用的木活字印刷技艺，至今已有800多年的历史，堪称世界印刷术的活化石。该村木活字印刷具有极高的历史人文价值，已列入全国非物质文化遗产名录。

China Wood Movable Type Printing Culture Village, a famous cultural relic site, is known as the only village that has still kept the wood movable type printing in China.

Movable type printing was invented by the great inventor Bi Sheng during Qingli reign of the Northern Song Dynasty (1041–1048), thus has a history of nearly 1,000 years. As the genealogy of *Wang Clan of Taiyuan **Prefecture*** recorded, the ancestors of Wang Clan used to live in Henan Province. In the late Tang Dynasty, one of the branches moved to Fujian. Since the Yuan Dynasty, Wang Famao started to print the genealogy by using the wood movable type printing. Later, they moved to Pingyang and then to Dongyuan Village, with their **patrimonial** printing techniques named "Ziji", the whole process of making genealogy by wood movable type printing. Since then, the techniques have been passed on from one generation to the next. The villagers **refined** on the techniques in practice and the village soon became the one renowned for its printing of genealogy.

In the village, there is a China Wood Movable Type Printing Culture Exhibition Hall, which was transformed from an ancient residence. The residence was built in the late Ming Dynasty and the early Qing Dynasty, covering an area of 1,670 square meters. Now, there are **elaborate** pictures and text materials and moulds. A master worker of making genealogy, is invited to display the whole printing process in the hall. The **typeface** on the mould is Song typeface, which has been used as the official type since the Ming Dynasty. The Song typeface printed on the Chinese art paper seems elegant and powerful. The tools include the **scorper**, the carving plate, the printing board, the brushes, the white wax, etc. And the whole process consists of 15 steps, including the paperwork of registration and composition, as well as the printing work of molding, picking, composing, checking, printing, trimming and binding. The mould is normally made from superior pyrus betulacfolia wood which is of fine texture, good **adsorption** and not easy to **cleave**. After being exposed and dried in the natural environment, the wood then will be made into the movable type and ready for composing. The whole process is exactly the same as the one recorded in *Agricultural Book* by Wang Zhen, an **agronomist** of the Yuan Dynasty.

The movable type printing in Dongyuan Village is the only known one in China which has been kept and is still in use. With a history of more than 800 years, it is indeed a living fossil of the world's art of printing. It is of a great value of historic humanity and has been listed on the National Non-material Cultural Heritage List.

★生词与词组 Words & Expressions

prefecture /'pri:fektjuə/ *n.* 府；专区；县	patrimonial /ˌpætri'moniəl/ *adj.* 祖传的
refine /ri'fain/ *v.* 改进	elaborate /i'læb(ə)rət/ *adj.* 精心制作的
typeface /'taipfeis/ *n.* 字体	scorper /'skɔːpə/ *n.* 雕刻刀
adsorption /æd'sɔːpʃən/ *n.* 吸附（作用）	cleave /kliːv/ *v.* 裂开，分开

agronomist /əˈɡrɔnəmist/ *n.* 农(艺)学家

◆ **知识拓展 Knowledge Extension**

活字印刷：印刷术是中国古代"四大发明"之一。中国早在 11 世纪就发明了活字印刷。活字印刷的发明是印刷史上一次伟大的技术革命。这种印刷方法使用可以移动的金属或胶泥字块，用来取代传统的抄写，或是无法重复使用的印刷版。活字印刷对世界文明进程和人类文化发展产生了重大影响。

毕昇(约 970—1051)：中国发明家。毕昇发明了胶泥活字印刷术，被认为是世界上最早的活字印刷技术。

第二节　旅游文化——山水文化

Section 2　Tourism Culture—Landscape Culture

山水从字面上看是山川大河的代名词，其实从广泛意义上讲，还应该包括花草树木、雨露云雾、溪泉烟岚等。山水特指地貌特征具有典型性，生态环境优良，有一定文化积淀，具有美学、文化、科学价值的自然景观的综合体。

Landscape literally means "mountains and rivers". However, in a broad sense, it covers plants and trees, rain and cloud, stream and spring, fog and mist, etc. Landscape refers in particular to the natural scenery with typical geomorphic features, fine ecological environment, cultural resources as well as value of aesthetics, culture and science.

我国山水景观的文化内涵十分丰富。山水景观中的亭台楼榭、塔廊桥殿等人文建筑，以及绘画、诗文、楹联、摩崖石刻、雕塑等均蕴含着巨大的艺术价值。自古以来，山水不仅是人们游览的圣地，还是人们创作的素材，灵感的源泉，山水也因此蒙上了浓厚的文化色彩。

The Chinese landscape is of abundant cultural connotation. The constructions such as pavilions, towers, corridors, bridges, halls, as well as the paintings, poetic prose, couplets, sculptures are all of great artistic value. Since ancient times, areas with beautiful landscape are not only people's sightseeing places but also the material of creative work and source of inspiration. Therefore, the landscape is also enriched by the culture.

1. 山地景观 The Mountain Landscape

我国山地景观数量巨大。其中东岳泰山、南岳衡山、西岳华山、北岳恒山、中岳嵩山自古以来就以其独特的地形地貌和深厚的文化底蕴备受关注，被称为"五岳"。山西五台山、四川峨眉山、浙江普陀山、安徽九华山被誉为中国四大佛教名山。还有在道教长期发展过程中形成的四大道教名山，即四川青城山、湖北武当山、江西龙虎山、安徽齐云山。此外，还有以风光旖旎著称的风景名山，如浙江雁荡山、辽宁千山、江西庐山、吉林长白山等。

The mountain landscape in China is of enormous amount. Mount Taishan in Shandong, Mount Hengshan in Hunan, Mount Huashan in Shaanxi, Mount Hengshan in Shanxi and Mount Songshan in Henan are considered the Five Great Mountains in China. They feature their unique topography and physiognomy as well as their rich culture, and therefore have been given much attention to. Mount Wutai in Shanxi, Mount Emei in Sichuan, Mount Putuo in Zhejiang and Mount Jiuhua in Anhui are known as the Four Great Buddhist Mountains in China. While there are Four Great Taoist Mountains, namely Mount Qingcheng in Sichuan, Mount Wudang in Hubei, Mount Longhu in Jiangxi and Mount Qiyun in Anhui. Besides, there are also mountains renowned for their beautiful sceneries, such as Mount Yandang in Zhejiang, Mount Qianshan in Liaoning, Mount Lushan in Jiangxi and Mount Changbai in Jilin, etc.

2. 水体景观 The Water Landscape

水体景观是另一类重要的旅游资源。其类型包括江河、湖泊、海滨、流泉以及熔岩瀑布。我国流域面积在 100 平方千米以上的有 5000 多条，1000 平方千米的有 1500 多条。主要河流有长江、黄河、珠江、黑龙江、辽河、淮河、钱塘江、漓江等。

The water landscape is another kind of important tourism resource, which includes rivers, lakes, beaches, springs and lava waterfalls. In China, there are more than 5,000 rivers with their drainage-basin areas exceeding 100 square kilometers. Among them, there are 1,500 rivers with their drainage-basin areas of 1,000 square kilometers. The main rivers are the Yangtze River, the Yellow River, the Zhujiang River, the Liaohe River, the Huaihe River, the Qiantang River, the Lijiang River and so on.

第三节 景点讲解技能——制造悬念法

Section 3 Narration Tactics of Scenic Spots—Suspense Creating

制造悬念法是指导游人员在讲解时提出令人感兴趣的话题，但又故意引而不发，激起旅游者急于知道答案的欲望，使其产生悬念。这种方法就是俗称的"吊胃口""卖关子"。让游客自己去思考、去琢磨、去判断，最后才讲出结果。这种"先藏后露、欲扬先抑、引而不发"的手法，一旦"发(讲)"出来，会给游客留下特别深刻的印象。但卖关子必须找到恰当的关口，即时机。悬念制造以前应有铺垫，即先有引人入胜的讲解，以引发旅游者强烈的兴趣和愿望。

制造悬念的方法很多，如问答法、引而不发法、分段讲解法等都可能激起旅游者对某一事物的兴趣，引起遐想，急于知道结果，从而收到制造悬念的良好效果。

例 1 河南少林寺

在介绍少林寺塔林时导游说："当年乾隆皇帝游历少林寺时带了 500 名侍从也没能查清楚少林寺到底有多少座塔。"说到这里，停下来，给旅游者留下一个问号，大家在想：到底多少塔呢？为什么 500 人也没有数清楚呢？塔林游览完毕导游员问："大家数清楚了吗？现在塔林有 255 座塔。当年乾隆皇帝来时这里古木参天、野草丛生，皇帝让一人抱一塔，有的两三人抱的是同一座塔而不知道，所以贵为天子也没弄清楚有多少座塔。"导游员用制造悬念来吸引游客的注意力，最后才把悬念揭开，使旅游者由衷地发出"原来如此"的感叹。

例 2 温州江心屿

当游客在前往江心寺时，导游人员可以不失时机地介绍："相信大家都知道杭州西湖的十景，实际上我们温州也有江心屿十景，那就是春城烟雨、瓯江月色、孟楼潮韵、远浦归帆、沙汀渔火、塔院筠风、海眼泉香、翠微残照、海淀朝霞和罗浮雪影。请大家边参观边思考，我们现在要去的江心寺会有十景中的哪一景？"这就给游客留下了一个悬念。游客到达江心寺后，导游人员再告诉游客："江心寺大殿前可南望鹿城，早晨烟雨如丝，古城空蒙隐现，春到江南，绿染枝头，正合'春风又绿江南岸'的诗意。前人题诗云：是烟复是雨，东风不开束，一夜霏空蒙，染得城头绿。大家现在就位于我们温州十景中第一景——春城烟雨的所在地。"由此，导游员用制造悬念的方法进一步激发了游客游览景区的兴致。

制造悬念是导游讲解的重要手法，在活跃气氛、制造意境、激发游客游兴等方面往往能起到重要作用，所以导游人员都比较喜欢用这一手法。但是，再好的导游方法都不能滥用，"悬念"不能乱造，以免起反作用。

◆ **综合练习**

请运用所学的"制造悬念法"讲解技巧，围绕温州某一景设计提问并分小组进行中英文讲解练习。

第四节 山水文化翻译技巧——景点名称翻译技巧

Section 4 Translation Skills of Landscape Culture

—Translation Skills of Names of Tourist Attractions

旅游景点(tourist attractions)是指风景区、文博院馆、寺庙观堂、旅游度假区、自然保护区、主题公园、森林公园、地质公园、游乐园、动物园、植物园及工业、农业、经贸、科教、军事、体育、文化艺术等各类旅游点。

汉语景点的名称，从其语法结构上分析可以表示为"专有名称+通名(种类名称)"的偏正词组形式。专有名称即指对景点的称呼，好比人的姓名和城市的名字，如："乾清宫""颐和园""云居寺"中的"乾清""颐和""云居"就是这三个建筑物的专有名称。通名(种类名称)就是指判断、辨别景点类别的名词，如："乾清宫"的"宫""颐和园"的"园"和"云居寺"

的"寺"。

1. 景点通名翻译 Translation of Generic Terms of Tourist Attractions

旅游景点通名一般都用英文直接翻译，英文单词首字母大写，其余小写。

1.1 植物园

译为 Botanical Garden，如"北京植物园 Beijing Botanical Garden"。

1.2 博物馆

一般名称译为×××× Museum，而 Museum 放置在后面，如"历史博物馆 History Museum"。某机构的博物馆译为×××× Museum of ××××(机构名)，如"大钟寺古钟博物馆 Ancient Bell Museum of Great Bell Temple"。

1.3 纪念馆

有两种译法：历史名人的纪念馆译为 Memorial，人名不加"'s"，如"吴运铎纪念馆 Wu Yunduo Memorial"；历史事件或事迹的纪念馆译为 Memorial Museum，如"新文化运动纪念馆 New Culture Movement Memorial Museum"。

1.4 故居

译为 Former Residence，如"宋庆龄故居 Former Residence of Soong Chingling"。

1.5 展览馆、陈列馆

译为 Exhibition Hall / Exhibition Center，而会展中心译为 Convention & Exhibition Center。

1.6 陈列室

译为 Exhibition Room / Display Room。

1.7 宫、院

译为 Palace，如"颐和园 Summer Palace"。有些宫译为 Hall，如"乾清宫 Hall of Heavenly Purity"。

1.8 殿、堂

译为 Hall，如"养心殿 Hall of Mental Cultivation""乐寿堂 Hall of Longevity in Happiness"。

1.9 寺

译为 Temple，如"云居寺 Yunju Temple"。

1.10 亭、阁

译为 Pavilion，如"寄澜亭 Jilan Pavilion"。

1.11 一般的佛塔

译为 Pagoda，如"五塔寺 Five-Pagoda Temple"；藏式塔译为 Dagoba，如"白塔寺的白塔 White Dagoba"。

1.12 牌楼

译为 Memorial Archway。

1.13 高山

译为 Mountain，如"太行山 the Taihang Mountain"或"Mt. Taihang"。比较小的山、山丘等译为 Hill，如"万寿山 the Longevity Hill"。

1.14 岛

译为 Island，如"南湖岛 the South Lake Island"。

1.15 湖

译为 Lake，如"昆明湖 the Kunming Lake"。

1.16 桥

译为 Bridge，如"玉带桥 Jade Belt Bridge"。

1.17 商店

译为 shop，如"旅游纪念品商店 Souvenir Shop""礼品店 Gift Shop"。

2. 景点名称翻译 Translation of Names of Tourist Attractions

中国自然景观和人文景观的名称大多不完全用音译，而是采取意译、音意兼译以及音译和意译结合等方法。

2.1 意译

专名和通名均意译，即"意译+意译"(Liberal Translation + Liberal Translation)。

玉佛寺	Jade Buddha Temple	碑林	Stone Forest
虎丘	Tiger Hill	钟楼	Clock Tower

2.2 音意兼译

专名音译，通名意译，即"音译+意译"(Transliteration + Liberal Translation)。

太和殿	Taihe Hall	少林寺	Shaolin Temple
黄山	Mount Huangshan		

使用音译和意译相结合的方法翻译景点名称时，景点名称如属汉语"单名"，为了照顾音节和外国人的习惯读法，最好把名字后面的"湖""山""园"等同时音译出来。如：太湖 the Taihu Lake，豫园 Yuyuan Garden 等；如果景点名称是"双名"，则不必音译后面的词。如：

洞庭湖 the Dongting Lake，雁荡山 Mount Yandang，寄畅园 Jichang Garden 等。

2.3 音译和意译结合

大观园　Daguanyuan (Grand View Garden)

潇湘馆　Xiaoxiangguan (Bamboo Lodge)

孤山　　Gushan (Solitary Hill)

旅游翻译的一个主要目的就是对外介绍我国的文化。需要指出的是有些专有名称的直译译名，其所表达的只是字面上的意思，并不能完全表达出名称背后的含义，这就需要在具体的讲解中指明。例如：苏州著名的景点寒山寺，就不能译成 Cold Hill Temple，因其取自一古代诗僧寒山之名，故只能将其译成 Hanshan Temple；又如：拙政园(Garden of Humble Administrator)是明嘉靖年间御史王献臣辞职回乡后在元大宏寺遗址所建造的别墅，并借用晋代潘岳《闲居赋》中"拙者之为政也"一句为园名。如果采用音译的方法，不仅这其中的历史人物、典故将不为游客所知，其园名及游园的雅趣也无从体会了。

另外，景点翻译时需要注意"通译"问题。如："中山陵"的英文名称早已被确定为 Dr. Sun Yat-sen's Mausoleum，这一译名不但广为人知，也已被翻译界所接受。不能望文生义翻译成 Zhongshan Mausoleum，也不能简单翻译成 Sun Yat-sen's Mausoleum。Sun Yat-sen 之前没有加上表示对孙中山这位伟人足够尊重的 Doctor(博士)的缩写形式 Dr.，而我国官方在用英文宣传介绍孙中山的时候从来都是将其尊称为 Dr. Sun Yat-sen，"中山陵"的官方英文译名 Dr. Sun Yat-sen's Mausoleum 也由此而来。

◆ 课后练习 Exercises

把下列景点名称翻译成英语(Put the following Chinese names of tourist attractions into English)

1. 黄浦江
2. 城隍庙
3. 梅兰芳纪念馆
4. 香港会展中心
5. 人民大会堂
6. 峨眉山
7. 黄花岗七十二烈士墓
8. 紫禁城
9. 石林
10. 大雁塔

第五章 金华、嘉兴景域

Chapter Five Jinhua & Jiaxing Scenic Zone

第一节 旅游景点

Section 1 Scenic Spots

1. 赤松黄大仙风景区 Chisong Huang Daxian Scenic Area

赤松黄大仙风景区位于金华市赤松山，面积约 14.1 平方千米。赤松山山峻、水秀、石奇、洞幽，整个景区林木葱郁，风光旖旎。赤松山相传为赤松道人黄大仙得道升天之地，这传说为赤松山披上了一层神秘的传奇色彩。历代文人墨客寻仙觅踪，纷纷造访于此，更是留下了许多赞美此地的华丽章句。整个景区文化底蕴深厚，山山水水无不遍布着迷人的传说故事和仙人遗迹，与天然胜景相得益彰。

赤松山是道教三十六洞天中最后一个洞天，相传是赤松道人修身得道，飞升成仙的圣地，也是黄大仙文化的发祥地，在中国道教发展史上占据了极其重要的地位。赤松宫是整个赤松山的精髓所在，最早建于晋代，古称宝积观，历代香火鼎盛，有"江南道观之冠"之称誉，后几经修葺，现在依然保留着众多的古代道教文化遗迹，宫中有二仙殿、元机洞、元辰殿等古建筑。每日香客云集，香火不断。

与赤松宫遥遥相对，有卧羊山拔地而起。卧羊山，得名于黄大仙"叱石成羊"的故事。山中白石错落，点缀于湖光山色之间，树木葱茏之中，如群羊散牧，一派自然。五里之外，又有炼丹山，山中散落着传说中黄大仙炼丹所置的丹井、丹灶、丹龛等圣迹，仙风雅韵，风光无限，历来受人追捧。

赤松山作为黄大仙成仙得道的宝地，千年来都是信徒日夜向往的仙乡宗庙。黄大仙"普济劝善，度世救人"的精神，历来受到众多海内外人士的赞颂，黄大仙精神也世世代代被广为传诵，发扬光大。

Occupying an area of 14.1 square kilometers, the Huang Daxian Scenic Area sits on the Chisong Mountain of Jinhua City. With its steep mountains, clear water, grotesque rocks and secluded caves, the whole scenic area boasts with its lush woods and exquisite scenery. It is the place where Huang Daxian, a great Taoist Priest Deity in China, became immortal, which **renders** legendry colors to the land. For over centuries, it's been a popular destination for **literati** who strived to reveal fairy mysteries, among whom many left beautiful verses giving praises to the scenery here. The scenic spot has profound cultural deposits, fascinating legends and fairy relics here and there, which integrate with the enchanting natural beauty and complement each other.

The Chisong Mountain is the last among the 36 Taoism Fairylands. It is the place where Taoist Priest Chisong (namely Huang Daxian) became an immortal and Huang Daxian Culture originated. Thus it is of great significance to the history of China's Taoism development. The Chisong Palace is crowned as the quintessence of the whole Chisong Mountain. Dating back to the Jin Dynasty (265–420), the palace was first built and named Baoji Taoism Temple, winning not only a large number of **pilgrims** over years but also the **laudatory** title "No.1 Taoism Temple in South China". Despite of repeated repairs, it still preserves many relics of ancient Taoist culture such as the ancient architectures of the Erxian Palace, the Yuanji Grotto, and the Yuanchen Palace, which are crowded with continuously flowing worshippers every day.

Facing Chisong Palace from the opposite side, the Woyang Mountain soars above the horizon. Named after the legend of "turning rock into goat" by Huang Daxian. The scattered white rocks on the mountain, among the luxuriant woods, adding **radiance** and beauty to the landscape of lakes and hills, bear a resemblance of the scene of the grazing flocks, vividly capturing a picture of nature. Miles away is the Liandan Mountain, widely dispersed with **alchemy** stoves, **hearths** and shrines established by Huang Daxian, which is veiled with a fairy color and is shedding its extraordinary appeal over years.

As the blessed paradise where Huang Daxian achieved immortality, for thousands of years, Chisong Mountain has been the longing place for its disciples. And his spirit of doing merciful deeds has always been receiving **glorification** from home and abroad. His spirit has also been carried forward and further developed from generation to generation.

★生词与词组 Words & Expressions

render /'rendə/ v. 表达；描绘；给予
pilgrim /'pilgrim/ n. 香客，朝圣者
radiance /'reidiəns/ n. 发光；光辉
hearth /hɑ:θ/ n. 炉床，壁炉

literati /ˌlitə'rɑ:ti:/ n. 知识界，文人学士
laudatory /'lɔ:dətəri/ adj. 颂扬的
alchemy /'ælkimi/ n. 炼金术，炼丹术
glorification /ˌglɔ:rifi'keiʃən/ n. 赞颂

◆ 知识拓展 Knowledge Extension

黄大仙(约 328—386)：即赤松道人，著名道教神仙。本名黄初平，因在赤松山修炼成仙故又号赤松子。出生于浙江省金华兰溪黄湓村，一说出生于浙江省金华义乌赤岸，原是当地的一名放羊的牧童，在金华山中修炼得道升仙。黄大仙擅长炼丹和医术，在家乡造福黎民，又仙游各地，"普济劝善，助人为乐"，宋代敕封为"养素净正真人"，民间尊其为"治病救命，佑福保安"的财神和吉祥之神。全国各处的黄大仙祠香火鼎盛，信徒遍布世界各地。

2. 方岩风景区　Fangyan Scenic Area

　　方岩风景区位于金华永康城东 25 千米处，集雄、奇、险、秀、幽于一体，无论是险峰绝壁、洞府石室，还是平湖飞瀑、色彩丹霞都展现出独特的自然之美。景区内更有享誉江南的地方神明胡公大帝，以及独树一帜的南宋永康学派的发祥地五峰书院。

　　从方岩的南麓拾级而上，途径罗汉洞、百步峻，有飞桥栈道横跨危崖，内傍峭壁，外临深涧，盘亘虚空，迂曲有致。过飞桥，拾级而上，有巨石豁然中开，有八角重檐石亭一座，俗呼"天门"。飞桥和天门淋漓尽致地展示了方岩丹霞地貌的雄险诡奇。跨进天门，闲步走过商贩云集的天街，不远即至广慈寺。广慈寺原名大悲寺，初建于唐大中四年(850)，北宋治平二年(1065)改为广慈寺，由大殿、禅房、经楼等组成，大殿分前、中、后三殿，坐北朝南，逐进升高，殿与殿之间以天井分隔，以廊庑连接。后殿又名屏风阁。屏风阁的胡公祠是方岩香火最盛处。

　　从方岩旋回天门而下，绕寿山而行，一路曲折山径。寿山又名五老峰，峰岩如削，绝壁千丈，依洞傍山，筑有各式楼台殿阁，有寿山寺、丽泽祠、三贤堂、学易斋和五峰书院等遗址。五峰书院为南宋永康学派的发祥地。陈亮设帐授学于此，后声名鹊起，渐成气候。宋代著名学者朱熹、吕东莱和明代应石门、程方峰、程松溪等都曾在此讲学。除了自然风光，方岩风景区更有一年一度的方岩庙会，届时游人云集，节庆气氛浓郁欢庆，自然风光与人文气息得到完美的结合。

Fangyan Scenic Area, 25 kilometers east from Yongkang, Jinhua, is an integration of its original grandness, bizarreness, steepness, elegance and secludedness. With sheer **precipice**, deep caves, **cascading** waterfalls or overwhelming Danxia landform，it all without exception embodies its unique beauty of the nature. Apart from the natural spots, the ancestral temple of the well-respected local deity in Jiangnan lies in the spot, as well as the cradle land of the specially featured Yongkang School of the Southern Song Dynasty—Wufeng College together render colors to the fascination of Fangyan Scenic Spot.

Stepping up from the south of giant rock and crossing the scenic sights of Luohan Cave and Hundred-step Hill, there comes the Aerial Bridge which connects two cliffs, making people feel nervous and creepy. Another step makes it suddenly open up. "The Sky Gate" as people used to call, an eight-horn stone pavilion from which you can have a look at the splendid scenery, is right behind it. The Aerial Bridge and the Sky Gate make the most of the beauty of Danxia landform in Fangyan. After crossing the Sky Gate and wondering through the Sky Street that is converged with stores, the Guangci Temple would be just a few steps away. Previously named Dabei Temple and preliminarily built in 850 (4th year of Dazhong reign in the Tang Dynasty), it was renamed Guangci Temple in 1065 (2nd year of Zhiping reign in the Song Dynasty). Consisting of the main hall, the **Zenist** rooms and the Buddhist, **sutra** houses which are also divided into front, mid and back halls, the temple has itself lain in south-north direction, with its halls separated by courtyards and linked by corridors. The back hall is also called Pingfeng Pavilion, in which the Hugong

Ancestral Hall, the most flourishingly worshipped place in Fangyan sits.

Descending back from the Sky Gate and hoofing around the Shoushan Mountain, you will find the pathway is quite of **sinuosity**. The Shoushan Mountain, also named the Wulao Mountain, is rich in dangerous sharp crags and cliffs, on which various temples and pavilions sit, such as the Shoushan Temple, the Lize Ancestral Temple, the Three-sage Hall, the Xueyi Hall, Wufeng College, etc. Wufeng College, as mentioned above, is the cradle land of the specially featured Yongkang School of the Song Dynasty. Its popularity has been growing since Chen Liang, a famous thinker and a man of letter, taught here. Many other famous scholars, including Zhu Xi and Lü Donglai in the Song Dynasty, Ying Shimen, Chen Fangfeng and Cheng Songxi of the Ming Dynasty, ever gave lectures here. Besides, Temple Fair of Fangyan is held annually in Fangyan Scenic Spot. By then, it would be swarmed with visitors celebrating the festival, making a perfect integration of natural landscaping and social customs.

★生词与词组 Words & Expressions

precipice /'presipis/ *n.* 悬崖，峭壁	cascade /kæ'skeid/ *v.* 倾泻；流注
Zenist /'zenist/ *n.* 禅宗信徒	sutra /'su:trə/ *n.* 佛经，经典
descend /di'send/ *v.* 下去；下降	sinuosity /ˌsinju'ɔsiti/ *n.* 蜿蜒

◆ 知识拓展 Knowledge Extension

永康学派：南宋时期以陈亮为代表的学派。因陈亮为婺州永康人，故该学派被称为永康学派。此学派哲学上承认客观规律之实在，强调道存在于实事实物之中，提倡"实事实功"，反对道学家空谈义理，以为道义不能脱离功利。此学派除陈亮外，有倪朴、王自中、喻南强等。永康学派与永嘉学派观点比较一致。

五峰书院：位于浙江省永康市方岩镇橙麓村南寿山坑。建于固厚峰下的天然大石洞中，周围有鸡鸣、覆釜等五峰环抱。建筑壁北朝南，三开间，略呈方形，洞宽 12.75 米，深 11.3 米，总面积 175 平方米，屋高二层，屋内设直径 37 厘米的圆柱 18 根，柱础造型系明代风格。书院久经沧桑，因洞造屋，建筑十分牢固。人们习惯把五峰内的重楼、丽泽祠、学易斋、五峰书院等岩洞建筑统称为"五峰书院"，均为明代建筑，即洞支木构筑在天然石洞中，梁架穿斗式，横梁不加装饰，下有丁头拱，鼓形柱础，有覆盆。1997 年 8 月五峰书院被公布为省级文物保护单位。

3. 郭洞风景区 Guodong Scenic Area

被誉为"江南第一风水村"的郭洞村，因"山环如郭、幽邃如洞"而得名，有着丰厚的家族文化、生态文化和建筑文化的内涵。郭洞建村于宋代以前，繁衍发展至今 650 多年，是何氏家族聚居的血缘村落。

相传郭洞何氏后裔仿学仙修道宝图《内经图》巧设布局，砌城墙以形成水口，又密植大量珍稀树种于城墙内外，与危岩密布的西山相连。城墙东首建回龙桥，初建于元朝，重建于明隆庆年间（1567—1572），就如一把巨锁，聚气藏风，把郭洞风水紧紧包裹在内。桥下有宝、彰二溪流过，故郭洞古称"双泉古里"，至今城门还有石刻楹联："郭外风光古，洞中日月长。"水口和回龙桥体现了郭洞的风水设计灵魂。

郭洞民居多为明清时的建筑，古朴精美，保存完好，可以说是一部明代到清代直至民国的建筑编年史。其中以新屋里和何氏宗祠最为典型。新屋里建于明天启崇祯年间，已有 360 多年历史，三进，共 30 间，房雕图案古朴精美，寓意吉祥深刻，寄托了郭洞人对生活的美好祝愿。何氏宗祠建于明万历六十七年（1609），规模宏大，气象庄严，祠内的古戏台典雅古朴，匾额满梁，彰显了郭洞何氏传人耕读传世，尊师重教的一贯传统，丰富的古文化遗存令人赞叹。后院有与祠同庚的罗汉松，冠大形美，更为省内难得的古树珍品。

Hailed as "the Village of Best Fengshui (Geomancy) in Jiangnan", Guodong Village got its name because of the wall-like-mountain surrounding and the deep-cave-like seclusion. The Scenic Area is famous for its enriched family culture, **ecological** surrounding and architectural style. Since the Song Dynasty, Guodong Village has become a blood relationship village for more than 650 years **multiplication**. It is the residence of a big family, sharing the same family name He.

Legend has it that the **descendants** of Guodong Village with the family name of He imitated and settled the layout of Guodong according to the religious **doctrine** "Picture of Inner Scripture". The residents there built solid stone walls to form water gaps and planted massive rare species inside and outside the walls to gather influence on the fortune for the residents. At the east end of the wall, there came a bridge named Huilong Bridge which was initially built in the Yuan Dynasty, and rebuilt in Longqing Period of the Ming Dynasty (1567–1572). The wall and the bridge are designed to wrap the Fengshui of the whole village tightly, hoping to have all the good luck packed as people wish. Under the bridge there are Baoxi and Zhangxi two streams flowing through the village and thus they bring another interesting name "the Town of Two Streams" for the village. So far, this name can still be found in the stone-carved memorial archway with a couplet: "Outer the wall is a historic scenery; inner the cave is an everlasting life." The wall and the bridge perfectly represent the spirit of Guodong's design.

Guodong residential areas are composed of **considerable** buildings of the Ming and Qing dynasties which are well preserved and which represent an architecture chronicle of the Ming and Qing dynasties and of the Republic of China. Among all of them, the New House and He **Ancestral** Hall are particularly regarded as the model. Built in Chongzhen reign of the Ming Dynasty, the New House, occupying 30 rooms, is a three-lined house with more than 360 years' history. The rooms are beautifully carved by a variety of ancient patterns, symbolizing luck and best wishes to the people living in Guodong. He Ancestral Hall, magnificent and solemn, was built in Wanli reign of the Ming Dynasty (1609) and epitomizes the highlights in local culture. The transmission of farming and reading culture, and the spirits of showing respects to education, all these can be certainly found in every corner in the hall. And the giant podocarpus macrophyllus with the same age of the ancestral hall in the backyard is rare in Zhejiang Province.

★生词与词组 Words & Expressions

multiplication /ˌmʌltipliˈkeiʃn/ *n.* 繁殖

doctrine /ˈdɔktrin/ *n.* 教义，信条

ancestral /ænˈsestrəl/ *adj.* 祖先的

descendant /diˈsendənt/ *n.* 后代，后裔

considerable /kənˈsidərəbl/ *adj.* 相当多的

◆ 知识拓展 Knowledge Extension

风水："风"就是元气和场能，"水"就是流动和变化。"风水"本为相地之术，即临场校察地理的方法，也叫地相、古称堪舆术，是一种研究环境与宇宙规律的哲学。风水学认为人既然是自然的一部分，自然也是人的一部分，那么达到"天人合一"的境界是再平常不过的了。相传风水的创始人是九天玄女，比较完善的风水学问起源于战国时代。风水的核心思想是人与大自然的和谐，早期的风水主要关乎宫殿、住宅、村落、墓地的选址、座向、建设等方法及原则，原意是选择合适的地方的一门学问。是中国历史悠久的一门玄术。也称青鸟、青囊，较为学术性的说法叫作堪舆。

《内经图》：或称为《内景图》，是人体内脏的解剖图，其目的是要给予学习人体解剖、内脏关系的人以图示，富有道家养生方法图示的目的。

4. 金华斗牛 Jinhua Bullfighting

"斗牛"，又俗叫"操牛"，其历史可以追溯千年以外，特别是在清末民初的时候，斗牛在金华成为一时风潮，受世人追捧。

金华古有"操牛娱神"的习俗，往往在寺庙、殿阁落成或开光时，要以"斗牛"来娱神，希望通过"斗牛"敬神，得到"神"的保佑，以祈求消灾解难的目的。除此之外，斗牛的故事还可以追溯到三国时期，相传吴国孙权与鲁肃微服出巡东阳郡(今金华市)。孙权为培养当地百姓的勇武精神，便在东阳郡大兴斗牛之风。从那以后，婺城铜山村白鹤庙开创斗牛节，铜山也就成了金华斗牛的创始地了。由此可见，这种带有东方文明独特魅力的民间游乐活动在金华是世代相传的。

斗牛一般都放在春秋农闲期间进行，多选择周山环抱的水田为斗牛的场地。斗牛当天，战牛披红挂彩，由其主人护送进入斗牛场，届时鞭炮齐鸣，掌声轰隆。场中两牛怒目相视，夹尾低头，四角相接，奋力争斗；场边观者则呐喊助威，呼声雷动。斗牛结束后，随之而来的就是战牛的买卖。获胜的战牛一夜身价百倍。战牛交易俨若结亲，买主、卖主互称"牛亲家"，买卖仪式隆重，酷似嫁娶，成为当地一道奇趣民俗风景。

"金华斗牛"于每年重阳节隆重开角，并伴有斗牛大奖赛等奇趣赛事。

"Bullfighting" is nicknamed "cow parade", and its history can be traced back beyond the millennium, especially to the end of the Qing Dynasty, while bullfighting was popular there.

In the past time, Jinhua had a custom called "to entertain God by cow parade". It is usually held to celebrate the **completion** of temple, hall or the **consecration** ceremony so as to entertain God, hoping to be blessed by God and get off evils. In addition, the origin of the bullfighting can also be found from the story of Three Kingdoms Period. Sun Quan, the Lord of Kingdom of Wu with his advisor Lu Su, traveled incognito to Dongyang County (now Jinhua City). In order to train **chivalrous** spirit of the local people, he encouraged the people to hold bullfighting. Since then, the White Crane Temple starts the bullfighting festival, and the town of Tongshan becomes the cradle of Jinhua bullfighting. All in all, Jinhua bullfighting is such a beloved and recreational activity with unique charm.

In **slack** seasons of spring and autumn, people begin to put bullfighting on their schedule. It is generally held in the paddy fields surrounded by mountains as the bullfighting **venues**. On that day, the well decorated fighting bulls are escorted by their masters into the bullring, firecrackers explode and applause thunders. The bulls **glower**, and clip the end of horn corners each other, struggling to fight while the viewers at the sidelines shout as encouragement. After the end of that war comes the sale of bulls. Bull heroes have a sudden rise in social status over one night. The sale resembles a wedding that buyers and sellers call each other "bull relatives" just like marriage-relationship. This solemn ceremony has already become a unique local scenery.

"Jinhua Bullfighting" is held every year in Double Ninth Festival.

★生词与词组 Words & Expressions

completion /kəm'pli:ʃn/ *n.* 完成，结束

consecration /ˌkɒnsɪ'kreɪʃn/ *n.* 献祭，奉献

chivalrous /'ʃɪvlrəs/ *adj.* 有骑士风度的，彬彬有礼的

slack /slæk/ *adj.* 不活跃的；萧条的；冷清的

venue /'venju:/ *n.* 聚集地点；会场；体育比赛场所

glower /glauə(r)/ *v.* 怒视

◆ 知识拓展 Knowledge Extension

西班牙斗牛：起源于西班牙古代宗教活动(杀牛供神祭品)，13 世纪西班牙国王阿方索十世开始把这种祭神活动演变为赛牛表演(真正斗牛表演则出现在 18 世纪中叶)。现在西班牙有 300 多个斗牛场(最大的是马德里的文塔斯斗牛场，可容纳 2.5 万人)。每年 3 月至 11 月是西班牙斗牛节，有些时候每天都斗，通常以星期日和星期四为斗牛日。西班牙斗牛的牛(Spanish Matador)选用的一般是生性暴烈、天生好斗的北非公牛。它们由特殊的驯养场负责牛种培育，经过四到五年即可用于比赛。正式比赛的斗牛体重在四百到五百公斤之间。而见习斗牛士面对的一般是二三百公斤、三岁以下的牛。在表演中，没有被斗牛士刺死的牛最终也将被引入牛栏，被他人用剑刺死。

斗牛士：在西班牙乃至整个西语世界里，斗牛士被视为英勇无畏的男子汉，备受国人的敬仰与崇拜。这个独特的人群具备高雅、勇敢的灵魂，他们将技术和体力、柔美和勇猛完美地结合到了一起。现今西班牙斗牛士的服饰还是继承了 16 世纪前辈的传统。主斗牛士一般选用红色为主的衣着，上面镶有金边和一些金色饰物，使其在阳光下做动作时显得闪亮夺目，光彩照人。16 世纪的人习惯于盘发，因而主斗牛士都戴有头饰。红布和斗篷也是两件非常重

要的工具。三名斗牛士助手则手持斗篷。全套斗牛士的工具包括：一把长矛、六支花标、四把不同的利剑以及一把匕首。主斗牛士在表演的初始阶段一般选用不带弯头的利剑，并支撑红布，以引诱公牛，到了最后的刺杀阶段，亮相的是带弯头的短剑，斗牛士将其刺入公牛后背的心脏。此外，主斗牛士还配备十字头剑，用来刺入公牛中枢神经。

5. 揽秀园 The Beauty–Embracing Park

揽秀园是一座文物公园。嘉兴旧名秀州、秀水，此园以"秀水东会沪渎，西控语溪，襟带具区，独揽其秀"之意命名。

揽秀园以碑廊为中心。西为建筑园林，内有三进，第一进为门厅。第二进为水轩，与第三进有小桥相连。第三进正厅为五开间仿古建筑，设著名画家蒲华(又名蒲竹英，晚清书画家，海上派创始人)纪念室。在园中长达250米的碑廊上，陈列着嘉兴历代碑刻94块，其中有"清仪阁刻石""停云馆贴""小灵鹫山馆图咏"和相传为唐代吴道子手绘的观音画像石刻、元代重修嘉兴路总管府治记等，还有出自文徵明、赵子谦、何绍基、吴昌硕、任伯年之手的精品，具有极高的历史研究和艺术欣赏价值。

碑廊东侧为园林区，有菱香阁、三过亭、垂钓池等。其中，三过亭是为纪念宋代大文豪苏东坡三到嘉兴本觉寺而建的。菱香阁是一座歇山顶双层古建筑，和园外文星桥遥相呼应，显得尤为端庄，形成一幅和谐的江南水乡风情图。在揽秀园北园与南园之间为古建筑一条街。

在五曲长廊东首八角亭中，有一座高2.8米、阔1.3米的董其昌书"嘉兴府学重修明伦堂记"碑，碑刻于明万历三十九年(1611)，共1000余字，行笔流畅，风格秀逸，古朴潇洒，堪称一绝。

The Beauty-Embracing Park is a heritage park. The park was named after the description in a poem, "In the east the Xiushui River meets with the Hudu River and in the west this place connects to the Yuxi River, next to the Tai Lake and embracing all the beauty."

The stone tablet exhibition is the center of the Beauty-embracing Park, to the west of which is a garden, connecting three entries. The first one is a hall, the second a water pavilion connected with the third by a bridge, and the third the hall of a five-bay antique building where there is a memorial room for Pu Hua (also known as Pu Zhuying, the founder of over-sea style and calligraphy artist and painter of the late Qing Dynasty). Along the 250-meter stone tablet exhibition of the garden is an inscription corridor made up of 94 carved stone **inscriptions** in Jiaxing's history, among which are "Qingyige Inscription", "Tingyunguan Inscription", "Little Lingjiushan Inscription" and a **hand-painted** stone carving of the Goddess of Mercy said to be made by Wu Daozi, the famous painter of the Tang Dynasty, and the record by the general director who was in charge of the rebuilding of the park in the Yuan Dynasty. There are also masterpieces by the celebrated calligraphers and painters such as Wen Zhengming, Zhao Ziqian, He Shaoji, Wu Changshuo and Ren Bonian. The Park is of much significance in historical research and art appreciation.

East to the tablet exhibition is a garden in which there are the Lingxiang Pavilion, the Sanguo Pavilion which was built in memory of the great master Su Dongpo of the Song Dynasty, and the

Fishing Pool. The Lingxiang Pavilion is an ancient two-storey pavilion, decent and elegant, echoing at a distance with the Wenxing Bridge outside the garden, forming a typical flavor of Jiangnan. Between the south garden and the north is a street with ancient buildings.

On the east side of the corridor stands a pavilion named Bajiao Pavilion, in which there is a stone tablet of 2.8 meters high and 1.3 meters wide. On the stone tablet there is handwriting of Dong Qichang, counting for more than 1000 Chinese characters in an unconventional style of smoothness, elegance and simplicity, rated as a unique piece of calligraphy. The tablet is said to be carved in the 39th year of Wanli reign of the Ming Dynasty (1611).

★生词与词组 Words & Expressions

hand-painted ['hænd'peintid]　*adj.* 手工涂的，手工绘的

◆ 知识拓展 Knowledge Extension

歇山顶：即歇山式屋顶，宋朝称九脊殿、曹殿或厦两头造，清朝改今称，为中国古建筑屋顶样式之一。歇山顶共有九条屋脊，即一条正脊、四条垂脊和四条戗脊，故又名九脊顶。在规格上仅次于庑殿顶。由于其正脊两端到屋檐处中间折断了一次，分为垂脊和戗脊，好像"歇"了一歇，故名歇山顶。

开间：住宅设计中，住宅的宽度是指一间房屋内一面墙的定位轴线到另一面墙的定位轴线之间的实际距离。因为是就一自然间的宽度而言，故又称开间。

6. 卢宅明清古建筑 Lu's Curtilage, the Ancient Buildings of the Ming and Qing Dynasties

卢氏，婺州望族，自明永乐十九年(1421)卢睿中进士以来，500年间，科第绵延，其中不乏一代重臣。由于家世兴旺，于是卢氏家族相继建房置产，致房屋千间，院落连片，街巷纵横，占地达33万多平方米，即卢宅。卢宅，全称卢宅明清古建筑，是江南久负盛名的明清古建筑群。有美誉称："北有故宫，南有卢宅"，卢宅可谓是民间故宫。整个建筑群落古朴典雅、宏敞秀丽、气势非凡，显示出以血缘关系为纽带的卢氏宗族聚居结构，是反映东阳木雕浓郁的地方特色和封建士大夫传统风水意识的典型厅堂宅第，被国内外专家誉为"具有国际水平的文化遗产"。

卢宅的格局和故宫相仿，叫作"前堂后寝"，前堂是卢家的公共厅堂，供族内子孙举行祭祀、聚会、吉庆、议事等，后面则是家眷、仆人的生活起居空间。全宅由十余组按南北轴线布置的宅院所组成，主轴线沿照壁穿过风纪世家、大方伯、旌表贞节三座牌坊转折至肃雍堂、乐寿堂而止于世雍堂。肃雍堂轴线是主体建筑所在，纵深320米，以九进院落成工字形布局，严谨规整，左右对称，规模恢弘，构件雕饰华丽，融东阳木雕与彩绘艺术于一炉，集砖雕、石刻艺术于一体，是卢宅古建筑群之精华所在。肃雍堂内藏明清各式精美宫灯三百余盏，其中，现存一盏大堂灯高4.5米，重255斤，用了40万颗彩色玻璃珠穿就，已载入吉尼斯世界纪录。

卢宅的"九狮戏球"三架梁更是东阳木雕的绝品。古代艺术家采用深浮雕、透雕和圆雕

等技法，把狮子雕刻得形神兼备，栩栩如生，可以说古代东阳木雕的精华就藏在卢宅。

The Lu's clan, an **eminent** clan in Wuzhou, has been renowned as the cradle of scholars and high officials during the past 500 years since Lu Rui succeeded in the highest imperial examination in year of 1421. Thanks to the family prosperity, the Lus fed the needs to build houses one after another. The total area reached approximately 330,000 square meters, five hundred mu of field, as comes the name "Lu's **Curtilage**". Having long enjoyed a good reputation, Lu's Curtilage, according to a **commendatory** saying "just as there is the Forbidden City in the north, there is the Lu's Curtilage in the south", was described as a private deluxe palace. The architectural complexity lies in the **simplicity** and elegancy of ancient customs, **grandiosity** and majesty, showing the Lu's clan's compact **communal** structure based on the **kindred** bond. It also shares the features of strong local distinctiveness of woodcarving in Dongyang and traditional feudal **geomantic** conception embedded in curtilage of scholar-bureaucrats. The Lu's clan wins the crown of "cultural heritage with international standards" from the specialists at home and abroad.

Similar in layout with the Forbidden City which presented as is called "halls in the front, bedrooms at the back", Lu's Curtilage has its public reception hall in the front for matters relating to sacrifice, get-together, celebration and meetings, etc., and the living quarters at the back for daily life uses. The whole curtilage consists of more than ten pairs of houses setting symmetrically to an **axial** line. The main axis which crosses the three memorial archways, named "Fengji Shijia (Aristocratic Family of High Morality)", "Dafangbo (Gentleman of Generosity)" and "Jingbiaozhenjie (Honor of Virtue)", separately, along the gate-facing screen walls then turns to the Suyong Hall and the Leshou Hall and ends at the Shiyong Hall. The main buildings lie on the axial line of the Suyong Hall, which was laid out by nine entries as the shape of a section of I-shaped, being **symmetrical** and precisely ordered with 320 meters in length. Under the magnificence in scale and exquisiteness in enchasing, the buildings integrate the woodcarving of Dongyang and the patterning arts, stone-carving as well, which presents the cream of Lu's Curtilage. There are over three hundred palace lanterns in the Suyong Hall, among which the Guinness world record holder of the biggest lantern weighs 127.5 kg and measures 4.5 meters high, stuffed with 400 thousand colorful beads.

Lu's Curtilage's "Nine Lions Playing with Ball" can be named the top-notch masterpiece of woodcarving. The crafts men made the lions even more vivid than a real one with cameo, openwork and circular engraving techniques. The woodcraft wins another saying that "the treasure of Dongyang woodcarving lies in nowhere but Lu's Curtilage".

★生词与词组 Words & Expressions

curtilage /'kə:tilidʒ/ *n.* 庭园，宅地
commendatory /kə'mendətəri/ *n.* 评注，注释
grandiosity /'grændə'ɔsiti/ *adj.* 社会的，共享的
kindred /'kindrəd/ *adj.* 同宗的，同源的
axial /'æksiəl/ *adj.* 轴的，成轴的

eminent /'eminənt/ *adj.* 知名的；受人尊崇的
simplicity /sim'plisəti/ *n.* 简单，朴素，率直
communal /'kɔmju:nl/ *adj.* 社会的，共享的
geomantic /ˌdʒiə'mæntik/ *adj.* 风水的
symmetrical /si'metrik(ə)l/ *adj.* 对称的；匀称的

◆ 知识拓展 Knowledge Extension

卢睿(1390—1462)：字仲思，号愚斋，浙江东阳人。永乐十九年(1421)进士，授监察御史，廉政明决，不为利害所惑。

东阳木雕：因产于浙江东阳而得名，与"青田石雕""黄杨木雕""瓯塑"并称"浙江三雕一塑"。东阳木雕以平面浮雕为主，层次丰富而又不失平面装饰的基本特点。又因色泽清淡，保留原木天然纹理色泽，格调高雅，又称"白木雕"。东阳木雕自唐至今已有千余年的历史，是中华民族最优秀的民间工艺之一，被誉为"国之瑰宝"。东阳也被称为"木雕之乡"。

7. 磐安炼火 Pan'an Refining Fire

金华磐安有一种被称为"炼火"的古老民俗活动，因人赤脚在通红的炭火上表演而得名，故又称"踩火"。炼火起源于先民对火的崇拜。当某地遇到灾祸、瘟疫，或是有村民生病，往往就要请人主持法事来"踩火灭灾"。届时周边的民众聚集在广场上，堆积大量的木炭、干柴于八卦图案的圆形火坛上，炼火者赤膊、光脚，手执响铃、钢叉等，高歌狂舞，大声呐喊，适时冲进通红的火炭堆上奔跑，动作粗犷有力，场面壮观。乡民希望能借烈火驱赶妖魔鬼怪，祛瘟去邪，避祸消灾，整个仪式充满了远古先民对火的崇拜痕迹。

磐安的炼火活动在宋代进入鼎盛时期。炼火活动与"方岩胡公"等地方神祇信仰相结合，每年重阳节和胡公祭日均要举办大型炼火活动，兼具祈福、消灾等目的，逐渐形成一整套规范仪式。炼火盛会场景宏大，气势壮观，热闹非凡。整个炼火过程中还伴有各种民间特色舞蹈，山民念唱，侯阳高腔、婺剧乱弹等颇为难得的地方独特戏曲演唱也时常出现在炼火盛会中。

在 2005 年，磐安炼火便被列入浙江省第一批非物质文化遗产名录，而金华磐安县也被命名为"浙江省民间艺术炼火之乡"。

Pan'an Refining Fire is originally known as an ancient folk activity, referring to **sacrifice rituals** and worship of ancestors. It is named "Refining Fire", because the performer plays on the hot charcoal barefoot. When disaster, **plague**, or sickness occurs, a Refining Fire ceremony is often **presided** to get the evil away. On this occasion, people from nearby gather on the square. When a large number of charcoals and firewood burn on a round Eight Diagrams fire altar, the performer sings and dances wildly with bare feet, waving his bell and fork in hand, running into the fire and hoping to drive ghosts and misfortunes away. The whole ceremony shows worship of the ancient **ancestors** and the power of fire.

Pan'an Refining Fire was in the golden age in the Song Dynasty. Combined with the ceremony of "God Hu", one of the well-respected local gods, the annual Refining Fire is held on the Double Ninth Festival and the day in memory of God Hu, and gradually forms a set of principles. Refining Fire is a grand event of the momentum of **spectacular,** and the whole process of refining is accompanied by a variety of rough folk dances as well as traditional operas.

In 2005, Pan'an Reining Fire was included in the first batch of intangible cultural heritage in Zhejiang Province, while Pan'an County was also named as the "Hometown of Refining Fire in

Zhejiang Province".

★ 生词与词组 Words & Expressions

sacrifice /'sækrifais/ *n.* 献祭，用(人或动物)祭献

plague /pleig/ *n.* 瘟疫，灾害

spectacular /spek'tækjulə/ *n.* 壮观的场面；精彩的表演

ritual /'ritʃuəl/ *n.* (宗教等的)仪式

preside /pri'zaid/ *v.* 主持(会议、仪式等)

◆ 知识拓展 Knowledge Extension

侯阳高腔：地方戏曲剧种之一，多流行于浙江东阳、义乌、浦江等地，是金华婺剧三路高腔(侯阳高腔、西吴高腔、松阳高腔)之首，是浙江八大高腔系统中的独立分支，属单声腔剧种。侯阳高腔腔调古朴、粗犷，通俗易懂，旋律简单，很少用滚唱形式，同时保持了山歌体、上下句、一字一音，后半句高亢上扬、乡音土语，具有"一人启齿，众人帮唱"等特点。节奏与调式跟当地的山歌极为相似，保留了原始戏曲的古老状态。所唱曲牌带有较多民歌色彩，传统剧目有《白鹦哥》《梁山伯》《卖水记》等。

8. 绮园 Qiyuan Garden

绮园俗称冯家花园，位于浙江省海盐县武原镇花园弄，是清代富商冯缵斋的私家花园。其占地一万平方米，水面约两千平方米，树木遮盖面积达七千平方米，整个园林几乎为绿树所覆盖，园内树木近千株。其中古树名木 40 余株，均经数百年风雨。

绮园是一座典型的江南风格的园林，整个园林的建造，妙用了"水随山转，山因水活"的叠山理水园论。其特点是以树木山池为主，略点缀建筑，同时用大面积水域，以聚为主，散为辅；山为骨，水为脉；水随山转，山因水活。园内有潭影九曲、蝶来滴翠、晨曦罨画、海月小隐、古藤盘云、风荷夕照、美人照镜、百鸟鸣春等景点。其游径由山洞、岸道、飞梁、小船及低于地面的隧道等组成，构成了复杂的迷境，为江南园林所仅见。

园内假山分成前、中、后三区，有"横看成岭侧成峰"的诗境。园内建筑"潭影轩""小隐亭""滴翠亭""风荷轩"为建园点缀，更为游人提供休憩之处。园内小桥有九曲桥、四剑桥、罨画桥联结山水，更构成独立的景致。如四剑桥由三跨石板构成，为我国园林桥景的孤例，罨画桥为石拱桥，将园中湖水分为两界，拱旁有联"两水夹明镜，双桥落彩虹"，与周边景物构成如诗画境。绮园以她不同风格被园林艺术家誉为"浙中第一名园"。

Located on the Huayuan Lane, Wuyuan Town, Haiyan County of Zhejiang Province, the Qiyuan Garden, commonly known as the Fengs' Garden, was once owned by a wealthy businessman Feng Zuanzhai in the Qing Dynasty. It covers an area of 10,000 square meters with a water area of about 2,000 square meters and a forest of 7,000 square meters. In the garden, there are nearly one thousand trees, among which forty famous ancient trees have existed for hundreds of years.

The Qiyuan Garden is a garden of typical Jiangnan style. The construction of the whole garden is based on the theory of "water runs around the hills; hills are lively for the waters". The whole construction mainly focuses on trees, hills and lakes, dotted with a few buildings while a large area of water **converge** in which "gathering" is as its principal while "scattering" as its ancillary; hills as its bones while waters as its veins so as to make waters running around hills while hills alive due to waters. In the garden there are some scenic spots such as Zigzagging in Water, Dripping Green for Butterflies, Paintings in Dawn Sunshine, Curved Moon on the Sea, Twisted Vines around Clouds, Swaying Lotus at Sunset, Beauty in the Mirror and Birds Singing for Spring, etc. Caves, river paths, hanging beams, boats and underground tunnels are connected to constitute a complex magical place, which is totally uncommon in the gardens of Jiangnan.

Artificial hills in the garden are divided into three sections as the front, middle and back, taking on a poetic scene, that is, "Seen from across, they're ridges; seen from sideways, they're peaks". A lot of pavilions can serve as resting places such as the Pavilion Reflected in Water, the Pavilion for **Reclusion**, the Pavilion of Dripping Green and the Pavilion of Lotus in Wind. They not only decorate the garden but also provide open space for visitors to have a rest. The garden bridges such as the Zigzagging Bridge, the Four-sword Bridge, and the Yanhua Bridge connect the mountains and the lakes so as to form a separate scene. Of all the bridges the Four-sword Bridge consists of three stone **slabs**, the only one in all the garden bridges. The Yanhua Bridge is a stone arched bridge, which divides the lake into two halves, with a couplet reading, "A mirror sits between two lakes, a rainbow rests on two bridges". With the beautiful landscape and **picturesque** environment as the background, the Qiyuan Garden, for its **distinctive** style, has been described as "the No.1 of all the Zhejiang famous gardens."

★生词与词组 Words & Expressions

converge /kən'və'dʒ/ v. 聚合　　　　　　reclusion /ri'klu:ʒən/ n. 隐居
slab /slæb/ n. 平板　　　　　　　　　　　picturesque /ˌpiktʃə'resk/ adj. 如画的
distinctive /di'stiŋ(k)tiv/ adj. 有特色的

◆ 知识拓展 Knowledge Extension

冯缵斋(约 1840—1887)：晚清酱作业富商。

叠山理水园论：自古以来，中国园林以山水园的特色而著称。它是在山水创作的基础上，根据园景立意、构思和功能要求，因山就水布置亭台楼阁、花草树木，使之互相协调地构成符合自然规律的环境空间，以回归自然，并展现高于自然的艺术境界。山石和水体在园林中有着唇齿相依的关系，"水随山转，山因水活"恰好说明了造园中山与水的相互依赖关系。

9. 双龙风景区 Shuanglong Scenic Spot

双龙风景区素以林海莽原、奇洞异景、道教名山著称于世。"洞中有洞洞中泉，欲觅泉源卧小船"的双龙洞；口小肚大、银瀑飞泻的冰壶洞；深穿神异、一线幻天的朝真洞及叱石成羊、护宅生财的黄大仙，此"三洞一仙"被誉为"双龙四绝"。其中，双龙洞位于双龙风景区的中心，是整个景区的核心与象征。明代大旅行家徐霞客曾四游金华山，根据双龙洞"外有二门，中悬重幄，水陆兼奇，幽明凑异"的独特景观特点和价值，把它列为"金华山八洞"的第一位。

双龙洞两侧分悬的钟乳石一青一黄，酷似龙头，故名"双龙洞"。洞深 200 余米，由内洞、外洞及耳洞组成，并由巨大的石屏相隔，仅通水路。要从外洞进内洞，须平卧小舟，仰面擦崖逆水而入，素有"千尺横梁压水低，轻舟仰卧人回溪"的奇妙观感。水道十米有余，其洞中有洞，洞洞相通，泉水叮咚，奇景迭出。

进入内洞就宛如置身仙境龙宫，洞内石钟乳、石笋众多，造型奇特、颜色各异、幻化多变，有"黄龙吐水""彩云遮月""海龟探海"等四十余种景观，惟妙惟肖，使人目不暇接。游客至此，都会忘记尘世的喧嚣，体验"洞中方一日，人间已三载"的神奇。

冰壶洞因口小肚大、形似酒壶又寒气袭人而得名，俯首下视，深不见底。洞中瀑布从暗河飞泻而出，瀑声轰隆，声若惊雷。郭沫若有诗赞云"银河倒泻入冰壶，道是龙宫信是诬"。而朝真洞前临深壑，背依青峰，四周群峰挺立，宛若百僧朝圣求真，洞名即由此来。洞中钟乳高悬，石笋遍地，其中一根大石笋形似"观音"，称"观音大士像"。洞的上方有一"天窗"，透进一束阳光，宛如半月，也称"一线天"。

Shuanglong (two dragons) Scenic Spot gains its reputation for wide forests, fantastic cave landscapes and Taoist mountains. The four wonders in Shuanglong Scenic Spot are the Shuanglong Cave with a view of cave upon cave and an enjoyment of spring-exploring by rowboat, the Binghu Cave with as mall mouth but a big belly and a pouring water fall inside, the deep and mysterious Chaozhen Cave with a look at "rocks turning into sheep", and the Huang Daxian Temple bringing wealth to the people. Among them, the Shuanglong Cave lies in the centre of the scenic spot, being the centre and symbol of the area. The famous traveler Xu Xiake of the Ming Dynasty ever visited the Jinhua Mountain for four times, and he ranked the Shuanglong Cave the first among the total eight caves in the Jinhua Mountain according to its unique landscaping characteristics and value, which combines water and land with fancy in the overlapped suspending rocks.

Shining interlappedly with each other, the green and yellow **stalactites** from the two sides of the cave are like dragons' (long) heads, so comes the name "Shuanglong Cave". With two hundred meters in depths, it consists of inner, outer and ear caves, which are blocked off by rocks barriers, allowing only one little canal to pass through the hole. If entering the inner cave from the outer cave, people need to lie low on the rowboat, drifting against the current in and barely leaving any space between body and the rock barrier, which gives an amazing sensation combined with wonder and terror. Along over a 10-meter waterway, one cave contains or connects another, with a fair spring-drooping tone and a serial of wonderful inner world landscapes.

After entering the inner cave, visitors would be enchanted and amused by the diversely styled and variously colored stalactites and **stalagmites**. There are over forty vivid sights that the tourists' eyes feast on, such as "Yellow Dragon Spitting Water" and "Colorful Clouds Blocking the Moon" and "Sea Turtle Exploring the Sea". By experiencing the amazement of "a day in cave, three years in outer world", visitors could leave aside the hustle and bustle of urban life.

Binghu (icy flagon) Cave is named for its chill and flagon-like shape. The cave is so deep that one can hardly see the bottom. Splashing from underground river, the waterfall makes a deafening sound like a grumbling thunder which wins a highly compliment from Guo Moruo (a famous Chinese author, poet, historian and archaeologist). There is a different sight in Chaozhen (worship the verity) cave. It locates between **ravines** and skyrocketing hills, surrounded by uplifting hills as if there were hundreds of monks worshiping the verity. In the cave there are stalactites hanging down from the top and overspread stalagmites on the ground, among which there is a huge one in resemblance with Avalokitesvara, so it got its name "Avalokitesvara Figure". Sunshine permeates into the cave through a natural skylight, as though it's a half-moon, also named "Yixiantian" (narrow sky).

★生词与词组 Words & Expressions

stalactite /'stæləktaiit/ *n.* 钟乳石　　　　stalagmite /'stæləgmait/ *n.* 石笋

ravine /rə'vi:n/ *n.* 既深又狭、坡度很大的山谷　　rudiment /'ru:dim(ə)nt/ *n.* 雏形，萌芽

◆ 知识拓展 Knowledge Extension

　　道教文化：集中国古代文化思想之大成，以道学、仙学和神学为主干，并融入了医学、巫术、数理、文学、天文、地理、阴阳五行等学问，内容讲求长生不老，画符驱鬼。中国传统道教文化对中国社会产生了深远的影响，其"无为而无不为""见素抱朴""上善若水""道法自然"等思想的积极因素，有其独特的存在价值。

10. 武义"小黄山" "Little Mount Huangshan" in Wuyi

　　武义"小黄山"坐落在金华市武义县东南部，总面积 5 平方千米左右，奇松、怪石、云海、飞瀑"四绝"为景区的主要特色。因人们认为该景区像极了黄山，"小黄山"的美名于是就渐渐地越传越远。

　　武义"小黄山"的美在于那自然造化的鬼斧神工。奇松迎客，怪石险岭，天池飞瀑，尤其雨后初晴，秀丽的小黄山轮廓在薄雾之中时隐时现，朦胧之中，仿佛一幅泼墨山水画，意蕴无限。还有那江浙一带十分稀少的"悬棺"墓葬，更是为"小黄山"增添了一丝神秘色彩。

　　除了那秀美的自然风光，半山腰有一座畲族古村落，全为浙南老式泥墙瓦房民居，历史悠久，民族风情浓郁，堪称自然与人文景观的完美结合。游客可来小黄山畲族风情村旅游、休闲，体验畲族风情，和畲民一道生活，如边学畲族民歌边学做畲族特色小吃，品尝畲族农家菜、畲族米酒，住畲族农家院、族长的毛草寮，参与畲族婚嫁表演等。

　　武义"小黄山"的美在山，在水，更在那畲寨的曼妙风情。

"Little Mount Huangshan" Scenic Spot is located in south–east of Wuyi County, Jinhua City. It covers a total area of 5 square kilometers. **Wondrous** pines, unique rocks, sea of clouds, and the running waterfalls are the "Four Wonders" in the scenic area. It is **unanimously** acknowledged that it resembles the famous Mount Huangshan Scenic Spot, so the reputation of "Little Mount Huangshan" travels further and further.

The beauty of Wuyi "Little Mount Huangshan" is a canny workmanship of nature, such as wondrous pines welcoming guests, sharp cliffs with odd rocks and running waterfalls. The sketchy outline appears and hides in the mist after raining, just like a splash-ink landscape painting with unlimited implication. Besides, there is a mysterious **burial** custom called "Hanging Coffin", which is very rare in Jiangsu and Zhejiang provinces, adding a touch of mystery for the "Little Mount Huangshan" Scenic Spot.

In addition to the beautiful natural scenery, halfway up the hill there is a minority ancient village. The houses here are all of mud-material and have a long history and strong ethnic flavor. It is a perfect combination of natural and humanistic landscape. Visitors can come here to take a sightseeing and experience the life style of She (one of China's minorities), and even live with the local people. There are lots of things visitors can do, such as learning minority folk songs, learning how to do She snacks, tasting She delicacy and rice wine, living in the farmyard or the traditional She dwellings which are made of straw, and watching performances of traditional She wedding.

The beauty of Wuyi "Little Mount Huangshan" is not only in the picturesque nature, but also in the splendid folklore in the She village.

★生词与词组 Words & Expressions

wondrous /'wʌndrəs/ *adj.* 出色的　　　　　　　unanimously /juːˈnæniməsli/ *adv.* 无异议地
burial /'beriəl/ *n.* 掩埋，葬礼

◆ 知识拓展 Knowledge Extension

崖葬：包括悬棺葬和崖洞葬，是在崖穴或崖壁上安葬人的遗体的一种葬俗，也是露天葬的一种。崖葬是古代西南少数民族地区流行的一种古老的葬法，被认为是世界文化史上的一大奇迹。其葬法是利用天然岩缝或人工木桩把棺材悬置于峭壁之上，或者将棺材放在天然或人工凿成的岩洞这中，并岩壁上雕刻各种图案、铭文等。

畲族：我国人口较少的民族之一，原分布在闽、粤、赣三省结合部，是闽南、潮汕的主要原住民之一。元、明、清时期，从原住地陆续迁徙到闽东、浙南、赣东等地山区半山区，其中90%以上居住在福建、浙江的广大山区，大多使用接近于汉语客家方言的语言，通用汉文。山歌是畲族文学的主要组成部分，演唱形式有独唱、对唱、齐唱等。其中无伴奏的山歌是畲族人最喜爱的一种民歌方式。"双音"是畲族人擅长的二声部重唱的唱法，又称"双条落"。

11. 乌镇 Wuzhen

桐乡乌镇是闻名江南的历史文化名镇，已有一千多年历史。乌镇自古地处两省、三府、七县交界之地，"宛然府城气象"。古人称它为"姑苏留都之前户，嘉湖浙甸之后屏"。

乌镇素以水乡集镇著称。全镇河道如网，水街相依。纵横的溪塘穿街傍市。溪上众桥飞跨，塘畔绿树成荫，河中舟楫不绝，市间笑语阵阵，这一切给水乡乌镇增添了诗情画意。

乌镇的历史文化悠久，名胜古迹甚多。市河西岸的唐代银杏已有一千余年的历史。十景塘边的昭明太子读书处，为梁朝遗迹。市河东观前街上的修真观戏台，始建于乾隆十四年，是浙北水乡集镇保存下来仅有的古戏台。镇上还留下不少有清末民初建筑风格的古老民居。

乌镇分布着许多著名景点。乌镇镇东的立志书院是茅盾，即沈雁冰先生少年时的读书处，现辟为茅盾纪念馆，为国家级重点文物保护单位。镇上的西栅老街是我国保存最完好的明清建筑群之一。

传承千年的历史文化，淳朴秀美的水乡风景，风味独特的美食佳肴，缤纷多彩的民俗节日，深厚的人文积淀和亘古不变的生活方式使乌镇成了东方古老文明的活化石。

Wuzhen in Tongxiang is a famous town in Jiangnan area, with a history of over one thousand years and rich culture. Wuzhen is located in the north of Hang-Jia-Hu Plain and on the west side of the Beijing-Hangzhou Grand Canal. Wuzhen was once the place where two provinces, three prefectures and seven counties joined together, "like a capital". The ancients entitled it as "the gate of Gusu and the backyard of Jiaxing and Huzhou".

Wuzhen is famous for its intensive river networks, in which all the rivers are connected and all the rivers and streets are side by side. The streets in Wuzhen run along the rivers and shops are scattered along the streets. All the bridges over the rivers, green trees along the streets and the coming and going boats on the rivers, together with the laughter from the markets, make up a poetic painting.

There are many celebrated historical and cultural sites in Wuzhen. The ginkgo on the west bank of the Shihe River is over a thousand years old, dating from the Tang Dynasty. The study by the Shijing Pond is where Prince Zhaoming of the Liang Dynasty studied. The ancient Xiuzhen Temple Stage, on the Dongguan Front Street on the east bank of the Shihe River, was built in the 14th year of Qianlong reign and it is the only ancient stage preserved in the waterside villages in the north of Zhejiang Province. There are many old houses built between the late Qing Dynasty and the beginning of the Republic of China.

A great many famous scenic spots are scattered around Wuzhen. In the east of this town lies a Chinese-style **academy**, Lizhi Academy, where Mao Dun (Mr. Shen Yanbing, a noted writer) once studied in his teenage and now it is kept as Mao Dun **Memorial**, a major national **heritage** protection site. The Xizha Ancient Street is one of the best preserved building complexes built in the Ming and Qing dynasties. In 1991, Wuzhen was listed as one of Zhejiang's provincial historical and cultural towns and a national AAAA level scenic spot.

One thousand years of history and culture, simple beauty of landscapes, unique flavor of gourmet food, colorful folk festivals, profound humanity accumulation and constant way of life of people make Wuzhen a living fossil of ancient oriental civilization.

★生词与词组 Words & Expressions

academy /ə'kædəmi/ *n.* 学术，学院

memorial /mi'mɔːriəl/ *n.* 纪念碑

heritage /'heritidʒ/ *n.* 遗产，继承物

◆ 知识拓展 Knowledge Extension

昭明太子(501—531)：即萧统，字德施，南朝梁代文学家。梁武帝长子，死后谥"昭明"，故世称昭明太子。他编纂了中国现存最早的一部诗文总集——《文选》(《昭明文选》)，很多梁代以前的文学作品赖此得以保存。由于他与其父亲对佛教教义流通的贡献，禅宗寺庙时常以梁武帝与昭明太子父子合祀为护法神。

12. 西塘 Xitang

古镇西塘与其他五个中国江南古镇被列入了"江南水乡古镇"的名下，被选入世界遗产预备名单中。西塘古镇浓缩了中国古典江南水乡风情的特色，散发着静谧古朴的韵味。

西塘悠远的历史，从古镇独有的墨色和具有明清风格的古建筑群可见一斑。古镇的发展经历了从元代以集镇为特色到明清以商业为主，直至形成现有的格局的过程。廊棚、古桥和小弄是古镇的一大特色，也是最能吸引游客的景观。廊棚据说是旧时商人们的创意，随时间流淌其实用功能未减，审美价值凸显，因而成为镇上抢眼的一道风景线。

西塘有著名的五福桥、卧龙桥、来凤桥等。它们大多保持了宋、明、清的风格，桥梁工艺精湛，大都为单孔或三孔石柱木梁桥，自古被誉为"卧龙凌波，彩虹飞架"，目前保存完好的桥有 14 座。

曲径通幽的小弄与深宅大院相连，极能反映出古代大户人家的生活环境。这里的人们"以暗为安"，一条条的弄堂里，好几户人家都在宅弄里进出。最有名的一处特色景观是石皮弄，顾名思义，这个弄堂以石为材建成，所用的石板厚度都不过 3 厘米，长 68 米，最宽处不过 1.2 米。如今踏入小弄，说不定还有眼福看到主人的种种收藏呢。

Ancient Xitang Town, together with five other southern Chinese towns, is listed as one of the "Ancient Towns of Jiangnan", and has become a member of the preparatory World Heritage list. The tourists can experience the typical local living environment and customs of the towns of rivers and lakes, as well as the flavor of quietness.

Xitang's unique **pitch-black** and ancient buildings of the Ming and Qing style witness the long history of this place. The present pattern dates from the Qing Dynasty. Before that it had been first featured with a market town in the Yuan Dynasty and then with business in the Ming and Qing dynasties, and then it has developed into the town today. The outstanding attractions here are the streets with ceilings, ancient bridges and little alleys. Lang Peng, the streets with ceilings, created by the businessmen in the ancient times, are still in good condition, and remain a strong attraction because of their eye-catching aesthetic value.

Xitang boasts its many old famous bridges, such as the Wufu Bridge, the Wolong Bridge, and the Laifeng Bridge. Many bridges here are remained in the style of the Song, Ming and Qing dynasties, with **exquisite workmanship**. The bridges are mostly single-holed or three-holed wooden beam bridges, with stone pillars and wooden beams, well-known for being like "dragons lying on the waves and rainbows in the sky". There are still 14 well-preserved bridges up to now.

The winding little alleys, of which you even do not know the depth, are connected to the very large courtyards. This kind of layout reveals the exact ancient people's living environment, and was considered safe for its darkness in the ancient Chinese culture. (Darkness and safety are both pronounced as /an/ in Chinese). It was often like this—several lanes form a unit where several families live in and share the entrances and exits. The most famous landscape of the alleys is the 68-meter-long "Stone Alley". It gets the name because it is covered with pieces of stone with thickness of only three centimeters. The Stone Alley is only 1.2 meters at its widest point. At present, if you are lucky enough you may get a look at those valuables of the owners when walking through the alleys.

★生词与词组 Words & Expressions

pitch-black /'pitʃblæk/ *adj.* 乌黑的
workmanship /'wəːkmənʃip/ *n.* 手艺，技巧

exquisite /ik'skwizit/ *adj.* 精致的

◆ 知识拓展 Knowledge Extension

廊棚：其实就是带屋顶的街。西塘的廊棚有的濒河，有的居中，沿河一侧有的还设有靠背长凳，供人歇息，廊棚的顶有"一落水"，有"二落水"，也有过街楼形成廊棚的屋顶，虽然不同但都可以使商界贸易、行人过往免受日晒雨淋之苦。

13. 仙华山景区 Mount Xianhua Scenic Area

仙华山又名仙姑山，相传因轩辕黄帝少女元修在此修真得道升天而得名。主峰少女峰，海拔 720.8 米。整个景区山势峻伟，峰峦峭秀，迤逦连绵，美不胜收，共有奇峰 24 座，怪石异洞 14 个，大小景点 120 多处。明刘伯温有诗云："仙华杰出最怪异，望之如云浮太空。"故仙华山又有"第一仙峰"之称。仙华山景区现分为四个部分：北为石峰林立、怪石纷呈的"仙华峰林"景区；南有梅香数里的"梅坞香雪"景区；东为千岁宝掌和尚修行之地"宝掌幽谷"景区；西有山环水抱的"仙湖碧水"景区。如画似梦的自然风光与古老美丽的传说这两种巧妙的组合，使得仙华山"江南第一仙山"的美誉实至名归。

仙华山以奇、秀、险的山巅峰林为胜，多狭长、险峻的山峰峡谷。24 座奇峰中，轩辕少

女升天处——少女峰峰高形奇，顶有坪台，仙华八景之一的"华柱丹光"即此。玉尺峰，又称中峰，此峰陡壁如削，游人罕登，仙华八景之一的"中峰啸月"即此。而玉尺峰和玉圭峰对峙而立，如两把利刃直刺天穹。两山间距仅仅数米，最窄处仅一米有余，建有石门，题有"天门""广云路""广神游"字样。另外，玉尺峰的岩崖上有一个天然的反向太极图，阴阳分明，清晰生动，造就一处大自然的杰作。

岩洞又是仙华山一绝，通海洞和清虚洞是其中精华所在。清虚洞又名织绢洞，相传是昔日轩辕少女织绢所在地。洞内有泉一泓，入口清甜，被村民称为"仙水"。洞口崖际有康熙十二年(1673)洞名题刻。洞前筑有"九霄亭"。登九霄亭，可见一村郭阡陌，村子四面环山，如一个圆盆坐落在仙华山脚下。而通海洞深不可测，无人知道洞源所在何处，入洞清凉，传说洞风来自神秘海滨，"通海"之名神秘如斯。五峰西下是昭灵岩，崖壁高100多米，长400多米，蹲踞盘结，南北峻峭，岩脊上多奇石苍松，错落怪异。

Also named Mount Xiangu (female immortal), Mount Xianhua is renowned for the legend that Yuanxiu, the daughter of Xuanyuan, became fairy maiden here. And the highest peak is called Shaonü (young lady) Peak, with a height of 720.8 meters above sea level. The scenic spot has its magnificence with up to 24 sheer peaks, 14 **grotesque** caves and 120 viewing sights. "Mount Xianhua is worthy of the title of the most **bizarre** one, as it looks like a cloud flying in the sky", as described in the poem of Liu Bowen, the famous politician and writer of the Ming Dynasty. It consists of four parts: the north, the rocky hill-bristling "Xianhua Fenglin"; the south, the lush plum tree-blossoming "Meiwu Xiangxue"; the east, the Monk Baozhang cultivating land "Baozhang Valley"; and the west, the hills and water surrounded "Xianhu Bishui". With the beautiful legends perfectly combined with dreamland-like natural attractions, Mount Xianhua deserves its reputation, the No.1 fairy mountain.

Mount Xianhua is famous for the bizarre, beautiful and sharp peaks, among which most sit on long and narrow steep valleys. Among the 24 sheer peaks, the Shaonü Peak, where the Lady Xuanyuan Yuanxiu became an immortal has a flat roof on the top, which is one of the Top Eight Views of Mount Xianhua, called "Huazhu Danguang" (gorgeous post and red sunglow). The Yuchi Peak, also called Middle Peak, is infrequently traversed by the tourists due to its precipitous cliffs, which is also one of the top eight views, "Zhongfeng Xiaoyue" (Middle Peak Screaming at the Moon). The Yuchi Peak and the Yugui Peak stand against each other, which look like a pair of sharp blades pricking into the sky. The stone gate was formed on the narrowest space between the two peaks, about just one meter, marked "Sky Gate", "Guangyun Road (Vast Cloud Road)" and "Guangshen You (Carefree Tour)". Besides, there is a nature-formed vivid picturesque image of a reversed Taiji diagram with a clear distinction of Yin and Yang on the cliff of the Yuchi Peak, which is a masterpiece of the great nature.

Being a must of Mount Xianhua, stone caves have their most representative demonstration in Qingxu Cave and Tonghai Cave. Also called Zhijuan (weaving silk) Cave, Qingxu Cave is the place where Lady Xuanyuan weaved, as legend implies. Inside there is a sweet-taste spring, called "Holly Water" by the local villagers. And Emperor Kangxi had inscribed its name in the front of the cave in 1673. Stepping on the Jiuqiao Pavilion at the entrance of the cave, tourists can see a village surrounded by hills, just like a round **salver** sitting on the foot of Mount Xianhua. While Tonghai Cave is specially featured by its deep and mysterious depth—no one really knows where its end is. It is chilly inside the cave, and according to the legend, the breeze in the cave comes from a mysterious place, as comes the name. Going down the Five-Peak Rock to the west is Zhaoling Rock. With a height of over 100 meters and a length of up to 400 meters, the rock crouches steadily on the earth, on which are dotted with oddly shaped rocks and lush pines.

★生词与词组 Words & Expressions

grotesque /grəʊ'tesk/ *adj.* 奇形怪状的　　　　　　bizarre /bɪ'zɑː(r)/ *adj.* 奇异的
salver /'sælvə/ *n.* 托盘，盘子

◆ 知识拓展 Knowledge Extension

千岁宝掌和尚(? —657)：中印度人，因出生时，左手握拳，至七岁剃发始展掌，故取名宝掌。据传魏晋间东游中土，入蜀地参礼普贤。唐贞观十五年(641)，高僧宝掌禅师云游至今仙华山，建宝掌寺，临寂殁时自称活了1072岁，号称"千岁和尚"，又称"千岁宝掌"。

14. 盐官古镇　The Ancient Town of Yanguan

盐官镇是浙江省首批的十五个历史文化名镇之一，以其悠久的历史、灿烂的民俗文化、动人的民间传说和壮观的海宁大潮闻名于世。

盐官始建于西汉，原为海宁州州府，因吴王刘濞煮海为盐，在此设司盐之官而得名。在唐朝，盐官就以其发达的经济和盛行的宗教而名扬海内，是当时全国著名的三个繁荣县市之一。明清时期，由于"海宁陈家"疑案的出现，更使盐官名声显赫。民国首任总理唐绍仪甚至想把盐官定为国都，我们从中可以想象当年之繁华景象。

盐官镇处于钱塘江入海口的咽喉，一直是两浙的交通孔道，是重要物资集散地，城市经济自古繁荣。经济的繁荣也促进了文化的发展，使盐官人才辈出，仅清朝陈家就出现了"一门三人四阁老，六部五人七尚书"的奇迹。此外明代的戏曲家陈与郊、享誉海外的著名国学大师王国维、著名文学家陈学昭等都是盐官人，城内众多的名人故居更为之增添了风采。

名胜古迹众多是盐官的最大特色，除著名的海宁潮外，被列为省、市级以上的文物保护单位就达十余处，故有袖珍式历史名城之称。从规模宏大的海神庙到富有神秘色彩的镇海铁牛，从雕镂精细的汉白玉石狮到精巧多姿的唐代建筑，都为盐官增添了古朴、独特的风格。

The Ancient Town of Yanguan is world-famous for its long history, splendid folk culture and fairy tales, especially for its Haining surging tides. It is one of the first batch of approved 15 historical and cultural towns in Zhejiang Province.

The Ancient Town of Yanguan, established in the Western Han Dynasty, is where Haining Prefecture was originally located, which gained the name because the King of Wu, Liu Bi, boiled sea water for salt and assigned the officer of the Salt Division here. In the Tang Dynasty, Yanguan became famous at home and abroad because of its developed economy and **prevailing** religion as one of the three most **prosperous** cities and counties. It had an excellent reputation in the Ming and Qing dynasties for the doubtful case of "Haining's Chen Family". The first Prime Minister Tang Shaoyi of the Republic of China even wanted to transfer Yanguan into the capital of the country, from which we can imagine the prosperity of this place.

The Town of Yanguan is at the mouth of the Qiantang River estuary. It was once a vital communication line and very important commodity distribution center of North and South Zhejiang, and its prosperous economy has been like this for a long time. Economic prosperity promotes Yanguan's cultural development and cultivated many talented people to appear. Out of the Chen families in the Qing Dynasty, three persons once worked as cabinet members, and five persons worked in six ministry departments and took up seven ministers. The political achievements they made is like a miracle in most people's eyes. In addition, the great opera writer Chen Yujiao of the Ming Dynasty, the contemporary famous master of Sinology Wang Guowei and the famous writer Chen Xuezhao are all from Yanguan. All the former residences of celebrities have also lent charm to the town.

That there are many places of interest is the most **prominent** feature of Yanguan. In addition to the well-known Haining Tide, there are more than ten places listed as provincial or municipal conservation sites, so it is known as a pocket-like historic town. All the scenic spots, such as the large-scale Temple for Sea God, the **miraculous** Iron Ox used as the sea guard, the well-carved Marble Lions and the delicate buildings of the Tang Dynasty, give the Town of Yanguan a style of ancientness and uniqueness.

★生词与词组 Words & Expressions

prevailing /pri'veiliŋ/ *adj.* 流行很广的

prominent /'prɔminənt/ *adj.* 显著的

prosperous /'prɔsp(ə)rəs/ *adj.* 繁荣的，兴旺的

miraculous /mi'rækjuləs/ *adj.* 不可思议的

◆ 知识拓展 Knowledge Extension

吴王刘濞(bì)(前216—前154)：西汉诸侯王，汉高祖刘邦之侄，性情极为剽悍勇猛且有野心，在其封国内大量铸钱、煮盐，并招纳工商和"任侠奸人"，以扩张割据势力，图谋篡夺帝位。后被汉军击败，被杀，封国被中央废除。

尚书：最初是掌管文书奏章的官员。隋代始设六部，唐代确定六部为吏、户、礼、兵、刑、工，各部以尚书、侍郎为正副长官。

15. 诸葛八卦村 Zhuge Bagua Village / Zhuge Eight Diagrams Village

唐末五代时期，诸葛氏后裔为避中原战乱，开始南迁。到元朝中叶(1280)，第27世诸

葛大师以重金购地于兰溪高隆岗，以九宫八卦阵建村。到明代后半叶，已形成一个建筑独特、人口众多、规模庞大的村落，现居有诸葛亮后裔近4000人，是全国最大的诸葛亮后裔聚居地。

诸葛八卦村整个村落采用"九宫八卦"的形状修葺，以钟池为核心，向外辐射八条小巷，似连非连，曲折玄妙，俗称"内八卦"，而村外八座小山环抱村落，形成天然的"外八卦"。这种隐秘性与防御性兼具的设计使得整个村落千古流传，披上了浓厚的神秘面纱。

诸葛镇不仅布局奇特，镇中古民居也非常罕见。村内地形跌宕起伏，弄堂之间千门万户；古建筑群布局合理，错落有致；建筑雕刻工艺精湛，其"青砖、灰瓦、马头墙，肥梁、胖柱、小闺房"的建筑风格千年传承，全村形成了一个变化丰富而统一的整体。专家学者们称其为"江南传统古村落、古民居典范"。建筑群中最具代表性的是镇中的祠堂建筑。现存的大公堂、丞相祠堂是其中的佼佼者。

大公堂始建于明代，位于钟池北侧。大公堂前后五进，可容千人举行活动。至今堂内还珍藏着《诸葛氏宗谱》和《高隆八景图》两部重要的祖籍文献，对研究诸葛家族的变迁有重要意义。大公堂黑柱朱楣，飞檐拱斗，建筑用材十分讲究。其门庭飞阁重檐，高约10米，上悬一块横匾"敕旌尚义之门"。顶层有明英宗于正统四年(1439)所赐盘龙圣旨立匾一方，表彰诸葛彦祥赈灾捐谷千余石的义举。门两旁分书斗大的"忠""武"二字。

丞相祠堂是为纪念"武乡侯"诸葛亮而修建，与大公堂相距百米，是整个诸葛家族祭祖的祠堂，始建于明万历年间。丞相祠坐东朝西，平面按"回"字形布局，古朴浑厚，气势非凡。中庭是祠堂最精彩的部分，五开间，歇山顶敞厅，檐柱和山柱都是青石方柱，总共44根。中间四根合抱大柱，分别用柏木、梓木、桐木和椿木，谐音"百子同春"，祈求家族世代兴旺。中庭两边庑廊各七间，从庑廊拾级而上，两旁分列钟、鼓二楼。祠堂最后是享堂，中塑诸葛亮像，高2米余，两侧分侍诸葛瞻、诸葛尚及关兴、张苞像，气韵生动。

诸葛八卦村融合了"皖南徽派的建筑""浙江的房间格局""苏州的砖瓦门楼"，各个时期的古建筑错落分布于镇中的每个角落。像这样布局奇、规模大、年代早、数量多、种类繁、建筑精、保存好的江南古民居群落，具有极高的历史和科研价值。

In the late Tang Dynasty, the Zhuges migrated to the south to stay away from the **scourge** of war. In 1280 (the mid Yuan Dynasty), the 27th generation of Zhuge paid a lot for the land of Gaolonggang, Lanxi, and deployed the houses into the Eight Diagrams (Bagua, eight combinations of three whole or broken lines formerly used in divination Bagua) style. It has developed into a specially constructed, densely populated large-scale village in the late Ming Dynasty, now resided with about 4,000 descendents of Zhuge Liang, the Prime Minister of Shu Han during the Three Kingdoms, known as the largest populated community of Zhuge's descendents.

The whole village **radiates** from the centre of Zhong Pool with eight **occult** alleys full of twists and turns, which are called "The Inner Bagua"; and there are eight hills surrounding the village, being a natural "Outer Bagua". The obscurity and defensibility in design has been passed down over thousands of years, veiling the village with mysterious **tinges**.

Not only the layout is peculiar, but also its residences are exotic. Inside the village, the landform is full of bumps and holes; **innumerable** families living in alleys; the ancient building complex is logically outlined; the exquisite workmanship has been handed down through thousands of years under the surface of blue bricks, grey tiles, and standing walls. The village is called "model of traditional ancient residences in Jiangnan" by experts. The ancestral halls do the most representing work among the building complex, with the most famous two, Dagong Hall and Prime Minister's Ancestral Hall.

Located in the north of the Zhong Pool, the Dagong Hall was built in the Ming Dynasty. With five rows respectively at the front and back sides, the hall could bear over a thousand people in it. The ancestral documents "Zhuge's **Genealogy**" and "Eight Views of Gaolong" treasured up in the hall bear great significance of studying Zhuge's **vicissitude**. The hall is made up with black pillar and red lintel, particularly choosy in constructing materials. In the projecting part of the cornice, about 10 meters high, hangs a horizontal inscribed board noted "Gate of Loyalty". In the top floor there hangs a plague granted by Emperor Yingzong of the Ming Dynasty in 1439 (4th year of Zhengtong reign), to give praise to Zhuge Yanxiang's **altruistic** act of donating grain for disaster-striken area. Aside the gate, the Chinese "Loyalty" and "Valiancy" are inscribed respectively.

Prime Minister's Ancestral Hall was built in memorial of Zhuge Liang during the Wanli reign of the Ming Dynasty, being a hundred meters apart from Dagong Hall. It is the place for sacrificial activities of the Zhuges. Oriented south and north, it's laid out in accordance with concentric circles, **exuberating** the grand and vigorous manners. The best part of the building is the Middle Hall: about fifteen meters in width, open hall, four blue-colored square stone pillars. The four surrounding pillars are made by 44 different trees of cypress, catalpa, paulownia and Chinese toon, and the names of the trees combined together sound like "Bai Zi Tong Chun", which means "living with **posterities** of generation". Each side of the Middle Hall has seven wing-rooms. Stepping up from here, the bell tower and the drum tower sit on the opposite side. Deep inside the Middle Hall, there is a 2-meter-high vivid statue of Zhuge Liang, standing alongside with statues of Zhuge Zhan, Zhuge Shang, Guanxing and Zhangbao.

Integrated with "architecture of Huizhou style", "separating room-arrangement of Zhejiang" and "bricks and tiles style of Jiangsu", the village has diverse buildings from every time randomly distributed into every inch. Such well-reserved ecotone with peculiar layout, diversification and large scale bears great value in the study of history and scientific research.

★生词与词组 Words & Expressions

scourge /skə:dʒ/ *n.* 祸害
occult / ə'kʌlt/ *adj.* 隐秘的，秘密的
innumerable /i'nju:mərəbl/ *adj.* 无数的
vicissitude /vi'sisitju:d/ *n.* 变迁
exuberate /ig'zju:bəreit/ *v.* 充满

radiate /'reidieit/ *v.* 射出，向四周伸出
tinge /tindʒ/ *n.* 色彩
genealogy /ˌdʒi:ni'ælədʒi/ *n.* 系谱，宗谱
altruistic /ˌæltru'istik/ *adj.* 利他的，无私心的
posterity /pɔ'steriti/ *n.* 子孙；后裔

◆ *知识拓展* **Knowledge Extension**

八卦：我国古代的一套有象征意义的符号。用"—"代表阳，用"- -"代表阴，用三个这样的符号，组成八种形式，叫作八卦。每一卦形代表一定的事物。乾代表天，坤代表地，坎代表水，离代表火，震代表雷，艮代表山，巽代表风，兑代表泽。八卦互相搭配又得到六十四卦，用来象征各种自然现象和人事现象。

第二节　旅游文化——建筑文化

Section 2　Tourism Culture—Architectural Culture

建筑是一种物质载体，同时，它也展示着一个民族的哲学思想和伦理观念。中国传统建筑文化不仅反映了建筑的使用功能，而且还蕴含着浓郁的亲缘感情、尊卑意识等文化的内涵。中国传统建筑所折射的文化哲学思想和道德伦理理念如下。

Architecture is a physical carrier showing a nation's philosophy and ethics. Traditional Chinese architectural culture not only reflects the function of buildings in use, but also contains strong feelings of kinship, consciousness of superiority and inferiority, and other cultural connotations. Generally, Chinese traditional architecture reflects the cultural and philosophical ideas and the **ethical** philosophy is as the followings.

1. 群体的和谐性 Compatibility among Groups

有人认为，"间"是中国传统建筑平面布局的基本单位，由"间"而围合成庭院，进而由庭院组合成各种建筑群体。这种布局体系在民居、坊里、街巷、宫殿以及城市中都得到了体现。中国传统建筑多体现了严谨的"中轴"理念，各建筑在层层扩大、左右延展中呈现出和谐对称的态势。这就使得建筑布局处处体现出井井有条的秩序感和对称整齐的和谐性。

Some people think that the basic unit in the layout of traditional Chinese architecture is "Jian", a number of which are encircled into a courtyard and then courtyards into varieties of architectural groups. This composition concept is implied in the residences, lanes, streets, palaces and cities. Chinese traditional architecture embodies the concept of "axis", around which layers of buildings expand to the right and the left in a harmonious and symmetrical way. This keeps the architectural layout compatible, symmetrical and well-organized.

2. 组合的内向性 Introversion in Composition

以四合院为例，其住宅布局就以内向的房屋合围成封闭的院落，房屋对外的立面大多不开设窗户，仅有大门对外，从而使整个院落独立成一个小世界。小世界内，空间完整统一，气聚而不散，既同外界隔绝又适应了古代尊卑、长幼、男女、内外有别的礼法要求。四合院的形制独立于外部世界，内部却自成体系，折射出中华民族心理的内敛性和向心力。

For example, Siheyuan is a closed area made of inward-facing houses and rooms, with no windows on the outward-facing facades, except the front door. This makes the whole courtyard into a small world, inside which space is unitary and closed with no dispersing, both separating the courtyard from the outside world and adapting to the ancient etiquette requirements of differentiating noble and humble, young and old, men and women, internal and external areas. The pattern of Siheyuan makes it independent of the outside world but self-contained inside the courtyard, reflecting the Chinese nation's psychological characteristic of introversion and centripetal force.

3. 阴阳的融合性 Syncretism of Yin and Yang

受"阴阳合德"及"中和"思想的影响，中国古代建筑在体量和尺度上十分注意"适形而止"，不追求过分高大。中国传统建筑之宫殿，屋顶面积很大，屋檐宽，坚实的立柱将屋顶托起，整体上就呈现出阳刚之美。而立柱与屋顶之间则设置了巧妙的斗拱，在柱头上层层叠加，不仅减少了梁柱交接部的剪力，而且还形成了奇妙的韵律感。斗拱与屋顶向上向外夸张地卷起的飞檐翘角，形成飞动、轻巧、跳跃的阴柔美。大屋顶和立柱的阳刚，斗拱和飞檐翘角的阴柔，构成了阴阳融合、刚柔相济的造型。

Affected by the idea of "Yin and Yang integrated" and "Zhong He", the Chinese ancient buildings are "moderate and limited" in the shape and scale, which are not too tall or large. Chinese traditional palaces show a masculine beauty because of its large roof, wide eaves and solid columns holding up the roof. Between the columns and roofs brackets are set up cleverly, superimposed layer on layer in the stigmas, not only reducing the shearing force between the columns and the beams, but also creating a wonderful sense of rhythm. On the other hand, the cocked eaves with brackets and roofs literally rolled up outward show a feminine beauty because of the sense of flying, jumping and lightweight. The masculinity of large roofs and columns combines properly with the feminine beauty of brackets and the flying eaves and cocked angles, forming a picture of integration of Yin and Yang and combination of hardness and softness.

第三节 景点讲解技能——虚实结合法

Section 3　Narration Tactics of Scenic Spots—Combination of Landscape and Stories

虚实结合法是指在导游讲解过程中将典故、传说与景物介绍有机结合。虚实结合技巧中的"实"是指景观的实体、实物、史实、艺术价值等客观事实，而"虚"则是指与景观有关的民间传说、神话故事、趣闻轶事等艺术构造。在讲解中"虚"与"实"必须有机结合，以"实"为主，以"虚"为辅。"虚"为"实"服务，以"虚"烘托情节，以"虚"加深"实"的存在，努力将单调的景物变成有意义的符号。当然，导游人员在讲解时选择"虚"的内容要"精"，要"活"。所谓"精"，就是所选传说是精华，与讲解的景观密切相关；所谓"活"，就是使用时要活，见景而用，即兴而发。不同类型景观解读的侧重点也会有所差异，我们将结合自然景观和人文景观这两大类来讲解虚实结合的导游讲解技巧。

1. 自然景观的虚实结合　Combination of Natural Landscape and Stories

自然景观的讲解是一个渐进的过程。在讲解自然景观时，导游人员不能脱离对景观本身具体特征的把握，必须时刻注意景观自然美和人文美的双重结合。在讲解景观的自然美时，导游可以通过视觉美、听觉美、嗅觉美、味觉美等表现形式，在色彩、声音，线条等方面进行介绍，给人以感官上的愉悦和心灵上的惬意。但由于不同游客自身条件的差异，以及对景观的深层次了解和文化内涵延伸度的不同，导游必须在客观、真实描述景物外在美的同时，适时加入人文背景和文化内涵的讲解，避免讲解过于平淡刻板、言而无物。

以杭州西湖为例："杭州西湖地处浙江省杭州市西部，位于杭州市市中心，旧称武林水、钱塘湖、西子湖等，宋代始称西湖。西湖风景区以西湖为中心，分为湖滨区、湖心区、北山区、南山区和钱塘区五个地区，总面积 49 平方千米。整个景区绿荫环抱，山色葱茏……"这样的景点介绍虽然是就事论事，但却平淡无味、单调枯燥、流于形式，丝毫不能引起游客的兴趣和共鸣。但是如果导游在讲解西湖时，不断加入"白娘子和许仙在断桥上'千年等一回'的故事"，或"东坡肉"的来历等故事，效果就会截然不同。

2. 人文景观的虚实结合　Combination of Cultural Landscape and Stories

人文景观的讲解离不开对实物具体特征的把握，主要包括布局、功能、造型、质地、文饰、色彩以及与之相关的匾额楹联等方面的解读。相对于自然景观而言，人文景观与社会生活有更加密切的联系，所以在介绍人文景观时不能脱离当时的历史背景孤立地去欣赏它们。人文景观往往承载着人类的文化，表现了人类各种文化内容，成为文化的凝聚、积累和表征。

正是靠着人文景观，才使相当一部分各时代各地区的文化得以保留和显现。因此，导游员在讲解人文景观时候，要在尊重科学和历史的前提下，穿针引线，将各种文化因素，如神话传说、奇闻趣事等很好地融入讲解当中，以求产生艺术感染力，使那些随着岁月渐渐消逝的因素能清晰生动地展现在游客的眼前。

以诸葛八卦村为例，导游在介绍诸葛八卦村地理位置、村落布局、历史渊源等客观事实的同时，加入诸葛亮"三顾茅庐""舌战群儒""草船借箭""白帝托孤"等历史故事的讲解，同时适当阐述八卦村布局的相关风水玄术："以钟池为中心，有八条小巷向四面八方延伸，直通村外八座高高的土岗，其平面酷似八卦图。小巷又派生出许许多多横向环连的窄弄堂。这些小巷纵横相连，似通非通，犹如迷宫一般。整个村落形成围绕一个中心呈放射状的九宫八卦形布局。"这些内容的介绍无疑就会激起游客极大的兴趣。诸葛亮的丰功伟绩，智勇双全和诸葛八卦村的诡秘悬疑很好地调动了游客的好奇心。

◆ **综合练习**

请运用所学的"虚实结合法"讲解技巧，小组练习用中英文讲解金华或嘉兴的某一景点及其相关的景点文化。

第四节　建筑文化翻译技巧——汉语分句的翻译技巧

Section 4　Translation Skills of Architectural Culture

—Translation Skills of Chinese Clauses

汉语句子根据其复杂程度可以分为单句和复句。单句是只含有一套主谓宾定状补句子成分的句子；复句是由两个或两个以上的单句组成的句子。组成复句的单句往往称为分句，分句是单句，同时又不能与复句中其他分句密切关联。在复句的背景中，分句才具有了其全部含义。

准确识别汉语分句　Correct Distinguishing of Chinese Clauses

首先需要认识清楚的是，汉语句子的单句或复句的认定，不是看句子的长短或字的多少，关键在于正确划分句子的成分。汉语复句中分句之间往往存在一定的逻辑关系，并借助一定的关联词体现。所以，把握住关联词通常是认识汉语分句的关键所在。汉语复句中常用的关联词根据其体现的逻辑关系可以分为如下类别。

1.1 并列关系

体现并列关系的关联词通常有：也，还，又，既……又……，一边……一边，一方面……另一方面，不是……而是……，等等。例如：

到了晚上，在天风海涛亭一带，既可赏月又可观赏十万军声半夜潮。

In the evening at the Haitao Pavilion people can appreciate the moon and watch the mid-night wave with great roar.

1.2　递进关系

两个分句中，后一个分句表达的意思比前一个更进一层时，两个分句间为递进关系，常用到的关联词语有：更，而且，甚至，尤其，特别，何况，不但(不仅，不只，不光)……而且(并且，也，还，甚至)……，……尚且……，何况，等等。例如：

南湖不仅风景如画，而且还是中国共产党诞生的见证和象征，是"中共一大会址"的有机组成部分。

The South Lake is not only a sightseeing spot, but the witness and symbol of the Communist Party of China's coming into being, as well as an important part of the meeting places of the First National Congress.

1.3　选择关系

由两个或两个以上的有选择关系的分句组成。选择关系的复句分两种。一种是有取舍的选择，即对两种可能的情况有所取舍，常用的关联词有：是……而不是……，与其……不如……，宁可……也不……，等等。另一种是无取舍的选择，即只提供几种可能的情况，常用到的关联词有：或者……，或者……，或者……，也许……，等等。这几种可能性是相容的，并不相互排斥；有的结构中，两种可能性之间是不相容的，不能同时存在，常用到的关联词有：不是……就是……，要么……要么……，等等。例如：

这个景点拥有的是独特的文化遗产，而不是房子和树。

This attraction involved unique culture heritage, rather than buildings and trees.

1.4　转折关系

由两个有转折关系的分句组成。后一个分句的意思转到相反的意思上去，这样的复句中通常用到这些关联词：虽然(尽管，固然)……但是(可见，却)……，然而，不过，等等。例如：

然而，1937年，缘缘堂却毁于侵华日军的炮火中，悲愤至极的丰子恺在逃难途中写下了《还我缘缘堂》《告缘缘堂在天之灵》等檄文，痛斥日寇的暴行。

However, in 1937, the house was destroyed by a big fire in the Japanese invasion of China, because of which Feng Zikai was extremely indignant and wrote *Return Me My Yuanyuan House* and *Mourn for My Yuanyuan House* to denounce the Japanese atrocities on his way of fleeing from a calamity.

1.5　因果关系

由两个有因果关系的分句所组成，这类复句有两种类型。一种是说明因果关系，有的是前因后果，有的是由果溯因。常用的关联词有：因为，由于，所以，因此，因为(由于)……所以……，之所以……是因为……，等等。另一种是推论因果关系，前一个分句提出一个依据或前提，后一个分句表示有这个依据或前提可以推出的结论，一般用"既然……就……"等关联词来表示。例如：

由于嘉兴地处上海、杭州、苏州的中心，地理位置极其优越。

Since Jiaxing is the center of Shanghai, Hangzhou and Suzhou, it has become the backyard of these big cities.

1.6 假设关系

一般由两个有假设关系的分句组成，前一个分句假设存在或出现了某种情况，后一个分句说明有这种假设的情况产生的结果，常用的关联词有：如果，假设，假若，倘若，要是，等，并且常与"就"，"便"，"那么"等搭配使用。例如：

如果把西湖比作浓妆艳抹的窈窕情女，南北湖便是未施脂粉的纯真村姑。

If the West Lake is compared to a beauty made up quite much, the Nanbei Lake is a pure and simple country girl without any make-up.

1.7 条件关系

前一个分句提出条件，后一个分句说明在这种条件下产生的结果是，这样的复句关系称为条件关系，其中常用到的关联词有：只要，只有，除非，等等，他们常会和"就"，"便"，"才"等搭配使用。例如：

市民只需出示身份证就可以免费参观爱国主义景点。

On presentation of one's own identification card, the citizens may visit the patriotism attractions for free.

◆ 课后练习 Exercises

把下面的段落翻译成英语(Put the following Chinese paragraph into English)

茅盾故居主体是四开间两进深的二层楼房，共 16 间，面积 414.25 平方米。另外楼房后有小园，有平房三间，近 100 平方米。这所楼房东西两个单元购进时间有先后，东单元称"老屋"，西单元称"新屋"。两单元外貌一样，前后两进，楼上楼下都门、路相通，浑然一体。茅盾故居建立后曾设 7 间陈列室，陈列茅盾的 150 幅照片和反映他的生平及业绩的实物。故居共有珍藏品 276 件，茅盾照片 400 余件，当代名家的书画 200 余件。这些文物近年已移至立志书院展出。

第六章　湖州景域

Chapter Six　Huzhou Scenic Zone

第一节　旅游景点

Section 1　Scenic Spots

1. 安吉竹博园 Anji Bamboo Museum

安吉是中国第一竹乡。安吉竹博园是竹乡旅游的经典之作，王牌景点。到竹博园游览，可以一览世界各国的奇篁异筠，洞悉千载的竹子加工利用史。清风摇曳，竹影婆娑，占地80万平方米的园内，遍植约389种竹子。置身其间，仿佛走进竹的海洋，它们有的伟岸凌空，有的低矮匍匐；有的细如棒针，有的叶大如帛；有的色彩斑斓，有的古怪扭曲。

秋冬观竹，可观竹的形态，观竹竿的颜色和形状，观竹叶形。而春夏之际观看竹笋，则更是兴趣盎然。且不说笋壳呈黑绿色的乌芽笋、紫红色的金竹、青色的四季竹、花色的角竹，也不说形如红缨枪的枪刀竹、甜的甜笋、苦的苦竹，单说那哺鸡竹和黄甜竹，就让人瞧上半天了。

这里除了安吉的乡土竹种45种外，还聚集了从福建、江西、广东、北京等全国17个省市的移植引种，更有与泰国、美国、日本等各国交流的一些竹种，成为世界上规模最大，品种最齐全的竹子王国，被誉为"竹类大观园"。每个竹种都有自己的一块园地，片片竹林汇成了一片大竹海，我们徜徉其中，仿佛进入了竹的海洋、竹的世界。

中国竹子博物馆是 6000 年竹文化的浓缩，是中国一流、世界领先的竹子专业博物馆。全馆占地 12000 平方米，分历史厅、资源栽培厅、文学艺术厅、工艺集萃厅、国际陈列厅等八个展厅。竹编《清明上河图》《兰亭序》，以及世界最粗最大的巨龙竹、实心的古里竹等都在此陈列。博物馆以丰富的展品和翔实的史料，介绍了中国丰富的竹资源、悠久的竹历史和光辉灿烂的竹文化。

Anji is the hometown of Chinese bamboo and its bamboo museum is the best scenic spot in the bamboo hometown. Here you can enjoy various kinds of bamboos in the world as well as the colorful history and application of bamboo. Within an area of 800,000 square meters, there are about 389 bamboo species. It forms a sea of bamboo: some are straight and high; some are bent and low; some are with huge leaves; some are of various colors; some are odd and twisty.

In autumn and winter, you can observe the shape and color of bamboo; while in spring and summer, you can enjoy the **bamboo shoots**. You will be **dazzled** at the variety of the bamboos such as dark-green Wuya bamboo shoot, green Siji bamboo, colorful Jiao bamboo, sweet bamboo, bitter bamboo, etc.

Apart from the 45 native bamboo species, other species are **transplanted** and introduced from 17 provinces and cities of Fujian, Jiangxi, Guangdong, Beijing, etc. Some bamboo species are also exchanged with those from foreign countries such as Thailand, America, Japan, etc. It becomes the biggest kingdom of bamboo in the world. Every species has its own field, and various fields form a sea of bamboo.

The Bamboo museum, with the **essential** of 6,000 years' bamboo culture, is the best special bamboo museum in China and among the leading ones in the world. With an area of 12,000 square meters, it includes eight halls, namely History Hall, Cultivation Hall, Literature and Art Hall, Craftsmanship Hall, International Exhibition Hall, etc. Here the famous painting of "**Riverside Scene at Qingming Festival**" and famous calligraphy of "**The Preface to Orchid Pavilion**" are made on bamboo. With various exhibitions and **substantial** historical materials, the museum introduces plenty of bamboo resources, long bamboo history and **glorious** bamboo culture.

★生词与词组 Words & Expressions

dazzle /'dæz(ə)l/ v. 使惊讶
essential /i'senʃ(ə)l/ n. 精华
glorious /'glɔːriəs/ adj. 光荣的
The Preface to Orchid Pavilion 《兰亭序》

transplant /træns'plɑːnt/ v. 移植
substantial /səb'stænʃl/ adj. 大量的
Riverside Scene at Qingming Festival 《清明上河图》
bamboo shots 竹笋

◆ 知识拓展 Knowledge Extension

孟宗哭竹：三国时候，吴国有个孝子，姓孟名宗，字恭武。很小的时候，他的父亲便去世了。从此，母子俩相依为命。孟宗一直很孝顺他的母亲，对母亲侍奉有加。母亲年纪渐渐大了。有一次，母亲病得很厉害，很想吃鲜笋做的汤，但这时都快冬至了，天很冷，哪里还会有笋长出来啊。孟宗心里焦急万分，可是束手无策，便忍不住跑到竹林里。他双手抱着毛竹，想着卧床的老母，不禁两行泪簌簌往下落，孟宗越想越难过，竟大声哭了起来。或许是他的一番孝心感动了天地，突然间，眼泪滴落的地方裂开了，从地上露出了几茎竹笋，孟宗看了破涕而笑，抹掉脸上的泪珠，兴高采烈地把这些竹笋带回家去。他做竹笋汤给母亲吃，母亲吃了新鲜味美的汤后，疾病居然立刻就好了。孟宗的一片孝心都感动了天地。

2. 百间楼 Hundred-Room Residence

百间楼是南浔至今为止保存得最为完整，并留有传统风貌的沿河居民群落，是南浔古街古镇的典型代表。百间楼全长 400 余米，距今已有 400 多年的历史，明朝中期始建于西南岸，在此后约 200 年时间中，东北岸也陆续建造起幢幢民宅。

百间楼相传是明代礼部尚书董份为他家的女性仆人居家而建，始建时约有楼房百间，故称"百间楼"。

百间楼的特色是依河立楼，顺河道蜿蜒逶迤，由石桥相连。楼房为传统的乌瓦粉墙，形成由轻巧通透的卷洞门组成的骑式长街。各楼之间有形式各异的封火山墙，有云墙，有包墙，有马头墙。河埠石阶，木柱廊檐，与映在河水中的倒影，连同隐约的渔歌，构成了一幅江南水上人家的绮丽画卷。

百间楼大宅三到四进，但大多数为只有一个天井的两进屋。小巧的天井，雕花的木窗，别致的砖雕，古朴的厢房，无不洋溢着江南水乡独特的神韵和灵气。石灰剥落的老墙上垂下几丝青藤，平添几分情趣，廊屋顶上摆着几盆花卉、盆果，与晒衣竿上晾着的衣服和谐地消融在氤氲而又古香古色的小楼氛围里。

尽管没有浮雕，也没有壁画，但从任何一个角度看去，百间楼都是一幅如诗如画、精巧绝妙的杰作。那是水墨画的韵味！

The Hundred-Room Residence is one of the riverside architectural **complexes** that has been preserved intact up to the present and is the most vivid **epitome** of the old streets and **dwelling** houses in Nanxun. It is more than 400 meters long with a history of over 400 years. The first house of the Hundred-Room Residence was built on the southwest bank of the river during the middle period of the Ming Dynasty. In the following 200 years, many dwelling houses were put up one after another on the northeast bank.

One **hearsay** is that it is the dwelling house built by Dong Fen, **the Minister of Rites** of the Ming Dynasty, for the women servants of his family. Altogether there are about one hundred rooms on the banks of the river; therefore it is called the Hundred-Room Residence.

One of the features of the Hundred-Room Building is that it was built along the river, and twisted and turned along the river course. The houses are connected with stone bridges. Covered with black tiles and white eaves, dwelling houses on either bank are **stringed** by a stretching street, looking at each other across the river. Walking along the river, we can meet towering area-separating walls standing one after another; some look like heaps of clouds and others are bag-shaped or horse-head-shaped. Those arched doorways, eave-covered corridors with pillars, stone steps stretching down the river bank, **wharves** and piers and all their **inverted** reflections in the river echo so nicely and harmoniously with the creak from the **oars** and the faint fishermen's singing in the distance, composing **scrolls** of **idyllic** wash paintings of the scenery typical in watery regions.

Some of the houses of the Hundred-Room Residence are in three to four lines while others have two lines of rooms and a dooryard. If you push open the gate, you will be greeted with an exquisite dooryard, **lattice** windows, distinctive brick carvings and wing-rooms with antique flavors. Several lianas come down from the old wall with lime flaking off, which is very interesting. The potted flowers and miniature trees on the roof, together with the clothes hanging on the rod, have been harmoniously combined into the scenery of the house, which is covered in an air of antiquity and elegance.

Although there are no relief sculptures or mural paintings, the Hundred-Room Residence with tier upon tier of houses looks picturesque and imposing from all angles. What a nice Chinese ink and wash painting it is!

★生词与词组 Words & Expressions

complex /'kɔmpleks/ n. 建筑群
dwelling /'dweliŋ/ n. 住宅
string /striŋ/ v. 用线串
inverted /in'və:t/ adj. 反向的；倒转的
scroll /skrəul/ n. 画卷
lattice /'lætis/ n. 格子框架

epitome /i'pitəmi/ n. 缩影；典型的人或事物
hearsay /'hiəsei/ n. 传闻
wharf /wɔ:rf/ n. 码头
oar /ɔ:/ n. 浆，橹
idyllic /i'dilik/ adj. 田园风光的
the Minister of Rites 礼部尚书

◆ 知识拓展 Knowledge Extension

董份(1510—1595)：字用均，号浔阳山人，又号泌园，浙江乌程县(今湖州)人。明嘉靖十六年(1537)举乡荐，二十年(1541)进士，改庶吉士，授翰林院编修，参与纂修会典。转右春坊右中允，管国子司业事。世宗斋居西宫时，钦点其为翰林学士，得乘骑出入宫廷之中，斋醮仪上"天神"表文多出其手。

3. 藏龙百瀑 Canglong Waterfalls

藏龙百瀑景区位于浙江省安吉县东南部，系天目山麓支脉。

藏龙百瀑是浙江最大的瀑布群，有三折重叠，落差为60多米的"长龙飞瀑"；有彩虹横卧的"虹贯龙门"(人称小黄果树)；更有神形皆备的"神龟听瀑"——真可谓瀑瀑相连，一步一景。藏龙百瀑不仅以瀑布众多而闻名，同时还有一块万吨巨石悬挂在两座悬崖之间，人称"仙人桥"，有千钧一发之险，还有望仙石、老鹰石、天生悬石，石石相望，形象逼真。俗话说深山藏宝，景区内有多种野生动物和近百种国家保护树种。夏天天气凉爽，宁静幽雅，有十里不打伞之奇，峡谷无蚊之妙；冬天百瀑冰凌，天造奇观，雪景迷人，堪称"江南哈尔滨"。从山顶俯瞰，只见一个山谷，口狭肚大，呈宝葫芦形，山谷之中有一村落，名为"藏龙山寨"。

藏龙百瀑景区内的藏龙山寨，村子不大，约300余人，建村历史不长，仅200年左右。据称，该村祖先均为太平军余部。藏龙百瀑地势之险以长龙山为最。19世纪中叶，忠王李秀成率领的太平军在长龙山上与清军战斗了4年多。

藏龙百瀑景区内物产丰富，尤以四大"仙物"闻名，其一谓"仙茶"，尤以"白茶王"闻名。其二谓"仙水"，山顶的藏龙山泉是天荒坪电站的唯一水源，也是上海人民的母亲河黄浦江的源头之一。其三谓"仙桃"，藏龙百瀑连绵的山核桃林上万亩，清朝时安吉山核桃被征为朝廷贡品。其四谓"仙药"，据查藏龙百瀑景区内有珍稀药材近百种，相传明代名医李时珍曾到此采药。

Canglong Waterfalls Scenic Spot belongs to one branch of the Tianmu Mountain.

It is the largest waterfall cluster in Zhejiang Province, including "Long Dragon Waterfall", a three **overlaps** and 60 meters fall, and the "Dragon Gate" and "Super Tortoise Listening to the Waterfall", etc. In addition to its famous waterfalls, it is also well-known for "Fairy Bridge", a huge stone of 10, 000 tons hanging between two cliffs. There are a lot of wild animals and nearly 100 tree species in the protection list of the country. In summer it is cool and quiet without any mosquitoes. In winter it is famous for its marvelous ice slush waterfalls and attractive snow scene, which has the reputation of "Harbin in Jiangnan". Overlooked from the top of the mountain, a **gourd-shaped** valley appears, in which there is a village named "Mount Canglong Village".

The village is not big, with 300 people and of 200 years history. It is said that the ancestors were the **Taiping Army**. It was a strategic place for troops because of its unique location. The Changlong Mountain is the steepest. In the middle of the 1800s, under the leadership of Li Xiucheng, Taiping troops fought against the Qing troops for more than 4 years.

Canglong Waterfalls Scenic Spot is abundant in products, especially famous for its "four immortal products": immortal tea, especially "King of White Tea"; immortal water, especially the Canglong Fountain on the top of the mountain, which is the sole source of Tianhuangping Hydroelectric Power Station and one of the sources of the Huangpu River in Shanghai; immortal **pecan**, with 10,000 mu area of pecan trees which were the best **tributes** of the Court in the Qing Dynasty; and immortal medicine, with 100 rare **medical herbs**, and it is said the the famous doctor Li Shizhen in the Ming Dynasty once collected medical herbs here.

★生词与词组 Words & Expressions

overlap /əuvə'læp/ *n.* 重叠
pecan /pi:kən/ *n.* 山核桃
Taiping Army　太平军

gourd-shaped /'guədʃeipt/ *adj.* 葫芦状的
tribute /'tribju:t/ *n.* 贡品
medical herb　药草

◆ 知识拓展 Knowledge Extension

长毛：此处指太平军。清朝统治者对太平天国军队的蔑称。因太平军反抗清政府剃发留辫的规定，一律蓄发，故称。

清妖：太平天国的宗教理论认为，世间人之所以有痛苦，是因为清朝统治者是地狱派来为害世间的妖魔，因此参加太平天国起义的人都称清朝为清妖。

4. 顾渚茶文化景区　The Guzhu Mountain Tea Culture Resort

顾渚山海拔 355 米，面积约 2 平方千米，属水口乡顾渚村。这里东临太湖，垂嶂叠岭，大涧中流，太湖水蒸气沿谷底蒸腾而上，具有天造地设的产茶条件。顾渚山是我国茶文化的发祥地，曾是茶仙陆羽研究茶道的主要场所，我国历史上的第一个贡茶院也诞生于此。这一切都可以凭"顾渚摩崖石刻"中颜真卿、张文规、杜牧、韩允寅等唐宋名人留下的大量石刻为证。

顾渚山特产紫笋茶，品质上乘，口味独特，闻名于世，在唐代还被列为贡品，专设贡茶院。顾渚山题刻和贡茶院遗址是研究茶种植业、制茶业和茶文化的珍贵资料。顾渚贡茶院位于长兴县顾渚山侧的虎头岩，始建于唐大历五年(770)，它是督造唐代贡茶顾渚紫笋茶的场所，也可以说是有史可稽的中国历史上首座茶叶加工场。

顾渚茶文化景区的主要景点有大唐贡茶院、寿圣寺、霸王潭等。寿圣寺始建于三国赤乌年间，距今已有 1700 多年历史，盛唐时寺院规模达到鼎盛。寺院主要建筑有天王殿、大雄宝殿、三圣殿、七如来殿和五佛楼、大悲殿功德堂、念佛堂等。寺院现存遗迹有雌雄千年古银杏各一棵，千年古井一口，刻有"古寿圣寺"的石砖墙一处，以及数方宋代柱础。

Covering an area of 2 square kilometers, the Guzhu Mountain is located in Guzhu Village in Shuikou Town in Changxing, with an altitude of 355 meters. The Guzhu Mountain has an excellent environment for tea production, for it **overlooks** the Taihu Lake in the east, which makes it continually moistened by the water vapor from the Taihu Lake. The Guzhu Mountain is the **cradle** of Chinese tea culture and it once was the main place for Lu Yu (the Sage of Tea) to study tea. It also gave birth to the first Tribute Tea House in history, which can be seen from a large number of stone carvings by men of letters in the Tang Dynasty such as Yan Zhenqing, Zhang Wengui, Du Mu, Han Yunyin, and so on.

It has been famous for the production of **purple bamboo-shoot tea** which is distinctive for its high quality and flavor. In the Tang Dynasty, purple bamboo-shoot tea was listed as a tribute to the imperial palace, and Tribute Tea House was established. The carvings and the site of Tribute Tea House provide precious material for the research of tea plantation, production and tea culture. Guzhu Tribute Tea House was established in the year of 770 in Hutou (Head of Tiger) Rock by the Guzhu Mountain, which was the production place of purple bamboo-shoot tea in the Tang Dynasty, and also considered to be the first tea-processing workshop in Chinese history.

The main scenic spots in the Guzhu Mountain Tea Culture Resort include Tribute Tea House built in the Tang Dynasty, Shousheng Temple, King Pond, etc. Shousheng Temple was built in the Three Kingdoms Period with a history of more than 1,700 years, and flourished in the glorious age of the Tang Dynasty. The main constructions in the temple include Tianwang Hall, Sansheng Hall, etc. Two ginkgos trees and a well with a history of more than 1,000 years as well as several column bases built in the Song Dynasty can also be found here.

★生词与词组 Words & Expressions

overlook /ˌəuvəˈluk/ v. 俯瞰

cradle /ˈkreidl/ n. 发祥地

purple bamboo-shoot tea 紫笋茶

◆ 知识拓展 Knowledge Extension

陆羽(733—804)：一名疾，字鸿渐、季疵，号竟陵子、桑苧翁、东冈子，又号"茶山御史"。汉族，唐朝复州竟陵(今湖北天门市)人。一生嗜茶，精于茶道，以著世界第一部茶叶专著《茶经》闻名于世，对中国茶业和世界茶业发展作出了卓越贡献，被誉为"茶仙"，尊为"茶圣"，祀为"茶神"。

紫笋茶："紫笋"一名，由陆羽《茶经》"紫者上，笋者上"而得名。紫笋茶白毫显露，芽叶完整，外形细嫩紧结，色泽翠绿，香气浓郁，滋味鲜醇，汤色淡绿明亮，叶底细嫩，很有特色，从唐肃宗年间起被定为贡茶。

霸王潭：传说楚汉争雄之时，楚霸王项羽屯兵水口地界，见山水风景优美，独自上山游猎，因口渴难忍，环顾四周，见山间一条小涧自石中流出，霸王跪下就喝，在石板上留下两个深深的膝盖印。

5. 红房子 Red House

红房子是崇德堂的俗称(又称刘氏梯号)，位于南浔镇南西街的幸福桥东端，是南浔"四象"之首刘镛的三子刘安注(字渊叔，号梯青)的居处。整个建筑始建于光绪三十一年(1905)，于光绪三十四年(1908)竣工。

整座建筑全部由红砖建成，这就是俗称红房子的来历。红房子由南、中、北三部分组成。中部建筑以传统儒家文化思想理念的厅、堂、楼、厢为主体；南、北部中式建筑融入西欧罗马式建筑，其中北部欧式建筑立面尤为壮观。在这里，人们可以看到波斯的木质百叶窗，罗马的蓝晶石柱子，欧洲的彩色玻璃，法国的印花地砖，加上壁炉，全然是 18 世纪欧洲的建筑风格。大宅高敞恢弘，以精美的砖雕、木雕、石雕见胜。当时刘梯青虽然既是高官又是商人，但较早接受了西方文化，使东、西文化在这里完美交融结合。宅后原辟一草地为网球场，一边角上饲养奶牛。东西潭边钟楼上曾有一口巨大的自鸣钟，远近都能听到它的声音。

刘氏梯号宅后的留园，种树栽花，叠石为山，坡植白皮松，蓄水栽荷，且有楼、亭、阁、榭和欧式小洋房。留园得名是因为"留"正好与"刘"同音。

刘氏梯号与南浔其他豪宅相比，具有线条简洁、布局通畅、西风较浓等特点，同时也是建筑史上民族文化和外来文化的一次有力的碰撞。

Red House, alternatively named Chongde Manor or the Home of Liu Tiqing, is located on the east end of the Xingfu Bridge near the Nanxi Street. As a matter of fact, Tiqing is the **literary name** of Liu Ansheng (styled Yuanshu), the third son of Liu Yong, one of the four wealthiest merchants in Nanxun (Four Elephants). The entire residence was built in the 31st year of Guangxu reign of the early Qing Dynasty (1905) and was completed in the 34th year of Guangxu reign (1908).

The entire residence was built of red bricks and that is the origin of the name "red house". It consists of 3 parts: the southern part, the central part and the northern part. The central construction contains halls, pavilions, **wing-rooms**, which are in consistent with the traditional conception of the Confucius culture while the south and north combine architecture styles of both Western Europe and Rome. The construction in the north section is especially magnificent. With wooden Persian **blinds**, **granite** Roman pillars, European **stained glass**, French floor tiles with flower patterns and a fireplace, the grand building in the north is a construction exactly in the European style of the 18th century. The whole construction boasts lofty and magnificence characterized by the exquisite brick carvings, wood carvings as well as stone carvings. Although Liu Tiqing was a high-ranking official and wealthy merchant in those days, he accepted the western **ideology** and culture earlier than people of the same age, which can be clearly seen in his former residence of a mixed style. In the manor there used to be a **tennis court**, a cattle farm on one of the corners and a **chime clock** on the building near the pond.

Behind the Red House is Liu Garden, with green trees, beautiful flowers, rockeries, pines and lotus as well as pavilions, towers and European buildings.

Compared with other manors in Nanxun, the Red House has a linear and simple style, spacious layout and westernized buildings. Actually it is also a powerful collision between national culture and foreign culture in the history of architecture in the world.

★生词与词组 Words & Expressions

wing-room /'wiŋr'u:m/ *n.* 厢房	blind /blaind/ *n.* 窗帘；百叶窗
granite /'grænit/ *n.* 花岗岩	ideology /ˌaidi'ɔlədʒi; id-/ *n.* 理念
literary name 号	stained glass 彩色玻璃
tennis court 网球场	chime clock 自鸣钟

◆ 知识拓展 Knowledge Extension

南浔"四象"：即"四象八牛七十二墩狗"为代表的南浔富商，清光绪年间，出现在湖州南浔民间及江浙一带。所谓"四象""八牛""七十二狗"者，皆资本雄厚，或自为丝通事，或有近亲为丝通事者。财产达百万以上者称之曰"象"。五十万以上不过百万者，称之曰"牛"，其他在二十万以上不达五十万者则譬之曰"狗"。南浔"四象八牛"之说，属于民间说法，根本无正规的统计和详细记载，七十二墩狗仅仅是泛指。"四象八牛"之说，表明南浔自南宋淳祐十二年(1252)建镇，浔溪、南林、设镇官、南浔，耕桑以富，行商坐贾荟萃，为江南雄镇。

刘湖涵：南浔"四象"刘镛之子，刘梯青的哥哥，当时上海房地产大王。

刘安泩(1876—1950)：字渊叔，号梯青，是南浔"四象"之首富刘镛的三子。他不仅是文物收藏家，也是实业家，在上海、杭州等地拥有不少房地产。他还与庞赞臣等人集资28万两，于1927年在余杭塘栖创办崇裕丝厂，产品销往欧美及东南亚等地区，为当时浙江乃至全国一流的大型缫丝厂(新中国成立后，该厂更名杭州新华丝厂，属国有大型缫丝企业)。刘梯青在杭州湖滨路上的别墅小方壶斋据说是因他的一件青铜器藏品而得其名。

6. 金钉子地质公园 Golden Spike Geological Park

地层的年代分为前古生界、古生界、中生界和新生界。每个界又分为多个系。系与系之间的全球标准就俗称为"金钉子"。"金钉子"就是所谓的一种永久性纪念标志的代名词。地质"金钉子"，是距今 2.5 亿年左右的二叠系至三叠系的地质时代的地层、生物。二叠系至三叠系的界线层型剖面，也是古生态到中生代的界线层型剖面。它是根据 1972 年 11 月 16 日联合国教科文组织在巴黎通过的《联合国保护世界文化和自然遗产公约》，由世界遗产委员会负责实施，旨在以整个国际社会的集体性援助来参与保护具有突出价值的文化和自然遗产。

长兴灰岩是地质学上的专用名词，它是"二叠系到三叠系地质连续剖面"的代名词，这是由著名地质学家葛利普在 1931 年命名的，得到世界公认。其标准地层剖面位于浙江省长兴县西北角青塘山麓，紧临长牛省道，距县城 21 千米，交通便捷。经国际地质科学联合会认定，长兴灰岩代表了世界晚二叠纪的最高层位，是全球二叠系至三叠系界线层型标准剖面。

长兴灰岩—"金钉子"地质公园是长兴三大古生态奇观之一，在地质学界具有无可替代的至高地位。

The age of the **strata** is divided into the former Paleozoic, Paleozoic, Mesozoic and Cenozoic. Each sector is divided into multiple sub-sectors. The global standard between the sub-sectors is known as the "Golden **Spike**". As a term for a kind of permanent memorial sign, the so-called "Golden Spike" refers to the stratum and life-form of 250 million years before. The boundary **stratotype profile** between **Permian System** and **Triassic System** is also the boundary stratotype profile between the **Paleozoic Era** and **Mesozoic Era**. It is conducted according to the *United Nations Convention of Protection of the World Cultural and Natural Heritage* passed by United Nations Educational Scientific and Culture Organization (UNESCO) in Paris on November 16, 1972 and was carried out by **World Heritage Committee**, aiming to help the precious cultural an natural heritage by the collective assistance of the entire international society.

Changxing **limestone** is a proper name in geology, a name for "the continuous geological profile from Permian System to Triassic System". It was named by the famous geologist Grabau in 1931 and was approved by the whole world. The standard stratotype profile is located in Qingtang Mountain in the northwest of Changxig County of Zhejiang Province, and has convenient transportation, near to the Changniu Provincial Highway, 21 kilometers to the town. According to the confirmation of International Union of Geological Sciences, Changxing limestone represents the highest stratotype of the late Permian Period and is a standard boundary stratotype profile between Permian System and Triassic System.

Changxin limestone—"Golden Spike" Geological Park is one of the three ancient ecological wonders of Changxing, and has an irreplaceable high position in the geological field.

stratum /'strɑ:təm/ *n.* 地层

stratotype /'strætətaip/ *n.* 层面

limestone /'laimstəun/ *n.* 石灰岩

Triassic System 三叠系

Mesozoic Era 中生代

spike /spaik/ *n.* 尖状物

profile /'prəufail/ *n.* 纵剖面图；侧面；轮

Permian System 二叠系

Paleozoic Era 古生代

World Heritage Committee 世界遗产委员会

◆ 知识拓展 Knowledge Extension

金钉子：地质学上的"金钉子"实际上是全球年代地层单位界线层型剖面和点位(GSSP)的俗称。"金钉子"一名源于美国的铁路修建史。1869 年 5 月 10 日，美国首条横穿美洲大陆的铁路钉下了最后一颗钉子，这颗钉子是用 18k 金制成，它宣告了全长约 2858 千米的铁路胜利竣工。鉴于这条铁路的修建在美国历史上具有里程碑的意义，对美国政治、经济、文化的影响极其深远，特别是对于美国西部开发战略的实施具有举足轻重的作用。为纪念这一事件，美国在 1965 年 7 月 30 日建立了"金钉子国家历史遗址"。全球年代地层单位界线层型剖面和点位在地质年代划分上的意义与美国铁路修建史上"金钉子"的重要历史意义和象征意义具有异曲同工之处，因此，"金钉子"就为地质学家所借用。

葛利普(Amadeus William Grabau)(1870—1946)：德裔美国地质学家、古生物学家、地层学家。他是古生态学的创始人之一，他把自己的后半生完全贡献给了中国古生物学、地层学的伟大事业。

7. 嘉业堂藏书楼 The Jiayetang Library

嘉业堂藏书楼是我国近代著名私家藏书楼之一，同时也是中国私家园林的典型代表。藏书楼主人原为"江浙巨富"、南浔"四象"之一刘镛之孙刘承干。清末代皇帝溥仪奖予一块九龙金匾"钦若嘉业"，刘承干为报恩取"嘉业"两字，故名嘉业堂藏书楼。

书楼与小莲庄仅一河之隔。楼的前面建有一个小园，园内中央为一个约 12000 至 16000 平方米亩的荷叶状的荷花池，周围假山围绕，小园外面以一衣带水替代围墙，使藏书楼建筑、花园景色与四周风光浑然一体。池中心有一人造小岛，岛上有一个亭子名曰"明瑟亭"。有石桥与岛相连至岸边，两侧各有一亭，分别名曰"浣碧亭"和"漳红亭"。明瑟亭旁竖有一太湖石，3 米多高，称为"啸石"，若风吹过，会发出巨响，极似虎啸。藏书楼总体设计为中西合璧园林式布局，寓肃穆的书楼于幽雅的园林之中。

藏书楼系砖木结构，是一座回廊式的两层建筑物，平面呈"口"字形，共有书库 52 间。在全盛的 1925 年至 1932 年间，楼内收藏的珍本善本有宋元刊本 200 种，清刻本 5000 种，地方志 1200 余种，丛书 220 余种，抄本 2000 种，其他 1200 余种，大量的是清人文集和各种史书。此外还有碑帖数千种。

刘承干不仅以收藏古籍而闻名全国，还以雕版印书蜚声海内。1951 年 11 月，刘承干把藏书楼捐献给国家，由浙江省图书馆接收。现有藏书十余万册，雕版片三万。嘉业堂藏书楼能保存至今，难能可贵。

The Jiayetang Library distinguishes itself as an **imposing** and representative library of the private libraries in China, whose founder is Liu Chengan, the grandson of Liu Yong, one of the "Four Elephants (Millionaires)" and one of the richest merchants in Nanxun. The library and one of its halls are named after the boards **inscribed** and **bestowed** by Puyi, Emperor Xuantong of the Qing Dynasty.

The Jiayetang Library is separated from the Little Lotus Villa only by a river. With a lotus-leaf shaped lotus pond of about 12,000 to 16,000 square kilometers as the center scatted with rockeries, the courtyard in front of the library is surrounded by a river in the shape of a belt, which combines harmoniously the building with scenery and nature. Three pavilions respectively called "Mingse Pavilion", "Huanbi Pavilion" and "Zhanghong Pavilion" form a state of **tripartite** confrontation. A giant stone near Mingse Pavilion, named "whistling stone", is more than 3 meters high and when the wind blows, it makes the sound of a roaring tiger. With unique layout, the whole architecture has combined an exquisite garden and a **solemn** library into a harmonious unity.

The library is a two-storey building which combines harmoniously Chinese and western elements. The square house is a brick-wood construction. It totally has 52 rooms. During its most flourishing period (from 1925 to 1932), the library has housed 200 block-printed editions of the Song and Yuan dynasties, 2,000 block-printed editions of the Ming Dynasty, 5,000 block-printed editions of the Qing Dynasty, more than 1,200 local **chronicles**, over 220 series, 2,000 **transcriptions**, several thousand **rubbings** from stone inscriptions as well as more than 1,200 other kinds of books, most of which are literary corpuses and history records.

Apart from collecting books, Liu Chenggan was also fond of block printing. In November 1951 Liu Chenggan contributed the Jiaye Library to the country, which was taken over by Zhejiang Library. It's really a miracle that the Jiaye Library has been preserved well up to the present.

★生词与词组 Words & Expressions

imposing /im'pəuziŋ/ *adj.* 庄严的
bestow /bi'stəu/ *vt.* 授予
solemn /'sɔləm/ *adj.* 严肃的；庄严的
transcription /træn'skripʃn/ *n.* 抄写；抄本

inscribe /in'skraib/ *v.* 写，刻，题
tripartite /trai'pɑ:tait/ *adj.* 三重的；分三部分的
chronicle /'krɔnik(ə)l/ *n.* 编年史
rubbing /'rʌbiŋ/ *n.* 拓本

◆ 知识拓展 Knowledge Extension

刘承干(1882—1963)：刘镛的长孙，藏书楼创始人，字贞一，号翰怡，清光绪三十一年考中秀才。刘承干自幼嗜好读书、买书、校书、写书、藏书，还爱好目录版本学。他自谓"世守中垒旧业"，平素交游知名人物。辛亥革命期间，刘承干乘大批古籍抛售之机，不惜巨资，大量购书。因为"窃好斯文"的刘承干深知藏书之不易，于是决心在小莲庄刘氏家庙的旁边建造一座藏书楼。藏书楼于1920年初冬动工，1924年岁尾竣工，"康金十二万，拓地二十亩"。

藏书楼建成以后，他又不惜重金，陆续增添，自称藏书最多时有 13 万部 60 万卷以上，内有宋本、元本 200 种，清本 5000 余种，方志 1200 种，抄本 2000 余种，其中很多为海内孤本、善本。

8. 莫干山 Mount Mogan

莫干山属天目山余脉，相传是干将莫邪铸剑之地。主峰塔山海拔 700 多米，风景秀丽。莫干山素有"清凉世界"之美誉，被誉为"江南第一山"，与北戴河、庐山、鸡公山并称为中国四大避暑胜地。

莫干山已有 2000 多年的开发历史。莫干山有句地方谚语："三胜竹云泉，三宝绿净静"。"三胜"指竹胜、云胜、泉胜；"三宝"指绿宝、净宝、静宝。莫干山遍山竹海，日本冷杉和宋代银杏高大挺拔，景区植被覆盖率高达 92%。莫干山上多云雾，多风雨。雨后大雾更是一绝，山腰以下全被云雾吞没，塔山之顶飘浮于云层之上，如大海中的小岛，又像空中楼阁，虚无缥缈，好似仙境一般。"泉胜"则是由于莫干山山高林密多清泉。剑池、龙潭是大泉，其余中泉、小泉、微泉，遍山皆是。无须"山中一夜雨"，也堪"树梢百重泉"。淙淙潺潺，叮叮咚咚，嘀嘀嗒嗒，到处是泉水的歌声。至于莫干山的"绿宝"，则是菁密林茂，是个绿色的海洋。"净宝"是讲水和空气洁净。"静宝"是指环境一片幽静。

莫干山中心景区包括塔山、中华山、金家山、屋脊山、莫干岭、炮台山等，既可看日出、云海，更可观瀑布、清泉。莫干山人文景观丰富多彩，明清之际，曾有"水乡佛国"的说法。清末民初兴建的数百幢别墅，掩映在竹林绿荫之中，非常清幽，被称为"世界建筑博物馆"。

Mount Mogan belongs to Tianmu Mountain Range. It is said that it is the sword-casting site of Ganjiang and Moye in history. The highest peak in the mountain range has an altitude of more than 700 meters. With beautiful scenery, it has the fame of "cool world" and is regarded as "the No. 1 mountain in Jiangnan", and together with Beidaihe, Mount Lushan and Mount Jigong, it is one of the four **summer resorts** in China.

With a history of more than 2,000 years, Mount Mogan has developed its own unique scenery sights. There is a famous local saying about Mount Mogan, "Three **Specialties**: Bamboos, Clouds and Springs; Three treasures: Being green, clean and quiet." The whole site is covered with various kinds of vegetation, such as bamboos, Japanese **firs** and gingkoes in the Song Dynasty. Rains and mists are frequently seen in Mount Mogan. The heavy mist after a rain is unique. Halfway down, the mountainside is covered by clouds and the peak floats above the cloud, just like a small island in the ocean; like a **castle in the air.** Springs can be seen here and there among the high bushes, of which Jianchi, Longtan are big springs. The **bubbling** and **rippling** of the spring can be heard everywhere. As to the treasure "Green", it indicates that Mogan Mountain is covered with green bushes and bamboos, just like a green ocean. "Clean" means clean water and air, and "quiet" refers to the quiet atmosphere.

The central scenery site includes Mount Tashan, Mount Zhonghua, Mount Jinjia, Mount Wuji, the Mogan Ridge, Mount Paotai, etc., where people can not only enjoy the sunrise and cloudy sky but also the waterfalls and clear springs. Mount Mogan also has **diversified** human landscape, and in the Ming and Qing dynasties, it was entitled "Buddhist Place in the Town of Water". Hundreds of villas built at the end of the Qing Dynasty are hidden among the shades of bamboo bushes; that's why Mount Mogan is called "Architectural Museum in the World".

★生词与词组 Words & Expressions

speciality /ˌspeʃi'æliti/ *n.* 特色
bubbling /'bʌbiŋ/ *n.* 冒泡的
diversified /dai'vəːsifaid/ *adj.* 多样化的
castle in the air 空中楼阁

fir /fəː/ *n.* 冷杉
rippling /'ripliŋ/ *adj.* 起涟漪的
summer resort 避暑胜地

◆ 知识拓展 Knowledge Extension

干将莫邪：古代汉族神话传说。干将，春秋时吴国人，曾为吴王造剑。后与其妻莫邪奉命为楚王铸成宝剑两把，一曰干将，一曰莫邪(也作镆铘)。干将将雌剑献予楚王，雄剑传给其子。后干将被楚王所杀。其子成人后，将楚王杀死为父报仇。

9. 南浔小莲庄 Little Lotus Villa in Nanxun

小莲庄也叫"刘园"，位于南浔镇西南万古桥西，为南浔著名经典园林之一，占地27亩(约1.8公顷)。它是晚清南浔"四象"之首富刘镛所筑的私家花园，始建于清光绪十一年(1885)，后经刘家祖孙三代40年的努力经营，由刘镛的长孙刘承干于1924年建成。因慕元末湖州籍大书画家赵孟頫所建莲花庄之名，故称小莲庄。

小莲庄群体建筑由刘氏义庄、家庙和园林三部分组成。园林分外园、内园两部分。外园以十亩荷花池为中心，形如瓢，古称"挂瓢池"，植荷历史已逾200年。内园的主体是一座用太湖石堆砌的假山群。内园山坡上仅种两种树，东面的翠松和西面的红枫，更添园内的秋韵。据称该园林的设计是缘于唐朝诗人杜牧的诗《山行》："远上寒山石径斜，白云生处有人家。停车坐爱枫林晚，霜叶红于二月花。"

外园西面为碑刻长廊，长廊壁间嵌置《紫藤花馆藏前》《梅花仙馆藏套》及刻石四十五方。整条碑廊正、草、隶、篆各体皆备，书艺高妙，文采风流，刻工精绝，堪称史料与艺术价值兼备的珍品。旁边为净香诗窟，是主人邀集文人雅士吟诗酬唱之处。

位于园林西部的刘氏家庙，始建于清朝光绪十四年(1888)，建成于光绪二十三年(1897)，为刘家祭拜祖先的场所。家庙高厅广屋，雕饰华美，尽显豪门富贵之气。刘氏家庙门前两座东西相对的石牌坊，东边一块是"积善牌坊"，因为当时四川、安徽等地闹饥荒，刘家出巨款资助，光绪皇帝颁赐"乐善好施"准予建坊；西边一块"贞节牌坊"是清宣统皇帝旌表刘镛的大公子刘安澜的夫人邱氏等女子恪守妇道，守节不改嫁，而准予建坊。

小莲庄园林各处建筑分别成景，构思精妙，匠心独具。

As one of the most famous gardens in Nanxun, Little Lotus Villa, also named "Liu Garden", is located in the west of the Wangu Bridge of Nanxun Town. Covering an area of 1.8 hectares, it is the private garden of Liu Yong, the richest of the "Four Elephants" (Four Millionaires) in the late Qing Dynasty. The constructing project of the Little Lotus Villa got started in 1885 and, with the **unremitting** efforts of three generations of the Liu Family, has **gone through** 40 years of **elaboration** and was finished in 1924 by Liu Chenggan, Liu Yong's eldest grandson. As a matter of fact, the villa **was named after** the Lotus **Manor** in Huzhou City, the residence of Zhao Mengfu, a master of painting and calligraphy of the Yuan Dynasty.

The group-constructions in the Little Lotus Villa consist of three parts, namely, the Manor of the Liu Family, the Ancestral Temple and the Garden Area. The Garden Area can be redivided into the Outer Garden and the Inner Garden. The Outer Garden, originally named "Guapiao Garden" for its shape of "piao" (the Chinese name for a **gourd ladle**), features a 10 mu lotus pond and is more than 200 years old. The most distinctive symbol of the Inner Garden is a large **rockery** of Taihu Stone. **Emerald** green pines planted on the east slope and **intoxicating** red **maples** on the west slope have decorated the garden with charming scenery of autumn; it is said that the construction philosophy follows the artistic conception of one poem of Du Mu, a famous poet of the Tang Dynasty. The poem，titled as "**Strolling** in the Mountains"，goes "Strolling along the slanting stone pathway, I arrive at the mountain in cold winter; dimly I catch sight of the houses far away over the white clouds. I stop my coach at maple woods to gaze my fill; the frost-bitten leaves look redder than early spring flowers."

In the west of the Outer Garden is the extending Corridor of **Steles**, which is made up of the *Tablets of **Wisteria** Hall* and the *Tablets of Plum Hall*. With marvelous scripts, **untrammeled** literary grace and the carving skills, 45 steles of various styles can absolutely be rated as treasures of historical and artistic value. Beside the Corridor of Steles is a four-side hall called "Jingxiang Poetic Hall", which used to be the place where the host invited some men of letters for reciting and composing poems.

In the west of the garden is the Ancestral Temple of the Liu Family, which is full of rich and abundant **connotation** of the ancestral culture. The construction started in the 14th year of Guangxu reign of the Qing Dynasty (1888) and was finally completed in the 23rd year of Guangxu reign of the Qing Dynasty (1897). It was used to sacrifice the ancestors and was boasted spacious rooms with exquisite design and luxurious style. There are two archways in front of the Ancestral Temple of the Liu Family. The eastern archway is the "Charity Memorial Archway" commemorating the deed that the Liu Family once relieved the people in famine in Sichuan and Anhui provinces with large sums of money. It was said to be authorized by Emperor Guangxu of the Qing Dynasty. The western archway is the "Chastity Memorial Archway" authorized by Emperor Xuantong of the Qing Dynasty to confer honors on the virtuous widow of Liu Anlan, the elder son of Liu Yong.

The little Lotus Villa is a work of nature and always provides visitors with an exquisite and refreshing atmosphere with **ingenious** design and uniqueness of the villa.

★生词与词组 Words & Expressions

unremitting /ʌnri'mitiŋ/ *adj.* 不懈的

manor /'mænə/ *n.* 庄园

ladle /'leid(ə)l/ *n.* 长柄勺

emerald /'em(ə)r(ə)ld/ *n.* 翡翠绿

maple /'meipl/ *n.* 枫树

stele /sti:li/ *n.* 石碑

untrammeled /ʌn'træmld/ *adj.* 无阻碍的

ingenious /in'dʒi:niəs/ *adj.* 设计独特的

be named after 以……命名

elaboration /iˌlæbə'reiʃn/ *n.* 精心制作

gourd /guəd; gɔ:d/ *n.* 葫芦

rockery /'rɔkəri/ *n.* 假山

intoxicating /in'tɔksikeitiŋ/ *adj.* 令人陶醉的

stroll /strəul/ *v.* 漫步

wisteria /wi'stiəriə/ *n.* 紫藤

connotation /kɔnə'teiʃn/ *n.* 内涵

go through 经历

◆ 知识拓展 Knowledge Extension

南浔民谣云："刘家的银子，张家的才子，庞家的面子，顾家的房子"，谓之南浔四象，指的是清光绪年间，出现在湖州南浔民间及江浙一带的南浔富商刘镛、张颂贤、庞云曾和顾福昌。南浔也以名家辈出、古宅群落而声名远播。

刘镛(1825—1889)：名介康，一字贯经，因排行第三，人称"刘三东家"。刘镛以其精明发家，成为著名的"南浔四象"之首。据传刘镛的资产达两千多万两银子之多。

10. 吴昌硕纪念馆 Wu Changshuo Memorial

吴昌硕纪念馆位于安吉县。吴昌硕(1844—1927)，安吉彰吴人，我国近代书画金石艺术大师，首任杭州"西泠印社"社长。父吴车甲，善诗，尤擅金石篆刻，对吴昌硕青少年时代有极重要的影响。吴昌硕自幼酷爱诗词篆刻，青少年时代在家乡耕读中度过。

吴昌硕纪念馆于 1986 年 9 月建成。该馆系仿古三层建筑，用蓝绿色琉璃瓦覆盖，建筑面积 972 平方米。底层为吴昌硕生平事迹和代表作品展。正中安放着吴昌硕半身铜像。一楼为临时展厅，可供举办各类展览。二楼陈列当代书画艺术家为纪念吴昌硕大师所作书画展和安吉史迹陈列馆，设有"吴昌硕生平图片展"及"吴昌硕作品展"。三楼收藏吴昌硕先生早、中、晚期不同风格的书画作品，包括水墨、彩色写意花卉、人物、石鼓文、篆书、行书、对联、扇面，以及诗稿、信札。还有吴昌硕生前的生活用品、文房四宝、刻刀笔筒、镇纸等原物。三楼还辟有《诸乐三作品陈列室》，陈列诸老的书画作品。此外馆内还收藏有近现代书画名家王一亭、沈尹默、沙孟海、陆维钊、陆俨少、方介堪、钱君、谭建丞等书画作品近 400幅。纪念馆编辑出版了《馆藏吴昌硕作品集》《吴昌硕》等。

Wu Changshuo Memorial is located in Anji County. Wu Changshuo (1844—1927), a great master of painting and calligraphy in modern China, was born in Zhangwu, Anji, and assumed the first chairmanship of **Xiling Seal Art Society** in Hangzhou. His father Wu Chejia was good at poem and was especially an expert in seal cutting on metal or stone. The background of Family Wu had a profound influence for the development of Wu Changshuo in his youth. From young he was keen on poems and seal cutting, and he spent his youth time in his hometown on farming while studying.

Wu Changshuo Memorial was established in September, 1986. With an area of 972 square meters, the memorial is a three-floor building with ancient style covered by **bluish green glazed tiles**. The first floor exhibits the achievements and representative products in his life. In the center is his **bronze bust**. The first floor is a contemporary exhibition hall and can be used to hold various kinds of exhibitions. The second floor displays calligraphies and paintings by modern artists for memorizing Master Wu Changshuo and historical development of Anji with "The Life of Wu Changshuo" and "the Works of Wu Changshuo". The third floor shows paintings and calligraphies of different styles of Master Wu in different periods, including ink, colored freehand brushwork of flowers, drum-shaped stone inscriptions, figures, seal character, cursive scripts, couplets, fans covers and poems and letters. It also displays the original articles of basic necessities, four treasures of the study, graver and brush holder and paperweight that Wu Changshuo used when he was alive. In addition, it collects 400 products of some famous modern painters and calligraphers such as Wang Yiting, Shen Yinmo, Sha Menghai, Lu Weizhao, Lu Yanshao, Fang Jiekan, Qian Jun, Tan Jiancheng, and so on. The Memorial has published *The Collection of Works of Wu Changshuo*, *Wu Changshuo*, etc.

★生词与词组 Words & Expressions

bronze /brɔnz/ *n.* 青铜
Xiling Seal Art Society 西泠印社
glazed tile 琉璃瓦

bust /bʌst/ *n.* 半身雕塑像
bluish green 蓝绿色的

◆ 知识拓展 Knowledge Extension

吴昌硕(1844—1927)：字昌硕，别号仓硕、老缶、苦铁等，汉族，浙江安吉人。中国近、现代书画艺术发展过渡时期的关键人物，"诗、书、画、印"四绝的一代宗师，晚清民国时期著名国画家、书法家、篆刻家，与任伯年、赵之谦、虚谷并称为"清末海派四大家"。吴昌硕的艺术独辟蹊径、贵于创造，最擅长写意花卉，他以书法入画，把书法、篆刻的行笔、运刀、章法融入绘画，形成富有金石味的独特画风。他以篆笔写梅兰，狂草作葡萄，所作花卉木石，笔力敦厚老辣、纵横恣肆、气势雄强，构图也近书印的章法布白、虚实相生、主体突出，画面用色对比强烈。

西泠印社：创立于清光绪三十年(1904)，由浙派篆刻家丁辅之、王福庵、吴隐、叶为铭等发起创建，以"保存金石，研究印学，兼及书画"为宗旨，是海内外研究金石篆刻历史最悠久、成就最高、影响最广的学术团体之一，有"天下第一名社"之盛誉。社址坐落于浙江省杭州市西湖景区孤山南麓，1913年，近代艺术大师吴昌硕出任首任社长。

11. 新市古镇 Xinshi Ancient Town

新市古镇位于德清县东部，古称仙潭，至今已经有 1600 多年的历史，古镇因水成市，因水成街，又因水被分割成 18 块，再由架在河面上充满浓郁水乡情调的 72 座桥梁连成一片，36 条各具特色的弄堂贯穿于街市之间，构成典型的"小桥、流水、人家"的诗意画卷。

新市宗教历史悠久。自东晋至晚清的千余年间，佛教、道教文化兴旺，先后建成的寺庙庵堂达 30 多处。随着历史的变幻，这些建筑大多已遭战乱毁坏，目前保存完好的有觉海寺和刘王庙两处。觉海寺是一座风景优美、香火旺盛的千年古刹，民间有"先有觉海寺，后有灵隐寺"的说法。刘王庙，是为纪念南宋抗金名将刘锜所建。

新市古镇浓郁的民俗文化和商贸文化堪称别具一格。它是中国古代"丝绸之路"的发源地之一。当地民俗文化中最著名、最具影响力的，当属蚕花庙会。相传，越国美女西施自会稽送蚕花至新市镇。从此，新市蚕桑丰收，物泰民丰。为追念西施，每逢清明，新市人便会举行蚕花庙会。

新市有很多特色美食，首推羊肉，其中"张一品"的牌子最响，原料考究，酱料独特，美味可口。此外，茶糕及芽麦圆子，也是新市小吃中一大特色。

西河口是新市一条典型老街，南始陈家潭北至朱家桥，长约 1000 米。西河口水街的西边，历代为临水而建的靠街楼，基本保持清末民初水乡老街之特色。古朴优雅的石库墙门、精美的砖雕民居、独特的封火墙、石砌的堤岸河埠，向你诉说着一个个凄美动人的故事。

The Xinshi ancient town is located in the east of Deqing County and it has a long history of 1,600 years. In ancient times it is named Xiantan, with 18 parts separated by water, 72 bridges and 36 featured lanes through downtown streets, which form a typical poetic picture of "bridges, water and families".

Xinshi has a long history of religion. From the Eastern Jin Dynasty to the late Qing Dynasty, when Buddhism and Taoism were popular, more than 30 temples were built, among which Juehai Temple and Liuwang Temple are reserved till now. Juehai Temple is an ancient **monastery** with elegant landscape. There is a saying in the folk that "Juehai Temple was established before Lingyin Temple". Liuwang Temple was established to memorize a heroic general in the Southern Song Dynasty.

Xinshi Ancient Town is well-known for its places of interest, glorious culture and famous **elites**. It is particularly famous for its **folk culture** and commerce culture. It was one of the origins of the "Silk Road" in ancient China. Among the folk culture, the most influential activity is Silkworm **Temple Fair**. It is said that Xishi, the beauty in Yue Country, once sent silk flowers from Kuaiji to Xinshi. Thereafter, people in the town had a great harvest in silkworms and lived a happy life. In order to memorize Xishi, the Silkworm Temple Fair is held every year in Tomb-sweeping Day.

The town has many specialities, such as mutton. The Brand "Zhang Yipin" is the most famous, cooked with special raw material and **seasonings**, which is delicious. Besides, tea cakes and **malt** dumplings are also famous.

Xihekou is a typical street in the town with a length of 1 kilometer. In the west of the street the buildings have **retained** the flavor of the Qing Dynasty with simple elegant stone gates, delicate engraved brick houses, unique fire seal, and stone **embankment**.

★生词与词组 Words & Expressions

monastery /'mɔnəst(ə)ri/ *n.* 修道院；寺院	elite /ei'li:t/ *n.* 精英
seasoning /'si:zəniŋ/ *n.* 佐料；调味品	retain /ri'tein/ *v.* 保留
embankment /im'bæŋkmənt/ *n.* 河堤	folk culture 民俗文化
temple fair 庙会	

◆ 知识拓展 Knowledge Extension

张一品酱羊肉：浙江湖州德清县新市著名的老字号品牌，已有100多年的历史。早在清朝末年，宁波人张和松在继承传统羊肉烧法的基础上，采用新的烹调方法，终于使他烧的羊肉受到顾客的欢迎。到了20世纪30年代，其子继承父业，在经营上比其父更高一筹，不仅烹调考究，选料均用两岁到四岁的肥壮湖羊，而且每一锅他都要亲自品尝，因此生意越来越兴旺。他还请一秀才取店名。秀才看到该店正朝一家"当铺"，过去有"一品当朝"的美句，又想到该店的羊肉也应在同行中独占鳌头，于是取名"张一品"。

12. 中国湖笔博物馆 China Huzhou Writing Brushes Museum

中国湖笔博物馆位于湖州莲花庄路，是集湖笔历史文物陈列、工艺流程展示、精品博览和销售，以及元代大艺术家赵孟頫生平与书画作品展览于一体的具有很强地域特色和传统文化的人文博物馆。整个景点分两个部分：湖笔博物馆和赵孟頫艺术馆。湖笔博物馆主题部分设：湖笔源流厅，陈列湖笔历史文物；湖笔工艺厅，展示湖笔传统制作工艺流程、制笔技工现场操作；湖笔陈列厅，汇集王一品斋笔庄、善琏湖笔厂等生产的百余种各式精品湖笔。许多名人、学者、大师对湖笔作出了高度评价。

湖笔，与徽墨、宣纸、端砚并称为"文房四宝"，是中华文明悠久灿烂的重要象征。作为一家历史悠久的笔庄，王一品斋笔庄不仅荣膺了"中华老字号"的称号，其生产的"天官牌"湖笔也深得名家的喜爱。

赵孟頫艺术馆于2001年9月建成开馆。建筑外观为歇山顶卷棚，飞檐翘角，亭廊楼榭皆为仿古建筑。它是集元代大艺术家赵孟頫生平与书画作品展览于一体的地域特色传统文化博物馆。馆内根据历史记载复原了他的书房"松雪斋"，更陈列了代表他艺术进展不同时期的书画作品以及其老师、朋友、家人、学生的作品，从一个侧面展示了中国文化的继承和发展。

China Huzhou **Writing Brushes** Museum is located on Lianhuazhuang Road. This **human landscape** is a traditional cultural museum with special local color, which integrates the exhibition of historic relics, process flow and the best products, the sale of Huzhou writing brushes as well as the exhibition of the works of the great calligrapher Zhao Mengfu. The museum consists of two parts, namely, Huzhou Writing Brushes Museum and Zhao Mengfu Art Gallery. The major parts of Huzhou Writing Brushes Museum include the following: the origin exhibition hall, which shows historic relics of Huzhou writing brushes; the technique exhibition hall, which shows the traditional process flow in making Huzhou writing brushes and the onsite performance of the technicians; the exhibition hall of Huzhou writing brushes, which collects about 100 best Huzhou writing brushes made by the factories of Wangyipinzhai Brushes and Shanlian Brushes and others of the city. Many celebrities, scholars and masters speak highly of Huzhou writing brushes.

Huzhou writing brushes, together with Huizhou ink, Xuancheng paper and Duanzhou ink slab, are called "**the Four Treasures in Study**", which are the significant symbols of long and splendid Chinese civilization. Huzhou writing brushes of the brand "Tianguan", made by Wangyipinzhai Brushes, are the most popular among masters.

Zhao Mengfu Art Gallery was opened in September, 2001. The architecture, especially its pavilions, lanes and buildings, is of ancient style. It is a museum integrating the great calligraphy works of Zhao Mengfu, the calligrapher in the Yuan Dynasty. With reference to the history record, his study "Songxue Study" (literally meaning Pine and Snow Study) was restored. The exhibitions reveal his works at different times as well as the calligraphy works of his teachers, family members, friends and students. The museum inherits and reflects the Chinese culture.

★生词与词组 Words & Expressions

human landscape 人文景观	writing brush 毛笔
ink slab 砚，调墨台	the Four Treasures in Study 文房四宝

◆ 知识拓展 Knowledge Extension

湖笔：产于浙江湖州南浔区善琏镇。湖笔选料讲究，工艺精细，品种繁多，粗的有碗口大，细的如绣花针，具有尖、齐、圆、健四大特点。尖，指笔锋尖如锥状；齐，笔锋撮平后，齐如刀切；圆，笔头圆浑饱满；健，笔锋挺立，富有弹性。湖笔分羊毫、狼毫、兼毫、紫毫四大类；按大小规格，又可分为大楷、寸楷、中楷、小楷四种。湖笔，又称"湖颖"。颖是指笔锋尖端一段整齐透亮的部分，笔工们称之为"黑子"，这是湖笔最大的特点。

赵孟頫(fǔ)(1254—1322)：字子昂，号松雪道人，汉族，宋太祖赵匡胤的第 11 世孙、秦王赵德芳的嫡系子孙，吴兴(今浙江湖州)人。元代著名画家，楷书四大家(欧阳询、颜真卿、柳公权、赵孟頫)之一。赵孟頫博学多才，能诗善文，工书法，精绘艺，擅金石，通律吕，解鉴赏。特别是书法和绘画成就最高，开创元代新画风，被称为"元人冠冕"。他也善篆、隶、真、行、草，尤以楷、行书著称于世，绘画山水、人物、竹石、鸟兽均享有盛名，在我国艺术发展史上占有重要地位。书法代表作有《洛神赋》《赤壁赋》等。

王一品斋笔庄：中国最老的一家前店后坊的专业笔庄，以生产"天官"牌湖笔名扬中外。相传清乾隆年间，湖州有一个姓王的笔工，以制笔卖笔度日，朝廷大试之时，他随考生一起跋涉千里进京叫卖。有一名考生忘了带笔，正在焦急之际，见来了卖笔人，忙买了王笔工的一支羊毫笔，匆忙进了考场，考试时这名考生得心应手，下笔有神，竟中了头名状元，一时轰动京城。书生们纷纷争购王笔工的毛笔，称他的笔为"一品笔"，称王笔工为"王一品"。从此，他的名声大振，乾隆六年，王笔工在湖州城里开了一爿笔庄，店名就叫"王一品斋笔庄"。店主人在底楼顶塑了一个天官金身像，与王一品斋互相映衬，而王一品毛笔的笔杆上端都有天官标记，天官就成了王一品的商标。

13. 中国扬子鳄村 Chinese Alligator Village

中国扬子鳄村占地 0.67 平方千米，现有大小鳄鱼 500 余条，是国内第二大扬子鳄自然保护区，位于长兴县泗安镇尹家边村。它由扬子鳄自然繁殖母子湖、鳄鱼系列池、钓鱼馆、人鳄共乐园、鳄鱼标本陈列室、扬子鳄度假村组成。

扬子鳄仅存于我国，且分布区窄小，数量稀少。扬子鳄可以为研究大陆漂移、生物进化等世界性课题提供科学依据，对于保护生物多样化，维持生态平衡有重要意义。

中国扬子鳄村，包含了扬子鳄自然繁育研究中心，除了拥有大小不等的 500 余条扬子鳄外，还新增设了以暹罗鳄、尼罗鳄为主体的鳄鱼馆，分自然繁育、休闲、垂钓、观赏等四大功能区，拥有观鳄楼、垂钓台、休闲亭、绿色长廊、翠竹茶楼等，形成了独具一格的"楼台亭闲""廊桥轩舫"等江南古园林景观。

现在，长兴已建设好扬子鳄繁殖中心，正在落实放归自然计划。

Covering an area of 0.67 square kilometer and with more than 500 crocodiles altogether, **Chinese Alligato**r Village in Yinjiabian Village of Si'an Town in Changxing County is the second largest Chinese alligator **nature reserve** in China. It consists of several parts such as the **Breeding** Lake of Chinese Alligator, the Crocodile Lake, the Fishing Pool, the Crocodile Park, the Exhibition Hall of Crocodile **Specimen** and the Chinese Alligator Resort.

Chinese alligators are uniqe to China and live in a few areas. The amount of Chinese alligator is small. Chinese alligator can provide scientific evidence for the study of some global subjects such as the **continental drift**, biological evolution, etc., which plays a significant role in maintaining the ecological balance.

Chinese alligator village includes the study center of Chinese alligator breeding. Besides more than 500 Chinese alligators, there are also other crocodiles such as **Siamese crocodile**, Nile crocodile, etc. The village is divided into four sections, namely breeding, entertainment, fishing and watching and has several unique buildings such as the Viewing Building, the Fishing Tower, the Entertainment Pavilion, the Green Gallery, the Green Bamboo Tearoom, etc., and these altogether form a typical building style of garden sceneries.

Now the breeding center has been set up and Changxing government is launching a program of "**releasing** crocodiles back to nature".

★生词与词组 Words & Expressions

breeding /'bri:diŋ/ *n.* 繁殖　　　　　　specimen /'spesimin/ *n.* 标本

release /ri'li:s/ *v.* 释放；放开　　　　　　Chinese alligator 扬子鳄
nature reserve 自然保护区　　　　　　　　continental drift 大陆漂移
Siamese Crocodile 暹罗鳄

◆ 知识拓展 Knowledge Extension

扬子鳄：或称作鼍(tuó)，是中国特有的一种鳄鱼，也是世界上最小的鳄鱼品种之一。它是一种古老的、现在生存数量非常稀少、濒临灭绝的爬行动物。因其生活在长江流域，故称"扬子鳄"。在扬子鳄身上，至今还可以找到早前恐龙类爬行动物的许多特征。所以，人们称扬子鳄为"活化石"。因此，扬子鳄对于人们研究古代爬行动物的兴衰和研究古地质学和生物的进化，都有重要意义。我国已经把扬子鳄列为国家一类保护动物。

暹罗鳄：属于中型鳄鱼。分布于东南亚，如越南、柬埔寨、泰国、印尼等国，生长在低地的淡水湖、沼泽和河川等，主要以鱼类为食。

尼罗鳄：一种大型的鳄鱼，体长 2～6 米，平均体长 4 米，有不确切的最长纪录达 7.3 米。尼罗鳄主要分布于非洲尼罗河流域及东南部。成体有暗淡的横带纹。前颌齿 5，上颌齿 13～14，颌齿 14～15，齿总数为 64～68。幼体呈深黄褐色，身体和尾部有明显的横带纹。尼罗鳄体色为橄榄绿色至咖啡色，有黑色的斑点。其下颚第四齿由上颚的 V 字形凹陷中向外面突出。尼罗鳄非常强壮，尾巴强而有力，有助于游泳。成年尼罗鳄的体重可达一吨。

14. 张静江故居 The Former Residence of Zhang Jingjiang

张静江故居位于南浔镇东大街 108 号，系其父张宝善所建造而成。张静江，字人杰，1877 年 9 月 19 日生于南浔，他是江南"四象"之一张颂贤的孙子。早年在他随驻法公使赴欧途中，结识了孙中山，曾为反清革命筹集活动经费，与孙中山结下了深厚的友谊。孙中山与他初遇时即称他为奇人，后他因其忠诚热心称其为革命圣人。"二次革命"失败后，张静江又前往东京、巴黎，支持孙中山改建国民党。他曾历任国民党中央执行委员、浙江省政府主席等职。1938 年，他先避居汉口，后经香港到美国，寓居纽约。1950 年 9 月 3 日病逝。

张静江故居是典型的江南建筑风格，一进门是正厅，也称"尊德堂"，用来接待客人。匾上的三个字是通州张謇所题，中堂的画是谢公展的佳作，两侧则是孙中山题写的对联，抱柱联是同治、光绪的老师翁同龢所题。边厅为双层结构，用来招待普通宾客。二厅三厅陈列记录着张静江的生平事迹的各种照片、书札、任命状等文物，还有与孙中山等名人的来往信件。故居还有明代著名书法家董其昌手写的刘伶《酒德颂》板屏六块，系用银杏木镌刻。两边的诗句为清朝书法家赵子谦所写，乃国内罕见的珍贵历史文物。厅堂两座砖雕，雕刻十分精细，门楣上写有"有容乃大"等，为南浔近代实业家兼收藏家周梦坡所书。

The former residence of Zhang Jingjiang is situated at Number 108, Dongdajie Street, Nanxun. It was built by his father named Zhang Baoshan. Zhang Jingjiang, **alternatively** named Zhang Renjie, was born on September 19, 1877 in Nanxun. He is the grandson of Zhang Songxian one of the "Four Elephants". On his way to Europe with French **envoy**, he contracted friendship with Dr.

Sun Yat-Sen and later continuously provided money to him for the **bourgeois** democratic revolution to **overthrow** the Qing Dynasty，thus he had built a good relationship with Dr. Sun Yat-Sen. When they first met each other, Dr. Sun Yat-Sen regarded him as an **eccentric** person. Later he got the title of "**Saint** of Revolution" for his loyalty and enthusiasm. When they lost the Second **Punitive** War against Yuan Shikai, Zhang Jingjiang went to Tokyo and Paris in order to support Dr. Sun Yat-Sen to rebuild Kuomingtang. Afterwards, he **assumed** the posts of the officer of the Central Executive Committee of Kuomingtang and Chairman of Zhejiang Province, etc. He **secluded** himself in Hankou to avoid politics in 1938 and later went to America via Hongkong. On September 3, 1950, he died of illness in New York.

The residence is of typical style in Jiangnan. Stepping into the residence, you can see the Zunde Hall, the board hung over which was inscribed by Zhang Qian, who came first in the highest imperial examination at the end of the Qing Dynasty. It is a hall used to serve the guests. The painting hung in the middle of the hall of his former residence was drawn by Xie Gongzhan. The **antithetical couplets** hung on the wall were authentic characters written on scrolls by Dr. Sun Yet-Sen. The other antithetical couplets on the pillars were characters written on scrolls by Weng Tonghe, the teacher of Emperor Tongzhi and Emperor Guangxu of the Qing Dynasty. With double-decker structure, the side hall is used for entertaining ordinary guests. In the second and third halls are various photographs, books and appointment letters as well as letters with Dr. Sun Yet-Sen. The residence has six screen plates with the poem *On Drinking Morals* carved on it. The poem was composed by Liu Ling in the Jin Dynasty and was written by Dong Qichang, a famous calligrapher in the Ming Dynasty. The plates are made of gingko wood with poems on both sides written by Zhao Ziqian, a famous calligrapher in the Qing Dynasty, which is precious historical relics. In front of the main hall are two finely carved sculptures. The modern **industrialist** and collector Zhou Mengpo's inscriptions such as "Tolerance is a Virtue" are carved on the brick **lintel**.

★生词与词组 Words & Expressions

alternatively /ɔl'tə:nətivli/ *adv.* 作为选择的
bourgeois /ˌbuəʒwɑ:/ *adj.* 资产阶级的
eccentric /ik'sentrik/ *adj.* 古怪的
punitive /'pju:nitiv/ *adj.* 处罚的, 严厉的
seclude /si'klu:d/ *v.* 隔绝；隐退
lintel /'lint(ə)l/ *n.* 楣；过梁

envoy /'envɔi/ *n.* 使节、公使
overthrow /ˌəuvə'θrəu/ *v.* 推翻
saint /seint/ *n.* 圣人
assume /ə'sju:m/ *v.* 担任
industrialist /in'dʌstriəlist/ *n.* 实业家
antithetical couplet 对联

◆ 知识拓展 Knowledge Extension

二次革命：又称癸丑之役或赣宁之役，是孙中山等国民党人于民国二年(1913)在中国发动的反对袁世凯的武装革命，又称为"讨袁之役"。

谢公展(1885—1940)：江苏丹徒(今镇江)人。1929 年与郑午昌等组织蜜蜂画社，又任西湖

博览会艺术审查委员、中华国货展览会艺术审查委员、教育部艺术教育委员等职。善画花鸟虫鱼，尤擅画菊花，有"谢家菊"之称。

竹林七贤：魏正始年间(240—249)，嵇康、阮籍、山涛、向秀、刘伶、王戎及阮咸七人常聚在当时的山阳县(今河南辉县、修武一带)竹林之下，肆意畅饮，世谓竹林七贤。

周梦坡：又名周庆云，南浔"八牛"之一，近代实业家兼收藏家。

15. 张石铭旧宅 The Former Residence of Zhang Shiming

张石铭旧宅，又称懿德堂，是江南巨富、南浔四象之一张颂贤之孙张均衡所建。张钧衡，字石铭(1871—1927)，吴兴南浔人，清光绪二十年(1894)举人。虽为商人，但酷爱收藏古籍、金石碑刻和玩赏奇石，为南浔清末民初大藏书家之一。

张石铭旧宅总占地面积 6500 平方米，建筑面积 7000 平方米。整个大宅由典型的江南传统建筑格局和法国文艺复兴时期的西欧建筑群组成。建筑群之间相互联通，巧妙结合，反映了 19 世纪末中西方在经济、文化、艺术中的联系与沟通。大宅气势宏伟，富丽典雅，风格独特，可称江南最大的具有中西建筑风格的私家民宅。旧宅有五落四进和中、西各式楼房 100 余间，风格奇特、结构恢宏，工艺精湛，尤其是众多精美生动的木雕、砖雕、石雕以及从法国进口的玻璃刻花等，都具有很高的艺术欣赏、民俗建筑和文物价值。

进门即为内厅(轿厅)，二进正面为大厅，厅后为堂楼(女厅)。楼上供女眷居住，楼下为女主人接待理事之用。雕砖门楼，楼厅装修极为精致，扇窗装有法国进口的彩色花玻璃，以蓝色为主。后进天井中有一形似苍鹰的英德石，名"鹰石"，高约 1 米，苍鹰欲从石盆中展翅高飞，生动真切，做工精良，实乃江南罕见之珍品。旧居以前后划分，第三进为内厅，内厅两侧的漏明廊窗为木刻芭蕉叶，玲珑剔透，栩栩如生，故亦称"芭蕉厅"。第四进的大厅是一个设有化妆间、更衣室的豪华舞厅，地砖均从法国进口。

张石铭旧宅中西合璧的建筑风格体现了封建主义和现代主义的碰撞，被称为"江南第一巨宅"。

The Former Residence of Zhang Shiming, also named Yide Manor, was built by Zhang Junheng, the grandson of Zhang Songxian, one of the "Four Elephants" in Nanxun. Zhang Junheng (1871–1927), styled Shiming, in 1894 succeeded in the imperial examinations at the provincial level. Though a businessman, he was crazy about paintings, **calligraphic** works and **tablet** inscriptions and became one of the most famous **bibliophiles** in Nanxun during the end of the Qing Dynasty and the beginning of the Republic of China.

The Former Residence of Zhang Shiming covers an area of 6,500 square meters and occupies a construction area of 7,000 square meters. The whole manor well combines typical traditional architecture style of Jiangnan and the complex blocks of Western European style. It is ingeniously connected, reflecting the communication of Chinese and western economy, culture and art in the 19th century. The manor boasts imposing and elegant style, and can be regarded as the largest private houses with a harmonious combination of Chinese and western style of construction. The residence with grand halls, elegant decorations, and unique styles has more than 100 separate rooms, and their **carvings** as well as the **glass cuttings** imported from France reveal both high artistic and **relic** value.

Through the entrance hall is the inner hall called "Jiaoting", another hall behind it with French windows is "Tanglou"(rooms for women). The rooms upstairs are for women guests to live in while the hall downstairs is for the hostess to serve guests. The hall is decorated with brick carvings in an exquisite style and the windows of the rooms look crystal and elegant with **cyanite** cut glass. In the courtyard of the residence, there is a Yingde stone named "Eagle Stone". With a height of about 1 meter, it looks like an eagle getting ready to fly from a stone basin. Vivid and lifelike, it is of wonderful workmanship and has been regarded as a rare treasure. The third line is an inner hall. In window frames along both sides of the veranda there are vividly carved stone **plantain** leaves, so the hall is also called "Plantain Hall". The middle hall in the fourth line is a grand ballroom with private dressing rooms. All decorative materials including the **floor tiles** were imported from France.

The harmonious combination of Chinese and western styles of the residence also reveals the collision between feudalism and modernism. It is reputed as the No. 1 House in Jiangnan.

★生词与词组 Words & Expressions

calligraphic /ˌkæli'græfik/ *adj.* 书法的
bibliophile /'bibliə(u)fail/ *n.* 藏书家
cyanite /'saiəˌnait/ *n.* 蓝晶石
wood carvings 木雕
stone carvings 石雕
floor tiles 地砖

tablet /'tæblit/ *n.* 碑；牌匾；药片
relic /'relik/ *n.* 文物
plantain /'plæntin/ *n.* 芭蕉；车前草
brick carvings 砖雕
glass cutting 玻璃刻花

◆ 知识拓展 Knowledge Extension

张颂贤(1817—1892)：字竹斋，祖籍徽州休宁，清康熙年间迁居南浔(今湖州市南浔镇)。善经营，成巨富，为南浔"四象"之一。据传他的财富仅次于刘镛家，占四象之第二位。

第二节　旅游文化——特产文化

Section 2　Tourism Culture—Native Specialty Culture

湖州美食和特产历史悠久，源远流长。清代诗人袁枚在《随园食单》中多次提到湖州特产，如南浔酒、水蜜桃、甘蓝、桔红糕、鼎盛糕及其他当地特产等，并给予很高的评价。这些美食和特产展现给我们一个中国南方特色城市——湖州。

Specialties and delicacies of Huzhou have a long history. Yuan Mei, a poet in the Qing Dynasty has highly praised Nanxun Wine, juicy peach, turnip cabbage, Juhong cake and Dingsheng

Cake and many other local dishes in Huzhou. All these specialties and delicacies constitute a unique city in Jiangnan—Huzhou.

1. 绣花锦菜 Xiuhuajincai Cabbage

南浔绣花锦菜属南浔古镇所独有。外形与普通青菜相似，只是菜茎稍细，菜叶的边缘有细细的锯齿形，叶面上的脉络富有一种曲线美。此菜炒熟以后依旧碧绿。品尝此菜，菜香糯软，风味独特。

南浔绣花锦菜，只生长在南浔方圆十里之内，十里之外这种菜就变种，有形而无香。

Xiuhuajincai Cabbage is one of the specialties unique to Nanxun, Huzhou. It looks like pakchoi at first sight. It has saw-toothed leaves, curvy nervure and stems thinner than those of pakchoi. Even after being fried, it still keeps verdurous. Tasting savory and soft, it never spoils people's appetites.

The Xiuhuajincai Cabbage can only grow well in Nanxun district. Those out of the circumference of 5 kilometers will mutate and lose the taste.

2. 南浔香大头菜 Nanxun Savory Kohlrabi

南浔香大头菜已有两百多年历史。早在清朝雍正年间(约 1729)，香大头菜已经在国内市场很受欢迎，同时远销菲律宾、新加坡、马来西亚及印度尼西亚等国。南浔香大头菜香甜、脆嫩、爽口，色、香、味俱佳。

Nanxun Savory Kohlrabi keeps being the best and has already gone through a history of more than 200 years. Dating back to the reign of Emperor Yongzheng of the Qing Dynasty (around 1729), it was already sold well on national markets as well as such foreign countries as the Philippines, Singapore, Malaysia and Indonesia. It is tender, tasty and refreshing.

3. 南浔臭豆腐 Nanxun Fermented Bean Curds

民间谚云："臭南浔，辣乌镇。"乌镇人爱吃辣，南浔人却爱吃"臭味"。臭豆腐干虽有臭气，但吃起来香，其味甚佳。用南浔人的话来说，这是"纯正的南浔风味"。

As the folk saying goes, "Odoriferous Nanxun and Spicy Wuzhen". Wuzhen is famous for its spicy food while Nanxun has become well known with its permented bean curd. Though the bean curds smell odoriferous, they really have a good taste. Nanxun folks praise it as "a pure Nanxun local taste".

4. 桔红糕和鼎盛糕 Juhong Cake and Dingsheng Cake

桔红糕和鼎盛糕是南浔传统特产，至今已有百余年历史。桔红糕，软而不黏，色泽桃红，桔味醇正，香糯可口。

Juhong Cake and Dingsheng Cake are two special local products that have undergone a history of more than one hundred years. The rosy Juhong Cake tastes soft, sweet, goluptious but not glutinous.

5. 熏豆茶 Smoked Bean Tea

熏豆茶主要以熏豆、茶叶、陈皮、炒芝麻等"茶里果"配制，是南太湖地区的传统土特产品，农家待客素有自制和饮用此茶的习俗，春节期间常用来招待客人。

Smoked bean tea, made from smoked beans, tea leaves, salted orange peel, fried sesame, etc., is one of the traditional snacks in the south of the Taihu Lake. People of Nanxun have the tradition to make and drink this kind of tea and like to entertain guests with smoked bean tea during the Spring Festival.

第三节　景点讲解技能——问答法

Section 3　Narration Tactics of Scenic Spots

—Questions & Answers

问答法一般分为"我问客答、客问我答、自问自答和客问客答"等四种常见的导游讲解方法。它不仅可以避免导游员在讲解时自说自话的局面，而且能使旅游团队内的气氛活跃，关系融洽，更可满足各种游客的求知欲，解答他们的疑难问题，从而给人难以忘怀的回味。

1. 我问客答法 Guide–guest Approach

我问客答即由导游员提出问题，并引导游客回答或讨论的方法。我问客答法要求导游员善于提问题，所提的问题游客不会毫无所知，但会有不同的答案。游客的回答不论对错，导游员都不应打断，要给予鼓励，最后由导游员讲解。

导游员采用我问客答法时，所提问题必须是在游客似懂非懂的程度上，或者是难度不大，但要动脑筋才能回答。例如，在游览南浔百间楼时，导游可以问游客，为什么叫百间楼。游客可能会猜到一共有一百间，但不知道具体的其他细节。导游可以再进一步补充：百间楼相传是明代礼部尚书董份为他家的女性仆人居家而建，始建时约有楼房百间，故称"百间楼"。

2. 客问我答法 Guest-guide Approach

客问我答即游客提出问题，导游员回答游客问题的方法。

导游员要欢迎游客提问，要善于有选择地将提问和讲解有机地结合起来，这样可以减少导游员的"独角戏"，增加游客与导游交流的机会。但导游员要掌握主动权，不要让游客的提问干扰了自己的讲解和安排，不能游客问什么就答什么，一般只回答一些与景点相关的问题。

在整个旅游过程中，游客的问题涉及面很广，其难度也有深浅，同时也具有随时性。导游员对实在回答不出的问题也应谦虚，想尽办法做到既不失面子，也使游客得到心理上的满足。例如在游览安吉竹博园时，游客可能对竹博园的故事很感兴趣。有游客主动要求导游讲关于孟宗哭竹的故事(参见"安吉竹博园"的注解)，导游可以根据典故娓娓道来。

3. 自问自答法 Guide-answer Approach

该法是导游员常用的一种导游方法。自问自答法是由导游员自己提出问题并作适当停顿，让游客猜想，但并不期待他们回答。首先吸引游客的注意力，促使游客思考，激起游客的兴趣，然后导游员才作简洁明了的回答或生动形象的介绍，给游客留下深刻印象。

此法"自问"实际和"我问"相似，而"自答"不是自说自话。自问自答法在掌握节奏和速度上要比我问客答法来得快些，其关键在于动作、表情和眼神上。这种方法通常适用于很难的、客人回答不出来的问题，类似一种疑问式的停顿。导游员使用这种方法是为了吸引游客的注意，接下来要讲解的内容是比较重要或关键的。例如游览南浔广惠宫的提问：中国庙宇山门口，一般是不放石狮子的，为什么广惠宫前的广惠桥旁边有两座石狮子呢？

4. 客问客答法 Guest-answer Approach

即游客提问，由导游员引导其他游客回答问题的方法。该法是问答四法中难度最大的方法，导游员如果使用得当不仅能调动游客的积极性，而且能活跃旅游团队内的气氛，加强导游员与游客以及游客与游客之间的关系。

客问客答法一般是在导游员使用以上"三法"中产生的。当游客向导游员提出问题后，导游员不马上给予解答，而是故意让游客来回答，要注意的是：导游员要有意让那些活跃分子以及稍有名气的"群头"来回答，这样那些人如果回答正确，心中自然高兴；如果回答不对，当导游员讲出正确答案时，那些人也会哈哈一笑了之，只有在这时得到的知识，脑海中才能久久难忘，像烙印一般。

同时，导游员运用客问客答法的时间、地点和团队气氛要把握好，反之会适得其反。一般在旅游团队中游客玩得高兴时，或者对某些问题颇感兴趣时效果会更好。而当游客处于疲倦和无聊之中时，对回答问题之类是不感兴趣的。

由于旅游团队的层次各有不同，因此，导游员在掌握客问客答法时要注意问题的内容和性质，对于知识性、趣味性和健康性等的问题尽可讨论，甚至可以辩论。

有时当游客提出某一问题的时候，导游员不立即给出回答，而是把这个问题又转给其他的游客，让其他的游客来回答，这样能调动游客的积极性。此时，导游要注意扮演好"导演"角色。

◆ **综合练习**

请运用所学的"问答法"讲解技巧，围绕湖州地区某一景点或特产设计提问并分小组进行中英文讲解练习。

第四节　土特产文化翻译技巧

Section 4　Translation Skills of the Culture of Native Specialty Products

有道是："穿在法国，吃在中国。"中华美食文化源远流长，且不说那些名贵的菜肴了，单是小吃及地方特产，就足够让外国人食欲大开了。而中国物产丰富，各地的土特产也纷繁复杂，令人应接不暇，实在是不胜枚举。现选择土特产中"吃"与"喝"的部分，介绍土特产的翻译技巧。

1. 土特产翻译的要点　Translation Keys

根据土特产的定义与特点，土特产的翻译要抓住以下两点：

1)土特产的名称的基本内容翻译，包括"地名"与"产品名称"的翻译。

2)如有必要，要简略介绍其独特性，以展示其优于同类产品的关键要素，其中以前者为要，后者为辅。以"北京烤鸭"为例，"北京烤鸭"普遍译成"Beijing Roast Duck"。其中，地名"北京"直接音译，"烤鸭"意译，因为北京烤鸭历史悠久，本身已经具有很强的知名度，无须注释即可理解。

2. 土特产翻译的技巧　Translation Skills

土特产因为其"独一无二"的独特性，很难在英语文化中找到对应词，一般采用以下翻译方法。

1)产品名+地名+style

(1)直译(产品名)+音译(地名)+ style

白沙油鸭 The Oil Duck, Baisha Style

(2)意译(产品名)+音译(地名)+ style

肇庆鼎湖上素 Super Vegetarian Food, Dinghu Style

(3)音译(产品名)+音译(地名)+ style

北京二锅头 Erguotou (Superior 500ml 56°), Beijing Style

2)地名+产品名

(1)音译(地名)+直译(产品名)

内江蜜饯 Neijiang Succade

(2)音译(地名)+意译(产品名)

长兴紫笋茶 Changxing Purple Bamboo-shoot Tea

(3)音译(地名)+直译(产品名)+注释

带有历史典故、人物故事的土特产多用此种翻译方法。

秦邮董糖 Qinyou Sugar Named after Dong Xiaowang

3)约定俗成

天津狗不理包子 Go Believe

◆ 课后练习 Exercises

把下列土特产翻译成英语(Put the following specialities into English)

1. 湖州鳜鱼　　　　　　　2. 长兴紫笋茶

3. 西湖牛肉羹　　　　　　4. 太湖百合

5. 南浔绣花锦菜　　　　　6. 南京板鸭

7. 黄桥烧饼　　　　　　　8. 清蒸武昌鱼

9. 金华火腿　　　　　　　10. 糟鸡

第七章 台州、衢州、丽水景域

Chapter Seven Taizhou, Quzhou & Lishui Scenic Zone

第一节 旅游景点

Section 1 Scenic Spots

1. 长屿硐天 Changyu Cave

长屿硐天风景区，位于温岭市，系北雁荡山余脉，山峦海拔在 150 米左右，属低山丘陵。长屿因峰峦蜿蜒起伏，犹如海上一座狭长的岛屿而得名，为省级风景名胜区，系规模最大的人工开凿石硐。1998 年 4 月被列入世界吉尼斯世界纪录，2002 年 4 月被国家旅游局评为国家 AAAA 旅游区。

风景区总面积 16.18 平方千米，由四大景区组成，其中八仙岩、双门硐以硐群景观为主；崇国寺和野山景区则是人文景观和自然景色为一体的旅游景区。崇国寺始建于东晋咸和年间 (约 326)，距今已有 1600 多年的历史。

长屿硐群为南北朝以来人工开采石板后形成的石文化景观，历经 1500 余年，共凿出了 28 个硐群，1314 个硐体，洞套洞，被誉为"中华第一洞"。长屿硐天虽没有自然溶洞般的钟乳、石幔，然而依势取石留下的石硐风景或如古钟，或如覆锅，或如巨兽，千姿百态。硐内石架悬桥，宛若岩石的迷宫。

此外，硐内有与德国巴尔沃岩洞媲美的自然音乐厅，在洞中演奏，不用电声设备就具有立体声效。2002 年，这里成功举办了"中国首届岩洞音乐会"。

长屿硐天集雄、险、奇、巧、幽为一体，可谓"人力无意夺天工"，是我国独有的风景。

Located in Wenling City, Changyu Cave (Long Island Cave) is a branch of Mount Yandang and belongs to the low hilly and **mountainous** region with its altitude of about 150 meters. It is said that it has such a name just because it is **zigzagging** like a long and narrow island. As a provincial scenic spot, it is the largest artificial cave in China, listed among the Guinness World

Record in April 1998, and appraised as one of the AAAA Grade tourist areas in China in April 2002.

With a total area of 16.18 square kilometers, it is composed of four major scenic areas, of which the Eight-fairy Rock and the Two-door Cave are attractive for their cavern sceneries, while Chongguo Temple and Yeshan Scenic Site are famous for both cultural and natural landscape. Built in the Eastern Jin Dynasty (about 326), the Chongguo Temple has a long history of over 1,600 years.

Being the **cavern** sight built up through quarrying for more than 1,500 years, this area has 28 cavern groups and 1,314 caverns jointing one another. And it is reputed as the First-level Cave of China. Although there are no natural lava stalactites and rock curtains here, the caves have remained different figures, some are like clocks, some are like covered pans, and others are like huge monsters. Besides, in the cavern, there are so many rocks and stone bridges that they make the whole place a rock maze.

Moreover, in the cave there is a natural music hall which is as charming as the Barvaux Cave in Germany. Although there are no **electronic** and vocal **instruments**, you can still play a concert here. And in 2002 it managed to hold the China's first cavern concert.

Changyu Cave has been called "the result with no intention of humans", and it has been a unique landscape in our country. It is an integrated landscape with majesty, danger, peculiarity, ingeniousness and quietness.

★生词与词组 Words & Expressions

mountainous /'mauntinəs/ *adj.* 多山的
cavern /'kævən/ *n.* 洞穴
instrument /'instrəmənt/ *n.* 设备

zigzagging /'zigzægiŋ/ *adj.* 之字形的
electronic /i.lek'trɔnik/ *adj.* 电子的

◆ 知识拓展 Knowledge Extension

崇国寺：据《太平县志》记载，晋咸和(326—334)年间，有一闽僧航海经过此处(当时崇国寺前是大海)，见林壑中发出奇特光彩，立即登岸插竹标记，而后于此建寺并取名为普光寺。至宋大中祥符元年(1008)改名崇国寺。清顺治年间，逐步增建殿宇。康熙年间，增建佛殿三进及钟楼一座，广置田业，规制宏敞，一时为刹院之冠。道光元年冬遭火灾，寺院烧毁，寺僧忠义奋志18年才得以恢复。民国以来，崇国寺长期失修，"文化大革命"中又遭浩劫，仅留金刚殿。20世纪80年代初，寺庙再次修建，至今雄姿似初。这所古寺建造至今已有1660多年历史，仅迟于我国著名的杭州灵隐寺4年，较佛教天台宗发源地浙江天台山国清寺早268年。

2. 大鹿岛海上森林公园 Dalu Island Marine Forest Park

大鹿岛海上森林公园位于玉环县东南15千米的洋面上，由大鹿、小鹿两岛组成，以浅滩相接，合称大鹿岛。总面积为1.75平方千米，海岸线长5.45千米。传说天庭有一只神鹿，为盗绿色种子撒播人间，遭霹雳击顶，坠入海中。岛因传说而得名，也因山形似花鹿昂首于海面而命名。

大鹿岛是唯一的海岛森林公园。岛上树木茂盛，四季常绿，苍翠欲滴，犹如镶嵌在万顷碧波中的一颗绿宝石，故有"东海碧玉"之美称。据统计，岛上森林覆盖率已达 87.5%，林木蓄积量达 3300 多立方米，有银杏、香樟、黑松、红杉等 204 科 534 属近 1000 种植物，构成良好的植被。大鹿岛已成为全省森林最好、植物最丰富的海岛。

大鹿岛山体主要是晚侏罗纪的火山基岩，经亿万年的海浪冲刷和剥蚀风化，形成奇异的岩石、洞穴和礁滩，景观各具形态。这里有罗汉岩、将军洞、狮子岩、石鱼等景观。

大鹿岛的森林、四周浩瀚的大海和沿岸的礁滩岩雕，组成了独具风韵的山海形胜，目前已形成 20 处名胜景观，77 个景点。其中龙游洞、索桥风月、八仙过海、五百罗汉、寿星岩、渔翁老洞、乱石穿空、千佛龛为岛上八大景观，各具特色。

岛上还有刘海粟、沙孟海、陆俨少等名家巨匠所书的摩崖题刻，号称"森林艺术岛"。此外，岩礁上生长着众多的海螺、牡蛎等海生贝类，可供观光者拾取，烹煮品尝，别具情趣。

Dalu Island (Great Deer Island) Marine Forest Park is located in the ocean 15 kilometers southeast of Yuhuan County and **is composed of** both Dalu (Big Dear) and Xiaolu (Little Deer) Islands which are connected with **shoal**, hence the name Dalu Island. Its total area is about 1.75 square kilometers with a coastline as long as 5.45 kilometers. It is said that a fairy deer **was stricken by** the lightening and fell into the sea because of having stolen the seeds and **sowed** them on the earth. The island got its name from the legend, and also from the mountains of which shapes are like a deer raising its head above the sea level.

Dalu Island is the only marine forest park at the national level. The trees are so **lush** and evergreen that the Island looks like an **emerald** in the sea. Therefore, it has got the reputation as "the Jade in East China Sea". According to **statistics**, the forest coverage rate of the island has reached 87.5% and the forest reserves have amounted to more than 3,300 cubic meters. There are nearly 204 fields, 534 sections and 1,000 kinds of plants, such as ginkgo, **camphor**, black pine, **sequoia**, etc., forming good vegetation. Dalu Island has already become the best island which has the richest kinds of plants in Zhejiang Province.

The hill part of Dalu Island is mainly made up of the late Jurassic volcanic bedrocks which have been **eroded** for millions of years thus producing fantastic and different rocks, caves and **reefs**, etc. Here are a lot of famous scenic spots, such as Arhat Rock, General Cave, Lion Rock, Stone Fish and so on.

The forest, sea, beach and rock carvings have made Dalu Island a unique scenic site which now has 20 places of great interest and 77 spots, of which Dragon-Flying Cave, Rope Bridge, Eight Fairies Crossing the Sea, 500 Arhats, Longevity God Rock, Fisherman Cave, Quarry Stones and 1,000 Buddha Niches are considered to be the top-8 famous scenic spots on the island. Each of them has its own features.

Besides, Dalu Island is an island of art and full of rock carvings carved by some well-known artists such as Liu Haisu, Sha Menghai, Lu Yanshao, etc. Furthermore, tourists here can have a lot of fun in picking many shells such as conches, oysters and so on.

★生词与词组 Words & Expressions

shoal /ʃəul/ *n.* 浅滩

lush /lʌʃ/ *adj.* (草等植物)茂盛的

statistics /stə'tistiks/ *n.* 统计资料

sequoia /si'kwɔiə/ *n.* 红杉

reef /ri:f/ *n.* 暗礁

be stricken by 遭受……损害

sow /səu/ *v.* 播种

emerald /'em(ə)r(ə)ld/ *n.* 绿宝石

camphor /'kæmfə/ *n.* 香樟

erode /i'rəud/ *v.* 腐蚀

be composed of 由……组成

◆ 知识拓展 Knowledge Extension

礁滩：地质历史时期或现在由于海相沉积作用，在海水或波浪的搬运下，沉积物堆积形成的岸，通常由生物碎屑和沙砾充填，是重要的油气资源指示标志。

3. 方山—南嵩岩 The Fangshan Hill–Nansong Rock

方山—南嵩岩地处温岭大溪镇，系北雁荡山余脉，总面积 9.88 平方千米，以古火山口火山地貌为基础，集危岩绝壁、奇峰深谷、飞瀑溪涧、田园风光等自然景观与人文景观于一体，气势雄伟，地貌奇特，风光清丽，被人们称之为"神山仙境""空中花园"，可与雁荡山、天台山媲美。

方山—南嵩岩，由方山、南嵩岩、狮峰三大景区组成。历史文化源远流长，被古人誉为"东南第一名山"，是明朝礼部侍郎、国子监祭酒谢铎的故里。王羲之、徐霞客等历史名人都曾游历过此地，并留有优美的诗句。景区于 2004 年 11 月被评为国家森林公园，在 2005年被列为世界地质公园。

方山景区周围 5 千米皆壁立千仞，气势磅礴，难于攀登。远观山体雄隐、如桌如台，故称方山。山顶坦荡开阔，约 47 万平方米的山场平旷如野，恍若空中平原，天外琼台，堪称天下第一大顶。山顶四季犹如一座天然的巨大空中花园。方山整体千变万化的地貌和危崖怪石，可探险、寻幽、揽胜，具有很高的游赏价值。

南嵩岩景区地貌断层交错，陡峭的地势，短促的河流，形成了极为雄险而丰富的崖谷景观，奇峰突兀。景区内四时苍翠，朦朦胧胧，尤其是枫树湾内，秋季时节，满山红叶，桂花飘香。南嵩岩的嵩岩讲寺是浙江临济宗的一个著名大道场，藏于深山大谷之中，隐于茂林修竹之间，名僧辈出，留下许多悠远的胜迹遗踪。

狮峰景区素以壮奇见称，有很多名胜景点。主景点狮子头峰高 309 米，山势雄伟，景区崖壁奇绝，景点之间以栈道连接，内贴绝壁，外临深谷。洞穴景观奇特，烟火洞主洞有 200余平方米，俨然一座天然的大雄宝殿，主洞有三个岩穴通往各方，盘曲幽深，最为神奇，让游人叹为观止。

The Fangshan Hill–Nansong Rock lies in Daxi Town of Wenling and comes down in one continuous line with the Northern Mount Yandang. With a total area of 9.88 square kilometers, and the foundation of the ancient volcano **crater** landscape, the Fangshan Hill–Nansong Rock has both natural and artificial scenic spots such as **perilous** rock cliffs, deep valleys, waterfalls and streams as well as country sights. Because of these magnificent, unique and beautiful sceneries, it is known as "mountain **paradise**" and "sky gardens", compared to the Yandang and Mount Tiantai.

Made up of three parts: the Fangshan Hill, the Nansong Rock and the Lion Peak, Fangshan Hill–Nansong Rock with a long history and profound culture, **was reputed as** "the most famous mountain in the south–east of China" and the hometown of Mr. Xie Duo, an official in the Ming Dynasty. Wang Xizhi, Xu Xiake and other celebrities had been here and left some wonderful poems. It was appraised as a National Forest Park in November 2004 and a World Geological Park in 2005.

The Fangshan Hill is surrounded by sharp cliffs and steep hills within 5 kilometers. It looks like a desk or a table viewed from a long distance away, so it is called Fangshan (Square Mount). The top is broad and level, with a 47-hectare peak looking like a plain in the air. So it is considered to be the biggest peak on earth and it is like a beautiful garden with different sceneries in four seasons. Besides, its **changeable** landforms and strange rocks make it very explorative and enjoyable.

The Nansong Rock has a lot of cliffs, peaks and valleys. Autumn is the best season to come here for it is full of maple trees and sweet **osmanthus** trees. The Songyan Temple is a famous temple hidden in the deep valley and a lot of Buddhist monks have been living here, leaving a lot of ancient historical tourist spots.

The Lion Peak is magnificent and fantastic. It has many great places of interest. The main place is the Lion-head Peak which is about 309 meters high. It is huge and steep. Walking on the narrow footway planked over a cliff, you can enjoy and explore the natural scenery. Besides, the Fireworks Cavern is over 200 square meters and looks like a natural big palace. Three main caves lead to different directions in the zigzagging deep cavern, making it **attractive** to the tourists.

★生词与词组 Words & Expressions

crater /ˈkreitə/ *n.* 火山口
paradise /ˈpærədaiis/ *n.* 天堂
osmanthus /ɔzˈmænθəs/ *n.* 桂花
be reputed as 被认为……

perilous /ˈperiləs/ *adj.* 危险的
changeable /ˈtʃein(d)ʒəb(ə)l/ *adj.* 易变的
attractive /əˈtræktiv/ *adj.* 有吸引力的

◆ 知识拓展 Knowledge Extension

谢铎(1435—1510)：明朝藏书家、文学家。字鸣治，号方石。他博通经史，文学造诣极深。为"茶陵诗派"重要作家，又是理学家。他的理学思想对浙中阳明学派有深远影响。

侍郎：官名。西汉侍郎为郎官之一，掌守宫廷门户，充当车骑随从皇帝。明侍郎升至正三品，清侍郎升至从二品，与尚书同为各部堂官。

国子监祭酒：中国清朝中央政府官职之一，品级为从四品。该官职隶属于清朝最高学府：国子监。主要任务为掌大学之法与教学考试，其上为监事大臣，辖下有监丞等辅佐官职。

4. 景宁畬乡 Jingning Shexiang Town

景宁畬乡大均村是一个小小的古村，人口仅为 400 有余。据悉大均古村始建于唐末，这一千多年来始终是瓯江支流的小溪流域水陆交通枢纽，商贸经济繁荣，耕读文化氛围浓厚，形成了大均人重"三杆"的民俗，即笔杆、秤杆、竹杆(撑篙)，大均人多靠写契、写文书、做生意和撑船撑排谋生。在建筑上形成了明清风格的古朴的前店后院式山区商贸古街风貌和石板街面，享有"小溪明珠""景宁最高学府""浙南芙蓉镇"之美称。此外畬民还有他们自己的语言，其婚嫁特色服饰等有浓郁的民族特色。

景宁封金山是南宋畬民迁来景宁的聚居地，亦是蓝姓畬民入浙的最早发祥地。相传当年农民垦地时掘出了黄金，由此封金山被畬民视为畬族传说中的"桃花源"。畬族风情名胜丰富，有深受游客喜爱的活泼风趣的婚俗演绎，还有众多保存良好具有欣赏价值的畬族文物。封金山上有一瀑布，时而奔腾呼啸，急浪翻滚，时而又飞流细雨。山上另一著名景点是一老屋，相传此屋建于清朝，三进两厢类似三室两厅结构，屋内雕刻自然精细，总体保存良好，是山间不可多得的古民居建筑。

封金山大峡谷有面积约 33 万平方米的桃林，还有天然巨石，石下巨鳞，有温泉流出。石面有奇文。如果敲击这块神奇的石头的不同部位，它还会发出悦耳的声音。此外，封金山也有着许多神话传说，这些传说故事赋予封金山更多的神奇魅力。

Lying in Jingning Shexiang Town, Dajun Village is a small old village of which the population is only about 400. Dajun Village's construction began at the end of the Tang Dynasty. It has been the land and water transportation hub in the stream basin, **tributary** of the Ou River for one thousand years, where the trade and economy is rather **brisk**, and study and plantation are paid great attention to. Therefore, Dajun people **attach great importance to** the folk costumes of "three **rods**", namely the pen, the weighbeam and the bamboo punt-pole. The local people often make a living by writing contracts, doing records management, doing business or **propelling** the boat. In terms of architecture, local buildings have gathered simple and original trade streets and pavements laid with **flagstones** into one organic whole. Dajun Village also enjoys the reputation of "the pearl of little stream", "the highest institution of Jingning", "the lotus town of South Zhejiang". The She People have their own spoken languages; besides they also have their traditional wedding fineries with distinctive characteristics.

The Mount Fengjin (the Gold Mountain) is the vast melting-pot to which She people of the Southern Song Dynasty migrated and it is also the earliest cradle for the Lan people. It is said that farmers found gold when they ploughed land; therefore, the Mount Fengjin was considered to be an ideal place for the She people to live in. The town displays its rich and unique natural scenery and ethnic folklore such as the marriage custom, which is quite lively and is deeply loved by tourists. Meanwhile, many cultural relics are well kept there. We can also see a waterfall in the Mount Fengjin. It **splashes** over the rock. Sometimes, it falls rapidly with high-wind and pressing-waves, at other times the waterfall flows gently like a drizzle. Another famous scenic spot is the old house with three rooms and two halls built with stones. It is said that this old stone house was built in the Qing Dynasty. Its carvings are natural and exquisite and the whole house is well kept. It is a rare ancient residential building in the mountain.

About 330,000 square meters of peach trees are planted in the Mount Fengjin Valley. There is a natural huge stone in which spring water flows out. Some remarkable articles are carved on the stone. The **miraculous** stone makes **euphonic** sounds as long as you knock at different positions of the stone. Moreover, the Mount Fengjin is also the cradle of folk tales, making the place more charming and attractive.

★生词与词组 Words & Expressions

tributary /'tribjut(ə)ri/ *n.* 支流
rod /rɒd/ *n.* 杆
flagstone /'flægstəun/ *n.* 石板
splash /splæʃ/ *v.* (指液体) 溅落
euphonic /ju:'fɒnik/ *adj.* 好听的

brisk /brisk/ *adj.* 兴隆的
propel /prə'pel/ *v.* 推动
emphasize /'emfəsaiz/ *v.* 强调
miraculous /mi'rækjuləs/ *adj.* 奇迹般的
attach great importance to 重视

◆ 知识拓展 Knowledge Extension

畲族：我国典型的散居民族之一。他们自称"山哈"。唐代，畲族居住在福建、广东、江西三省交界地区。包括畲族先民在内的少数民族被泛称为"蛮僚""峒蛮"或"峒僚"。南宋末年，史书上开始出现"畲民"和"拳民"的族称。畲，意为刀耕火种。新中国成立后，改称"畲族"。畲族极少部分使用畲语，属汉藏语系苗瑶语族。畲族无本民族文字，通用汉字。全国只有一个畲族自治县，位于浙南山区，景宁畲族源于唐永泰二年(766)，从闽迁居浙西南时落户景宁，距今已有1200多年历史。因此，景宁又称为中国畲乡。

5. 孔氏南宗家庙 The Confucius South Ancestral Temple

浙江衢州孔氏南宗家庙是全国重点文物保护单位。衢州孔庙是全国主要的两家孔氏家庙之一，素称"南宗"(北宗位于山东曲阜)。

南宗孔庙于宋宝祐元年(1253)始建，明正德十五年(1520)迁于现址，历经多次修葺。1998年经过全面修缮，作为衢州市历史博物馆对外开放。主体建筑有头门、大成门、大成殿、东西两庑、思鲁阁、圣泽楼等。

据史载，北宋末年，宋都汴京(今河南开封)陷入金兵之手。宋高宗赵构仓促南渡，孔子第四十八代裔孙、衍圣公孔端友，负着孔子和亓(qí)官夫人(孔子夫人)的一对楷木像(据传为孔子学生子贡所刻)，离开山东曲阜南迁，定居于衢州。宋宝佑三年(1255)，敕建孔氏家庙，为南宗。孔子后裔子孙已在衢州度过了800多个春秋。衢州作为孔子后裔的第二故乡，向来有"南方圣地"之称。

事实上，全国唯一的"一城三孔庙"中的"一城"指的就是柯城。在衢州市区县学街县学公园内，还有一专门记载衢州"一城三孔庙"(衢州府孔庙、西安县孔庙、南宗孔氏家庙)的"石书"。

曲阜的孔氏家庙只有一个用处，就是用作孔氏家族祭祖的场所。而衢州的家庙承担着两个任务，一是官方祭孔场所的官庙；二是孔氏祭祖的专祠。由此可见，衢州孔庙同时具有官庙和家庙两种身份。

The Confucian South **Ancestral** Temple is a cultural relic site under the national protection. Being one of the two Confucian family temples in the world, the Temple is commonly called the South Temple with the other one in Qufu of Shandong called the Confucian North Ancestral Temple.

The temple was built in Baoyou reign (1253) of the Song Dynasty and was moved to where it is in Zhengde reign of the Ming Dynasty (1520). The temple was repaired many times in history. In 1998, after full **reparation**, it was open to the public as a historical museum. Its main buildings include the First Gate, Gate Dacheng, Dacheng Palace, Dacheng Hall, East and West Corridor Rooms, Silu Pavilion, Shengze Pagoda, etc.

According to the records of history, Capital Bianjing was occupied by the forces of the Jin Dynasty at the end of the Northern Song Dynasty. Emperor Gaozong ran away to the south and built the Southern Song Dynasty. Kong Duanyou, an offspring of Confucius, carried Confucius' and his wife's wooden figures, left Qufu for Quzhou and lived there ever since. In 1255, he built the temple in Quzhou where his descendants lived for more than 800 years. Therefore, Quzhou was the second hometown for Confucius' descendants and the temple was **dignified** with the name South Shrine.

Actually, "one city" in the old saying "Three Confucian Temples in One City" refers to Ke City (the old name of Quzhou). And now in one park of Quzhou, there are still some stone carvings recording the information about "Three Confucian Temples in One City" in Quzhou.

The Confucian Family Temple in Qufu has only one role that is to be used as a place for the whole family to **worship** their ancestors. However, the Confucian Family Temple in Quzhou has two tasks one is to be the **official** temple where the officials can worship the Confucius, and the other is an ancestral temple for the Confucian family. Therefore, the Confucian Temple in Quzhou has both official and personal status. Its connotation includes both the official Confucian Temple and the Confucian Family Temple.

★生词与词组 Words & Expressions

ancestral /æn'sestrəl/ *adj.* 祖先的
dignify /'dignifai/ *v.* 使显得威严
official /ə'fiʃl/ *adj.* 官方的

reparation /ˌrepə'reiʃ(ə)n/ *n.* 修复
worship /'wəːʃip/ *v.* 崇拜

◆ 知识拓展 Knowledge Extension

柯城：泛指衢州府城。衢州府城是府、县二级共城的一座古城。明代余敷中在《太末集》中认为，衢城称柯城来源于烂柯山，因为衢南"九龙山右支渡河会黄坛诸山，经柯山逶迤入府城"而得名。

6. 临海桃渚风景名胜区 Linhai Taozhu Provincial Scenic Site

桃渚地貌独特，海景雄奇，为省级风景名胜区。由因戚继光抗倭而闻名于世的国家文物保护单位桃渚古城、小雁荡武坑、天下奇观珊瑚岩等众多景观组成，面积约 150 平方千米，有 200 多个景点。

桃渚古城始建于明洪武年间(1387)，是明代浙东沿海用于抗倭的 41 个卫所中唯一保存完好的石头古城。城周长 1366 米，高 4.5 米，城门狭小，外面筑有瓮城。城墙以条石及石块垒筑而成，上面苔痕斑斑。古城内外，古迹众多，风景优美。后所山上有"眺远""镇海"石刻、抗倭亭、烽火台；城内有抗倭陈列馆、古城一条街等。桃渚城在明代的抗倭战争中发挥过十分重要的作用。戚继光在台州抗倭八年，功勋卓著。

桃渚城是风景优美的旅游胜地，城四周山水俱佳。据说南宋文天祥落荒从海道过此，看到了桃渚雄奇的风景赞其为"海上仙子国"；武坑是一片由火山熔岩形成的峰林，峰奇崖峻，有小雁荡之称。几十处峰岩既高又怪，乌龟、展旗、仙人担等各种形态，惟妙惟肖；联辉、玉镜等洞穴各有特色；火焰山一线瀑、珍珠瀑等更是美不胜收。

珊瑚岩总面积约 5 平方千米，是一处国内罕见的火山熔岩柱状节理地质景观，这里还是侏罗纪江南翼龙化石的发现地，对研究我国东南沿海地区古代的地理气候以及地质地貌有很高价值。

Taozhu is a provincial scenic spot which has unique **geographic** features and wonderful sea-views. It covers about 150 square kilometers and has almost 200 sites, including the Ancient Castle of Taozhu famous for Qi Jiguang, a general of the Ming Dynasty fighting against ancient Japanese **pirates**, Wukeng Sight Area which is also called the Small Mount Yandang, and Coral Rock Sight Area.

The Ancient Castle of Taozhu was firstly built in 1387, during the Hongwu reign of the Ming Dynasty. It is the only well-preserved ancient stone city among the 41 defending spots which were used to fight against the Japanese pirates in the eastern coast of Zhejiang Province. The city is 1,366 meters in perimeter and 4.5 meters in height, with a narrow gate and a small town outside for defence. The wall is made of bar stones and rocks, with a lot of moss on it. Both inside and outside of the ancient castle are there a lot of wonderful historical sites. On the back mountains of the castle, there are stone carvings titled "Tiaoyuan" (far-looking) and "Zhenhai" (sea-protecting, Japanese Pirate Resistant Booth, and beacon towers. While in the inner city, there are exhibition houses storing the war materials of defending against the Japanese pirates and a street of the ancient city. Taozhu Castle has played a very important role in the war against Japanese pirates. General Qi Jiguang had been in Taizhou for eight years since 1555 and had won a lot of battles against the Japanese pirates.

Taozhu Castle is also a beautiful scenic spot which has been surrounded by mountains and rivers. It is said that the famous general Wen Tianxiang in the Southern Song Dynasty had praised

Taozhu as the fairy place.

Wukeng Sight Area, also called the Small Mount Yandang because of its odd and steep peaks, is actually a pit formed by **volcanic** rocks. Scores of peaks are as vivid as turtles, flag-flying, stone barbell; and caverns are unique with their own features such as Lianhui and Yujing Caves; while the Volcanic String Waterfall and the Pearl Waterfall are much more beautiful.

Coral Rock Sight Area covers about 5 square kilometers. It is a rare domestic **lava columnar** joint geological landscape. It is also the place where the **fossil** of **pterosaur** of Jurassic Period were discovered. So it enjoys a high value of studying the climate, geography as well as geological features of ancient China's southeastern coastal areas.

★生词与词组 Words & Expressions

geographic /dʒiə'græfik/ *adj.* 地理的

volcanic /vɔl'kænik/ *adj.* 火山的

columnar /kə'lʌmnə/ *n.* 圆柱

pterosaur /'terəsɔː/ *n.* 翼龙目动物

pirate /'pairət/ *n.* 海盗

lava /'lɑːvə/ *n.* 火山熔岩

fossil /'fɔs(ə)l/ *n.* 化石

◆ 知识拓展 Knowledge Extension

嘉靖皇帝(1507—1566)：即明世宗朱厚熜，明朝第十一位皇帝。早期整顿朝纲、减轻赋役，对外抗击倭寇，后史誉之谓"中兴时期"。执政后期崇信道教，此后不再理政。嘉靖四十五年(1566)驾崩，谥号钦天履命英毅圣神宣文广武洪仁大孝肃皇帝。葬于北京十三陵之永陵。

7. 龙游石窟——世界第九大奇迹 Longyou Grottoes—The Ninth Wonder of the World

龙游石窟景区为省级文物保护单位，于 2003 年 12 月被国家旅游局列为国家 4A 级旅游区。

龙游石窟是一处气势恢宏、瑰丽壮观、世界罕见的古代地下人工建筑群。根据专家初步断定，龙游石窟的开凿年代最晚不迟于西汉时期。龙游石窟不仅具有很高的社会学、历史学、考古学、古建筑学、工程地质学和岩石力学等多学科的研究价值，而且也具有巨大的教育价值、文物保护价值和旅游开发价值。

龙游石窟于 1992 年 6 月被发现。据勘察，在方圆 0.38 平方千米的土丘上至少分布了大小 36 个洞窟，洞窟面积从 1000 平方米至 3000 平方米不等，每个洞窟从矩形洞口开始垂直向下延伸，高度约 30 米，顶部呈"倒斗形"，窟内均科学地分布 3～4 根巨大的"鱼尾形"石柱，与洞顶浑然一体，洞壁、洞顶和石柱上都均匀地留下了古人似乎带有装饰意图的凿痕。1–5 号洞窟已开发并对游人开放，其余仍保持原状。

龙游石窟具有令人震撼的精美凿纹和诸多古代工程科学技术亮点，因重重谜团而备受国内外有关专家学者和旅游业内人士的高度关注，这些谜团不仅有许多至今难以解开的人文方面的谜团(例如开凿目的、年代等问题)，而且在工程"设计"、施工和得以保持长期稳定的原因等方面也存在不少值得用岩石力学和工程地质学原理解释的悬念。龙游石窟以其庞大的规模，复杂的建筑工艺被誉为"世界第九大奇迹"。

Longyou **Grottoes**, a key cultural relics protection site of Zhejiang Province, became the AAAA Grade national tourist area in December 2003, chosen by the National Tourism Administration.

It is an **enormous** underground architectural complex, full of mysteries. According to the judgments of experts, it was dug no later than the Western Han Dynasty. Longyou Grottoes not only has high research value in multi-subjects such as sociology, history, **archaeology**, ancient architecture, engineering geology and rock mechanics, etc., but also has great value in education, cultural relic protection and tourism exploration, etc.

Longyou Grottoes was found in June 1992. It is found that 36 caves of all sizes from 1,000 to 3,000 square meters lie in a mound that occupies an area of only 0.38 square kilometer. Each cave extends down vertically from the top **rectangular** hole with a height of about 30 meters. And the top which looks like an inverted funnel blended naturally into those 3 or 4 huge stone pillars which are shaped like a fish tail scattering in the cave. All those walls, tops and stone pillars **are engraved with** some decorative carvings. At present No.1 to No.5 grottoes have been explored and are now open to the tourists while others are still in their original forms.

Its beautifully carved marks and engineering research values have attracted tourists and experts all over the world. It contains not only **humanity** mysteries such as why and when it was built, but also gives rise to arguments on how it was designed and constructed, considered the low level of rock mechanics and geology at the time. Longyou Grottoes is reputed as the Ninth Wonder of the World.

★生词与词组 Words & Expressions

grotto /'grɒtəʊ/ *n.* 洞穴
archaeology /ˌɑ:ki'ɒlədʒi/ *n.* 考古学
humanity /hju:'mænəti/ *n.* 人文

enormous /i'nɔ:məs/ *adj.* 巨大的
rectangular /rek'tæŋgjulə/ *adj.* 长方形的
be engraved with 刻上

◆ 知识拓展 Knowledge Extension

　　世界八大奇迹：指埃及金字塔、希腊奥林匹亚宙斯神像、希腊罗德岛太阳神巨像、巴比伦空中花园、希腊阿尔忒弥斯神庙、土耳其摩索拉斯陵墓、埃及亚历山大港灯塔、中国秦始皇陵兵马俑。

8. 廿八都古镇——遗落在大山里的梦 The Twenty-eighth City—Dreamland in the Mountains

　　廿八都地处江山市仙霞岭高山深谷之中，地势险要。四方关隘拱列，东有安民关，南有枫岭关，西有六石关，北有仙霞关，易守难攻。浙闽赣三省边界的地理位置和历史上的频繁战争、屯兵、移民，使廿八都成为"方言王国"和名副其实的"百姓古镇"，镇上有 13 种方言和 142 种姓氏。

廿八都之名源于 1071 年，北宋时在浙江南部设都 44 个，这个小镇排行 28，因此得名"廿八都"。1991 年 9 月 15 日被浙江省人民政府批准为省级首批历史文化名镇。

小镇古建筑风貌依旧。古镇至今仍保存有两段较完整的约 1 千米长的古商业街道和 36 座民居古建筑。镇上的一条古街，是 19 世纪保存下来的，窄得无法通行汽车，但两边店铺密集，户户相挨。十余幢公共建筑，二十多幢古民居基本保持明、清两代建筑风貌。其建筑风格与浙皖一带的水乡民居不同，融合了浙式木雕、徽式砖雕、赣式灰墙、闽北客家式甚至还有洛可可式等建筑风格。尤其是"文昌阁"，建筑内还保存了大量文化价值相当高的壁画以及保婴局的碑文，称之为"民间建筑博览馆"。其规模之大，艺术水平之高，保存之完整，实属国内罕见。

Located in the deep valleys and high mountains of Jiangshan City, the Twenty-eighth City is a very important, **strategic** and difficult place for access. It has one gateway in each direction, the Anmin Gate in the east, the Fengling Gate in the south, the Liushi Gate in the west and the Xianxia Gate in the north. Therefore, it is easy to hold but hard to attack. Moreover, the geographical position at the border of three provinces as well as the **frequent** wars in history, station **troops** and **migration** have made it become a **dialect** kingdom and an ancient town for ordinary people for it has 13 dialects and 142 family names.

The Twenty-eighth City got its name in 1071 because during the Northern Song Dynasty, the central government set 44 branches in the south of Zhejiang Province, and it happened to be No. 28. And on September 15, 1991, it was approved by the Zhejiang Provincial People's Government as one of the provincial historical and cultural towns.

At present, the town still keeps a lot of its original buildings and constructions. For example, it still has two main complete ancient **commercial** streets for about 1 kilometer and 36 old **vernacular** buildings. As for the ancient commercial street which survives from the 19th century, it is so narrow that even a car is difficult to pass. However, both sides of it are lined with shops and residential houses. Although 10 more public buildings and 20 more ancient residential houses still keep the styles of the Ming and Qing dynasties, the structures are quite different from those of the regions of waters and lakes in other parts of Zhejiang and Anhui provinces, for they blend with various other styles, such as Zhejiang wood-carving style, Anhui brick-carving style, Jiangxi grey-wall style, Fujian Hakka style and even rococo style. In Wenchang Pavilion, highly-valued **frescoes** and **epigraphs** are kept in such a big scale that it is even rare in China. For this reason, it is reputed "the Museum of Public Constructions".

★生词与词组 Words & Expressions

strategic /strə'ti:dʒik/ *adj.* 有战略意义的
troop /tru:p/ *n.* 军队
dialect /'daiəlekt/ *n.* 方言
vernacular /və'nækjulə/ *n.* 本地的
epigraph /'epigrɑ:f/ *n.* 碑文

frequent /'fri:kwənt/ *adj.* 时常发生的
migration /mai'greiʃ(ə)n/ *n.* 迁移
commercial /kə'mə:ʃ(ə)l/ *adj.* 商业的
fresco /'freskəu/ *n.* 壁画

◆ 知识拓展 Knowledge Extension

都城：指封"邑"之城。而大城为"都"，小城为"邑"。所以，古代都城指国家(包括诸侯国)的首都及较大的城市。后人亦称国都(各国及诸侯国首都)为"都城"。现特指"首都"。

9. 皤滩古镇　Potan Ancient Town

皤滩乃永安溪独一无二的五溪汇合点，即朱姆溪、万竹溪、九都溪、黄榆溪和永安溪同点汇入的永安溪，故皤滩有夜观五月(指五个月亮倒影)之景。皤滩又是水陆交汇之地，沿灵江、永安溪的水路在皤滩拢岸，通往浙西的苍岭古道也在皤滩起步。由于其连接东南沿海与浙西内陆的优越地理位置，早在公元998年，这里就因水路便利而成为永安溪沿岸一个繁华的集镇。

经过了千年的沉淀和积累，皤滩仍保存有1.5千米长的鹅卵石铺砌的"龙"型古街。古街形似一条龙，西龙头，东龙尾，中段弯曲成龙身。龙头所对是五溪汇合点，而龙尾所在处矗立着一座国内罕见的砖雕坊，高3.5米，跨度8米，砖头的外表上刻着一组组玲珑剔透、栩栩如生的龙凤、麒麟、仙鹤、花卉、人物等图案。古街两旁至今还保存着260多家店铺，还有不少书香门第，其中以长门堂和何氏里门堂为突出。

此外，皤滩的桐江书院和无骨花灯都蕴涵着千年的文化内涵。桐江书院是南宋哲学家、教育家朱熹送子求学的地方，号称"江南第一书院"，已成为广大游客旅游观光、接受传统文化熏陶的一处胜地。皤滩无骨花灯，始于唐盛于明，灯身没有骨架，全由用绣花针绣成各种花纹图案的纸片粘贴而成，且轻巧能飞，有"中华第一灯"之誉。

Potan is a unique **convergence** of five streams called Zhumu, Wanzhu, Jiudu, Huangyu and Yong'an. Therefore, tourists can enjoy the scenery of five **inverted** images of the moon on the five streams at night. Potan is at the crossroad of the land and the sea. It gathers the water route of Lingjiang and Yong'an Stream. The Cangling Trail which leads to the west of Zhejiang starts from here too. Because of its superior geographic location connecting the southeast coast with the western Zhejiang inland, it had been a bustling **littoral** market along Yong'an Stream for its **facilitated** waterway since 998.

1,000 years have passed, and Potan still preserves 1.5-kilometer-long "dragon" type ancient pebbled street. The west is the dragon head, east the dragon tail, and middle the curved body. The head just faces the connecting point of five streams, and on the tail stands a rare brick archway which is 3.5 meters in height and 8 meters in span and with a lot of lively designs carved on it, such as dragon and phoenix, unicorn, crane, flowers and personage, etc. On both sides of the street there are more than 260 shops as well as some families of scholars, among which Changmen Hall and Heshilimen Hall are **highlighted** for their unique features.

In addition, Tongjiang Academy and Needle-**pierced** Boneless Lantern have a history of over 1,000 years. Tongjiang Academy, "the Best Academy in Jiangnan" was the school where the well-known philosopher and educator of the Southern Song Dynasty Zhu Xi had his son once

浙江景点文化双语教程

studied. It has been a resort where thousands of tourists can tour and sightsee, or learn traditional culture. Needle-pierced Boneless Lantern started in the Tang Dynasty and bloomed in the Ming Dynasty. It had no framework and was made by needle-pierced paper so that it was light and could fly high, hence the **reputation** of "First-grade Lantern of China".

★生词与词组 Words & Expressions

convergence /kən'və:dʒəns/ *n.* 集中
littoral /'lit(ə)r(ə)l/ *adj.* 沿海（湖）的
highlight /'hailait/ *v.* 突出
reputation /repju'teiʃ(ə)n/ *n.* 名声

inverted /in'və:tid/ *adj.* 倒转的
facilitated /fə'siliteitid/ *adj.* 便利的
pierce /piəs/ *v.* 刺穿

◆ 知识拓展 Knowledge Extension

麒麟：中国古籍中记载的一种动物，外形像鹿，头上独角，全身有鳞甲，尾像牛尾，与凤、龟、龙共称为"四灵"，是神的坐骑。古人把麒麟当作仁兽、瑞兽。雄性称麒，雌性称麟，常用来比喻杰出的人。麒麟文化是中国的传统民俗文化。盼麒麟送子，就是中国古代的生育崇拜之一。麒麟主太平，带来丰年、福禄、长寿与美好。玄学称麒麟是岁星散开而生成，故主祥瑞，含仁怀义。

桐江书院：宋乾道年间(1165—1172)方斫建，位于今台州蟠滩乡山下村与板桥村之间。当年的桐江书院前有鼎山叠翠，后有溪水萦回，东有鉴湖烟柳，西可登临道渊山，确是环境清幽的钟灵毓秀之地。桐江书院创办后，名闻遐迩。"四方之学士文人，负笈从游者尝踵相接。"朱熹、王十朋等历史名人新笔题写的"鼎山堂""桐江书院"匾额沿存。朱熹曾两次巡视仙居，并满怀激情地留下了"鼎山堂"三个字。这个真迹匾额至今还保存着。

无骨花灯：起源于唐朝，当时人们把花灯称为"唐灯"，也有人叫它"神灯"。此灯造型别致，工艺独特，灯身没有骨架，全由用绣花针绣成各种花纹图案的纸片粘贴而成，且轻巧能飞。制作这种花灯的工艺比较复杂，要经过绘图、粘贴、烫纸、剪样、装订、凿花、拷背、刺绣、竖灯、装饰等十道主要工序。1996 年 10 月份获 "96 中国民间工艺品博览会" 金奖。同年 12 月份又荣获 "96 澳门第四届国际文化艺术品展览会" 金奖。

---

10. 庆元古桥 The Ancient Bridges in Qingyuan

庆元木拱廊桥不但具有全国数量众多、历史悠久、历史沿革具连贯性的特点。庆元有四座知名的古桥梁：菇城镇的咏归桥，五大堡乡的濛淤桥、兰溪桥，竹口镇的后坑桥，均为大跨度伸臂木拱桥，历史悠久，结构独特，造型优美。

咏归桥在庆元县松源镇北，有十余米长，桥名语出《论语·先进》。咏归桥建桥 500 多年来，历遭洪水、大火，几经兴废。咏归桥木构伸臂起拱，成弓状木拱桥，木拱不用一枚铁钉，桥面铺设石块，平坦坚固。桥北首为两层建筑，名曰"补天阁"，昔有衣带飘风的女娲塑像。

濛淤桥在庆元县五大堡乡濛淤村，始建于元代，屡毁屡修。现存桥体系 1986 年重修。

濛淤桥为本拱伸臂廊桥，长 36 米，宽 4.5 米。现系县级文物保护单位。

兰溪桥位于庆元县五大堡乡西洋村，始建于 1574 年，1794 年重修，1984 年按原貌迁建今址。全长 48.4 米，宽 6 米，是全国现存单孔跨度最大的木拱桥。虽历经百年风雨，仍保存完好，系全省现存同类桥梁的最早实例，颇具研究价值。1997 年列入省级文物保护单位。

后坑桥始建于 1671 年，1885 年重修。长 36 米，宽 5 米，为县级文物保护单位。

The ancient wooden arch bridges in Qingyuan own the characteristics of the large number, the long history, and the coherent in historical evolution in China. There are four famous ancient bridges in Qingyuan, which are the Yonggui Bridge in Gucheng Town, the Mengyu Bridge and the Lanxi Bridge in Wudabao Town, the Houkeng Bridge in Zhukou Town. These bridges have a long history and are all beautifully shaped and **particularly** constructed.

Located to the north of Songyuan Town, Qingyuan County, the Yonggui Bridge, named after a well-known sentence from *The Analects of Confucius,* is more than 10 meters long. It has a history of more than 500 years. The bridge has gone through many floods and fires and has been rebuilt many times. It is an arched wooden bridge, which **stretches** out like a bow. The constructors built the whole bridge without a nail, but it is still solid and **smooth**. There is a two-floor garret named as Mending the Sky Attic in the north of the bridge. Once a statue of a goddess named Nüwa who was dressed beautifully was put here.

The Mengyu Bridge is located in Mengyu Village, Wudabao Town, Qingyuan County. It was founded in the Yuan Dynasty, and has been rebuilt many times. The existing part was rebuilt in 1986. The Mengyu Bridge is an extended arched bridge which is 36 meters in length and 4.5 meters in width. And now it is a historical and cultural site under the county government's protection.

The Lanxi Bridge, located in Xiyang Village, Wudabao Town, Qingyuan County, was built in 1574 and rebuilt in 1794. And in 1984 it was removed to its present location keeping its original appearance. It is 48.4 meters in length and 6 meters in width and it is the longest existing wooden arch bridge with only one opening in China. It has experienced a lot, yet it remains intact. And it is of great value in research on the other bridges in the same era. It became a provincial cultural relic protection unit in 1997.

The Houkeng Bridge was founded in 1671, and rebuilt in 1885. It is 36 meters in length and 5 meters in width. It is a historical and cultural site under the county government's protection.

★生词与词组 Words & Expressions

particularly /pə'tikjuləli/ *adv.* 特别，尤其　　　　**stretch** /stretʃ/ *v.* 延伸
smooth /smu:ð/ *adj.* 光滑的

◆ 知识拓展 Knowledge Extension

女娲：又称女阴、女娲娘娘、娲皇、女阴娘娘，史记女娲氏。一说她的名字为风里希(或为凤里牺)。是中国历史神话传说中的一位女神。女娲人首蛇身，不但是补天救世和抟土造人

的女神，还是一个创造万物的自然之神，神通广大，化生万物，每天至少能创造出七十样东西。她以黄泥仿照自己抟土造人，创造人类社会并建立婚姻制度；后因世间天塌地陷，于是熔五彩石以补天，斩鳌足以立四极，留下了"女娲补天"的神话传说。女娲是中华民族伟大的母亲，她开世造物，因此被称为大地之母，是被民间广泛而又长久崇拜的创世神和始祖神。

11. 蛇蟠岛 Shepan Island

蛇蟠岛位于三门湾蛇蟠洋，素有千洞岛之美称。岛上气候宜人，特别在盛夏季节，海风徐徐，凉气习习。岛上主要景观为因长期采石而留下的 1300 多个洞穴，因其姿态各异，使得洞洞为景，千姿百态，妙趣无穷。高楼岩洞，俗名强盗岩洞，传说以前住过强盗，故有此名。洞极深广，足可容纳两个篮球场。洞中有一"凸"字形裂口穿破顶洞，仰视可见蓝天白云。

岛上的海盗村景区是目前国内唯一一个以海盗为主题的海岛洞窟景区，其独特的海盗文化吸引了众多的游客。这里不仅汇集了千百年来中国海洋史上赫赫有名的"东海枭雄"，也招来了世界史上"盗"名远扬的"海上魔王"弗朗西斯·德雷克及"海盗女皇"卡特林娜等北欧海盗。遍布岛上的奇洞深穴，神秘诡异，令人惊叹，石自天生，洞由人掘，天之工巧，人之灵性，成就了千洞之美。

此外，在岛上品尝蟹肉也是一大乐趣。三门青蟹向来以"壳薄、膏黄、肉嫩、味美"闻名。三门县的青蟹养殖与捕捞已有 200 多年历史，占浙江产量的二分之一，全国的五分之一。三门中国青蟹节于每年的 9 月举行，蟹肥膏黄，正是品尝蟹肉的最佳时机。

Located in Shepan Waters, Sanmen Bay, Shepan Island is the biggest one among the islands in Taizhou and is called the Thousand-Cavern-Island. The island has good weather, especially in summer. You can feel the coolness from the gentle sea breeze. Its main scenery is the 1,300 caves which have been left for long years' **quarry**. These caves are totally different so that each can be an independent interesting scenic spot. The Gaolou Cave, also called the Robber Cave, is said to have been **occupied** by the **robbers**. The cave is as deep and broad as two basketball playgrounds. Through a "凸" shaped cleft which **penetrates** the top of the cave, the tourists can look up at the blue sky and the white clouds.

At present, the Pirate Village is a unique national island cavern taking pirate as the theme of the scenic spot, whose distinctive pirate culture has attracted a lot of visitors. There are not only the "East Sea Formidable Men" during the thousands of years in Chinese ocean history, but also Francis Drake, the well-known "Sea Devil" in the world as well as Katrina the "Pirate Queen" and other European pirates, etc. These special caves are mysterious and surprising. The stones are natural and the caves are dug by humans. So the Thousand-Cave-Island is made by the exquisiteness of the heaven and the intelligence of humans.

Besides, it is fun to taste **crabs** on the island. Sanmen Crab is famous for its thin shell, yellow cream, fresh and tender flesh and beautiful taste. The farming and fishing of crab in Sanmen County is of over 200 years of history and its products account for half of the output in Zhejiang and one fifth of the country. The Chinese Crab Festival is held in Sanmen every September and it is the best time to enjoy the crabs.

★生词与词组 Words & Expressions

quarry /ˈkwɔri/ *n.* 采石场　　　　occupy /ˈɔkjupai/ *v.* 侵占

robber /ˈrɔbə/ *n.* 强盗　　　　　　penetrate /ˈpenitreit/ *v.* 穿过

crab /kræb/ *n.* 螃蟹

◆ 知识拓展 Knowledge Extension

海盗：是指专门在海上抢劫其他船只的犯罪者。这是一门相当古老的犯罪行业，自有船只航行以来，就有海盗的存在。特别是航海发达的 16 世纪之后，只要是商业发达的沿海地带，就有海盗出没。由于海盗的特殊性、神秘性，海盗已经成为人们观念中带有传奇甚至魔幻色彩的存在。

12. 天台山 Mount Tiantai

天台山素以"佛宗道源，山水神秀"闻名于世，是中国佛教天台宗和日本天台宗的发祥地，也是中国道教南宗的祖庭，1992 年被列为浙江省十大旅游胜地，2000 年底又被国家旅游局评为全国首批 4A 级旅游区。

天台山自古闻名，景点也各有特色，可概括为古、清、奇、幽四个字。天台山自然景观得天独厚，人文景观悠久灿烂，大致分为 13 个景区，较为著名的有国清寺、石梁飞瀑、赤城山、寒山湖、华顶景区等。各景天然成趣，别具一格，各擅其胜，美不胜收。其中尤以石梁飞瀑、华顶归云等景致为最。

石梁飞瀑，位于方广寺前。两崖峭壁对峙，山腰间一块巨石横亘其间，因巨石颇似屋梁，故称石梁。梁面宽约 0.3 米，梁下有一飞瀑三折穿梁而出，从 40 多米高的峭壁上呼啸而下，色如霜雪，势若雷霆，极尽雄伟奇丽。

华顶是天台山主峰，海拔 1110 米。峰顶四周常有白云缭绕，晓雾昏烟，云气氤氲盘结，故有"华顶归云"之称。华顶现辟为国家森林公园，是浙东南地区著名的夏季避暑胜地。园内的云锦杜鹃是一片占地三百亩树龄百年的原始杜鹃林。每年 5 月开花，树之古、林之广、花之艳，堪称华夏奇观。此外，天台山有隋梅、唐樟，有被称为"长生不老药"的乌药和"救命仙草"的铁皮石斛等，盛产中药材，有白术、茯苓、石斛等名贵药材 1000 余种，还有大灵猫、云豹等珍稀野生动物。天台是中国最早产茶地之一。

Mount Tiantai is the **birthplace** of both Tiantai-sect of Chinese & Japanese **Buddhism** and Southern-sect of Chinese **Taoism**, and is well-known for its wonderful landscapes. It was listed as one of the top 10 tourism resorts of Zhejiang Province in 1992 and **was appraised as** one of the first national 4A Grade scenic spots at the end of 2000 by the National Tourism Administration.

Mount Tiantai has been famous since the ancient times. In the mountain, each scenic spot has its own distinctive features which can be characterized as being ancient, clear, **amazing** and quiet.

With unique natural scenic spots and long **brilliant** artificial and cultural sights, Mount Tiantai can be roughly divided into 13 districts. There are some key scenic spots such as the Guoqing Temple, the Shiliang Waterfall, the Chicheng Hill, the Hanshan Lake and the Huading Peak, etc. Each scenic spot has its unique fun and view and among them the Shiliang Waterfall and the Huading Peak are the best.

The Shiliang Waterfall (the Stone Beam Waterfall) is situated in front of the Fangguang Temple. A huge stone, 0.3 meter in width, looks like a **beam** that crosses two banks of cliff and divides a waterfall into three folds. It then falls from the 40 meters high cliff to the ground with the icy color and an imposing manner, hence the name Shiliang Waterfall or Shiliang Icefall.

Huading is the main peak of Mount Tiantai, with 1,110 meters above the sea level. Clouds, dawn fog and dusk smog are always winding and **twisting** on the top of the peak, hence the name "Cloud Gathering Peak". And now Huading is not only a national forest park, but also a famous summer resort in the southeast of Zhejiang. In the park, there is an original azalea forest which has been there for 100 years taking about 50 acres. Every May, those Yunjin azalea trees will bloom. And it is considered to be one of Chinese wonders for its ancient trees, broad areas and beautiful flowers.

Moreover, Mount Tiantai has many rare plants and precious wild animals. For example, the rare plants include the plum trees in the Sui Dynasty, cypress trees in the Tang Dynasty, lindera aggregata and dendrobium candidum walls. As for the wild animals, there are viverra zibetha and neofelis nebulosa, etc. Tiantai is one of the earliest places to produce tea. It not only has its local famous Yunwu Tea, but also Sado as the eastern tea culture. Besides, Mount Tiantai has more than 1,000 kinds of Chinese **herbal** medicines such as atractylodes alba, poria cocos and dendrobium nobile, etc.

★生词与词组 Words & Expressions

birthplace /'bəːθpleis/ *n.* 出生地
Taoism /'tauˈizəm/ *n.* 道教
brilliant /'briliənt/ *adj.* 明亮的
twist /twist/ *v.* 蜿蜒
be appraised as 被评为

Buddhism /'budiz(ə)m/ *n.* 佛教
amazing /əˈmeiziŋ/ *adj.* 令人惊奇的
beam /biːm/ *n.* 横梁
herbal /'həːbl/ *adj.* 药草的

◆ 知识拓展 Knowledge Extension

国清寺：位于天台山麓，始建于公元598年，取"寺若成，国即清"之意，遂名国清寺，是中国和日本以及韩国佛教天台宗的发源地，现为我国重点文物保护单位。国清寺总面积73000平方米，建筑面积2万余平方米，由数十个大小不同、风格各异的院落和建筑群组成，多为清代重建，分布于五条轴线上。有四殿(弥勒佛殿、雨花殿、大雄宝殿、观音殿)，五楼(钟楼、鼓楼、方丈楼、近塔楼、藏经楼)，四堂(妙法堂、安养堂、斋堂、客堂)，二亭(梅亭、清心亭)，一室(文物室)，成为我国最完整的大型寺院之一。

国清三隐：分别为唐朝天台山国清寺三位高僧：寒山、拾得、丰干。

13. 通济堰 Tongji Weir

通济堰建于南朝萧梁天监四年(505)，距今已有 1500 年历史，是我国最古老的大型水利工程，也是迄今为止所知世界上最早的拱坝，为国家级重点文物保护单位。

通济堰位于丽水市西南 25 千米的堰头村，由拦水大坝、渠道、分水闸(概)组成水利灌溉体系。大坝拱形，长 275 米，宽 25 米，高 2.5 米，初为木条结构，南宋时改为石坝，是一个以引灌为主，蓄泄兼备的水利工程。上游集雨面积 2150 平方千米，引水流量为 3 立方米/秒，方方能拦入堰渠 20 万立方米，灌溉着整个碧湖平原中部、南部 20 多平方千米粮田。通济堰的堰史、堰规、筑堰有功者，均刻碑立于世。整个水利工程，连同碑刻，是研究我国古代水利工程的珍贵资料。

通济堰是古人在我国水利工程史上的一大不朽杰作，不但名垂我国水利史册，而且领先国外同类水利工程。

通济堰风景秀丽，古迹多处。大坝西侧建有一座詹南司马祠，俗称"龙庙"，祠内保存着宋、元、明、清及民国时期的碑刻 16 方，记录着历代修建情况及堰规、堰图等。许多文人墨客都为通济堰树过碑，撰写过文章。

在堰头村四周分布着南宋参知政事何澹及其亲属的九座雄伟壮丽的墓园，坟堂前当年曾伫立着石马、石羊、石狮等雕件，拱卫着通济堰。

Tongji **Weir** was built in the 4th year of Tianjian reign in the Liang Dynasty (505), having a history of 1,500 years till now. Furthermore, it is a key national protection site for it is the oldest large-scale hydraulic project in China, and the oldest arch dam worldwide as well. Tongji Weir is a marvelous construction in the history of **irrigation** construction of ancient China.

Tongji Weir is located in Yantou Village, which is to the south-west of Lishui and 25 kilometers away from the center of the city. It is composed of the dam, the ditch and the distribution gate. The dam is arched and 275 meters long, 25 meters wide and 2.5 meters high. It was firstly built of battens, and later of stones in the Southern Song Dynasty. It is a water conservancy project for irrigation, flood storage and flood **discharge**. The upper reaches of the river can collect 2,150 square kilometers of rain and the flow rate of the **diversion** work is 3 cubic meters per second. And it can store 200,000 cubic meters of water every day to irrigate more than 20 square kilometers of farming land in the central and southern parts of Bihu Plain. What's more, the history, stipulation and names of the water conservancy engineers are all carved on the stone stele to make their offsprings commemorate them. The whole **water conservancy project** and the stone carvings are all precious materials for the research on our national ancient water projects.

Tongji Weir is a masterpiece in the history of water engineering in ancient China. It is not only crowned with eternal glory in our country, but also is in the lead of the same kind of irrigation projects around the world.

Tongji Weir has beautiful sceneries and many places of historic interest. In the west of the dam there is an ancestral temple called Zhannan Sima Temple with another name Dragon Temple. In the temple, there are 16 carvings which record the reconstruction and the **specification** and have the pictures of Tongji Weir during dynasties of the Song, Yuan, Ming, Qing and the Republican Period. And many **literati** in the ancient times had written essays about this place.

Moreover, Yantou Village is surrounded by 9 graveyards of the official He Dan and some of his relatives in the Southern Song Dynasty. Once there were a lot of stone **sculptures** such as stone horses, stone sheep and stone lions, etc. standing in front of those graveyards to surround and protect Tongji Weir.

★生词与词组 Words & Expressions

weir /wiə/ *n.* 堰
discharge /dis'tʃɑːdʒ/ *n.* (气体、液体从管子里)排出
specification /ˌspesifi'keiʃən/ *n.* 规格
sculpture /'skʌlptʃə/ *n.* 雕刻

irrigation /ˌiri'geiʃn/ *n.* 灌溉
diversion /dai'vəːʃ(ə)n; ˌdi-/ *n.* 转移
literatus /ˌlitə'rɑːtəs/ *n.* 文人学士
water conservancy project 水利工程

◆ 知识拓展 Knowledge Extension

何澹(1146—1219)：字自然，南宋龙泉人，曾任兵部侍郎、右谏大夫等职。开禧元年(1205)奏请朝廷调兵 3000 人，疏浚处州通济堰，将木坝改为石坝；修筑保定村洪塘，蓄水灌溉 2000 余亩；修撰《龙泉县志》，开龙泉地方志之先河。著有《小山集》，收入《永乐大典》及现代唐圭璋编《全宋词》。

14. 吴子熊玻璃艺术馆 Wu Zixiong Glass Art Museum

吴子熊玻璃艺术馆是我国第一家玻璃雕刻艺术馆，由我国著名工艺美术大师吴子熊创办。馆内陈列着大师 40 多年来创作的艺术精品，具有极高的文化内涵。

以砂轮作笔，用玻璃作画，玻璃雕刻艺术是我国民族工艺美术之林的一朵奇葩，也是浙江最有特色的工艺美术，文化品位很高，内涵十分丰富。

吴子熊自幼失去双亲，11 岁因无钱上学，开始流浪生活。新中国成立后，他成为海门玻璃厂第一代玻璃雕刻工人。40 多年来，他凭着坚韧不拔的顽强意志和孜孜不倦的艺术追求，在透明的玻璃上潜心琢磨，苦苦探索，将玻璃雕刻艺术推上一个新境界，成为这一领域的佼佼者。他的作品，集东西方艺术为一体，既有传统意蕴，又有现代气息，具有极高的艺术性。

吴子熊玻璃艺术馆建立的目的是揭示顽强的生命力。它告诉人们，不管是无生命的玻璃或者是有生命的人，也不管处于荒郊的"物"或者成为流浪的"人"，只要你自身过硬，在一定条件下都会成为稀世奇才。吴子熊玻璃艺术馆的基本组成是梦幻般的玻璃艺术世界及吴子熊大师的传奇人生。馆内珍藏着 3000 多件晶莹剔透的雕刻作品，美不胜收。

Wu Zixiong Glass Art Museum, the first national glass carving museum, was set up by Wu Zixiong, a well-known master of arts and crafts. The museum **displays** his fine works with great cultural connotation.

The glass carving which uses the **grinding** wheel to carve pictures on the glass is a wonderful technique in our national arts and crafts and it is also the most **distinctive** art in Zhejiang Province. In the museum, there are a lot of wonderful works created by Master Wu Zixiong as well as his son and his apprentices over the years. Therefore, the museum is a cultural place.

Wu Zixiong was an **orphan** and began to **wander** around at the age of 11 because he had no money to go to school. After New China was founded, he became a glass carving worker of the first generation in Haimen Glass Factory. For over 40 years, with his persistent, tireless and **indomitable** will of the art, he devoted himself to the glass sculpture and improved this art to a new level, making him a leading person in this field. His works, uniting Eastern and Western styles of art together, have both traditional meaning and modern taste and enjoy high artistic quality.

The museum is set up to expose the vitality of human beings. It tells people that whether the **inanimate** glass or the living person or whether the material in the lonely wild countryside or the wandering person, if you have skills, you will become a useful person under a certain condition. Wu Zixiong Glass Art Museum is composed of the **fantastic** glass world and the legendary life of Master Wu. There are more than 3,000 crystal and beautiful carving works in this museum.

★生词与词组 Words & Expressions

display /ˌdis'plei/ *v.* 展示
distinctive /dis'tiŋ(k)tiv/ *adj.* 有特色的
wander /'wɔndə/ *v.* 徘徊
inanimate /in'ænimət/ *adj.* 无生命的

grinding /'graindiŋ/ *adj.* 磨的
orphan /'ɔ:fən/ *n.* 孤儿
indomitable /in'dɔmitəb(ə)l/ *adj.* 不气馁的
fantastic /fæn'tæstik/ *adj.* 奇异的

◆ 知识拓展 Knowledge Extension

玻璃雕刻：顾名思义，就是在玻璃上雕刻各种图案和文字，立体感较强，可以做成通透的和不透的，适合做隔断和造型也可以上色之后再夹胶。玻璃雕刻分为人工雕刻和电脑雕刻两种。其中人工雕刻利用娴熟刀法的深浅和转折配合，更能表现出玻璃的质感，使所绘图案给人呼之欲出的感受。雕刻玻璃是家居装修中很有品位的一种装饰玻璃，所绘图案一般都具有个性"创意"，反映着居室主人的情趣和追求。

15. 仙居风景名胜区 Xianju Scenic Spot

仙居风景名胜区，为国家重点风景名胜区，总面积 187.8 平方千米，含神仙居、景星岩、十三都、公盂、淡竹五大景区，山川秀丽，风光迷人，被称为"仙人居住的地方"。

仙居风景名胜区的典型代表是神仙居景区，总面积 15.8 平方千米，景观丰富而集中，奇峰环列，山崖陡峻，峰崖的相对高差多在 100 米以上。这里有将军岩、睡美人、飞天瀑等景点80 多处。景区上游瀑布群和龙潭群众多，仅五百米范围内就拥有连续十一级飞瀑和形态各异的深潭，为国内罕见。神仙居的一山一水、一崖一洞、一石一峰都能自成一格，有不类他山，异乎寻常，出人意料，匪夷所思的景观形态。一字蔽之："奇"。即峰奇、山奇、石奇、崖亦奇。

景星岩总面积 27.3 平方千米，海拔 742 米，像一艘巨型的大轮船停泊于此。景星岩景区不仅自然景观秀丽，同时有着十分丰富的人文景观，唐代以来就有宏大的净居寺，此外和尚圆寂塔、读书堂等名胜古迹也源远流长。

十三都景区内有海拔 904 米、高 120 多米的天柱岩，它像一柄利剑，直刺苍穹。"索桥飞架"和"绝壁天书"两个景点也引人入胜。铁索桥长 40 多米，宽不到 2 米，被称为"钢丝桥"。"绝壁天书"则是一座人迹罕至的"千尺石岩"。岩壁上刻有名闻遐迩、被视为"天书"的全国八大古文字难解之谜之一的仙居韦羌绝壁蝌蚪文。

公盂景区以岿巍著称，地型构造呈多级梯状，海拔为 1200 米左右，整个公盂巍峨鼎立，气势峥嵘，山崖连着山崖，横亘无际，各峰离立，自为一体，石林崖壁，各有风采。主要景点有柯九思故居、公盂崖、竹林、神龙瀑等。神龙瀑一瀑四折三潭，高达七八十米，每瀑每潭，景色各异，自有风采。

淡竹原始森林景区总面积 80 平方千米，拥有 2000 多种野生动植物品种，其中属国家保护和珍稀濒危的野生动植物有 100 余种，包括南方红豆杉、白颈长尾雉、娃娃鱼等，被专家誉为省内罕见的天然植物"绿色基因库"和植物"博物馆"，享有"天然药物宝库"之美誉。

Xianju Scenic Spot is a national key scenic spot of China with a total area of 187.8 square kilometers, and is made up of five major scenic sites such as Shenxianju, Jingxingyan, Shisandu, Gongyu and Danzhu. Because of its fantastic and charming sceneries, it is reputed as "the living place of the Immortals".

Shenxianju is the **representative** scenic spot of Xianju and covers an area of 15.8 square kilometers. Its landscape is rich and **concentrated**, with winding peaks and steep cliffs of which relative height difference is more than 100 meters. There are over 80 famous scenic spots, such as the General Rock, the Sleeping Beauty as well as Flying Waterfall, etc. In the upper part of the area, there are a lot of **domestically** rare waterfalls and unique dragon pools since it has 11 continuous waterfalls within 500 meters. Generally speaking, its mountains, waterfalls, cliffs, caves, stones and peaks are all particular, unimaginable and **remarkable**. In short, they are amazing.

Jingxingyan, with a total area of 27.3 square kilometers and an altitude of 742 meters, looks like a huge ship **anchoring** there. This scenic spot has both beautiful natural sceneries and rich artificial sceneries, such as Jingju Temple in the Tang Dynasty, Monk Parinirvana Pagoda and Reading Hall, etc.

In the scenic spot of Shisandu, there is a long pillar rock which looks like a sharp sword **stabbing into** the sky, with an altitude of 904 meters and a height of 120 meters. Besides, there are two other famous scenic spots. One is an iron bridge which is more than 40 meters in length and less than 2 meters in width, named as the Steel-wire Bridge by the local people. The other is an about 300 meters deep trackless rock which is fully carved with mysterious characters called tadpole, considered to be one of the eight ancient characters in China.

Gongyu Scenic Spot is grand and steep. Its altitude is about 1,200 meters and it is full of different cliffs and rocks which have their own unique features. Its main spots are Hometown of Ke Jiusi, Gongyu Cliff, Bamboo Forest, Dragon Waterfall, etc. Dragon Waterfall is as tall as about 80 meters and has four folds and three deep pools. Each fall and each pool has their own special sceneries.

Danzhu is famous for its **primeval** forest. It is about 80 square kilometers and has almost 2,000 kinds of wild animals and plants, of which 100 kinds, such as South Taxus, White Neck's Pheasant and giant salamander, etc., are rare, precious and endangered or under the national protection. Danzhu is praised by experts as "a green gene pool", "a plant museum" as well as "the treasure house of natural medicines".

★生词与词组 Words & Expressions

representative /repri'zentətiv/ *n.* 代表
domestically /də'mestikli/ *adv.* 国内地
anchor /'æŋkə/ *v.* 抛锚
stab into 刺入

concentrated /'kɔnsəntreitid/ *adj.* 密集的
remarkable /ri'mɑ:kəbl/ *adj.* 不寻常的
primeval /prai'mi:vl/ *adj.* 原始的

◆ 知识拓展 Knowledge Extension

仙居蝌蚪文：也叫蝌蚪书、蝌蚪篆，是在浙江省仙居县淡竹乡韦羌山附近一个高达百余米的高山陡壁蝌蚪崖上人工凿刻的形似日纹、月纹、虫纹、鱼纹等奇异的图案符号。蝌蚪文为书体的一种，因头粗尾细形似蝌蚪而得名。蝌蚪文的名称是汉代以后才出现的，意指先秦时期的古文。目前中国已发现的有待破解或正在破解的原始文字或符号共八种，即：仓颉书、夏禹书、夜郎天书、贵州的红崖天书、四川的巴蜀符号、云南的东巴文、浙江绍兴禹庙的岣嵝碑文字和浙江仙居蝌蚪文。从发现的时代看，仙居的蝌蚪文发现的年代最早，也最难解读。其他七种文字均有据可查，而唯独蝌蚪文扑朔迷离，至今还未见其篆文摹本。

柯九思(1290—1343)：元代文物鉴藏家，画家。字敬仲，号丹丘生，别号五云阁吏。浙江仙居人。能诗善画，墨竹师法文同，为湖州竹派的继承者，有《清閟阁墨竹图》(藏故宫博物院)、《双竹图》(藏上海博物馆)传世。著有《丹丘生集》《竹谱》等书。

第二节 旅游文化——民俗文化

Section 2　Tourism Culture—Folk Culture

民俗文化，是在普通人民(相对于官方)的生产生活过程中所形成的一系列物质的、精神的文化现象。总体上说，民俗文化包括物质民俗、社会民俗和精神民俗。它具有普遍性、传承性、变异性和社会的一致性。台州、衢州、丽水三地区历史悠久，具有丰富多彩的地方民俗，比较突出地表现在以下几个方面。

Folk culture refers to a series of traditional and typical substantial and mental cultures which have been produced in the lives of the ordinary people. Generally speaking, folk culture is divided into substantial culture, social culture and mental culture. It is universal, inheritable, variable and coherent with the society. Taizhou, Quzhou and Lishui have a long history and colorful local folk cultures which are represented in the following aspects.

1. 传统工艺琳琅满目 Various Traditional Arts & Crafts

台州仙居的针刺无骨花灯被列入国家级非物质文化遗产保护名录；衢州的石雕、木雕和砖雕闻名遐迩；丽水的"三宝"青田石雕、龙泉宝剑、龙泉青瓷，被列为全省非物质文化遗产。这些非物质文化遗产与当地百姓生活密切相关，是民族个性、民族审美习惯的"活"的显现。

The Needle-pierced Boneless Lantern made in Xianju has been elected as the national intangible cultural heritage. And the stone carving, wood carving and brick carving made in Quzhou are also well-known. Besides, Qingtian Stone Carving, Longquan Sword and Longquan Celadon which are called "Three Treasures" in Lishui have been listed as the provincial intangible cultural heritage. Those intangible cultural heritages are closely related to the local people's daily life, and they vividly reflect the nation's personality and aesthetic habits.

2. 乡土建筑别具一格 Unique Country Constructions

台州的古村落、古镇、古街、古城、寺庙、园林等建筑形式多样，具有很高的历史价值、科学价值和艺术价值。衢州有被称为"遗落在大山里的梦"的廿八都古镇，不仅拥有众多风格各异保存完好的明清古建筑，而且在一个小镇中还存有 13 种方言、140 多种姓氏、大小两座文昌阁等奇特现象。衢州市区至今仍保存着六座古城门、2000 余米的古城墙，护城河保存也较为完整。

The ancient villages, towns, streets, castles, temples and gardens, etc. in Taizhou have all kinds of styles and they have great values in history, science and art. The Twenty-eighth City, "the Dreamland in the Mountains" in Quzhou, has not only a lot of stylish and intact buildings made in the Ming and Qing dynasties, but also 13 local dialects, more than 140 family names as well as two Wenchang Pavilions in different sizes in the same town. In addition, Quzhou still preserves 6 ancient city gates, over 2,000 meters ancient walls and intact moat.

3. 佛道文化影响深远 Far-reaching Influence of Buddhism and Taoism Culture

天台山是佛教天台宗发祥地、道教南宗创立地。台州的佛、道教至今在国内外仍有重大影响，日本、韩国佛教天台宗信徒每年都要到国清寺朝拜祖庭，进行宗教文化交流。衢州有世界三大宗教的教堂、庙宇和道家的庙观。

Mount Tiantai was the birthplace of Tiantai-sect of Buddhism and Southern-sect of Taoism which still have great impact on the believers both at home and abroad. Every year, the Buddhists of Tiantai-sect from Japan and R.O. Korea will go to Guoqing Temple to worship their Buddha and exchange their religious ideas. Quzhou has many churches, temples and pagodas for the top three religions in the world.

4. 节庆活动多姿多彩 Colorful Festival Activities

除了春节、元宵、清明等与全国多数地方大同小异的岁时习俗以外，台州、衢州、丽水地区还有不少具有浓郁地方色彩的节庆活动，如仙居杨梅节、黄岩柑橘节、江山麻糍节等各类节庆活动吸引了众多的海内外游客。

Apart from the Spring Festival, the Lantern Festival, the Tomb-sweeping Day and many other festivals which have the same or similar customs with other places, Taizhou, Quzhou and Lishui still have their own local festivals which have attracted a lot of domestic and overseas tourists such as Waxberry Festival in Xianju, Oranges Day in Huangyan and Maci Festival in Jiangshan, etc.

5. 地方饮食特色鲜明 Distinctive Local Food

台州美食文化内容丰富，既有以天台、仙居、临海等地为代表的山地居民美食，又有以玉环、温岭、三门等地为代表的滨海居民美食；衢州有发糕、八宝菜和麻糍等特色小吃；丽水有青田糯米饭、缙云烧饼等经典小吃。

Taizhou has both mountainous food represented by Tiantai, Xianju and Linhai and sea food represented by Yuhuan, Wenling and Sanmen, etc. Quzhou has delicious local food such as steamed sponge cake, eight treasures dishes and maci, etc., while Lishui has Qingtian glutinous rice and Jinyun pancake, etc.

第三节　景点讲解技能——触景生情法

Section 3　Narration Tactics of Scenic Spots

—The Sight Stirring up the Feelings

所谓"触景生情法"就是见物生情、借题发挥的一种导游讲解方法。见到景色后，不是简单讲景色，而是引出话题，介绍事情，使游客不仅知其然，还知其所以然，如见到园林美景讲造园艺术，见到石林讲其形成原因，见到蒙古包讲蒙古包构成、特点等。触景生情法有两层含义。

第一层含意是导游员在讲解时不能就事论事地介绍景物，而是要借题发挥，利用所见景物制造意境，引人入胜，使游客产生联想，从而领略其中的妙趣。如旅游者到西安旅游，在从咸阳国际机场前往市区的途中看到一座座陵墓，导游人员便触景生情地讲道："中国的景色各有特色，北京看墙头，桂林看山水，上海看人头，到了西安，大伙看的就是各式各样的坟头。"一席话说得非常形象，给游客留下深刻的印象。

第二层含意是导游讲解的内容要与所见景物和谐统一，使其情景交融，让旅游者感到景中有情，情中有景。如当旅游团参观故宫太和门广场和高大巍峨的太和殿时，导游员可适当描述皇帝登基时的壮观场面：金銮殿香烟缭绕，殿前鼓乐喧天，广场上气氛庄严肃穆；皇帝升殿，文武百官三跪九叩，高呼万岁万万岁。

触景生情法贵在发挥，导游人员要通过生动形象的讲解、有趣而感人的语言，赋予没有生命的景物以活力，并注入情感，引导旅游者进入审美对象的特定意境，从而使他们获得更多的知识和美的享受。请看以下例子。

例 1　临海古城墙。导游在介绍古城墙时，不仅向游客讲解古城墙的地理、历史、构成及在历史上的重要作用，同时联系现实，向广大游客介绍古城墙在现今发挥的重要作用，即举办江南长城节，宣扬古城，发扬民族文化，展现临海古老文明的魅力，从而吸引更多的游客来游玩。

例 2　国清寺。导游在带领游客参观国清寺时，会看到寺内有一株隋梅，大可合抱，枝叶繁茂。见到这株隋梅时，游客会被隋梅的形状及其 1400 多年的历史所吸引。这时，导游在赞叹这株隋梅的同时，可以借题发挥，询问游客还知道哪几大古梅，都各自有什么特点。这样导游利用所见景物制造意境，引人入胜，使游客产生联想，从而领略其中的妙趣，并顺势向游客讲解我国的五大古梅，增加游客的兴趣和知识。

在运用该技巧时，导游要注意：首先，每讲解一个景点或讲一段话时，要明白自己表述的主旨，即要达到一个什么目的或要表达一种什么思想。不要就事论事，就景点讲景点，要扩展自己的视野，关注那些全局的、共性的东西。其次，讲解具有明显的互动性，是导游与游客之间相互作用的过程。因此，讲解时必须注意语言环境变化和游客的反应，随时调整自己的讲解。最后，讲解的各种方法和技巧不是孤立的，而是相互渗透、相互依存、互相联系的。讲解要在学习众家之长的同时，结合自己的特点融会贯通，在实践中形成自己的风格和方法，并视具体的时空条件和对象，灵活、熟练地运用，这样，才能获得不同凡响的效果。

◆ **综合练习**

请运用所学的"触景生情法"讲解技巧，围绕台州、衢州、丽水地区某一景点或特产设计提问并分小组进行中英文讲解练习。

第四节　民俗文化翻译技巧——菜谱的翻译技巧

Section 4　Translation Skills of Folk Culture

—Skills of Menu Translation

饮食文化为民俗文化的一种，特别是台州、衢州、丽水地区，地方饮食文化丰富，特色鲜明。因此，本节以菜谱翻译为例，主要探讨民俗文化中饮食文化的翻译技巧。

1. 烹饪的翻译　Cooking Translation

中餐菜谱不容易翻译，原因是中国人的饮食文化十分丰富，烹饪技术非常发达，对菜名又特别讲究。菜谱翻译的核心内容是菜肴是用什么原料做成的，因为外国人在餐桌上最关心的是吃什么东西。其次要讲清楚菜肴的各种用料、刀法和烹调方法。因此，要译好菜谱，首先需要了解一些菜肴的主要用料、刀法、烹调方法以及一些准备步骤。

1.1　常用刀法及用料形状的翻译　*Cutting Art & Material Shape*

切片 slice　　　　　　　　切丝 shred

切丁 dice　　　　　　　　切块 cube

切柳 fillet　　　　　　　切碎 mince

捣烂 mash　　　　　　　酿入 stuff

卷 roll　　　　　　　　　条 strip

段 segment　　　　　　　粒 grain

末 mince　　　　　　　　蓉(泥)mash

浆 thick liquid　　　　　汁 juice

整体 whole

1.2　中餐常见的烹调方法翻译　*Common Chinese Cooking Terms*

煮 boiling　　　　　　　　煲/炖 stewing

烧/焖/烩 braising　　　　煎 frying

炒 stir-frying　　　　　　爆 quick-frying

炸 deep-frying　　　　　扒 frying and simmering

煸 sautéed　　　　　　　煨 simmering

熏 smoking　　　　　　　烤 roasting/barbecuing/toasting

烘 baking　　　　　　　　蒸 steaming

白灼 scalding　　　　　　酱/醋 marinating

卤 spicy/stewed in gravy　酿 stuffed

涮 instant-boiled　　　　醉 liquor-preserved

加调味佐料的 seasoned　　加香料的 spiced

盐制的 salted　　　　　　腌制 pickling

去骨 boning　　　　　　　打鳞 scaling

剥/去皮 skinning　　　　脱壳 shelling

2. 菜谱翻译的技巧 Menu Translating Skills

2.1 直译法 *Literal Translation*

(1)以主料开头的翻译方法

① 介绍菜肴的主料和辅料

译法：主料(形状)+(with)辅料，例如：

牛肉豆腐 Beef with Beancurd

西红柿炒蛋 Scrambled Egg with Tomato

② 介绍菜肴的主料和味汁

译法：主料(形状)+(with, in)味汁，例如：

葱油鸡 Chicken in Scallion Oil

米酒鱼卷 Fish Rolls with Rice Wine

(2)以烹制方法开头的翻译方法

① 介绍菜肴的烹法和主料

译法：烹法+主料(形状)，例如：

烤乳猪 Roast Suckling Pig

炒鳝片 Stir-fried Eel Slices

② 介绍菜肴的烹法和主料、辅料

译法：烹法+主料(形状)+(with)辅料，例如：

仔姜烧鸡条 Braised Chicken Fillet with Tender Ginger

青椒炒肉丝 Stir-frying Pork Shreds with Green Pepper

③ 介绍菜肴的烹法和主料、味汁

译法：烹法+主料(形状)+(with, in)味汁，例如：

辣味烩虾 Braised Prawns with Chili Sauce

酱爆肉 Quick-fried Pork with Soy Paste

(3)以形状或口感开头的翻译方法

① 介绍菜肴的形状(口感)和主料、辅料

译法：形状(口感)+主料+(with)辅料，例如：

陈皮兔丁 Diced Rabbit with Orange Peel

时蔬鸡片 Sliced Chicken with Seasonal Vegetables

② 介绍菜肴的口感、烹饪法和主料

译法：口感+烹法+主料，例如：

香酥排骨 Crisp Fried Spareribs

水煮嫩鱼 Tender Stewed Fish

③ 介绍菜肴的形状(口感)、主料和味汁

译法：形状(口感)+主料+(with)味汁，例如：

茄汁鱼片 Sliced Fish with Tomato Sauce

椒麻鸡块　Cutlets Chicken with Hot Pepper

(4)以人名、地名命名的菜肴的翻译方法

一般全部译出，人名前最好加上头衔或职业，对于知之甚少或译出后外宾不能理解的，则去人名加味型。例如：

东坡肉　Poet Dongpo's Braised Pork

北京烤鸭　Beijing Roasted Duck

(5)菜名含器具的翻译方法

可译出器具，也可直译原料，但以译出器具为佳。例如：

锅仔甲鱼　Braised Turtle in Mini Pot

铁板牛柳　Veal Slices Fried on Iron Plate

2.2　意译法　*Liberal Translation*

(1)原料+with+佐料

以原料为中心词，有时捎带把烹调法也译出，再加上用介词 with 或 in 与佐料构成的词语即可。例如：

海米白菜　Chinese Cabbage with Dried Shrimps

鱼香肉丝　Shredded Pork with Garlic Sauce

(2)佐料+原料

即把佐料用作修饰语，放在中心词原料的前面。例如：

咖喱牛肉　Curry Beef

咕咾肉　Sweet and Sour Pork

(3)以"实"对"虚"法

即舍去中菜名里比喻意义、夸张等说法，而用平直、明白的英语译出。例如：

翡翠鱼翅　Double-boiled Shark's Fin with Vegetables

龙虎凤大烩　Thick Soup of Snake, Cat and Chicken

(4)音译加释义法

先按中文用拼音译出，然后再加以解释性的英译，使英译文保留点"中国味"。例如：

包子　Baozi——Stuffed Bun

馒头　Mantou——Steamed Bread

(5)"随机应变"法

风味菜肴，可按原料+地名+Style 方法译出。例如：

广东龙虾　Lobster Cantonese Style

麻婆豆腐　Bean Curd Sichuan Style

2.3　释译法　*Explanation Translation*

释译法通常采用直译加注，或者增加相关词语，把隐含的内容表达出来，使读者容易理解。例如：

"叫花鸡"的翻译：Beggar's Chicken——There's a legendary story connected to it. Long,

long ago, there was a beggar, who stole a chicken one day and was pursued by the owner. He was almost caught when he suddenly hit upon a good idea. He smeared the chicken all over with clay which he found nearby and threw it. After a long while, the beggar removed the mud-coated chicken from the fire. When he cracked open the clay, to his surprise, he found that the clay together with the feather had formed a hard shell in which the chicken had been baked into a delicious dish with wonderful flavor. That night he had a very enjoyable meal. Hence comes the name of the dish.

"佛跳墙"的翻译：Fotiaoqiang, a steamed abalone with shark's fin and fish maw in broth，refers to a famous Chinese dish. Lured by its delicious aroma, even the Buddha jumped over the wall in order to eat this dish, hence it is so named.

总之，菜谱翻译的主要原则是力求简明准确，能够说明菜肴的内容，能够使外国人明白即可。在准确的前提下，尽量把菜名翻译得优美一些会更好。

◆ 课后练习 Exercises

把下列菜名翻译成英语(Put the following Chinese dishes into English)

1. 蚝油鲍鱼片
2. 潮州烧鹅
3. 虾仁锅巴
4. 醋溜白菜
5. 美点双辉
6. 西湖牛肉羹
7. 麻辣鸡丁
8. 紫砂东山羊
9. 红烧鸡
10. 清蒸桂花鱼

第八章 浙江特色旅游产品文化

Chapter Eight   Distinctive Tourism Products in Zhejiang

第一节 杭州特产

Section 1   Native Specialty Products in Hangzhou

1. 昌化鸡血石 Chicken Blood Stone in Changhua

鸡血石主要用于制作印章、雕刻工艺品和原石欣赏等，是中国"印石三宝"之一。昌化鸡血石具有鸡血般的鲜红色彩和美玉般的天生丽质，是中国特有的珍贵宝石，历来与珠宝翠钻一样被人珍爱，被誉为中华"国宝"。

Chicken Blood Stone is mainly used for producing seals, stone carving crafts and the original stone appreciation, etc. It is one of the "three treasures of seal stone". Changhua Chicken Blood Stone has a bright scarlet color like chicken blood, and natural beauty like jade. It is a kind of precious stone unique to China, and has always been cherished by people just like diamond and jewelry and now has been known as "a national treasure" in China.

2. 王星记扇 Wangxingji Fan

王星记扇创始于清光绪元年(1875)，至今已有 100 多年历史，产品主要有黑纸扇、檀香扇、白纸扇、舞扇、绢扇、骨扇、香木扇、挂扇等 15 个大类 400 多个品种。王星记扇子精致细巧、玲珑光滑、清香四溢、高贵典雅，多次在国际博览会上得奖。

Wangxingji Fan was first produced in 1875 (the 1st year of the reign of Emperor Guangxu) with a history over 100 years. Wangxingji Fan produces 15 main categories, including over 400 kinds of designs, such as black paper fans, sandalwood fans, white paper fans, dancing fans, silk fans, bone fans, wood fans and wall fans, having won many prizes in World Expositions for the super quality of delicacy, exquisiteness, fragrance and elegance.

3. 西湖莼菜 West Lake Water Shield

莼菜叶片呈椭圆形，色暗绿，嫩茎和叶背部都有胶状透明物质。它产于淡水湖中，以"三潭印月"莼菜最为著名。食用部分就是沉没在水中尚未展开的新叶，用来调羹作汤，色泽鲜艳，汤纯味美，鲜嫩润滑，脍炙人口，被列为杭州名菜。

West Lake Water Shield, with oval shaped leaves, dark green color, is grown in the freshwater lake. The water shield planted around "three pools mirroring the moon" in the West Lake is the most famous one. Its edible part is the new leaves submerged in the water, which is cooked as a soup with bright color, pure and delicious taste, and freshness. It is listed as one of the most famous Hangzhou dishes.

4. 西湖藕粉 West Lake Lotus Root Powder

西湖藕粉作为杭州的名产，以余杭沾桥乡三家村所产的藕粉最为出名，故又称"三家村藕粉"。三家村及其周围数十里藕乡种植的藕具有孔小，肉厚，味甜的特点。西湖藕粉经冲泡后，是一种上好的滋补品。

West Lake Lotus Root Powder is known as a famous specialty of Hangzhou. The most famous kind is produced in Sanjia Village, Zhanqiao, Yuhang, so called "Sanjia Village Lotus Root Powder". The lotus root planted in Sanjia and its surrounding villages has such features as small holes, fleshy body, and sweet taste. Its powder is an excellent tonic after being brewed.

5. 西湖龙井 Longjing Tea

西湖龙井茶，因其色泽翠绿、外形扁平光滑、汤色碧绿明亮、香馥如兰、滋味甘醇鲜爽而闻名于世。它的产地集中于狮峰山、梅家坞、翁家山等地。龙井茶尤以一尖二叶的"明前茶"为佳品，芽叶柔嫩而细小，富含氨基酸与多种维生素。

Longjing Tea is famous all over the world for its fresh green color, flat and smooth appearance and sweet taste. The origins of Longjing Tea, rich in amino acids and vitamins, are in the Shifengshan Hill, Meijiawu, the Wengjiashan Hill, etc. Among all kinds of Longjing Tea, "Tea before Tomb-sweeping Day" with one bud and two leaves is the best.

6. 张小泉剪刀 Zhang Xiaoquan Scissors

张小泉的父亲张思家生产的"张大隆"牌剪刀质量上乘，在清乾隆年间被列为贡品。张小泉继承父业，苦心钻研，生意十分兴隆，便把招牌改为"张小泉"。张小泉剪刀以其嵌钢均匀、磨工精细、刃口锋利、经久耐用、物美价廉而闻名中外。

Zhang Dalong Scissors produced by Zhang Xiaoquan's father Zhang Sijia were of high quality and were identified as tribute during years of the reign of Emperor Qianlong in the Qing Dynasty. Digging into the study of scissors-making, Zhang Xiaoquan followed his father's step. With his business booming, he changed his scissors' name to Zhang Xiaoquan. Zhang Xiaoquan Scissors are well known in China and abroad for its uniformity, excellent grinding, sharp cutting edge, durability and low price.

第二节　嘉兴特产

Section 2　Native Specialty Products in Jiaxing

1. 嘉兴粽子 Jiaxing Glutinous Rice Dumpling

嘉兴粽子是嘉兴具有悠久历史的传统名点。嘉兴粽子具有糯而不糊、肥而不腻、香糯可口、咸甜适中的特点，嘉兴粽子尤以"五芳斋"的粽子最为出名。常见的嘉兴粽子品种有肉粽、豆沙、蛋黄等。嘉兴粽子滋味鲜美、携带方便、食用方便，有"东方快餐"之称。

Jiaxing Glutinous Rice Dumpling is a famous traditional snack with a long history. It is glutinous but not pasty, fat but not greasy, delicious, and moderately salty and sweet. The brand "Wufangzhai" is the most popular one in Jiaxing. The most common varieties of Jiaxing Glutinous Rice Dumpling include meat, sweetened bean paste, egg yolk, etc. It is entitled "Oriental Fast Food" for its delicious flavor, and convenience to carry and to eat.

2. 南湖菱 Water Chestnut in the South Lake

嘉兴南湖的菱形状圆而无角，绿皮白肉、壳薄味甜。南湖菱既可以生吃，也可以熟食。生吃则选色翠而鲜嫩，尤其是刚出水时口味更佳，熟食则选色黄褐之老菱，洗净后煮食，口味香甜浓郁，肉糯可口；南湖菱还可以用于制糕点、佳肴或酿酒、制糖。

The water chestnut in the South Lake in Jiaxing is round without any angle with green peel, white flesh, thin shell and sweet flavor. They can be eaten raw or cooked. The green and fresh ones are suitable for eating raw, especially those just picked from water; the yellow and brown ones are suitable for cooking after cleaning. They taste sweet and delicious. The water chestnuts in the South Lake can also be used for making cakes, dishes, wines and sugar.

3. 桐乡杭白菊 Tongxiang Chrysanthemum

桐乡杭白菊源于野生菊花，经过桐乡人对其不断的选优和精培，逐渐形成了杭白菊独特的品质。杭白菊花朵比观赏用的菊花略小，花瓣洁白如玉，花蕊灿如黄金，香气沁人肺腑，泡茶饮用则味甘而醇郁。

Tongxiang Chrysanthemum originates from wild chrysanthemum, and through the continuous selection and fine cultivation of the local people, a unique quality of chrysanthemum is gradually formed. The flower is slightly smaller than that of the ornamental chrysanthemum. The petals are as white as jade, and the stamens and pistils are as bright as gold. The aroma can touch the soul of people. When it is used for brewing tea, it is sweet and pure.

4. 西塘八珍糕 Xitang Bazhen Cake / Xitang Eight-treasure Cake

西塘八珍糕早在光绪年间已名闻遐迩。1920 年西塘老中医钟道生在古方的基础上结合自己临床经验改进制作为八珍糕，一直流传至今。西塘八珍糕因选料考究，做工精细，口感香甜，成为江南久负盛名的名点之一。

Xitang Bazhen Cake was famous as early as the reign of Emperor Guangxu in the Qing Dynasty. In 1920 a traditional Chinese medicine doctor Zhong Daosheng made some adaptations of the old recipe with his clinical experience and changed it into Bazhen (eight treasures) cake, which has been retained till today. Xitang Bazhen Cake is one of the famous snacks in Jiangnan for its sophisticated choice of materials, exquisite workmanship and sweet taste.

第三节　金华特产

Section 3　Native Specialty Products in Jinhua

1. 东阳木雕 Dongyang Wood Carving

东阳木雕有千余年的历史，其层次浮雕、散点透视构图、保留平面的装饰，形成了自己的特色。木雕作品多用本色透明清漆涂罩，以保留材质的天然本色。北京故宫精美绝伦的宫殿雕刻，杭州灵隐寺雄伟壮观的释迦牟尼大佛都出自东阳木雕艺人之手。

With a history of more than a thousand years, Dongyang wood carvings are characterized by the decoration of multilayered relief, scattering perspective composition and preserved surface. They are painted with transparent color in order to preserve the natural color and to show the superb skills better. The exquisite carving of the Forbidden City in Beijing and the majestic Buddha in Lingyin Temple in Hangzhou are their two good examples.

2. 金华佛手 Jinhua Fingered Citron / Jinhua Buddha's-hand Citron

明末清初金华开始栽培佛手。果实基部呈圆形，如常人双手抱着拳呈拜佛状，故被称为"佛手"，雅称"金佛手"。佛手成熟时色泽金黄，香气浓郁，切片沏茶，其香沁人心脾。放置室内，芳香馥郁，使人神清气爽。佛手还是一味名贵的中药材，具有治呕和胃等功能。

Fingered Citron has been grown in Jinhua since the late Ming Dynasty to the early Qing Dynasty. Its round base is like man's folded hands when worshiping Buddha, hence the name "Buddha's Hand", or "Golden Buddha Hands". Being ripe, they look golden yellow, taste refreshing and smell fragrant if put in the room. Fingered Citron is also a kind of precious traditional Chinese medicine. It has efficacy on relieving vomiting, comforting stomach and so on.

3. 金华火腿 Jinhua Ham

金华火腿始于唐，盛于宋，至今已有1200多年的历史，是金华市最负盛名的传统名产。金华火腿以皮色黄亮、香馨清醇、味鲜脆嫩和外形俏丽即色、香、味、形"四绝"而蜚声中外，位居我国"三大名腿"之首，是烹饪众多菜肴必需的原料之一，深受中外消费者所喜爱。

Jinhua Ham first originated from the Tang Dynasty and prospered in the Song Dynasty, with a history of more than 1,200 years. It enjoys great prestige home and abroad for its golden color, attractive flavor, delicious taste and pretty shape; hence it ranks the top of the three famous hams in China. It is also one of the most popular ingredients in cuisine in China and abroad.

4. 金华酥饼 Jinhua Shortcake

金华酥饼始于隋代，距今已有一千多年的历史，具有表里酥脆、内荤外素、油而不腻、鲜香可口和水分少易存放等特点。金华酥饼采用上白面粉、雪里蕻干菜、肥膘肉、菜油、芝麻、饴糖等为原料，用陶炉、木炭烘焙而成。因其馅心以干菜为主料，故又称干菜酥饼。

Jinhua Shortcake, with a history of more than 1,000 years, was invented in the Sui Dynasty. It is characterized by its crispness inside, meat and vegetarian ingredients, oily but not greasy taste, attractive flavor and easiness to preserve. It is made from top quality flour, dried legumes, fat, vegetable oil, sesames and maltose and it is baked above charcoal in pottery stoves. It is also named Dried Legumes Shortcake as dried legumes are its main ingredient.

第四节　丽水特产

Section 4　Native Specialty Products in Lishui

1. 龙泉宝剑 Longquan Sword

龙泉宝剑始于春秋战国时期，距今已有 2600 多年。在我国，龙泉剑亦成为宝剑之代名词。龙泉宝剑以"坚韧锋利，刚柔并寓，寒光逼人，纹饰巧致"四大特点而驰名于世。2006年龙泉宝剑的锻制技艺被国务院批准列入第一批国家级非物质文化遗产名录。

Longquan Sword, with a history of more than 2,600 years, dates back to the Warring States Period. Longquan Sword presents a name for outstanding swords in China. It is world-known for its sharpness, combination of pliability and toughness, shining brightness and elaborate decoration. It enjoys good selling both at home and abroad. And in 2006, its techniques were listed in the first national nonmaterial cultural heritage lists by the approval of the State Council.

2. 龙泉青瓷 Longquan Celadon

龙泉青瓷有"弟窑"或"龙泉窑"和"哥窑"之分，始于南朝，盛于南宋，久负盛名。青瓷以瓷质细腻，线条明快流畅、造型端庄浑朴、色泽纯洁而斑斓著称于世。龙泉青瓷于2009年9月30日正式入选联合国教科文组织的世界非物质文化遗产名录。

Longquan Celadon Ware, divided into "Di Kiln" or "Longquan Kiln" and "Ge Kiln", which has long enjoyed a good reputation, originated in the Southern Dynasties and prospered in the Southern Song Dynasty. It is famous for its delicate porcelain, simple and sprightly style, modest mold and pure color. Longquan Celadon is inscribed on the world nonmaterial cultural heritage of UNESCO on Sep. 30, 2009.

3. 青田石雕 Qingtian Carved Stone

青田石雕以名贵的青田石雕制而成。青田石，地质学称"叶蜡石"，是一种耐高温的矿物，具有色彩丰富、晶莹剔透，质地细腻，软硬适中，可雕性强的特点。石雕艺人依据石材的形状和颜色，巧妙构思，使作品具有独特的魅力，被誉为"在石头上绣花"，深受世人喜爱。

Qingtian Carved Stone is carved from the precious Qingtian stone which is geologically called "pyrophyllite", a kind of high-temperature resistant ore. It has such features as rich colors, transparency, fine texture, modest hardness and deformability. With imagination, stone carving artists enable the stones to be charming and attractive according to their shapes and colors. This skill also enjoys popularity as "embroidery on stone".

4. 庆元香菇 Qingyuan Dried Mushroom

庆元出产的香菇菇形圆整，富有光泽，菌褶密厚，香气浓郁，味道鲜美，素有"诸菌之冠，蔬菜之魁"的美称，庆元香菇自古为宫廷贡品，是宴席上的珍贵佳肴，曾获 1994 年"第五届亚太国际贸易博览会"金奖和 1996 年"第二届国际各行业产品畅销博览会"金奖。

Qingyuan Dried Mushroom are all in full shape, fresh color, full pulp, good flavor and delicious taste, hence the name "the champion fungi, the best vegetable". Since ancient times, it has been the tribute in royal court and the delicacy in feasts. It won the gold medals both in the 5th Asia-Pacific International Trade Fair in 1994 and in the 2nd International Best-selling Products Expo in 1996.

第五节 宁波特产

Section 5 Native Specialty Products in Ningbo

1. 奉化水蜜桃 Fenghua Juicy Peach

奉化水蜜桃的特点为果大皮薄、核紫肉厚、蜜汁丰富、甘美清香，其主要品种有黄玉露、玉露桃、玉露蟠桃等，以被誉为"琼浆玉露""瑶池珍品"的玉露桃为最上乘的品种。

Fenghua Juicy Peach is characterized by its big fruit and thin skin with a purple core and also by its attractive lovely luster with fresh and sweet flesh. The main varieties of Fenghua Juicy Peaches are Yellow Yulu, Yulu Peach and Yulu Flat Peach, etc. The most precious kind is Yulu Peach that is known as "the treasure in the Jasper Lake", a legendary place where a fairy queen lives.

2. 奉化芋头 Fenghua Taro

奉化芋头是奉化传统名特优农产品。俗话说"跑过三关六码头，吃过奉化芋艿头"，由此可见这芋艿头非同寻常。芋头近球型，外表棕黄，顶端粉红色，其特点为个大皮薄、肉粉无筋、糯滑可口，已成为宴请的必备佳肴。

Fenghua Taro is a traditional superfine agricultural product. The common saying "Walking off three terminals and six wharfs, you must have eaten the Fenghua Taro" fully shows that the taro is unusual. The taro is nearly spherical which has pale-brown appearance and pink color on its top. It is characterized by its large size and thin skin, soft flesh without gluten, and smooth and delicious taste, and has become a must-food in a banquet.

3. 宁波汤圆 Ningbo Tangyuan / Ningbo Stuffed Dumpling Ball

宁波汤圆是著名小吃之一，已有700多年的历史。宁波汤圆采用精白水磨糯米粉做皮，以细腻纯净的绵白糖、黑芝麻、优质猪板油和桂花等制成馅，汤圆皮薄而滑，白如羊脂，咬一口油香四溢，糯而不黏，因而享誉海内外。

Ningbo Tangyuan is one of the famous snacks, with a history of over 700 years. It takes fine white glutinous rice flour as its cover, with delicate soft sugar, black sesame, high quality pork fat and sweet osmanthus as its stuffs. The cover of Tangyuan is thin and smooth, white like suet. When you have a bite, the fat fragrance is overflowing; it is glutinous but not sticking. Ningbo Tangyuan is renowned all over the world.

4. 溪口千层饼 Xikou Layered Pancake

溪口千层饼已有100多年历史，其原料以面粉为主，加以重糖、芝麻、花生米。其外形四方，厚约两厘米，至少有27层重叠的薄片，层次分明，金黄透绿，酥足味醇，甜咸适中，风味独特，食后令人口齿留香，百食不厌。溪口千层饼多次获得国家和省级名特产品奖，

Xikou Layered Pancake has one hundred years' history. Its main material is flour, with sugar, sesame and peanuts in it. The two-centimeter-thick squarish pancake has at least twenty-seven overlapping sheets with clear layers. It is famous for its crisp and unique flavor with moderately sweet and saline taste, and with fragrance staying in mouth after eating. Nobody would refuse to eat it. The pancake has won several national and provincial awards as a special product.

第六节　衢州特产

Section 6　Specialty Products in Quzhou

1. 常山胡柚 Chanshan Pomelo

相传在常山澄潭有个自然村叫胡家村，是胡柚最早种植的地方，故名胡柚。常山胡柚果实美观，呈梨形、圆球形或扁球形，色泽金黄，肉质饱满，脆嫩多汁，酸甜适度，甘中微苦，鲜爽可口，且贮后风味变浓，品质更佳。

Legend says that there was a village named Hujia (Hu Family) in Chengtan, Changshan, which was the first place to grow pomelo, hence the name Hu Pomelo. Changshan Pomelo is beautiful in appearance with pear shape, round or flat ball shape and golden color. It is crisp and juicy, moderately sweet and sour, sweet with slightly bitterness, which is refreshing and delicious.

It will thicken the flavor with better quality after storage.

2. 开化龙顶 Kaihua Longding Tea

开化龙顶属于高山云雾茶，在清明至谷雨前，选用茶树生长健壮的一芽一叶或一芽二叶为鲜叶原料，烘干而成。制成后外形紧直挺秀，白毫毕露，有三绿之特点，即"干茶色绿，汤水清绿，叶底鲜绿"。

Kaihua Longding Tea belongs to the cloud and mist tea in top mountains. Before Pure Brightress (5th solar term) and Grain Rain (6th solar term), a robust tea bud and leaf or a bud and two leaves are used as fresh raw material, and then they are dried. The tea is elegant and straight after it is finished with disclosure of white hairs. There is "Three Green" for the tea, that is "green color in dry tea, green and clear soup, bright green leaves in the bottom".

3. 龙游小辣椒 Longyou Pepper

龙游小辣椒始产于 1851 年。王正丰酱园采"寸钉椒"，用家传秘方酱制而成，被御封为皇室贡品。龙游小辣椒具有色泽鲜亮，口感脆嫩，咸甜适中，风味独特等特点。

Longyou Pepper was first produced in 1851. Wang Zhengfeng Sauce & Pickle Shop used the "inch-pepper", and made the pepper with the secret family recipe sauce. It was labeled as the royal tribute. Bright in color, crisp in texture, moderate in sweet and salty flavor, with its unique feature, Longyou peppers are excellent appetizers.

4. 一品红椪柑 Yipin (Top-class) Red Mandarin Orange

"一品红椪柑"是柑中之精品，自明代起一直为皇家贡品。一品红椪柑果形端正，色泽鲜艳，肉质脆嫩，酸甜适中，清香爽口，营养丰富。

"Yipin (Top-class) Red Mandarin Orange" is the best among oranges. From the Ming Dynasty it has been labeled as articles of tributes to the imperial court. It is regular in shape and bright in color with tender and crisp flesh, moderate sweet and sour flavor, and rich in nutrition.

第七节　绍兴特产

Section 7　Specialty Products in Shaoxing

1. 枫桥香榧 Fengqiao Torreya Grandis

诸暨枫桥香榧早在唐代就享有盛誉。枫桥所产香榧外壳细，体秀气，具有壳薄仁满、种仁酥松细腻，质脆味香、营养丰富的特点，为我国稀有的干果之一，在国内外享有盛名。

Fengqiao Torreya Grandis in Zhuji City was very famous as early as in the Tang Dynasty. The torreya grandis grown in Fengqiao has thin peel and full nut, crisp and delicate, fragrant and rich in nutrition. As one of the rare kinds of nuts, it enjoys great reputation home and abroad.

2. 绍兴黄酒 Shaoxing Rice Wine

绍兴酿酒已有 2500 年的历史，声誉斐然，在清朝时被誉为全国十大名产之一。在 1910 年的南洋劝业会和 1915 年美国巴拿马万国博览会上曾荣获金牌和优等奖状。绍兴黄酒品种颇丰，色泽橙黄清亮，香气浓郁芬芳，滋味醇厚甘甜，营养丰富。

Shaoxing Wine, with a history of 2,500 years, has striking reputation. It was named as one of the top ten specialties in the Qing Dynasty. It won the gold medal on the Southeast Asia Commodity Exposition in 1910, and honors awards on the Panama Pacific International Exposition in the United States in 1915. Shaoxing Rice Wine has has many varieties, with orange color, fragrant aroma, sweet mellow taste and rich nutrition.

3. 绍兴乌毡帽 Shaoxing Black Felt Hat

戴乌毡帽曾是绍兴人的一个鲜明标志。乌毡帽采用普通羊毛为原料，进行反复锤炼、浆洗后，制成圆边、尖顶帽型，一般颜色为黑色，故名"乌毡帽"。乌毡帽以手感柔软、质地坚韧为优，具有吸水慢、干燥快、保温性好等特点，既可御寒，还可遮雨。

Wearing a black hat has been a clear sign of Shaoxing people. Felt hat, with ordinary wool as raw material, is made into steeple hat with rounded edges after being repeatedly tempered and starched; the general color is black, hence the name "Black Felt Hat". Felt hat has good qualities such as soft feel, hard and tough texture, slow water absorption, fast drying, good heat prevention; and it can be used to keep warm and hide from rain.

4. 崧厦霉千张 Songxia Fermented Bean Curd Sheet

崧厦霉千张具有鲜洁、清香、素淡的特点，是豆制品中的佳品，曾被皇宫誉为宫廷"奇菜"。乾隆皇帝品尝了崧厦霉千张，大加赞赏。

Songxia Fermented Bean Curd has fresh, clean and delicious sheets. It is among the list of best bean curd products, which was viewed as "wonder dishes" in the imperial palace. When Emperor Qianlong once ate it, he gave it a high praise.

5. 新昌小京生 Xinchang Small Peanuts

新昌小京生历史悠久，明清时已成为进京贡品，小京生由此得名。新昌小京生的特点是壳薄仁满，香而带甜，油而不腻，松脆爽口，色香味俱佳，有增强记忆力和延年益寿的功效，故有"长生果"之美称。

Xinchang Small Peanuts have a long history, and as early as in the Ming and Qing dynasties, they became one of the tributes to the court, and this is the origin of the name. With thin shell and full nut, this kind of peanut is fragrant and sweet, oily but not greasy, crisp and refreshing, which is a good combination of color, aroma and taste. It can enhance memory and longevity, and thus it gets the name of "longevity nut".

第八节 台州特产

Section 8 Specialty Products in Taizhou

1. 楚门文旦 Chumen Pomelo

楚门文旦别名玉环柚，迄今已有 120 余年种植历史。它成熟时底部平而稍凹，蒂部凸起，果皮橙黄，肉嫩汁多，含有糖分和多种维生素，是加工罐头、果汁的好原料。

Chumen Pomelo, also named Yuhuan Pomelo, began to be planted about 120 years ago. When it is ripe, its bottom will be flat with a little depressed and the base of the fruit will be a little raised. Its skin will be bright orange with juicy flesh inside. It contains much sugar and various vitamins, so it is a good raw material to be made to canned food or fruit juice.

2. 万年藤杖 Ten Thousand Years Cane

万年藤杖又称"华顶杖"。它由深谷中的苍郁古藤删削而成，其中寿命最长的可达千年以上。万年藤杖外涂栗色本山漆，晶莹光亮。也可不涂漆，保持天然本色。佛教天台宗把万年藤杖当作方丈身份的标志。

Ten Thousand Years Cane is also called Huading Cane. It is sharpened by luxuriant, old rattan and the oldest one can be longer than one thousand years old. The stick can be painted to chestnut color or keep the natural color. Tien-sect of Buddhism, the Ten Thousands Years Cane is regarded as the sign of an abbot.

3. 仙居三黄鸡 Xianju Sanhuang Chicken

仙居三黄鸡又名仙居鸡，明朝开国皇帝朱元璋品尝此鸡后评曰："此鸡喙黄、爪黄、羽黄，可称三黄鸡。"因而得到朱元璋的钟爱，列为贡品，"三黄鸡"的名字也由朱元璋钦赐。如今，在国家农业部编撰的《中国家禽品种》中，仙居三黄鸡也被排在首位。

Xianju Sanhuang chicken, also named Xianju Chicken, got its name from Zhu Yuanzhang, the emperor who founded the Ming Dynasty, because its beak, feet and feature are all yellow. In the past, the chicken won Zhu Yuanzhang's favour and was a tribute. Now, Sanhuang Chicken is also the first in the list of *Chinese Poultry Species* which was written by the Ministry of Agriculture.

第九节　温州特产

Section 9　Specialty Products in Wenzhou

1. 凤尾鱼 Anchovy

凤尾鱼是温州的著名特产，因其尾部分叉，呈红色，尖细窄长，犹如凤尾而得名。凤尾鱼营养丰富，肉质醇厚，细嫩鲜美，含有大量蛋白质、脂肪和碳水化合物，还富有猪肉和牛肉中少有的磷酸。

Anchovy is one of the specialties in Wenzhou. It is named after its phoenix-shaped tail in red, sharp, narrow and long forked shape. Anchovy is rich in nutrition with mellow and tender flesh, which is abundant in protein, fat and carbohydrates, and contains phosphate that is rare in pork and beef.

2. 黄杨木雕　Boxwood Carving

黄杨木雕是一种立体圆雕艺术，发源于温州乐清，因以黄杨木做雕刻材料而得名，是我国木雕工艺的一个主要品种。黄杨木雕具有精巧细腻，刀法明快，疏密得体，形神兼备的特点，给人以古朴典雅的美感。

Boxwood Carving, as a three-dimensional circular engrave art, is originated in Yueqing, Wenzhou. It is named after the boxwood material for carving, and it is one of the main wood carving arts in China. It is characterized by delicate nature, bright blade skill, appropriate space and vivid unity of form and spirit, giving a kind of simple and elegant beauty.

3. 楠溪香鱼　Nanxi Sweet Fish

香鱼，是楠溪江盛产的一种奇特、名贵的淡水鱼，因其背脊上长有一条满是香脂的腔道，能散发出浓郁的芳香而得名。香鱼鱼肉细嫩多脂，味鲜且有香味，是上等食用鱼类，素有"淡水鱼之王"的美誉。

Sweet fish is a special and rare freshwater fish in the Nanxi River. There is a cavity full of balsam in its ridge, which generates strong fragrance, thus it gets its name. The sweet fish with its fine flesh and greasy, fresh and fragrant flavor ranks the first-class fish category and has the reputation of "The King of the Freshwater Fish".

第十节　舟山特产

Section 10　Specialty Products in Zhoushan

1. 金塘李　Jintang Plum

金塘李因盛产于定海金塘而得名，距今已有 130 多年栽培历史。具有皮青心红，果大核小，肉厚质脆，汁多味甜等特点。其富含有多种维生素，具有开胃之功效，无论是鲜果，还是蜜饯制品，都有很高的营养价值。

Jintang Plum is known for it abounds in Jintang. It has a history of more than 130 years. It has features of green skin and red core, big shape and small core, thick flesh and crisp taste, plenty of juice and sweet taste. It has several kinds of vitamins for increasing one's appetite. Both fresh fruit and preserved ones have high nutrition.

2.马目泥螺 Mamu Mud Snail

泥螺又名"吐铁"，遍布于舟山各港湾海涂，尤以定海马目一带质量上佳，素有"马目泥螺呑山虾"之说。马目泥螺以壳薄、肉软、鲜嫩而著名。

Mud snail, also called "Tutie" which is everywhere at all bays of Zhoushan. Among them, the bullacta exarata at Mamu Town of Dinghai Area is the top grade, which has long enjoyed the saying "Mamu Mud Snail, Qiaoshan Shrimp". Mamu Mud Snail is known for its thin shell, mild meat and tender taste.

3. 舟山大黄鱼 Zhoushan Big Yellow Croaker

"舟山大黄鱼"是国内最有名的海水鱼类。舟山群岛海域是大黄鱼的主要产地之一。大黄鱼肉质鲜嫩，营养丰富，既可鲜食，也可制成鱼鲞、鱼松和罐头食用。用黄鱼剖晒成的"舟山白鲞"，味甘性平，营养丰富。

Zhoushan Big Yellow Croaker is the most famous ocean fish, one of whose main origins is Zhoushan Islands. It is nutritious because it has nutritional components of protein. It could be eaten freshly, and also made into dried fish, dried fish floss and canned fish. "Zhoushan dried fish" made by yellow croaker is healthy and nutritious.

◆ 课后练习 Exercises

任意选择你喜欢的三种浙江特色旅游产品，阐述为什么作此选择。

参考文献

Bibliography

包惠南. 中国文化与汉英翻译[M]. 北京：外文出版社，2004.

陈刚. 旅游翻译与涉外导游[M]. 北京：中国对外翻译出版公司，2004.

陈刚. 西湖赞诗[M]. 杭州：浙江摄影出版社，1996.

陈腊娇，冯利华，沈红，孙立峰. 古村落旅游开发模式的比较：金华市诸葛八卦村和郭洞村实证研究[J]. 国土与自然资源研究，2008(5)：121-123.

仇专专. 从文化角度论中国旅游景点名的英译[D]. 湖南师范大学，2009.

杜思民. 旅游景点名称的英译探究[J]. 焦作大学学报，2007(1).

顾雪梁，李同良. 应用英语翻译教程[M]. 杭州：浙江大学出版社，2009.

顾雪梁. 英语学习宝典[M]. 杭州：浙江大学出版社，2011.

胡念望. 温州揽胜[M]. 上海：上海书画出版社，2005.

黄成洲. 汉英翻译技巧[M]. 西安：西北工业大学出版社，2008.

贾文波. 应用翻译功能论[M]. 北京：中国对外翻译出版公司，2004.

教育部《旅游英语》教材编写组. 旅游英语[M]. 北京：高等教育出版社，2002.

金华旅游公司主编. 浙江旅游丛书：金华游[M]. 杭州：浙江摄影出版社，2011.

金惠康. 跨文化旅游翻译[M]. 北京：中国对外翻译出版公司，2006.

李艺. 从跨文化交际谈中文旅游文本的英译[D]. 重庆大学，2007.

卢红梅. 华夏文化与汉英翻译[M]. 武汉：武汉大学出版社，2008.

罗开富. 湖州人文甲天下[M]. 北京：经济日报出版社，2006.

名吃特产编委会. 中国名吃特产指南[M]. 北京：外文出版社，2008.

谭燕. 浅析旅游景点名称的翻译[D]. 湖南师范大学，2011.

王连文. 旅游翻译二十讲[M]. 北京：旅游教育出版社，1990.

王敏，吴攀升. 古村落旅游发展策略探讨：以浙江金华古村落为例[J]. 桂林旅游高等专科学校学报，2006(1).

吴育红. 旅游材料汉英翻译中文化信息的转化[J]. 湖州职业技术学院学报，2008(1)：66-68.

肖乐. 旅游景点英语翻译中的跨文化意识探析[J]. 湖北社会科学，2008(5)：121-123.

杨晋. 浅谈旅游景点翻译中美学特征的体现[D]. 四川外语学院，2012.

一山. 自驾车游浙江[M]. 杭州：浙江科学技术出版社，2004.

臧维熙. 中国旅游文化大辞典[M]. 上海：上海古籍出版社，2000.

张航. 旅游景点标示语的语言特点和汉英翻译策略思考[J]. 济南职业学院学报，2010(1).

张基珮. 外宣英译的原文要适当删减[J]. 上海科技翻译，2001(3)：21-24.

张建庭. 西湖十景(西湖全书)[M]. 杭州：杭州出版社，2005.

张明清. 导游业务与技巧[M]. 北京：高等教育出版社，2003.

浙江旅游指南[M]. 杭州：浙江人民出版社，1988.

浙江移动公司. 浙江历史文化旅游名筑(珍藏册)精装本[M]. 杭州：浙江移动公司，2012.

周琰. 民俗文化对口译的影响及应对策略[D]. 上海：上海外国语大学，2009.

走遍中国编写组. 走遍中国·浙江[M]. 北京：中国旅游出版社，2006.

图书在版编目(CIP)数据

浙江景点文化双语教程：英汉对照/顾雪梁等主编.
—杭州：浙江大学出版社，2016.8
ISBN 978-7-308-15923-4

I. ①浙… II. ①顾… III. ①旅游点—介绍—浙江省
—教材—汉、英 IV. ①K928.705.5

中国版本图书馆 CIP 数据核字(2016)第 123472 号

浙江景点文化双语教程
顾雪梁　钱建萍　徐中意　主　编

责任编辑	韦　伟
责任校对	张远方
封面设计	项梦怡
出版发行	浙江大学出版社
	(杭州天目山路 148 号　邮政编码 310007)
	(网址：http://www.zjupress.com)
排　　版	杭州中大图文设计有限公司
印　　刷	杭州日报报业集团盛元印务有限公司
开　　本	787mm×1092mm　1/16
印　　张	15.75
字　　数	407 千
版 印 次	2016 年 8 月第 1 版　2016 年 8 月第 1 次印刷
书　　号	ISBN 978-7-308-15923-4
定　　价	39.00 元